THE
RECONSTRUCTION OF
AMERICAN LIBERALISM,
1865–1914

THE

RECONSTRUCTION OF

AMERICAN LIBERALISM,

1865–1914

NANCY COHEN

THE UNIVERSITY OF NORTH CAROLINA PRESS

CHAPEL HILL & LONDON

© 2002

The University of North Carolina Press

All rights reserved

Manufactured in the United States of America

Set in Minion Type by Keystone Typesetting, Inc.

The paper in this book meets the guidelines for
permanence and durability of the Committee on
Production Guidelines for Book Longevity of the Council
on Library Resources.

Library of Congress Cataloging-in-Publication Data

Cohen, Nancy, 1963–

The reconstruction of American liberalism, 1865–1914 /
Nancy Cohen.

p. cm.

Includes bibliographical references (p.) and index.

ISBN 0-8078-2670-7 (cloth: alk. paper) —

ISBN 0-8078-5354-2 (pbk.: alk. paper)

1. United States—Politics and government—1865–1933.
2. Reconstruction. 3. Liberalism—United States—History—
19th century. 4. Liberalism—United States—History—20th
century. 5. Progressivism (United States politics). I. Title.

E661 .C65 2002

320.51'3'0973—dc21   2001041457

06   05   04   03   02   5   4   3   2   1

FRONTISPIECE

"Around Columbia's May-Pole: Dancers at Cross-Purposes,"
cover illustration of Harper's Weekly, *April 30, 1887.*

TO CAMILLE AND HELENA

CONTENTS

ACKNOWLEDGMENTS

I have often imagined with pleasure the moment when I would be able to express in writing my gratitude to the many people who have sustained and aided me in this project.

First I would like to thank the librarians and archivists of Columbia University, the Rare Book and Manuscript Library of Columbia University, the New York Public Library, the Bentley Historical Library of the University of Michigan, the Massachusetts Historical Society, and the Los Angeles Public Library. Financial support of my dissertation from Columbia University, the Whiting Foundation, the Bentley Historical Library of the University of Michigan, and the Massachusetts Historical Society helped make this book possible.

This work has been vastly improved by a number of people who read and commented on various versions of the manuscript. David Montgomery and Ira Katznelson generously gave their time to read my dissertation and thus helped me conceptualize its revision. Discussions with Melvyn Dubofsky during my year at Binghamton University challenged me to reexamine some of my conclusions; his comments on parts of chapter 7 helped me clarify and refine my interpretation. John M. Cooper Jr., in his careful reading of the manuscript, spotted a number of omissions and pointed me toward several additional fruitful leads. Wilfred M. McClay offered invaluable criticism that compelled me to tackle the difficult task of pursuing my argument to its logical and necessary conclusion. Early on I was aided by the advice and comments of my fellow graduate students at Columbia University: Celia Azevedo, Aaron Brenner, Anthony Kaye, Kevin Kenny, Manisha Sinha, Jeffrey Sklansky, and Michael West. Michelle Adams has been my guide in legal history and constitutional interpretation. I have also benefited from the experience and craftsmanship of several people at the University of North Carolina Press. This project was first taken on by Lewis Bateman. With a deft touch, he saved me from many of the pitfalls of a first book and allayed my anxieties of authorship. Charles Grench has kindly given of his aid, advice, and experience, and I am deeply appreciative of his commitment to this book. Ruth Homrighaus and Paula Wald have expertly guided the manuscript through the editorial process.

Three of my former teachers at Columbia merit special recognition. Elizabeth Blackmar dedicated many hours to close reading of successive drafts of my dissertation and to conversations with me about late-nineteenth-century history. Up until I finished writing this book, her questions have provided grist for the mill. I consider myself lucky to have experienced her renowned devotion to her students. Eric Foner encouraged and inspired me throughout, read several versions of most chapters, kept me on track, and shared his broad knowledge of the period to gently steer me toward a deeper understanding of my subject. My deepest appreciation goes out to my adviser, mentor, and friend, Barbara J. Fields. In so many ways, this project would have been inconceivable without her. She has been unstinting in her generosity, nurturing me as a writer, scholar, and teacher. But even more important, she has provided me with a model of intellectual integrity graced by warmth, humor, and compassion. My debt to her is immense.

For most writers, as I have learned through experience, long projects grow into a constant obsession. But if my truth be told, most of my waking hours have been spent making life, rather than writing history, despite the everpresent nagging on the conscience of an unfinished book. It is with delight that I can finally put in writing my thanks to the people who have made life more pleasurable and meaningful during the years of writing. Susan Margolin has been a constant source of strength, wisdom, and friendship. Nazila Shokrian has provided many forms of sustenance, but most especially in her knack for finding the words that comfort, heal, and encourage. Michelle Adams has been there at a few critical moments with her keen common sense and nonjudgmental support and has enlivened countless hours with talks of history, politics, and life. Elaine Charnov has given warmly of her friendship and hospitality and has shared with me many adventures in America's greatest city. I extend special thanks to those friends in the guild, Aaron Brenner, Anthony Kaye, Rona Peligal, Thaddeus Russell, Manisha Sinha, and Marla Stone, for providing friendship in which my love of history does not seem quite so odd. Many other friends and relatives have given me great joy in their friendship and made my life richer. With appreciation to each, I thank Janet Cohen, Janice and Howard Fineman, S. Beth Atkin, Emily Alejos, Kirsten and Luis Barajas, Maren and Rick Candaele, Laura Coblentz, Lisa Hacken, Melissa Kaye, and Neal Smith.

Finally, I would like to thank my parents for the manifold ways in which they made this book possible. My mother, Suzanne F. Cohen, passed on her love of literature and her conviction that her daughters must pursue their dreams. My father, Nathan L. Cohen, died before I began this long journey, but the memory of his skepticism about sacred truths and his hatred of cant have helped keep me on my path. I doubt he would have agreed with many of my conclusions, but I believe he would have spotted the family resemblance.

To Kerry Candaele, for his eagle-eyed scrutiny of the meaning of every word, for the questions that lifted me out of many an intellectual morass, for the many diversions he has provided, and for his faith in me, I am enormously grateful. To our daughters, Helena and Camille, who have taught me to see the world through new eyes, I dedicate this book.

THE
RECONSTRUCTION OF
AMERICAN LIBERALISM,
1865–1914

This association of poverty with progress is the great enigma of our times. It is the central fact from which spring industrial, social, and political difficulties that perplex the world, and with which statesmanship and philanthropy and education grapple in vain. From it come the clouds that overhang the future of the most progressive and self-reliant nations. It is the riddle which the Sphinx of Fate puts to our civilization and which not to answer is to be destroyed. So long as all the increased wealth which modern progress brings goes but to build up great fortunes, to increase luxury and make sharper the contrast between the House of Have and the House of Want, progress is not real and cannot be permanent. The reaction must come. The tower leans from its foundations, and every new story but hastens the final catastrophe.

HENRY GEORGE, *Progress and Poverty* (1879)

It is one of the marks of a civilized, as distinguished from a barbarous state of society, that in the former what we call property is protected equally, whether it consists of lands and houses, or of mere evidences of value— paper credits, or bonded debt. If in the era of progress to which the farmers' movement proposes to introduce us, we are going back to a condition of society in which the only sort of property which we can call our own is that which we can make our own by physical possession, it is certainly important to every one to know it, and the only body which can really tell us is the Supreme Court at Washington.

E. L. GODKIN, "The Farmers and the Supreme Court," *Nation*, January 28, 1875

On this one issue, the problem of progress in a regime of consolidated capital—depends the future of humanity. In so far as principles decide the event, it appears that man has the power forever to progress.
This result will be gained if human evolution does not turn backward and ensure a survival of the hopelessly unfit among industrial types.
Such a reversal of the order of nature has not elsewhere occurred.
We are justified in putting faith in evolution.

JOHN BATES CLARK, "The Theory of Economic Progress,"
AEA *Economic Studies* 1, no. 1 (1896)

INTRODUCTION

On hearing of General Robert E. Lee's surrender at Appomattox, James Russell Lowell—abolitionist, Radical Republican, future liberal reformer, and the poet laureate of New England letters—wrote to his coeditor at the *North American Review* of his elation at the Union's victory. "There is something magnificent in having a country to love. It is almost like what one feels for a woman. Not so tender, perhaps, but to the full as self-forgetful."[1] Lowell, transported by the thought of a democratic people overwhelming the slave power and abolishing the barbarity of slavery, imagined that the purified nation would be reconsecrated on its ideals of liberty and human equality. With the licentious slave-holding aristocracy defeated, the marriage of true love could be consummated.

But love is demanding and lovers sometimes capricious. Eleven years later, at the celebration of the nation's centennial, Lowell's Columbia, betrayed, "found it hard to hide her spiteful tears."[2] While living American women continued to be excluded from politics, the ideal of woman merged with the ideal of nation. Victorian American men seem to have had a penchant for expressing their political desires, fears, and frustrations through the figure of Columbia. On the eve of May Day, 1887, an illustration of the approaching ravishment of Columbia adorned the cover of the *Harper's Weekly*—"A Journal of Civilization" and the most widely read magazine among the American middle class. In the cartoon, Columbia sits on the pedestal of a maypole decorated with stars-and-stripes bunting and a liberty cap. She is quite alarmed, for around her a burlesque of a maypole dance is taking place. The dancers, instead of cooperating to weave an orderly pattern around the pole, are kicking, kneeing, slashing, and snarling at one another. To the side, winged Hermes appears, bearing the government's message to railroad corporations that they will be controlled by a higher power. But he has just met up with the railroads, and his classically athletic limbs are tangled up in the railroad's iron legs. Who might win the contest between the modern machine and the elegant, agile, but ancient messenger? Front and center the main struggle goes on. A swarthy, whiskered, apelike laborer, wielding a large knife and a satchel of "anarchy dynamite," plunges headfirst from his severed ribbon into an abyss. "Labor" has just passed him in the circular procession—had he used his saw to cut the alien anarchist's bond to Columbia? "Labor" now goes knee to boot with

"Capital," as Columbia is framed by their ribbons; they stare each other down with menacing glances, and she casts a pleading gaze on the viewer.[3]

The *Harper's Weekly* illustration was a revealing representation of the fate of the ideal of national harmony that Lowell had evoked at the moment of Union victory. By 1887, an observer of national life had to render its discord. Coming round the bend were Congress and the railroads, figuring the impending upsurge over the problem of monopoly. The lead dancers in the 1887 maypole dance were capital and labor, just as the "labor question" had become the national preoccupation. As the eight anarchists convicted of the Haymarket bombing awaited execution, no one could mistake the seriousness of the danger posed to Columbia as she sat ensnared in the closing web of conflict.

When Lowell had first expressed his optimism, he knew that the consummation would require a thorough reconstruction of the South. Only later did he and others realize that forces unleashed during the war had raised issues about the reconstruction of the North in equally powerful ways. Most obviously, the stimulus given to industrial growth by the Union war effort laid the foundations, ultimately, for the rise of corporate capitalism. In the decades after the war, the ongoing transformation of the economy deeply affected the daily lives of Americans.

Nevertheless, the Union war machine nurtured an equally potent and politically significant force by mobilizing the citizenry under the banner of patriotism, free labor, and democracy. The Northern populace had been called on to make the ultimate sacrifice, to give their lives and fortunes for the higher good of the nation. They had been appealed to with the claims that only through the preservation of the Union could their interests and their most expansive dreams of a more perfect society be realized. They had been warned that defeat would spell the end of all they valued. Emotions and identifications thus fostered could not simply be turned off when they were no longer needed. The heartfelt patriotic rhetoric that permeated Northern society during the war not only cemented the loyalty of the vast majority of the population to the state but also, unintentionally, heightened their expectations about what the nation could do for them. Most important, as the events of the next three decades would show, wartime appeals to the superiority of "free labor civilization" gave warrant to a vision of America as a producers' democracy.

As the cartoonist's metaphor of national peril conveys, the decades after the war, the "Gilded Age," were ones of endemic, ideologically suffused social conflict. It has long been recognized that the disruptions caused by breakneck industrialization sparked conflict and that much of it revolved around economic questions that pitted workers and farmers against the propertied classes.

HARPER'S WEEKLY.

JOURNAL OF CIVILIZATION.

VOL. XXXI.—No. 1584.
Copyright, 1887, by HARPER & BROTHERS.

NEW YORK, SATURDAY, APRIL 30, 1887.

TEN CENTS A COPY.
$4.00 PER YEAR, IN ADVANCE.

"*Around Columbia's May-Pole: Dancers at Cross-Purposes,*"
cover illustration of Harper's Weekly, April 30, 1887.

But to appreciate fully the meaning and significance of social conflict, it is important to keep in mind the legacy of the war, in all its dimensions. If the core of Northern patriotism resided in the complex of ideas that historians have termed "free labor ideology," then it appears logical to propose that the movements of the postbellum decades were asserting historically specific claims about the linkage between producerism and democracy that they believed had been validated in the war.[4] They, as well as their opponents, claimed the mantle of the victorious Union and true democracy. The stakes were high, as in many ways the national government found itself in a situation akin to that of a consolidating postrevolutionary regime, pressed on one side by counter-revolutionists (in the South) and on the other by the popular forces it had itself authorized.

In this specific economic, political, and cultural context, a new problem emerged as the preeminent one. Were the values of democracy and the social relations of capitalism reconcilable, and if so, on what terms? Revolving around this question, the social conflict of the Gilded Age upended the political values and identities of an earlier America. Among the many ideological shifts and changes of the era, none left a larger and more portentous legacy than the transformation of liberal ideology, which resulted in the creation of modern American liberalism.

This work offers a new narrative of the origins of modern American liberalism and, in doing so, forces a reconsideration of its character. A new set of problems and questions about society, economy, and state arose after the Civil War: among them, the first real confrontation with the implications of universal suffrage and mass democracy, the transformation of the majority of the citizenry into wage earners, the rise of the corporation as a new type of property, the devastating fluctuations of the international market economy, and the growth of the administrative capacity of government. These were distinctively the problems of a new America, a modern America, and Gilded Age liberals faced them squarely and honestly—if not without their own particular interests. Contrary to most accounts, I demonstrate that the distinctive values and programs of modern liberalism were formulated by Gilded Age liberals, not in the very different context of the Progressive Era.

The reconstruction of liberalism hinged especially on the response of postbellum liberal political intellectuals to two of the most important political questions of their age: the "labor question" and the "monopoly question." As new social movements of workers and farmers arose, protesting the economic developments of the era and demanding change in the name of democracy, the liberals of the Gilded Age reacted. Their trepidation over democratic majoritarianism in the new landscape of organized labor, agrarian populism, and large financial and industrial capital prompted them to reevaluate earlier political ideas and commitments. At the same time, even as large numbers of Americans decried the rise of monopoly and economic inequality, liberals were among the first to look upon economic consolidation with a favorable eye, appreciating the progress it wrought.

As an abundant literature makes clear, by 1900 the producers' movements that had been so characteristic of nineteenth-century America had gone down to defeat, and corporate capitalism had risen to dominance over the American economy.[5] Gilded Age liberals had been in the vanguard of analyzing, explaining, and legitimating these innovations. Through a three-decades-long examination and debate about the nature of American society, they invented a new liberalism that posited an active role for the state in society and economy, even as it justified constraints on democracy and the ascendancy of corporate capitalism. In doing so, liberals played a critical role in legitimating corporate capitalism and politically insulating it from democratic challenge—in reconciling corporate economic dominance and its attendant asymmetries of power with American democracy.

It was this legacy that was bequeathed to twentieth-century liberals, and, to a large degree, the progressives and their successors built on, rather than razed, the foundation left to them. During the Progressive Era, even as the basic institutions of the capitalist economy and representative, constitutional government were preserved, the minimal state of an earlier liberalism was abandoned in favor of one with the power to intervene in the market and to promote social welfare. The progressives' new liberalism, most historians conclude, was fundamentally reformist; it sought to use state power to regulate the capitalist economy and to improve the living conditions and "security" of the citizenry, without abolishing private property or revolutionizing liberal-democratic political institutions. In a period of turmoil, the poles of revolution and reaction had been averted: neither socialism, corporatism, nor authoritarianism had overthrown America's liberal, constitutional democracy, even if in the scheme of international social reform, American new liberalism was a pale copy of its competitors.[6] This new liberalism continued to be politically hegemonic through much of the twentieth century, as the New Deal, Fair Deal, and Great Society elaborated and extended the ambitious but tentative innovations of the Progressive Era. From Woodrow Wilson's New Freedom to Lyndon Johnson's Great Society reigned modern American liberalism; its decline was evident by the mid-1960s, as movements from both left and right challenged the settled routines of reformism and state activism. The victory of Ronald

Reagan, at the head of a professedly conservative movement, signaled the apparently irreversible defeat of the now aged modern liberalism.

The birth, career, and fate of modern liberalism are thus deeply implicated in the political history of the twentieth-century United States. But it is important to emphasize that the origins of modern liberalism lay in the Gilded Age, when the alternatives were clearer and sharper, the balance of social forces more equal, and the possibility of a different outcome greater. This book turns to the Gilded Age to examine the reconstruction of liberal political ideology, its causes and consequences, and its deeper implications for American governance and culture in the late nineteenth century and beyond.

In seeking to examine the reconstruction of American liberal political ideology, and the process by which the relationship between liberalism and democracy was redefined, it is necessary to say a few words about the definition of terms. It is quite obvious that, in its long historical career, liberalism has had a varied and changing existence. What distinguishes liberalism from other traditions, and what gives the long history of liberalism a unity? The political uses to which liberalism has been put have differed historically, and likewise, there are alternative approaches to the scholarly analysis of liberalism.

The values of liberalism are the commitment to freedom, tolerance, self-rule, the rule of law, and justice. Debate begins on the question of the assumptions underpinning liberalism. Liberalism understands human beings as rational, autonomous, and equal and conceives of history as progressive. But it also expresses a distinctive sociology. Breaking with the dominant tradition in Western thought, which viewed human beings as fundamentally social beings contained within and subordinate to the social body, liberalism defined man as an autonomous being, human because of his ownership of his own person and his own capacities and free in his lack of dependence on the will of others. The individual possesses himself and hence possesses rights upon which neither society nor the state can trespass. (The male pronoun is indicative of the inherently gendered conception of the individual within liberalism, as political theorists now routinely acknowledge.) The ambiguous portrait of the individual in the texts of political liberalism lends itself to different interpretations. The concept of the self-possessed individual can have democratic or libertarian implications: the former if the equality among individuals is emphasized; the latter if the person's possession of self is emphasized. Conversely, as is suggested in John Locke's much debated use of the metaphor of property for all rights, the self-possessed person is the propertied man, and the primary purpose of government can be seen as the protection of the property owner's liberty in the market and the inequality of possession in society. The complicated relationship between liberalism and democracy, in part, is rooted in this tension within liberal theory.[7]

Individualism is, as the historian Anthony Arblaster observes, "the metaphysical and ontological core of liberalism."[8] It may be possible in theory to preserve a commitment to the rights of the individual person while dispensing with the individualistic premises of liberalism, as some contemporary philosophers have attempted to do.[9] Nevertheless, a historical analysis of liberalism must recognize that in practice this has not yet occurred and that the current resurgence and popularity of free market ideology suggests that the prospects for the success of this project in the near future are not bright. The priority of the claims of the self-possessed, self-interested individual over that of society continues to be the pivotal determinant of the scope of governance in liberal societies, and it is clear that this is what distinguishes liberalism from its competitors. In the Anglo-American tradition, furthermore, market freedom has been understood as one of the essential rights of the free individual. The central political ideas of liberalism flow from the premise of individualism. Positively, liberalism asserts that the ultimate end of politics is to give scope to the individual's pursuit of self-rule, self-satisfaction, and self-realization. Negatively, no matter how far modern liberalisms have gone toward accepting state action and "positive liberty," there remains the assumption of an inherent conflict between the society and the individual. From this analysis derives the bias against collective action; the defense of individual autonomy, privacy, and rights; the commitment to rule based on consent; and the conception and enforcement of a sharp division of social space between private and public realms.[10]

As a historical practice, liberalism has been powerfully shaped by the opponents it has faced in its long history. Liberal philosophy and politics were born in a reaction against monarchical absolutism, and liberalism's central principles can be understood as the repudiation of conservatism, its organic worldview, and its defense of hierarchy and order, tradition and religious dogma, authority and obedience. Liberals represented the party of progress against the party of order, and the opposition between liberalism and conservatism remains one of the critical divides in world politics. The union of liberalism and democracy, on the other hand, is a very recent development, despite the contemporary tendency to conceive of the two as synonymous. Only in the late eighteenth century, in the American and French Revolutions, did democracy appear to any significant social force to be a positive principle of social organization. Likewise, it was not until then that the egalitarian and democratic potential within liberal theory was discerned. By the early twentieth century, the liberal regimes of the Western world were also representative democracies, but the advance of political democracy had been bitterly contested and resisted in many countries. (The United States, in which political democracy and liberal constitutionalism coexisted early, is the exception in this regard.) Thus, the emergence of democratic forces in the age of revolution created a new dynamic in the historical development of liberalism. And as modern labor and socialist movements arose in the developing economies of the transatlantic world, liberalism faced challenges from the left that were in certain respects more threatening than those from its right. Not only were the democratic and socialist lefts able to mobilize a mass constituency, but they also claimed to be the true heirs of the Enlightenment legacy of freedom, equality, and progress— a claim that was aided by the resistance many European liberals mounted against the democratization of politics. The history of liberal politics, thus, is a tale of relationships, most important, of the triangular struggle for power between liberals, conservatives, and socialists. The period with which this work is concerned, the late nineteenth century and the first decades of the twentieth, was an era of revision in liberalism throughout the transatlantic world. It was also an age when conservatives were weak, the contest between liberalism and socialism accelerated, and the widening of the franchise to include the propertyless was a central issue in European politics.

The ambivalent relationship between liberalism and democracy derives not only from problems inherent in liberal theory and the history of liberal practice but also from the varied meanings democracy has contained in its history. It is relatively simple to define democracy: democracy is rule by the people. But what is meant by each term is far from clear. First, who are the people? If democracy entails political equality of the citizenry, what are the principles for inclusion and exclusion? Second, what are the conditions and preconditions for democracy? Is it sufficient that all individuals are formally equal and possess equal civil and political rights? Or must legal equality be linked to concrete opportunities to participate in civil society and governance? Must formal legal equality be buttressed by substantive material equality for equality and democracy to be more than an abstraction? Third, what are the procedural requirements for a legitimate democracy? What is the scope of participation and decision making? What is the relationship between the people, representatives, and rulers? Is it sufficient that there be fair and free competitive elections, that representatives be accountable to the people, and that the state be neutral toward the diverse interests in society? Or must there be avenues for participation in decision making by the average citizen, and if so, in what range of decisions should the people participate? Fourth, in what social spheres must democratic procedures operate and substantive democracy result for a society rightfully to claim to be democratic? Historically, the contention on this subject has focused on the relative importance of political democracy and economic democracy, with a persisting undercurrent of attention to gender inequality and democracy within the family. At the heart of all these questions is the primary one: What is the object or purpose of democracy? Is formal political equality the means used by society to achieve a higher end, such as individual liberty or economic progress or the general good, or are substantive self-rule and equality ends in themselves? Are the purposes of democracy fulfilled if all individuals have the opportunity to participate in the political process for the purpose of protecting their private interests? Or, rather, must there be a substantive material equality among all citizens for democracy to survive, and as a corollary, is the object of democratic government to preserve substantive material equality? Or is the claim that democracy is a superior form of government based solely on an instrumental defense, that in an imperfect world democracy is the most fair and most efficient type of government?[11] The history of democracy is marked by conflicts over these and related questions. As we shall see, debates about democracy were explicitly formulated during the social conflicts of the Gilded Age, and through them, American liberal political ideology and the practices of liberal democracy were transformed.

Liberal democracy has been one of the most frequently studied subjects in the historiography of the United States, and the changes that occurred within liberal politics and thought between the end of the Civil War and the beginning of World War I have attracted many analysts. The dominant interpretation, with few exceptions, is that progressive liberals after the 1890s rejected the "classical" liberalism of their Gilded Age forebears and that, in doing so, they created a new liberalism and defined the parameters of modern liberalism. Richard Hofstadter's typology in his influential *Age of Reform* is characteristic of this view. To Hofstadter, the Gilded Age "Mugwump type" was "a conservative in his economic and political views" and a " 'liberal' in the classic sense." Ignoring "the serious abuses of the unfolding economic order," he was "dogmatically committed to the prevailing economics of *laissez faire*." Progressive reform was born out of the revolt against the outmoded ideas of the mugwumps by their successors.[12] Even as Hofstadter fundamentally reoriented the historical debate about progressivism, he largely accepted the value judgments that the progressive historians had first enshrined in the discussion. Sidney Fine, in what remains a frequently cited intellectual history of the origins of modern liberalism, *Laissez Faire and the General-Welfare State*, made explicit the teleology on which the typology was based:

> Industrialization and urbanization intensified old problems and brought with them a host of new ones. . . . Although, for the most part, the intervention of government was required for the solution of these issues, existing theories with respect to the role of the state constituted an intellectual barrier to the development of any realistic program of state action. . . . What was needed was a new philosophy of the state, a new liberalism embodying something of the spirit of Jeffersonianism but ready to use government as an agency to promote the general welfare. Industrial America made necessary the evolution of the general-welfare state.

Having asserted a rigid distinction between the liberals of the Gilded Age and those of the Progressive Era, Fine praised the right-thinking and righteous modern liberals and condemned the illiberal Gilded Age liberals.[13] The negative portrayal of the Gilded Age mugwump classical liberal, in sharp contrast to the new progressive liberal, is likewise conveyed in the most widely cited history of the politics of Gilded Age liberalism, John Sproat's *"The Best Men."*[14]

Thus, the history of liberalism in the postbellum decades has been dominated by the tale of the rise and fall of the only American generation of doctrinaire classical liberals, who sacrificed the humanitarian core of liberalism at the altar of laissez-faire. One of the objects of this study is to reassess the conventional portrait of Gilded Age liberals and hence to reconsider the question of the relationship between Gilded Age and Progressive Era liberalism and its implications for questions about the substance and character of progressive reform and modern liberalism. As I shall demonstrate, a closer examination of the ideology of Gilded Age liberalism and attention to the cultural networks through which it was elaborated and disseminated reveal that the liberalism of the Gilded Age was both more complicated and more influential in the formation of modern liberalism than is generally perceived.

Most historians of Progressive Era modern liberalism accept that the distinction between old and new liberalism is coincident with the dominance of old or new liberals. The best recent work on the ideology and social theory of the liberal progressives, such as that of James Kloppenberg, Mary O. Furner, and Daniel T. Rodgers, has deepened our understanding of modern liberalism by illuminating the distinct and competing strains within progressive thought and by situating the rise of social reform and new liberalism in the overarching transatlantic context. But the analysis of the character of progressive thought is dependent on a contrast (implicit or explicit) with the "laissez-faire" liberals of the Gilded Age. Even when these historians look for originators in the post-bellum decades, they exclude from their purview the alleged "classical" liberals of the Gilded Age or ignore the close connection between them and some of their new liberal protagonists.[15] The implications of a revision of the existing genealogy of modern liberalism is one of the subjects explored in this book.

As these debates attest, the history of American liberalism must be told through the people who shaped it. Before a political ideology becomes common sense and in little need of explicit formulation, it is a body of ideas and assumptions, problems and solutions, that emerges out of the common intellectual production of particular individuals. The reconstruction of American liberal political ideology between the end of the Civil War and the Progressive Era was the accomplishment of two generations of nationally prominent liberal political intellectuals, Gilded Age liberal reformers and the first American generation of professional social scientists. Contrary to the prevailing historiographical interpretation, the proto-progressive social scientists did not overthrow the classical liberals.[16] Rather, after a cultural struggle in the 1880s, liberal reformers and social scientists ended up collaborating with each other to forge the new liberalism.

Gilded Age liberal reform was both a political and an intellectual movement. The political movement of liberal reform included prominent politicians; the nation's most renowned writers and scholars; the editors of leading newspapers, magazines, and journals; the heads of the main publishing houses; presidents and professors of the most prestigious colleges and universities; and a significant segment of the nation's financial and industrial elite. A full roster of the liberal reform constituency reads like a *Who's Who* of American "respectable" culture: among them were Senator Charles Sumner, Governor and near president Samuel J. Tilden, President Grover Cleveland, Mark Twain, James Russell Lowell, William Dean Howells, Charles Eliot Norton, Henry Adams, George William Curtis, Edwin Lawrence Godkin, Joseph Medill, Horace White, Daniel Coit Gilman, Andrew Dickson White, Francis Amasa Walker, William Graham Sumner, Thomas McIntyre Cooley, Simon Newcomb, Edward Atkinson, John Murray Forbes, and Andrew Carnegie. In their editorships of *Harper's Weekly*, the *Nation*, the *Atlantic Monthly*, the *North American Review*, and *Scribner's Monthly*, they held a virtual monopoly on the periodicals read by the refined Northern middle class. Their opinions of political affairs received wide broadcast in the *Chicago Tribune*, *New York Evening Post*, *New York Times*, and many other urban dailies.[17]

Among the most influential in formulating, articulating, and publicizing the ideas and ideology of their movement were Godkin, Curtis, Charles Francis Adams Jr., Atkinson, David Ames Wells, Walker, Sumner, White, and Carroll Davidson Wright. (Throughout this work, I refer to these men as liberal reformers or liberal reform political intellectuals.)[18] Politically, these men shared doubts about the new tendencies of American democracy. Personally, they shared a common social world. With few exceptions, they were heirs of prominent Yankee Protestant families. At a time when only a tiny minority of Americans received even secondary education, most of the leaders of liberal reform had graduated from college, in which they had been formally educated in the canons of English liberal political philosophy, Scottish moral philosophy, and English classical political economy. The vast majority of them came from families that were prominent in abolitionist, antislavery, and Unionist organizations.[19]

Notwithstanding personal conflicts and intellectual differences, liberal reformers forged a cohesive group culture, creating political associations, social clubs, and institutions for intellectual community. They quite consciously banded together in voluntary organizations to influence the public sphere.[20] They founded the American Social Science Association and met within it to discuss their most serious intellectual work. They edited newspapers, magazines, and journals and owned publishing companies; they read one another's writings, wrote letters to one another about them, and republished the best and most persuasive articles as pamphlets to disseminate to a broader audience. They created a multitude of political reform clubs locally and nationally and tried on several occasions to create a liberal political counterforce to the two major parties, most famously in the Liberal Republican movement of 1872 and the mugwump bolt of 1884 that helped elect Democrat Grover Cleveland to the presidency. Some were active businessmen, and many served in government positions, pioneering the field of administrative and investigative commissions in the 1860s, long before the rise of the modern liberal state. They also married one another's sisters and cousins and summered together in Saratoga, the Berkshires, or Newport; they spent many evenings in all-male clubs with politicians and businessmen, dining, smoking, and conversing as gentlemen. It is appropriate to observe that, until the 1890s, nearly every person who debated the subjects of state policy and economy *and* who was recognized as possessing cultural authority was a man. As the opening of this work illustrates, the language of patriotism included stock metaphors of femininity and sentimentality. Poets and cartoonists could be indulged when they reminded the Victorian middle class that its ideal of the masculine political sphere was suffused with dreams and fears of ideal femininity and sexual union. But when political intellectuals sat down to discuss politics, they did not invite women to the discussion, nor did they show awareness of the gendered inflections in their use of the prosaic terms of political economy, statistics, statecraft, political theory, and social science.[21]

Few in number and bumblers at the art of American party politics, self-styled liberal reformers were nevertheless effective lobbyists for their ideas. Without question, liberal reformers constituted a tiny minority of Americans. But numbers do not equal cultural and political influence. And liberal reformers wielded a very large share of both, particularly from the end of the Civil War until the mid-1880s. They held a presence in virtually every institution through which culture was disseminated to the Northern middle classes, and they controlled many of the most important forums of opinion formation. Derisively labeled "mugwumps" by their political opponents, despised by the working classes of their age for their elitism and the services they provided to capital, they are remembered for their adherence to an extreme individualism, laissez-faire, and social Darwinism. Few of their chroniclers have resisted the temptation to declare them irrelevant to nobler traditions of liberalism and the practical politics of their own time. But contrary to the conclusions of latter-day historians, liberal reformers, by virtue of their strategic positions in American culture, were able to frame the terms of political debate, determine the issues, and establish the values to which others had to conform. The very fact that debates about individualism and the relationship of the state to the market were at the fulcrum of Gilded Age politics testifies to the success of the ideological labors of these liberal intellectuals. Not only has their influence been understated, but the characterization of them as classical liberals is equally mistaken. As this work demonstrates, they were pioneering theorists of economic consolidation and the active liberal state. The politics and ideology of liberal reform are the subject of part I of this book.

Although liberal reformers entered directly into the fray of electoral politics, they always believed that their most enduring work would be cultural—the tutoring of public opinion. Thus, the most distressing opposition they confronted was that of the next generation of intellectuals, who they had hoped would carry on their legacy. It is this group of men who constitute the second generation of postbellum political intellectuals examined in this study. Almost to the man, they were reared in the same kind of middle-class, reform-oriented, Yankee Protestant families as the men of the first generation, albeit less privileged ones. They grew up reading the writings and attending the colleges of the liberal reformers. Yet the young intellectuals came of age in the

1870s, at a time when American capitalism had entered an endemic crisis and had generated astounding social misery and discontent. It also happened to be a time when the training and role of intellectuals were undergoing a transformation. Unlike their predecessors, who received the broad education of gentlemen, most often in the still religiously dominated American colleges, the young intellectuals were educated in the emerging social sciences at modern universities in the United States and Germany. In this they were exposed to more cosmopolitan influences than their predecessors, yet in institutions that encouraged a new kind of specialization. They became professional social scientists and began their careers by challenging the social theories and political practices of the liberal reformers and calling themselves socialists. Henry Carter Adams, John Bates Clark, Richard T. Ely, Edmund J. James, Edwin R. A. Seligman, Edward A. Bemis, and others tried to forge a new way, and they identified the ideas of their liberal reform forebears as obstacles in the path of progress. Indeed, they entered the public arena attacking liberalism and individualism and formed their own organizations, such as the American Economic Association, in the hope of countering the cultural power exerted by liberal reformers from the many institutions they controlled. It is unlikely that they foresaw how much their fate would be determined by the elder liberals. In the mid-1880s a bitter debate ensued between the two generations in which the young social scientists were forced back onto the terrain of liberalism or out of established positions of public power altogether.[22] The conflict of the eighties had the effect of defining limits of acceptable political debate, especially about socialism, collectivism, and the democratic collective action of the working masses. The winnowing out of the unrepentantly radical social scientists, and the reconciliation of most of the older liberal reformers and younger social scientists, set the stage for the forging of a new liberalism. The impact of the liberal reformers in the creation of modern American liberalism was more profound than historians have generally recognized, both in the cultural power they exerted against the young intellectuals and in the specific programs and principles they deeded to progressives. Liberal reformers played a significant role in shaping the American solution to the problem of the relationship between democracy and capitalism, at the moment when "progressivism," "new liberalism," and social democracy erupted into the political arena of the transatlantic world. The relationship between liberal reformers and young social scientists is explored in part II of this book. The concluding chapter explores the question of the influence on progressive social thought and political practice of the new liberalism forged in the debate between the two generations of postbellum intellectuals.

These two generations of late-nineteenth-century liberal political intellectuals confronted the problem of the relationship between democracy and capitalism and in doing so reconstructed American liberalism. The importance of the new liberalism they created lay, in part, in the articulation of specific policies for the liberal democratic state. But as important was its ideological legitimation of the novel economic, political, and social relationships attendant on the rise of corporate capitalism.

One of the fundamental achievements of the new liberalism was to render the dominance of corporate capital compatible with American democracy. It hardly needs to be stated that, in doing so, it promoted the class interests of corporate capitalists. The new liberalism can thus be viewed as an instance of bourgeois ideology, and the interpretation of the origins of new liberalism presented here hence raises the question of the social position of the intellectuals who forged a new liberalism. Although I think the question is secondary to the main purpose of this study, a brief exploration of the issue will help to highlight the differences between my interpretation and others of progressive new liberalism, especially the influential "corporate liberalism" thesis. The "corporate liberalism" school argues that forward-looking and class-conscious corporate businessmen served as the advance guard of modern American liberalism and that the project of forging the ideology of corporate liberalism was a critical element in their successful bid for hegemony.[23] I argue in this book, rather, that late-nineteenth-century liberal reform and social science intellectuals, who had little direct involvement in corporate enterprise, were the prime innovators of new liberalism and its legitimation of corporate capitalism. They also were a good twenty to thirty years ahead of their business counterparts.

What did it take to be an intellectual in nineteenth-century America, and how did one's social position affect one's ideas? Crosscutting influences are evident in the lives of the liberal reform intellectuals and are worth exploring by historians interested in the culture of intellectual production. The family histories of many liberal reformers reveal the marriages of Congregationalist preachers and professors to heiresses of merchant and industrial capital.[24] There were, apparently, quite a few fathers-in-law who were eager to underwrite a lifetime of good works. Perhaps marrying one's daughter off to a man of God eased some troubled souls. By virtue of the powerful Puritan legacy and the Calvinist ambivalence toward material success, Northern intellectuals gained a measure of autonomy.

Nevertheless, institutional support for intellectual work was extremely shallow in the nineteenth-century United States: there was no state bureaucracy to speak of, higher learning was an adjunct of the Protestant churches, and the separation of church and state made churches dependent on the financial support of their members. Those who desired to live a life of the mind, to investigate, interpret, and disseminate knowledge, required access to independent means or had to plunge into the emerging market as producers of intellectual commodities. Liberal reform intellectuals either were born into money, married it, or made it as entrepreneurs of the pen. And, in all three scenarios, investment in the emerging stock and bond markets served as the means of preserving wealth and respectability and funding future intellectual endeavors. Liberal reform intellectuals were owners of capitalist property, but unlike most men of their class, their work kept them at some remove from the day-to-day activities of business and the real conflicts between labor and capital in the Gilded Age. (The journalistic entrepreneurs among them present a partial, and interesting, exception.) Even if by profession they were somewhat autonomous from the central institutions of the capitalist market, they were still financially dependent on the success of their capital investments. Therefore, if it seems that Yankee capitalists sought something profound in their intellectuals that might have encouraged the latter to rise above narrow self-interest, Northern intellectuals were quite dependent on the ownership of capitalist property in ways that made them personally sensitive to threats to property rights. By profession and the social mission assigned to them, liberal reform intellectuals stood above the fray of class interests—or so they imagined they did. But they were also profoundly enmeshed—financially, personally, and emotionally—with the capitalist elite. They were, in a double sense, the conscience of the capitalist class.

Conversely, new opportunities to pursue intellectual work and earn a decent salary undoubtedly created the circumstances in which the younger social scientists believed they could chart a more critical and autonomous course. They discovered that they were wrong when wealthy trustees of their universities pushed to remove them, and several found themselves on trial. The history of the struggle for academic freedom in the United States is a case study in the social power of capital over nineteenth-century American intellectual life. I would venture to suggest that the ambiguous social position of American intellectuals was an important element in their ability to keep at half an arm's length the promptings of particularistic self-interest and play the role of avant-garde theorists of new social and political relationships. But it also seems reasonable to observe that the virulence of the liberal reformers' defense of propertied individualism, and the social scientists' acquiescence to their elder liberal opponents, demonstrate that matters of self-interest and self-definition were never absent.[25]

A final explanation of the place and role of the intellectuals on whom I focus is necessary. The selection of the individuals arose out of the problems I chose to analyze, and my use of the phrase "political intellectual" is meant to suggest a specific category that is not adequately covered by the category "intellectual" or the currently popular "public intellectual" (although for stylistic reasons, I often use the unmodified noun "intellectual"). The analysis of political ideology requires that ideas be taken seriously, but it is rarely the most original or deepest thinkers of an age who wield the most influence in shaping ideology. A study of ideology requires that a person's influence in shaping public opinion be given greater weight than the intellectual quality of his or her work. Whereas much of what follows analyzes intellectual production, it is a different type of work than many intellectual histories, in which the main object is to trace and analyze specific ideas or to understand the work of exceptional thinkers. The subjects of these kinds of works are those individuals who formulated the ideas in question in the most precise, logical, and rigorous form, and intellectual histories thus tend to focus on the most capable and renowned thinkers of an age and often have in view the recovery of these ideas for contemporary purposes.[26]

The history of political ideology, which is more about power and culture than about the quality of ideas, demands a different approach. It should begin with social history, broadly construed, and pay particular attention to the dialectical relationship between power, politics, and culture. Rarely are those who reveal the most about political ideology in their intellectual work the best thinkers of their time. Nevertheless, they are often incisive or prescient observers, who offer complex assessments, descriptions, or prescriptions that merit close analysis. In this way, they frequently stood out in their own time, even if to a later generation their ideas seem to be of purely historical interest. Godkin, the editor of the flagship Gilded Age liberal journal, the *Nation*, was no John Dewey. But Dewey was not an influential political thinker before the late 1890s, in part because he spent the Gilded Age in his study wracking himself with the problem of Hegelian idealism.[27] In contrast, Godkin spent four hours a day writing about current politics, economics, culture, mores, and art while bringing to bear on them a well-trained and well-honed intellect. According to the pragmatist philosopher William James, "To my generation, [Godkin] was certainly the towering influence in all thought concerning public affairs, and indirectly his influence has certainly been more pervasive than that of any other writer of the generation, for he influenced other writers who never quoted him, and determined the whole current of discussion."[28] And so, Dewey was no Godkin. It would be tendentious to deny political writers such as Godkin the title "intellectual" and even worse to consign them to the irrevocably derogatory category "ideologue"—though it is impossible to deny that, at times, they descended to this level of discourse. Nevertheless, within the broad universe of publicists and political intellectuals, there were some who were more capable than others. After an exhaustive study of the writings and publications of each generation of intellectuals, I have concluded that a close analysis of the work of a few of these particularly capable thinkers reveals more than would an effort to summarize the ideology through as many examples as possible. Likewise, the central figures in this narrative are not necessarily the ones who are most familiar in the historical literature. Some of the lesser-known writers of the era (such as David A. Wells and Henry C. Adams) receive more attention than the more renowned (such as William G. Sumner and Richard T. Ely). The book is structured accordingly. I hope that what I have sacrificed in breadth has been regained through depth.

In the winter of 1872, Mark Twain and his good friend Charles Dudley Warner began writing a send-up of post–Civil War America. Their *The Gilded Age: A Tale of Today* (1873) indelibly marked the era as one of crassness, corruption, and deceit, and their name for the age has stuck—against all rescue efforts to the contrary. It is important to keep in mind that the book told a story already in process. Although it has been convenient for textbook publishers and standardized test writers to date the dawn of the Gilded Age to 1877, the novel suggests otherwise. The Gilded Age was the era of the reconstruction of the North, and it, too, began with the end of the Civil War.

Twain and Warner were associated with the liberal reform movement. No group in Reconstruction America appeared more driven than they to root out the corrupted political norms parodied in *The Gilded Age*. But liberal reform did not begin, as has often been asserted, as a reaction against the political corruption of Republican politicians.[29] It was, rather, one of the harvests of the unforeseen discord among Radical Republicans over matters in the North. Before the sordidness and corruption of party politics captured the minds of liberal reformers, the growth of a Northern labor movement had already jolted them out of the self-satisfaction they enjoyed as the tribunes of the triumphant Union.

The spring of 1865 brought the future leaders of liberal reform a brief interlude of exuberance and confidence, during which they persuaded themselves that the problems of America had been permanently resolved. The conflict that had dominated national politics since the birth of the Republic had ended; the age of slavery and freedom had closed. To liberal Radical Republicans, all the classic antinomies between equality and liberty, democracy and property, seemed to have dissolved in a patriotic transcendence. But that moment would not last. With its passing, the Gilded Age movement for "liberal reform," and the postwar reconstruction of American liberalism, would commence.

POLITICS & IDEOLOGY IN GILDED AGE LIBERAL REFORM

THE EDUCATION OF ECONOMIC MAN

THE "LABOR QUESTION," RADICAL REPUBLICANISM,
AND THE ROOTS OF LIBERAL REFORM

The citizens of New York City were awakened on the Fourth of July, 1865, by the blaring sounds of patriotism. At dawn, and for an hour after, city church bells peeled and the guns in the Battery fired salutes. In the early hours of the morning, military bands gathered at street corners, playing the songs of the war to call out the city's Union veterans and militia to assemble for the day's main attraction, the military parade to Union Square. Thousands of Union flags flew from rooftops and ship masts, and floral wreaths adorned many windows, spelling out blessings for survivors and odes to the dead. At ten in the morning, with bands playing, the soldiers began to march. They wore grayed Union Blues, carried shredded battle standards, and exposed wounds for all to see—their dismembered bodies offered up as the negative for the tableau of the reembodied nation. Starting the procession on Twenty-third Street, they proceeded north on Madison Avenue and then returned down Fifth Avenue. As they made their way along the two fashionable avenues of the parade route, the sidewalks crowded with thousands of celebrants, they could see that most of the lavish residences had been taken over for the day by those who made the lives of New York's bourgeoisie suitably gentle; cooks, chambermaids, butlers, and coachmen leaned out from the windowsills, raining shouts and flowers on the heads of their compatriots. The fervor of the citizens reached a crescendo when, at precisely eleven o'clock, the column swung out of Fourteenth Street into Union Square and the soldiers saluted the Democratic mayor and Common Council.

After the review, as the various regiments dispersed to smaller gatherings in their honor, Tammany kept up the party for the rest of the city's residents. Throughout the day bands and orators, vying to make themselves heard over a seemingly inexhaustible supply of fireworks, filled the dozens of public squares of the city to entertain and educate the citizens. "Never have we seen the great masses evince more happiness," wrote the *New York Tribune*'s reporter, who evidently saw himself at some distance from this kind of public. "If patriotism is to be judged by the amount of noise made, there can be no question that the denizens of New York are the most patriotic people in the universe." While Independence Day undoubtedly gave those New Yorkers who remained in the city an opportunity to demonstrate their heartfelt patriotism, their boisterous celebrations attested as much to the pleasure provided by a day off from work and a great party given at someone else's expense. The sheer relief felt at the end of a long war, the pride of a victory that was at many times in doubt, the pleasure of reunion with long-distant friends and relatives—all these emotions surely mingled with patriotism to give the 1865 celebrations of the Fourth a special intensity.[1]

Independence Day, under the auspices of Tammany Hall Democracy, had become a day when the streets and squares of New York City were taken over by the people as their own public space. Civic unity in this divided city was ostensibly achieved under the organizing sentiment of national patriotism.[2] But, in reality, as those who labored to produce the immense wealth of the United States' manufacturing and financial center participated in the public celebrations, many of their employers and other members of the city's elite made it an annual habit on the national holiday to escape from the muggy weather and the unkempt crowd. To each his own patriotism, as the New York elite gathered far from the raucous street festival at formal luncheons in Saratoga or Newport, where they regaled one another with fervent yet decorous patriotic orations.

Tammany was not, however, the only political agent wishing to guide popular sentiments. Republicans, after all, believed that the victory of the Union was theirs to claim. In the days surrounding the national holiday, the editors of the Republican-aligned newspapers in the city entered the competition for public influence through their columns, addressing those who might have missed the day's orations or learned the wrong lessons from them, instructing them about the uniqueness of this particular Fourth of July, its real symbolic import, and the true significance of the popular revelry. Horace Greeley, renowned and powerful editor of the *New York Tribune*, abolitionist, and champion of Western opportunity, linked nationalism to the principle of equality for all and hailed the return of the nation to the original purposes of the founding fathers. With the Union's victory and the abolition of slavery, he wrote, "our country . . . is far nearer to the realization of the hopes, the dreams, the sanguine predictions of her founders, than she ever was before. . . . May this day's observances do much toward bringing home to the understandings, the consciences of our people the truth of Equal Human Rights! and may that truth, thus reenforced, speedily make triumphantly the circuit of the globe!"[3]

Greeley's themes of national regeneration and secular millennialism, in which the nation, now redeemed, became the redeemer, echoed as Republicans aimed to trim popular patriotism to a fine figure. On the morning of July 5, the first issue of the *Nation*, a new journal established by influential abolitionist and antislavery leaders, appeared. Speaking not only to New Yorkers but to the refined middle class throughout the North, its premier editorial affirmed that Americans had good cause to celebrate this Fourth as no other had been celebrated before. The "moral and mental energy" of the country had been absorbed for half a century with the struggle over slavery—"one of the worst forms of barbarism"—and the conclusion of this conflict marked 1865 as a sacred turning point in the saga of inexorable progress. "It is not simply the triumph of American democracy that we rejoice over, but the triumph of democratic principles everywhere, for this is involved in the successful issue of our struggle with the rebellion. . . . We utter no idle boast, when we say that if the conflict of the ages, the great strife between the few and the many, between privilege and equality, between law and power, between opinion and the sword, was not closed on the day on which Lee threw down his arms, the issue was placed beyond doubt."[4]

Both the *Nation* and the *New York Tribune* expressed in their Independence Day editorials the characteristic zeal of Radical Republicans. Radicals, the virtual political representatives of the antislavery organizations, were a minority faction in the Republican Party but nonetheless influential nationally. (Although New York City was politically controlled by the Democratic Party and Radicals in the city had no local political power, New York City was the publishing capital of the United States and an important base for Radical publicity.) To Radicals, the nation had been vindicated by its successful prosecution of a war against slavery, and emancipation, in turn, proved the legitimacy of national power and its extension into new realms of activity. Specifically, they looked to the newly consolidated and newly powerful national state to complete the work of the war, which, as the *Nation* had argued, entailed not merely the end of "bloody strife" but more significantly "regeneration."[5] Radicals distinguished themselves from other Republicans by their insistence that the Reconstruction of the South on a sound foundation required the thorough integration of the freed slaves into the civil and political life of the nation, through the active intervention of the national government to guarantee and protect equal rights, equal justice, and equal suffrage for the freedmen and all

African Americans. Especially through their early advocacy of black suffrage, the Radicals set themselves apart from the rest of the Republican Party, constituting a distinct—if shifting—faction.[6]

The confident tone of the Radical press on Independence Day, proclaiming national triumph and the inexorable progress of freedom and democracy worldwide under the guidance of a purged and purified United States, belied the fear spreading in Radical circles in the summer of 1865. The moment of promise had been transmuted into the hour of danger by President Andrew Johnson's unanticipated betrayal of the Union cause in the face of widespread Southern resistance.[7] Accordingly, as Radicals faced the danger of national backsliding in the months after the war, they took to their press to marshal the Northern public for the last and most important battle of the long conflict: the battle for democracy.

To educated observers, as well as to the people at large in Europe and the Americas, the nineteenth century—for good or ill—was destined to be the century of democracy.[8] The anticipated triumph of democracy involved two related but potentially conflicting developments. First and most fundamentally, democracy required universal manhood suffrage. (Few yielded to the egalitarian logic inherent in the extension of the suffrage to include women.) Second, to some proponents, it also entailed the extension of the powers of the democratic state into new areas to accomplish the common good.[9]

The victory of the Union signified the triumph of democracy, but what exactly would democracy mean in the new order? While the Civil War invigorated convictions linking white manhood to democratic citizenship, it also profoundly disrupted the settled rituals of participation and, inevitably, each man's understanding of his worth as a citizen. In 1865, the civil status of white men in ten Confederate states hovered in limbo, even as black people, following the passage of the Thirteenth Amendment, stood poised to enter into the rights, duties, and privileges of American citizenship. Not only was the Confederate attempt at independent self-rule aborted and white Southerners' relationship to the old Union wholly out of their control, but for a civilization prone to settling disputes with violence and valuing martial virtues, the desertion of tens of thousands on the battlefield and the final defeat must have cut deeply into notions of manhood that had buoyed the ideal of the citizen since the Revolutionary era.[10] In the North, white men had consecrated the Union with their blood, deepening their bonds with the Union as well as bolstering their claims on the state. But one of every ten men who fought for the North was African American, and not a few white men had demanded a stop to the flow of white men's blood, unwittingly casting doubt on their fellows' devotion, if not their competence, with their unseemly declamations.[11]

Just as the Civil War had unsettled ingrained ideas about who was rightfully a citizen, so too had the exigencies of war violently recast the relationship of the individual American to the vastly more powerful national state. Most important, the federal government had exercised powers of revolutionary implications, given the principle of federalism and the tradition of minimal federal government. Without doubt, the most revolutionary of these acts was emancipation, begun extralegally by the army in some parts of the occupied South, furthered by Lincoln's Emancipation Proclamation, and constitutionally legitimated with the Thirteenth Amendment, which at once freed more than four million men, women, and children and wiped out more than four billion dollars' worth of slaveholders' property. Following emancipation, the next most novel innovation in American statecraft was the creation of the Bureau of Freedmen, Refugees, and Abandoned Lands, a federal agency to enforce emancipation and supervise the transition to free labor. Not only in occupied enemy territory but also in the North, the government insinuated itself into the daily lives of its citizens in an unprecedented fashion. Conscription and the suspension of the writ of habeas corpus were the most portentous of such acts, but they affected relatively few—though their exemplary force should not be underestimated. The government's assumption of control over the financial system through the creation of national banks, a national currency, and a large national debt had the most pervasive (and uneven) effect on Northerners. In addition, the Republican Party—virtually synonymous with the federal government after the secession crisis—took advantage of the absence of Southern delegations to enact the economic development program of its former Whig constituents and the homesteading program of its former Free Soil constituents. With the protectionist Morrill Tariff and its successors, the government not only raised revenue to fight the war but also nursed American large industry against its European competitors; with the Homestead Act and the Land Grant College Act, it provided for the settlement of family farmers on free land and the agricultural development of the West; with the Pacific Railroad Act, it oversaw the construction of a continental railroad that would guarantee the creation of a national market and the settlement of the frontier, along lines deemed favorable to particular interests in the North. (From 1863 to 1865, the U.S. government gave seventy-five million acres of the public domain to railroads.) Republican congressmen had overwhelmingly supported these measures to increase the instrumental powers of the federal government, and

Radical Republicans had been among the most enthusiastic backers. It remained to be seen, in 1865, whether the powerful state of wartime would be interpreted as a model to extend or an exception suitable only to a state of emergency.[12]

The conclusion of the Civil War thus placed questions about the definition of citizenship and the role of the national state at the epicenter of the Reconstruction era. Whereas all Americans who thought, spoke, or wrote about the settlement of the war faced these questions, Radical Republicans found themselves burdened with a greater need to justify themselves exactly because they advocated a sharper break with the past. After all, others could easily fall back on old arguments (generally constitutional ones) or old prejudices (often racist) to buttress their proposals for a reunion that would bring the Confederate states back into the Union on terms not far different from those in force before secession.

Radical Republicans, however, understood the Civil War as a revolutionary rupture with the past, and they refused to allow the likes of Tammany to define the future. Radicals demanded the extension of the suffrage to African American men in accord with a principled democratic universalism. In doing so, they unquestionably staked out the most advanced democratic position in the United States in 1865, given the peculiarity of Americans to perceive their own version of white manhood suffrage as a universal suffrage. (In Radical ranks, as well, were most of those who advocated woman suffrage on universalist grounds.)[13] Furthermore, Radicals unabashedly defended national supremacy and the increase of government power that accompanied it.[14] George W. Curtis, the editor of *Harper's Weekly* and the most widely read Radical publicist, believed that "the fear of consolidation or centralization which haunts some honest minds in this country curiously obscures them." The rights of the people would be better protected by the national government, for it embodied the popular sovereignty of the whole citizenry. True universal suffrage and an active national state would fulfill the democratic promise of the United States, advancing the nation into the vanguard of modern civilization.[15] For Radicals, therefore, the problem of democracy in 1865 was how to convince a war-weary, overtaxed, and unsympathetic public that, despite their brilliant victory on the battlefield, the national destiny could not be attained without taking—by the conventional standards of American political culture—two unsavory measures: admitting African American men to political equality with themselves, and strengthening the national state.

In taking up the task of persuasion, Radical publicists discovered that the two skeins of democratic expansion, the widening of the franchise and the extension of state power, were constructively entangled.[16] Conscious that they had to legitimate these political departures, they were caught unawares about matters on which they had assumed agreement—at least in the North. Since the Revolutionary era, Americans' conceptions of democracy had been interwoven with ideals of the just political economy: of what forms of property were legitimate, of what was proper in the economic transactions and relations among people, and of how the state preserved or disrupted productive activities. The vision of a free man's democracy had been central to the Civil War–era Republican Party's free labor ideology, which to many had won vindication with the Union's victory. A rough consensus in the North of the superiority of "free labor civilization" nonetheless masked profound disagreement about the character and definition of "free labor."[17]

The fundamental dividing line concerned the conditions of freedom. The producerist vernacular of free labor ideology, widely popular among Northern workers, artisans, and farmers, held that economic independence, gained through the ownership of real property or the possession of a skill that could provide a solid competence and independence, was a precondition of true freedom.[18] Producerism was buttressed by a popular version of the labor theory of value, that free men rightfully received the "fruits of their labor" and, conversely, that those who did not make a contribution to tangible production had no legitimate claims on its results. Alternatively, other Northerners, particularly those directing and financing the new industrial economy, claimed that freedom was constituted by the freedom to contract goods and services in the market. The promise of American society resided not in independence but in self-ownership and free contract. The boundary between the two visions, nevertheless, was permeable. For example, most property owners, large and small, held to a labor theory of value; they understood their wealth as the savings from their own labor and believed that constancy in the virtues of thrift, frugality, and industry had allowed them to prosper. Likewise, to workingmen and farmers, wage labor might be necessary and legitimate to get a start, but the legal regime of free contract was but a means to the larger goal of a society of roughly equal producers. Abraham Lincoln spoke to the consensus even as he unwittingly exposed the internal contradictions when, in a single speech, he extolled free society as one in which all had the freedom to choose an employer and asserted that, in the race of life, no man must remain a wage laborer for more than a brief period of capital accumulation.[19]

These once unspoken differences were forced into the open when, in 1865, Northern workingmen launched a movement for a legislated eight-hour workday. At the very moment that Radicals were heralding the irresistible advance of liberal-democratic civilization and a new era of national harmony and prosperity, workers and their allies ensured that the dawning era would be roiled by a new axial conflict, the status and condition of propertyless wage workers in a democracy.[20]

Since the days of Andrew Jackson's Bank War, the question of the relationship between democracy and capitalism had stood in the wings of American national political life; the eight-hour-day movement directed it onto the main stage. Before the war, for most native-born American men, the politician's rhetoric promising that wage earning was just a way station on the path to independent proprietorship still appeared true enough that Northerners could boast that they were free of the class conflicts that wracked the Old World.[21] But, as increasing numbers of American men and women, North and South, toiled as wage laborers from youth to death, the ideal of economic independence that had been embedded in the promise of American democracy receded more and more each year into the realm of mythology.[22]

Economic changes stimulated by the war made the matter of the worker's condition more salient than it had once seemed. But the politics of war, both grand and quotidian, determined that the labor question could become a preeminent national concern. While slavery remained a central institution in the nation, the problem of slavery and freedom overshadowed the problem of the status of the wage worker in a democracy. The way it did so was complicated—there were structural, political, and cultural constraints—and it is a subject that merits more probing by historians. At the very least, it is clear that those who did attempt to publicize the cause of wage workers in the late antebellum years were unanswerably reproached—how could free men complain when others were chattel slaves?[23] The contradiction at the heart of the U.S. polity, the union of two antagonistic civilizations in one political state, posed an insuperable obstacle to a sustained political engagement with the issues of wage labor.

The wartime appeal to the patriotism of Northern workers, however, was phrased in the cadences of producerist free labor ideology. The revolutionary nature of the war and the authorization of a popular mobilization had the unintended effect of enhancing the claims of producers, even as it deepened their attachment to the nation. At the close of the war, Northern workers, in the movement for "labor reform," rhetorically connected their struggle to the grand movement to preserve the Union and to abolish slavery.[24] Labor reformers defined the conflict between wage workers and their employers as a political question about the conditions for democratic citizenship. They insisted that the state intervene in the labor market to sustain laborers' capacity to act as citizens, no matter that such measures extended far beyond the traditions of limited government. In doing so, labor reform intersected with the Radical Republican activist program. Labor reformers thus compelled Radical Republicans to treat with them on the Radicals' own terrain. Was the labor movement a legitimate extension of the Radical Republican fight for free labor, equality, and democracy? Following the Radical model of state activism in other areas, should the state also regulate relations between workers and employers in the ostensibly free market?

Tensions always existed among Radicals about what exactly their expansive vision of democracy entailed besides black suffrage and equal citizenship. The encounter between the labor movement and Radical Republican politicians and publicists forced to the surface the contradictory ideological currents among Radicals. Radical Republicanism, as a cohesive political movement, would not survive its confrontation with the labor question.[25] The labor movement caused many onetime Radicals to disavow the general principles, methods, and goals of Radicalism. Likewise, the parallels these Radicals discerned between the political assertion of Northern workers and Southern freedmen alienated them from their own program of Reconstruction. The liberal reform movement crystallized in this reaction against the labor movement, bringing together disenchanted Radicals and some of their former antagonists among moderate and conservative Republicans and Northern Democrats.[26]

Among liberal reformers, those who had been Radicals faced the most acute dilemma in the rise of a labor movement organized and led by workers themselves. Coming from participation in humanitarian and democratic reform, they could not deny that many American wage workers lived and worked in deplorable conditions. Nonetheless, for them, class conflict, and its political incarnation as "class legislation," appeared even more ominous than growing economic inequality. To their dismay, workers created a mass political movement, which looked to the state to regulate relations between workers and capitalists and justified the measures in the name of democracy. Erstwhile Radicals, who themselves had been proponents of the active state, balked. They countered with an opposing model of the democratic citizen and a delimitation of the scope of political activity.

The new departure was in fact a repudiation of ideals that they had once held most precious. Former Radicals eased their consciences by insisting that their turnabout was a matter of science, not politics. Invoking the axioms of English classical political economy, they identified the education of economic man as the solvent of the social conflict that had arisen from the political agitations of discontented laborers. Hence, they moved on several fronts to educate workingmen into proper citizens of a liberal democracy. Universal manhood suffrage was a fact of life in the United States, or as Charles Nordhoff, a Republican moderate who would contribute much antidemocratic fare to the liberal reform movement, put it, "There are . . . Americans who do not think [popular government] the best kind of government; but probably no American out of an insane asylum imagines any other kind of government possible here just now."[27] Liberal reformers believed, however, that if citizens could be taught the scientific truth that the natural laws of the market could not be thwarted without putting civilization itself at hazard, they would stop trying to accomplish their redistributive purposes through the state. Once Americans had been molded into proper Economic Men, healthy and manly individual competition in the workplace and the political arena would displace the untoward social conflict of the "labor question."

Liberal reformers, furthermore, equated "economic man" with "citizen," thereby subordinating political activity to a normative model of economic behavior. Economic man proved himself in the competitive market. (Despite the evidence that ever increasing numbers of women were compelled to work for wages, economic man was always a man, while women workers were properly the object of benevolent charity work.)[28] He demonstrated his rationality by calculating his self-interest, all the time aware that natural economic laws determined and constrained his behavior. He certified his worth by the prosperity he achieved for himself and his family; his ruin lay in senseless political schemes that ignored the laws of the market. This subsumption of the citizen under the norm of economic man was rooted in the individualistic assumptions liberal reformers held about the appropriate social relations in a liberal-democratic society.

When put to the test, such assumptions ramified into new ideas about the proper role of the state. From 1865 to 1872, Northern workers agitated for state intervention in the relations between labor and capital, and they remained relatively indifferent to the liberal reformers' solutions to problems of the workingman and resistant to their leadership. In 1871, upheavals in two of the capitals of burgeoning international capitalism quickened liberal reformers' inchoate fears of a democracy controlled by the "proletariat."[29] In reaction, liberal reformers reevaluated their faith in the compatibility of democratic participation and active government. In its place they proclaimed the universal applicability of governance dictated by the doctrine of laissez-faire. The divisions in space on the Fourth of July, 1865, between New Yorkers in the streets and those who sought to lead them to higher moral ground prefigured the overt and direct confrontations that would lead some Radicals to question their Independence Day enthusiasm for democracy.

The eight-hour-day movement began in Massachusetts, and it was there that the rupture in the consensus over free labor ideology first became evident. As labor reformers argued that the movement for shorter hours was ratified by the values of "free labor," Radicals who disagreed were forced to make explicit their differences with the producerist critics of capitalist employers. Given the constellation of political forces and class conflict, once the Radicals asserted their opposition, they perforce abandoned the vernacular of free labor and began to invent a new justification for the market economy and the liberal democratic state.

Labor reformers, drawing on free labor ideology's linkage of free labor and the health of democracy, put forth two fundamental points in support of a legislated limit to the workday. First, long hours of work left no time, in the words of one workingman, "to comply with the public duties which we are having thrust upon us, or for the exercise of any personal gifts or longings for refined pleasures."[30] Striking a familiar theme in mid-nineteenth-century American culture, workers argued that the cultivation of personal character and the exercise of citizenship were what made a man a man and, accordingly, that a republic required men of character to sustain it. Producers in a democracy required the time to be active and virtuous citizens. Just as during the war Radicals had supported legislation to promote the common good, so now the state should limit the hours of labor in industry for the same purpose.[31]

Whereas the quest for self-cultivation could not but be lauded by middle-class Radical publicists, the second point workingmen made threatened the self-conception of these antislavery crusaders. Workingmen increasingly spoke of themselves in the idiom of liberty and slavery. Countering the platitudinous exaltation of the free laborer in the "free labor system," they provocatively questioned whether in fact they were not merely "wage slaves." Shorter hours not only would allow self-cultivation but would do so precisely because they would emancipate wage workers from the bondage that was renewed daily in and through overwork. Contending that labor "has aroused itself to a sense of its own dignity, and demands to be emancipated from the trammels which have hitherto degraded it, and that false political economy, which has made it the slave of capital," the labor reform movement drew new demarcations in the body politic.[32]

Labor reformers' claim on the Radical program of state activism found fertile ground in Massachusetts, where Radicals dominated the legislature and held the governorship. In 1865, the state legislature resolved to refer the question of eight-hour-day legislation to an appointed commission. The Special Commission on the Hours of Labor and the Condition and Prospects of the Industrial Classes was headed by Franklin B. Sanborn, abolitionist and Radical Republican, formerly one of the secret funders of John Brown's raid on Harpers Ferry.[33]

Sanborn was at the time the secretary of the American Social Science Association (ASSA), and the report of the commission was shaped by the new vogue for social science. The ASSA, founded in 1865, was modeled on the British Social Science Association, and its object was to promote the most current methods in social science and to apply scientific findings to the solution of social problems. The 1865 Massachusetts Commission on the Hours of Labor and the Condition and Prospects of the Industrial Classes was the ASSA's first experiment in fulfilling its charter to apply social science to the amelioration of social ills.[34] It also gave a preview of the notions that would displace free labor ideology for the Radicals who would become liberal reformers.

The commission concluded that the legislature should not adopt eight-hour legislation. It justified its position by asserting that legislation interfering in the contract between laborer and capitalist would violate the right of free contract. The essence of freedom was that adult men could voluntarily dispose of their power to labor and their property according to their own interests. A government that sought to "limit" this fundamental freedom "would be justly chargeable, either with gross folly or high-handed tyranny."[35] Admitting that many industries submitted workers to excessive hours, the commissioners insisted nonetheless that a reduction of hours would have to come through mutual, voluntary agreements between laborers and capitalists, not through politics or law.

The rub was how to orchestrate such a desirable agreement when workers and employers disagreed so profoundly on the subject. Capitalists insisted that honest workingmen had no interest in the eight-hour agitation and that the whole distraction had been fabricated by irresponsible idlers. Workers and labor reformers claimed that overwork degraded work in the eyes of the public, but they insisted through their rhetoric and action that they were men of character: their conditions of life impeded its flowering and its expression, but they themselves were not degraded. The difference in power between labor and capital required a political solution, according to them.

The commission ended up buffeted between these two poles, revealing not only a politic compromise but, more significant, a deep ambivalence about the character of workingmen and the instability in the conventional ideological categories about the nobility and virtue of free labor that had been forged in the antislavery struggle. The commissioners shared several of the producerist assumptions of the labor reformers, such as that the health of the community rested on the vitality of its producers, that all should receive the fruits of their labor, that consolidated wealth was a danger to democratic institutions, and that the community would profit if workers had more time to cultivate and educate themselves. But they held to the contractual definition of free labor, and whatever hopes they had for the elevation, advancement, and improvement of workingmen remained hostage to the exigencies of free contract. "Children and minors may be properly restrained for their own good. But when the season of pupilage is over, and the goal of manhood reached, then it is for the *man*, and not the *State* to say how many, or how few hours in the day he will use hand or brain for himself or those dear to him."[36] Liberty of contract separated the men from the boys.[37]

The commission's report was riddled with inconsistencies. Boston's main labor paper surmised that the odd contradictions of the report resulted from its being "the work of two minds," only one of which deserved its praise. Although the commission insinuated that there was something petulant, childish, and unmanly about the eight-hour-day movement, it nevertheless conceded much of the labor reformers' case. Overwork was extensive, sapping the vital energy of workers and causing injury and early death to many; the general good would ultimately be served by a lessening of the hours of labor; machinery should be employed to lighten labor rather than to shackle it; most workingmen would probably use their extra leisure for worthwhile pursuits; and the conditions under which many worked demeaned what should be noble—work.[38]

The commissioners had become entangled in the logical quandary at the heart of the concept of market freedom in a capitalist society, in which workers are doubly free. Given the presumption of freedom, all relations between men in a free society could be taken as evidence that rational men had voluntarily entered them. Therefore, if an individual seemed to suffer from one of his contracted relations, the problem could be traced to some deficiency in his character. In a section entitled "Whatever Lifts the Workman Elevates Work," the commissioners affirmed that more leisure time would serve as a means to elevate and honor work, while at the same time suggesting that the character of the worker determined the appropriate respect given to work. Such an ambiguity enabled them to claim that "many, in all departments of labor are now mere drudges, because they give themselves no time for anything but to drudge."[39] Nothing was amiss in the system; it was only that large numbers of individuals were insufficiently rational in the bargains they struck. Something was wrong, the commissioners gingerly implied, with the will of the working classes.

The condemnation of manual labor expressed in these observations about drudgery was one way to explain the collision between the ideal and the reality of the free labor system. Another way was to face more squarely that, with necessity impelling men to labor for wages, there was in practice an inequality between the wage laborer and the capitalist. This the commissioners refused. The commission's recommendation boiled down to one simple point: workers should prove that they were worthy of the leisure they demanded. Once they did, shorter hours would issue naturally from voluntary agreements between labor and capital, restored to their proper "harmony."[40]

"We must remind the Commission, the Legislature, and the public," concluded labor's *Daily Evening Voice*, "that the doctrine set forth in this report that the law is impotent to defend the laborer against the encroachments of the capitalist is not only ridiculous but dangerous. We have more hope of our institutions than to doubt for a moment not only that law can defend the rights of labor but that it will."[41] The commission's greatest evasion was of the questions that workingmen had inserted into the political arena. Was it possible for workers to cultivate their individual characters when overwork deprived them of the time and energy to do so? Could a nation of producers really value work when the conditions of work were degrading? Could workingmen perform their duties as citizens when all their waking hours were spent at work?

Whereas the labor movement sought to breach what it took to be the artificial boundary between the economic and the political, the commissioners hinted that workingmen would have to pass muster in the economic realm before they could be considered capable citizens: "Never was there a more glorious opportunity opened to the working men of any country, than of ours; but opportunity alone is not all that is needed; it is only as the opportunity is seized and used, wisely and manfully, by the working men themselves, that they can rise to the position of useful and honorable citizenship,—in itself higher than office,—or reach that goal of a true and noble manhood, that constitutes the only order of nobility recognized by the genius and spirit of our National Government."[42] Continuing with an exhortation to workingmen to prove themselves in the market, the commissioners left no doubt that they were speaking of economic opportunity. Workers were mistaken if they saw their political agitation as a demonstration of good citizenship. They had skipped a formative stage in the development of their manhood by failing to seize the opportunity the nation offered for their private pursuits. Paradoxically, political activity by and for workingmen became evidence of political immaturity. The market was the arena for competition, and conversely, politics was a matter of self-interested, individualistic assertion.

The 1865 Massachusetts labor commission, admitting the seriousness of the labor question and opposing eight-hour legislation, instead recommended that a nation of economic men be cultivated. Although the commissioners intended to situate their study in modern currents of social science, in fact the old and familiar question of moral character dominated their report. The commission's successor in 1866, headed by Amasa Walker, the author of the most popular textbooks on political economy in the United States, wholeheartedly accepted the dispensation of social science and more thoroughly jettisoned the old categories and prescriptions of antebellum free labor ideology.[43]

Walker, armed with the "dismal science," could not abide the rosy optimism of Sanborn's commission. There could be no exit from the harsh realities of the laws of political economy. Walker's analysis of the question of hours began with the premise that material progress was the essential condition of civilization. Therefore, "the great point to be aimed at in the culture of a people, is to secure the highest production of wealth, consistent with preserving intact all the natural powers of the laborer, and advancing his best and highest interests, his full and complete manhood."[44] The question was whether legislation could do anything to increase the worker's leisure. All the known laws of political economy—and Walker, unlike some more idiosyncratic American political economists, believed firmly in the English school—answered in the negative. Walker disagreed with the previous commission's argument that increased efficiency during shorter hours would prevent any decrease in production and wages. As a riposte, he explained how several immutable economic laws would negate the object sought by labor reformers. Simply put, the laws of economics were "above all human enactments."[45]

Perhaps it was workingmen's ignorance about obvious and fundamental scientific truths that made Walker so impatient with their claims. "All attempts to interfere with the laws of value must be ineffectual for any good object," he curtly announced; therefore, "the laborer can never be oppressed by being left at perfect liberty to work as he pleases, . . . he is never injured by *competition*, unless the laws or customs of the country deprive him of his just rights."[46] Walker concluded by recommending the familiar bourgeois verity for uplift: "Accumulations, however limited, promote not only the self-respect and independence of those who make them, but the respect and confidence of those who employ them. The amount of deposits in savings banks, so far as made by the working classes, forms *the best index* of the real progress of those classes, in pecuniary independence and in social improvement."[47] Acquisitiveness was the measure of character.

The reports by the two commissions encompassed the range of responses to the eight-hour-day movement by those who would join the liberal reform movement. Free contract was their foundational principle. Some would invoke an ideal of character—the rational, economic man—to reject workers' claims on the state; others would recite the litany of immutable natural economic laws to inform workers that any political victory would be Pyrrhic. These two propositions, first, that a man's character should be judged according to how well he performed according to the norm of the instrumentally rational, acquisitive economic man, and second, that the attempt to tinker with natural laws put civilization itself in danger, remained at the core of the liberal re-formers' reaction to the labor movement, even as their practical solutions to the labor question changed in response to the political development of labor reform.[48]

The Massachusetts commissions turned out to be more than academic ex-ercises. One of the first interventions of social science in practical politics, the commissions achieved a political victory, ensuring that Massachusetts would not pass hours legislation and thus not have to confront the consequences of it as a practical issue. That occurred in Illinois, when in March 1867 the state legislature enacted the first state eight-hour law in the nation. Labor's apparent legislative victory proved to be more ambiguous than workingmen might have desired, for several loopholes in the law allowed employers to excuse them-selves from its sanction. With the passage of this ambiguous law, the arena of struggle shifted from politics to the workplace. Chicago trade unions called for a general strike to compel employers to comply with the eight-hour law, while employers planned to keep their shops open for the usual number of hours until workers gave in. In doing so, they made Chicago, the largest and most prosperous city of the Midwest, the first site of struggle over the practical implementation of eight-hour laws.

When the general strike commenced on May 1, it was the leading Radical paper of the Midwest, the *Chicago Tribune*, that spoke for the city's business-men and, likewise, paced the shift from Radical Republicanism to liberal re-form. Horace White, the thirty-one-year-old editor in chief and co-owner, carried the paper's opinion to its mass readership. White would become, over the next three decades, a nationally prominent journalist, a Republican Party power broker, a leader of the liberal reform movement, the editor of the *New York Evening Post* (where he also covered the Wall Street beat), and one of the most respected writers in America on economics.[49] In the 1867 editorials he revealed a penchant for bringing economic theory to the people. Over and over again, White admonished the *Tribune*'s readers that the eight-hour law ignored the laws of political economy. By trying to put the legislature's law into effect, workingmen would be done in by a higher law. Either natural economic laws, such as the law of competition and the law of supply and demand, would effectively nullify the eight-hour law, or, if workers succeeded in reducing the working day to eight hours, Chicago's commerce and prosperity would be destroyed by competition from other states. White was a zealous popularizer: many of his editorials during the strike in May and June furnished simple arithmetical calculations of the costs of the strikes, designed to demonstrate how much the city stood to lose and how, in the end, workingmen and their families would suffer the most from the halt in production.[50]

More profoundly, White defined and expressed the fissure that had opened among those who had recently mobilized to win a war for Union and free labor. Underlying White's emphasis on the laws of political economy were two fundamental premises. First, capital accumulation was the essential material precondition of civilization, and the progress of civilization continued to depend on the further extension of the marvelous powers of capital. White cautioned, "Capital moves the world and keeps the hammer, the engine and the spindle at work, but it must be handled judiciously, and receive its remuneration, else its motive power ceases, and it flies away to countries which appreciate it more highly. . . . Every step that the world has taken from barbarism to civilization has been the result of capital, for capital is that which gives men the opportunity to think."[51] Although White still clearly held to a labor theory of value, in the context of a conflict between capital and labor, his notion of the preeminence of capital reversed the terms of priority and moral worth characteristic of American producerist ideology.

Not only were workingmen dishonoring the creator of their capacities and jeopardizing civilization, but they were also shaming themselves by violating the first principle of free society, the law of free contract. With the same logic as the Massachusetts commission reports but in a shriller tone, White viewed legislation interfering in the voluntary exchanges between adult men as "a restriction upon the inalienable rights of man." The eight-hour law was objectionable as a piece of "class legislation," yet, even more gravely, it sought "to regulate the private industry of adult male citizens, of sound mind, who, it may be fairly presumed, are competent to manage their own affairs."[52] Respect for the principle of free contract was the criterion by which to measure the legitimacy of workingmen's politics and self-organization. As long as trade unions merely aided workers, voluntarily joined together, "to defend their freedom of contract," they had some benefits.[53] But "the right of each man to labor as much or as little as he chooses, and to enjoy his own earnings, is the very foundation stone of free government. . . . Take this right from the workingman and he is as completely enslaved as the negro was five years ago."[54] Against the demonstration of collective action by workers, White held up the individualistic self-made man as the model for workingmen to emulate. Laborers had first to accumulate capital, and only the man alone, working hard and denying his current desires, could do so. When workers acted collectively in trade unions, they upset the harmony that had been achieved in the United States between natural economic law and free institutions. "Wages must be governed by the natural laws which control in such matters, it being only necessary to remove such obstructions and obviate such difficulties as prevent the full and fair operation of these laws. . . . Our institutions seek to secure to every man perfect freedom and independence, and then to leave his own welfare in his own hands." The rich meanings of freedom and independence in the American political tradition had been winnowed down, until what remained were free contract and freedom from restraint. In White's mind, the homilies of American equal opportunity and meritocracy merged seamlessly with the axioms of political economy.[55]

The eight-hour movement had ignited an inchoate debate about these very laws of political economy and their consequences for American democracy. Scholarly and popular political economy in the United States had shown an affinity for the optimistic varieties of classical political economy—especially the theory of harmony of interests stressed by Jean-Baptiste Say and Frédéric Bastiat—and had avoided the implications of Ricardian political economy, with its insistence on intractable conflict among the owners of land, capital, and labor.[56] With workingmen acting for their own class interest through strikes and political demonstrations and arguing that capitalists were putting the screws to them and stealing the full value of their labor, the conventional declarations by politicians, capitalists, and publicists of the harmony of interest between labor and capital were beginning to ring hollow.

Realism suggested that conflict would have to be admitted into the discourse of American political economy if it was to have any mooring in the political culture. The Massachusetts commissions had done little in this regard: Sanborn had been too optimistic, Walker too deterministic. In the midst of the

Chicago eight-hour strike, White became one of the pioneers among Radicals to navigate the storm of class conflict. In reality, White argued, capital and labor were mutually dependent on each other, but under the wages system each tried to wrest more than its value from the other, and conflict resulted. Nevertheless, an individual employer could not, as a general rule, gain more than his due because he had little control over the prevailing conditions of the market. Given that capitalists effectively received their fair share of the product of industry, the contention over its division "in great measure is caused by ignorance on the part of laborers. If they could be properly instructed in the elementary principles of political economy, strikes would terminate and all differences would be adjusted by committees of conference and arbitration between employers and employees."[57]

In other words, contrary to workingmen's opinion, there was no inherent injustice. But White understood that the perpetual disputes over wages and distribution were themselves corrosive of harmony and of social order itself. He proposed adopting a system of "co-operation" as the solution to class conflict. Workers would continue to receive daily wages, and employers would continue to receive a return on their investment equivalent to the prevailing rate of interest, but in addition, the profits above this level would be divided between employees and investors in the enterprise. Seemingly, the transparency and fairness of the division of the year's product would restore the knowledge of mutual dependence between capital and labor. White thought cooperation was "the true, and perhaps *only* method whereby the contention about compensation and profit can ever be settled between the owners of Capital and Labor."[58]

Before one deems White a protosocialist, it is important to understand what he meant by cooperation. It was not an anticapitalist or a collective system of economic organization. Rather, it accorded with the laws of political economy, and its day-to-day operation would serve to educate laborers about the inexorable market forces to which they must submit. Neither was cooperation an infringement on the rights of property. Indeed, it would augment the respect for property by rewarding workers with capital based exactly on the contribution of their labor. And most important, cooperation was not an attack on individualism. It was instead the best defense against the false collectivism of trade unionism that held Chicago business in its grip. White was sure that cooperation, "which recognizes labor as capital" with an individual reward for the labor one expended, would undermine the shiftless workers, who were always "the ringleaders in every proposition for a conflict with capital." Whereas trade unions gave "direct encouragement to mediocrity and idleness," thereby inducing workers to look for a false source of misery in the wrongs of capitalists, cooperation would "do more than anything else to encourage thrift, economy and permanency of interest among laboring men."[59] White warned that workers, through their collective power in the workplace and in the democratic state, were tumbling headlong into the Anglo-American breed of communism, "agrarianism."[60] Cooperation offered an alternative. Through it, the laws of political economy would be respected, workers would receive elementary education in the science of political economy, capital and labor would be restored to their proper harmony, and capital could continue on its civilizing mission.

By word and implication, White had condemned the behavior of the workers of Chicago in engaging in the strike for the eight-hour day. An antilabor position was of course commonplace among conservatives, and it would become so among the liberal reform movement within a few years. It was, in 1867, potentially tricky business for a Radical Republican publicist with a mass audience to say such things. Many of the striking workingmen would have been veterans of the Civil War, and most would have been mobilized to sacrifice for it with appeals to their commitment to a union in which "free labor" flourished. White indeed went to some length to preserve an image of the honorable workingman amid his campaign to discredit the labor movement, its methods, and goals. His first assay at the problem explained the strike by workers' misguided loyalty to one another. The honorable workingman was one whose tender domestic affections spurred him to excel in the tough, competitive market. The harmony between the two sides of his private life—family and work—would guarantee him a prosperous, secure, and happy future. Economic man, in popular culture, was a family man. Unfortunately, according to White, the righteous married men "were tied hand and foot by fellowship" with the strike leaders, "unmarried men . . . who can flit with the swallows, and return with the wild geese,—whose wants are only of the present, who have no wives and children dependent upon them . . . who have no such heart promptings and no such home incentives to work."[61] As the strike ended in failure, White indulged in nastier rhetoric, suggesting to workingmen that they examine how they had been injured by the "demagogues," the "miserable creatures who have set themselves up as special 'advocates' of the workingmen."[62] Cooperation offered a way to reconstitute the unity of free labor civilization and the harmony of capital and labor, even as White had revealed how far some had traveled.

By the end of May, the strike to enforce the eight-hour-day law had collapsed under the weight of employer resistance, the city police force (cheered on by White, it is worth noting), and its own internal weakness. The *Chicago Tribune* and Horace White moved on to other pressing events. White casually shrugged off his strike-born fascination with cooperation, the logical and practical flaws of his plan left unexplored. What, in fact, gave workers a claim on a share of the profits, if capital's rate of profit was naturally inscribed in economic law? How could increases in productivity be shared, and not infringe on property rights, when the fundamental dynamic of industry was to produce more and more? White's own argument pointed to a definition of property as a social and political creation, although he did not discern this in his formulation. Nor did he recognize his own uneasiness with the logic of the marketplace in his desire to curb the conflict inherent in competition. The tensions in the conception of property in cooperative schemes, as well as the dangers of actual cooperation to capitalist property, would become evident over the next five years, as workers in the United States and Europe shifted the definition of cooperation toward its affinity with modern socialism. And as this occurred, White and his like-minded colleagues would seek a safer solution to the labor problem.

The labor movement posed the question of the future of American democracy, a subject of great import to the Radical Republican publicists who defined the war as a test of democracy and viewed themselves as the most forward-looking democrats. The debate ignited by labor reformers, made concrete by the successes and failures of the eight-hour-day movement, forced Radicals to reckon with their own beliefs. As Radicals confronted the significance of the labor question for their own conception of democracy, the contradictory ideological tendencies among them rose to the surface and quite rapidly destroyed the Radical alliance. Liberal reform was forged in this political and ideological environment. But it was not the single route away from Radical Republicanism. How other Radicals interpreted the labor question and responded to the movement helps elucidate, by contrast, the character and nature of liberal reform.

The alternative—indeed, antithetical—trajectory of Radicalism was pursued by a few Radical politicians, such as the congressmen Benjamin Butler and Benjamin Wade, and by an indeterminable number of the foot soldiers of Radicalism. Among Radical intellectuals and publicists, this trajectory was most ably disseminated by Wendell Phillips. The renowned abolitionist had experienced a conversion in his political faith during the Civil War. He had begun his abolitionist career as a Garrisonian, abstaining from the morally polluted arena of politics. Once warfare against the slave South commenced, however, Phillips became an ardent supporter of political activity, as he began to see the opportunity for using the power of the national state to abolish slavery. Thus, politics became a means to achieve moral goals rather than a barrier to moral action. How deep a change of mind he had experienced was demonstrated at the June 1865 National Anti-Slavery Society meeting. William Lloyd Garrison sought to disband the abolitionist organization, arguing that with the constitutional abolition of slavery, their work had ended. Phillips insisted that the organization must continue its work; its new mission flowed necessarily from its old. Abolitionists must agitate for the rights of the former slaves, particularly their right to the suffrage. The members agreed and chose Phillips as their new president.[63]

Five months later, Phillips addressed a labor convention in support of the eight-hour day in Boston's Faneuil Hall. With this appearance he began an association with the labor reform movement that would last the rest of his life. While he viewed his participation in labor reform as a natural extension of abolitionism and radicalism, for this he would be reviled by many of his former Radical Republican allies. In 1865, having already taken a public position for the most radical of Radical Republican proposals—unconditional black suffrage, banishment of Confederate leaders, confiscation of Confederate land, and its redistribution to the loyal black and white population of the South—he now gave his blessing to the labor reform movement. "It is twenty-eight years next month since I first stood on this platform and addressed an audience of Boston citizens. I felt then that I was speaking for labor. If the speech which I make tonight be the last one I am privileged to make, I shall be glad that it is in the same strain—a speech for the laboring man and his rights."[64] Phillips thus linked the working class's campaign for the eight-hour day to the great moral cause of antislavery and then counseled labor reformers to adopt the techniques of abolitionist agitators.

Speaking with the humble assurance of one who had achieved victory after decades of struggle, Phillips pronounced, "Filtered through the ballot-box comes the will of the people, and statesmen bow to it."[65] Already in 1865 Phillips displayed his distance from many Radical Republican publicists by an unalloyed faith in the virtues of democratic activism. No natural laws of political economy or immutable facts of human nature stood in the way of the victory of rationally guided, popular direction of government to achieve a moral order in economic relations. Nevertheless, he shared the genteel prejudice that the refined, the "cultivated intellects" must be awakened to the subject of the labor question, for if they failed to weigh in on the issue, there was a danger that workingmen alone could not fully determine the truly moral and rational solution.[66] He rallied workers to make the power of their numbers felt in the political arena—but to do so in order to alert the natural leaders of society, who would then guide the nation toward the proper solution.

Pulled into the maelstrom of Massachusetts electoral politics by his new crusade, Phillips revised his understanding of political conflict and the significance of the labor question for democracy.[67] In a speech given in New York City in 1871, while he was engaged in complicated electoral maneuverings in Massachusetts, Phillips explicitly acknowledged that class conflict would necessarily be enacted in the political arena, given the current array of forces. "We stand at an epoch when the nature of the government is undergoing a fundamental change." Two powers were arrayed against each other in this new world: "the working masses that are really about to put their hands to the work of governing" and organized capital, the "moneyed corporation." He made it clear where his loyalties lay: "I confess that the only fear I have in regard to republican institutions is whether, in our day, any adequate remedy will be found for this incoming flood of the power of incorporated wealth." The "only hope of any effectual grapple with it is by rousing the actual masses, whose interests permanently lie in an opposite direction."[68]

Having pledged to stand by the working classes in the coming conflict, Phillips, like many other labor reformers and labor leaders, refuted point for point the attacks against the labor movement made by politicians, his erstwhile Radical allies, and capitalists. Inverting the claim that the laws of political economy rendered workingmen's demands moot, Phillips asserted that the law of supply and demand in fact justified the labor movement. As the working class was most subject to the fluctuations of the market, a movement with a particularistic object was necessary to protect those specially and uniquely affected. Not only was the pursuit of the much maligned "class legislation" thus legitimate, but so were the class-based organizations, trade unions, which pursued the goals of the working class. Here Phillips scathingly exposed the fiction of individual free contract and state neutrality maintained by capitalists in their attacks on unions. Labor had learned its methods of aggressive organization from capital, and Phillips warned, "While you combine and plot and defend, so will we." With the cadences of the Old Testament, as the Hebrew slaves appealed for divine justice against their oppressors, Phillips warned that as long as the privileges of capital were sheltered by the state, labor would defend itself. "Labor comes up and says, 'They have shotted their cannon to the lips; they have rough-ground their swords as in battle; they have adopted every new method; they have invented every dangerous machine; and it is all planted like a great park of artillery against us. They have incorporated wealth; they have hidden behind banks; they have concealed themselves in currency; they have sheltered themselves in taxation; they have passed rules to govern us; and we will improve upon the lesson they have taught us. When they disarm, we will—not before."[69]

Such a conception of politics as a conflict among irreconcilable powers was more robust than the one Phillips had presented to workingmen in 1865. Likewise, his idea of the solution to the labor question had deepened, and with it, his conception of equality. In 1865, he expected the solution to be derived from public debate, which would spur inquiry by the most educated and result in class harmony. Through this rationalistic and idealist approach, harmony among the classes would be achieved. In 1871, his recently evolved understanding of class division led him to advocate radical structural change. An archaic quality remained in his vision, which held up the ideal of a mythical New England of small towns where all were middling, independent producers. Nevertheless, he relished the truth that the labor movement intended to do exactly what the defenders of the money power most feared: "That's the meaning of the labor movement—an equalization of property—nothing else." To achieve a virtual equality of conditions, they would use the powers of the state to tax wealth out of existence and redistribute it to the poor and the worker. Phillips mocked those who would sacrifice the Republic to the whims of capital.

You will say, "Is that just?" My friends it is safe. Man is more valuable than money. You say, "The capital will go to Europe." Good Heavens! let it go.

If other states wish to make themselves vassals to wealth, so will not we. We will have a country equal from end to end. Land, private property, all sorts of property, shall be so dearly taxed that it shall be impossible to be rich; for it is in wealth, in incorporated, combining, perpetual wealth, that the danger of labor lies.[70]

Only the people, organized politically, could push forward the social transformations necessary to create the egalitarian democratic civilization for which the United States was destined. Since the war, Phillips had viewed political participation as educative; by the early 1870s, he had also come to believe that the moral and rational improvement of society would emerge inexorably from the crucible of political struggle. Phillips erected the political as the sphere in which men and women's true natures would flower, as they strove for a transformation that would usher in substantive equality and social justice.

Phillips was in a decided minority among onetime Radical Republican intellectuals. Most of them—and with the exception of Phillips, Frederick

Douglass, and the Woodhull sisters, all leading Radical political intellectuals—followed a different path, one that would lead them into a new liberal reform movement rather than an alliance with workingmen. To the majority of Radical publicists, Phillips's ideas were merely the ravings of a "sentimentalist," who understood neither the realities of the world nor the failings of human nature. Among these men, Edwin Lawrence Godkin was at once Phillips's most merciless critic, the most prolific writer on the labor question, and, by the late 1860s, the intellectual leader of the liberal reform movement.

Born in 1831 in Ireland, Godkin was the son of an Anglo-Irish Congregational minister and dissenting journalist, who, by the time Godkin was in his teens, had become an advocate of Irish nationalism and land reform. At Queen's College in Belfast, Edwin rejected his paternal legacy, developed a disdain for "sentimental" politics, became a confirmed religious skeptic, and discovered English political economy and the philosophy of utilitarianism. After college, he moved to London to study law but soon took up journalism instead, writing for a penny weekly, the *Workingmen's Friend*. In 1856, Godkin immigrated to the United States after determining that his prospects for a decent editorship in London or Ireland were not promising.[71]

From the time of his arrival in the United States, Godkin gave every indication of being a man on the make. And Godkin was just the kind of Englishman the educated, refined Northerner could love. He had earned his republican bona fides with a favorable portrait of the Hungarian revolutionary patriot, Louis Kossuth, in a book he published in 1853. Having met Frederick Law Olmsted and Charles Loring Brace, two prominent New Yorkers, in Europe, Godkin used them to gain admission to Northern high society. In 1859, Godkin married the daughter of a prominent antislavery Connecticut family and relative of the Beechers. Although his wife's fortune had been diminished by the 1857 panic and the death of her father, she nevertheless brought a modest inheritance and social standing to the marriage. In doing so, she made Godkin financially secure and solidified the social ties he had assiduously cultivated.[72]

On the eve of the Civil War, overwhelmed by his new domestic responsibilities, irritated by his in-laws, and still without an editorship, Godkin returned to Europe, staying there for two years. He returned to the United States shortly after Lincoln issued the Emancipation Proclamation, and he began regular newspaper writing again, his reputation enhanced by his defense of the Union in the hostile English press. Like so many others during these years, his political opinions fluctuated constantly. But Godkin's vacillation during these years was not just that shared by so many, that of trying to sort out the meaning of a revolutionary experience. Rather, he opportunistically cut himself to the figure he thought his potential American patrons would desire. His ability to do so ultimately landed him the job as the editor of the *Nation*.[73]

Godkin's reputation as the intellectual leader of Gilded Age liberalism became established in the period when he was most preoccupied with the labor question.[74] By 1866, he had alienated Radicals with his lukewarm support of black suffrage and had won total control over the *Nation*. He soon opened the pages of his weekly to new allies among Democrats and moderate and conservative Republicans, who had never shared Radicalism's enthusiasm for, respectively, a powerful national state or democracy. To Godkin, the labor question was the central problem of the postwar era: "How to raise the working classes nearer to the level of the rest of the community, in comfort, intelligence, and self-restraint, is now the great problem both of political and social science. As long as it is not solved, nothing is solved, nothing is settled, nothing can be called sure or lasting."[75]

Godkin took the evolving conception of the labor question current among the increasingly disaffected Radicals and pursued more thoroughly its political implications. As he reacted to the labor movement, his apprehensions about democracy, which had been undercurrents in his first extensive American writings, surged to the surface.[76] In doing so, he would eventually articulate one of the pillars of Gilded Age liberalism, the politics of laissez-faire.

Like his colleagues, yet even more dogmatically, Godkin perceived the individualistic, rational economic man as the epitome of human nature, not as a historical or cultural product. "There is no impulse implanted in human nature so strong and constant as the impulse to accumulate, to store up the fruits of one's industry for the purpose of procuring future enjoyment." Property, which grew from the unfettering of this instinct, stood as the foundation of civilization. If the instinct died out, which was hardly likely, "barbarism and anarchy" would instantly follow. But democracies, of which the United States was the exemplar in the modern world, gave fuller play to this instinct than any other form of government hitherto. Those who feared the power of the majority simply did not understand the ways in which democracy invigorated the "strongest passion . . . the passion for property" or "that the great peculiarity of democracy is not a taste for the spoliation of individuals or minorities, but for excessive individualizing." In accord with the blossoming individualistic spirit grew a tendency among democratic citizens to "leave things to nature, rather than regulate them by comprehensive legislation."[77] Contrary to the claims of the conservative tradition, democracy posed no risk to property; indeed, it was the system most hospitable to the flowering of individual liberty.

As the eight-hour movement spread and unionization accelerated, Godkin began to have greater doubts about the health of American democracy. Privately, he and his New York friends George W. Curtis and Charles Nordhoff were deeply troubled by the signs of the majority's passion for spoliation, manifested in eight-hour legislation, congressional debates about confiscation of the land of Confederates and its distribution to the freedmen, and Irish nationalist uprisings against the British in Canada launched from bases in the United States.[78] Instead of condemning the labor movement out of hand and calling for violent repression, as White had done in Chicago in the heat of battle, Godkin acted as if following the old adage that you catch more flies with honey than with vinegar. He would also conclude that cooperation and education in political economy were the surest solutions to the problems faced by laborers, but he arrived there by means designed to conciliate workingmen, ratchet down the level of conflict, and thereby engage the debate on a terrain more hospitable to a compromise on his terms.[79]

Godkin's most important strategic—and, in the long run, theoretical—move was to accord a limited legitimacy to trade unions. The strikes of 1867 in all the industrialized countries were merely a necessary stage of adjustment in the inexorable progress of modernity. Godkin explained that, although laborers in the civilized world had achieved legal contractual equality two centuries before, it was absurd to assert that contract was anything more than a formal, abstract right that in practice did not exist. Workers still labored under the compulsion of material needs, and this placed them in an unequal position to bargain with employers and effectively left them dependent once the bargain had been struck. The equality of the parties was a fiction, given the disparity in power, knowledge, and organization between laborers and capitalists. Viewed in this light, trade unions played a positive role by improving the bargaining position of workers against employers—themselves, Godkin insisted, collectively organized. Unions acted as collective evaluators of the individual worker's interest and, in doing so, served as the main actors in the last phase of the "emancipation" of workers into the regime of contract. Furthermore, workers acting under the guidance of trade unions tended to be more conservative about striking, and the unions educated their members about the nature of economic principles.[80]

There were a number of significant gestures in Godkin's granting of legitimacy to trade unions. First, his unqualified acknowledgment of the immediate conflict between workers and employers against the still reigning orthodoxy of their harmony of interests was a necessary step in bringing theory into some semblance of accord with the social world, and the manner in which he did so was far more serious than White's homilies on the self-made man. At the same time, admitting conflict served as well to defuse its potency, as with it Godkin offered up a means to direct conflict into less treacherous channels. Although Godkin, within a few years, would become one of the most dogmatic opponents of trade unions, at this time he discerned how the individualistic model could be renovated to include competition between collectivities organized according to the common self-interest of their members—an idea that would flourish in the Progressive Era and undergird the theory of business unionism and liberal pluralism. Second, by granting legitimacy to a force that could not be wished away, he opened up the potential for more sober intellectuals to lay down standards of behavior for participants in unions. This indeed was the real thrust of Godkin's argument. The role of trade unions should be to escort their members down the path to individualism; once this was accomplished, according to Godkin, there would be no need for unions, because equal bargaining power would have been established. In addition, the appropriate arena for trade union activity was the workplace, not the state. Improvement would come through participation in unions and contractual negotiations between organized workers and their employers, not through political movements seeking coercive legislation.

Godkin's relatively conciliatory stance toward workers, and his optimism about a solution to the conflict between labor and capital, depended on the accuracy of his prediction that the agitations by trade unions would give way to more economically rational and less political forms of behavior. If Godkin or others had any illusion that the solutions to the labor question they proffered in magazines, social clubs, and social science meetings would win over the working classes to right reason, the events of the years 1868 to 1872 dispelled them completely. This was the era of the first national and *international* organization of local trade unions, and American workers joined unions in record numbers.[81] Despite the tenuousness of these organizations in the United States, the range of activities they engaged in kept capitalists and the defenders of bourgeois society on the alert. As harbingers of the power of workers in a Western world in which democracy was emerging as the norm, Godkin understood that their influence could not be overstated.

Godkin, the immigrant who arrived in America equipped with the latest word in English philosophy, did much to infuse an antiexceptionalist perspective into American high culture. He was particularly knowledgeable about the labor movement in Europe and attuned to its ramifications for the United States.[82] From the beginning of the labor conflicts in the United States, Godkin had kept his eye on Europe so as to foretell America's future. Unlike many commentators of this period, he insisted that the United States was neither free from class conflict nor exempt from the harsher laws of political economy. Although he acknowledged the similarities and cultural affinities between the English and American trade unions, his interest was fixed on France, because, he argued, the French workers' movement was the most advanced in the world and their model would be followed by others. Early in 1868, he was cheered that in France the specter of socialism had been exorcised: "The wild dreams which led to the horrible struggle of June, 1848, have almost entirely passed away. The working-men as a body have ceased to expect anything from the state except liberty, and are completely absorbed in the experiment of co-operation." Godkin expected a liberal democracy to be established in France imminently, cooperative experiments were furthest advanced among French workers, and thus the ideal conditions for the harmonious progress of civilization seemed to be secured. He was so taken by the prospects that he even recommended some writings by French workers on political economy. His optimistic appraisals of the American labor movement up to this date grew out of his self-assurance that he could discern the course of necessary historical development.[83]

But even before Godkin had cause to regret his premature pronouncements about the conversion of French workers, the intensified political organization of American and European workers sowed doubts in his mind. From near and far came bad news: a bricklayers' strike in New York City, halting new construction in the nation's financial capital; the reelection of the infamous demagogue Ben Butler, backed by workingmen, over the challenge by a reformer; the formation of a labor party in Massachusetts and Greenback parties in the West; the founding of the International—even as many trades struck throughout the North and Northeast; Grant's effort to annex St. Domingo with its "semi-barbarous population."[84] "Even here, in what is supposed to be the fairy-land of working-men," Godkin ominously wrote, the advance of political liberty and democracy has been "welcomed by the working classes . . . because they . . . seemed to promise radical social changes, and above all a change in the relations of labor to capital [rather] than because the masses in any country share the love of Roman or political 'liberty.' . . . Working-men and women . . . all over the civilized world . . . are trying to find out what are the limits which human nature has placed on its amelioration." In their "experiments," they "absolutely refuse to be guided by either historians or philosophers."[85] Wherever these misconceptions of liberty and "human nature" surfaced, designs to redistribute property through legislation lurked, and civilization itself hung in the balance.

Just as French politics had once been a source for optimism, it became the occasion for a shift in political tactics and prescriptions once Godkin realized that his predictions had been wrong. This shift began in 1869, as Godkin explained the significance of the victory of the "radical democracy out-of-doors" over "moderate liberalism" in French elections of that year. Despite the intelligence of the French working class, the diffusion of pamphlets on political economy among them, and the success of cooperation, French workers rejected the "constitutional system" in pursuit of the wild dream of "a new social order." The significance of the radicals' election extended to every industrial democracy, revealing that "the principle of universal suffrage . . . will be followed by a movement which neither governmental coercion nor capitalist argumentation will be able to defeat . . . that is, no matter by what name it may be called, a legislative division of the profits between labor and capital."[86] The lesson from France was that cooperation was an elusive solution to the labor question and that those who wished to defend existing social institutions, even as they sought reform, would need to rely on surer methods.

Godkin's first move was to underscore the importance of education in political economy, elevating this above the structural reform of cooperation that he had formerly touted. As his hopes darkened, he took an increasingly dismal view of workers' capacities. In 1867, labor union leaders had been among the most capable and sensible men of the working classes; now, he thought, "a world governed by such lights . . . would be a world in which it is safe to say civilization of a high order could not last long, and in which the higher ends of human existence could only be very slenderly attained." He foresaw a long period of conflict that would produce "profound social and political convulsions." While arguing that higher education must be opened up to more individuals from the working classes, he minced no words about the inferiority of the masses who made up democracies. "The most pitiful spectacle of the modern world is the attempt . . . of the radical reformers to persuade us . . . that no matter how near the brute a human being may be as regards the condition of his mind, he is just as well fitted to deal with the most intricate problems of sociology as is the most patient student or investigator."[87]

Once the argument was joined on the level of the survival of civilization and workers were categorized as the new barbarians, any commitment to democracy logically had to be jettisoned. From 1868 to 1871, Godkin sketched out a theory of democratic politics characterized by a new series of oppositions. The key terms of the opposition were the "social," the "political," and the "scientific"; actual political activity took place, to speak metaphorically, in a triangular field marked off by these magnetic counterforces. The political was the most protean term in Godkin's schematic. When he attacked workingmen for wrongly seeking to accomplish *social* transformation through politics, he exalted the political as a special domain, in which individual competition safe-guarded liberty. The social, in this context, stood in as a code word for the infringement on private property rights—thus on individual liberty, which legitimate politics let alone.[88] But the political also represented the repellent world of increasingly corrupt, irrational, and incompetent American politi-cians, and at this point Godkin invoked the "scientific" as a power to wield against politics. Policy grounded in social science, "under the control of trained human reason" and carried out by professional civil servants, must replace the haphazard and sentimental lawmaking of the autodidacts and country lawyers of American legislatures.[89]

The scientific was the only unequivocally positive power in this triangular force field. His former optimism for a solution to the labor question had been rooted in faith that the three forces could be harmonized under the dominat-ing power of the scientific. Social transformation, as long as it respected the first principle of individual liberty and was ushered in under the force of natural law, with a little help from experts, was an expected part of historical progress. For example, the supersession of the regime of wages by cooperation would be a social transformation, but one that accorded with scientific law. Ideally, it would evolve gradually and voluntarily through negotiations be-tween labor and capital in the private sphere of the market. Neither party would seek the aid of the state, and thus the political, properly conceived as the arena for the protection of individual liberty, would be freed from corrupting influences. But as labor conflict and working-class political organization inten-sified from 1868 on, Godkin introduced a new theme, familiar to classical conservatism, that would sever any possibility of a concordance between the scientific and the social: "human nature" was intractable, and it was a "senti-mentalist" fiction to believe that institutions could be transformed when men remained woefully unchanged.[90]

Even as the notion of "social" change congealed into a fixed negative cate-gory in Godkin's thought, the political retained some of its multivalence. While always lamenting the defects of American politics, Godkin had insisted that individualistic democracies were superior to other forms of government be-cause they provided opportunity for all individuals to protect their interests. In addition, he had argued pragmatically for a moderately active state. For exam-ple, although he advocated free trade, on other issues he favored state action.[91]

Multiple crises in the first half of 1871, all of which Godkin connected to the international labor question, however, propelled him toward an unambiva-lently negative view of politics. Winter strikes in the coal fields of Pennsylvania threatened the fuel supply for the Northeast and pitted large capitalists against organized workers, while rumors began to circulate in the spring about the shaky and shady finances of Boss Tweed's New York.[92] But, ironically, these American conflicts gained their poignancy, for Godkin, from the revolutionary events in Paris in the spring of 1871. On March 26, 1871, following a series of repressive measures by the Monarchist National Assembly, which had come to power after France's humiliating defeat in the Franco-Prussian War, the Paris Commune was proclaimed. Composed of the forces of the French left, the commune attempted to institute socialism in the leading city of France and to encourage Communards to overthrow the regime in other French cities. In the two months of its rule, it enacted a number of measures that either undermined or abolished property rights, and it nurtured working-class and radical political organizations in Parisian civil society.[93]

In a dire tone, Godkin speculated that, regardless of the commune's defeat, its worldwide influence would be immense, as it would strengthen the labor movement and give heart to workingmen's aspirations to use political machinery for social revolution. The Communards were workers—not intellectuals or lawyers—and they had taken charge of government and maintained an army for two months, thereby giving "an air of practicalness to what all the rest of the world sneered at as unpractical." "Socialistic theories" would be regarded with even greater "repugnance" by rational men, but neither the commune's defeat nor its "excesses" would "weaken the faith of those who now hold these theories" or "lessen their attractiveness to the workingmen of the great manufacturing towns, not in France only, but everywhere." Most disturbingly, "patriotism," the glue that held individualistic societies together and made democracy less explosive, had been overcome by a "strong class feeling" among workers. Trade unions particularly were "rapidly wiping out national distinctions." To add to the problem, philosophers lent legitimacy to the Communards and other labor reformers. French Positivists and, alarmingly, even Godkin's old hero John Stuart Mill offered sophisticated theories for subversive designs. These intellectuals strengthened "the 'labor reformers' doctrine, that nobody should pocket any profit, rent, or interest which is not the product of his personal labor." Such an idea, "devoutly held by a great and increasing number of English and Continental workmen," Godkin believed "to be the seed of a barbarism compared to which that of the Dark Ages was respectable and hopeful." It was destined "to give the civilization of the Western world a severe shaking."[94]

The Paris Commune demonstrated not only that the working classes might wrest control of the state but also that conservatives had been right all along when they warned of the danger of popular rule to property. The Communards had achieved their brief reign through revolutionary activity. But with universal suffrage, a similar transformation could be achieved peacefully through the electoral process. In the United States in 1871, there were a number of illuminating examples of such an ascendancy of "class feeling" and designs to act politically on this sentiment. Labor reformers in Massachusetts, led by Wendell Phillips and Ben Butler and allied with Prohibitionists and advocates of woman suffrage, were giving the regular Republicans a serious run; the immigrant working class of New York City rallied for Tammany against a ticket of the city's "best men"; Republicans were once again dallying with the eight-hour question; white and black Republicans in Southern legislatures were enacting measures that favored small farmers and laborers against planters; and the Republican Congress passed a stiff Ku Klux Klan Act that extended federal intervention in the South in favor of the freedmen.[95] To Godkin, the signs were everywhere: democracy did, after all, threaten capitalist private property, the foundation of modern civilization.

The simplest solution, the restriction of the suffrage, was not a viable one, except in limited situations. By 1871 in the United States, universal manhood suffrage had been constitutionally secured, was ideologically hegemonic, and appeared impregnable in practice. If the radical momentum could not be arrested at its source, Godkin proposed that it could be stymied at its object: the state. On the day of the last meeting of the Paris Commune, Godkin published an editorial making what might seem to be remarkable connections between disparate historical events. "Thousands of demagogues are busy every day telling the workingmen of the civilized world of the power they now begin to possess over society, and the workingmen are not loath to exercise this power at the earliest possible moment." Referring to the International in Geneva and the commune in France, he warned that only "the wilfully blind now fail to understand the exact nature of the danger with which we are threatened; and to those who imagine that America is going to escape the convulsion, we recommend a careful study of the mining industry of Pennsylvania during the last ten years."[96]

According to Godkin, Pennsylvania industrialists were the most insistent and successful lobbyists for high protective tariffs. The tariff served their class interest, despite their high-sounding paeans to the American worker, and their political strength taught workingmen lessons about how to use the state to gain class legislation. To thwart class legislation, the state must be governed by the principle of laissez-faire. "Protectionism contains the germ of communism; what may be in the hands of the sober, thoughtful capitalist a means of stimulating a useful industry, becomes in the hands of ignorant and fanatical socialists a justification of an equal division of goods." Therefore, "the only salvation for modern society lies in making governments let people alone in all that relates to the exercise of their faculties." His earlier flexibility regarding the role of the state had to be rejected, as, "interference once begun, nobody can tell where it will end."[97]

The ideological underpinning of his new theory of the state was his old cherished one, the principle of individual liberty, and the right to private property was his sine qua non of liberty. The "only way in which the laboring classes of all countries can be prepared for the active and direct control of the body politics at which they are now aiming, is the steady and persistent preaching and *practice*, by all classes, of the doctrine that, in the choice and pursuit of a calling, there is nothing so good either for the individual or the nation as liberty."[98] Godkin defined liberty as market liberty, the "liberty to buy and sell, and mend and make, where, when, and how we please."[99] This liberty was so precious because civilization advanced by the actions of successful economic men: "The talent required for th[e] duty" of discovering profitable ventures, managing complex commercial enterprises, "is one of the rarest of gifts," and "the prosperity of the nation" depended on these capitalists' foresight and intelligence.[100] For now the United States remained a society governed by the principle of liberty. Contemplating the possibility, however, that some might try to use force to institute a society in which "the majority decided what I was to do, and how much I was to get for it," he intoned, "If war be ever lawful for any object whatever, it is lawful to wage war upon them, and destroy them to any extent that may be necessary to secure peace."[101] Once the national interest depended on the reign of entrepreneurship, the laissez-faire liberal state demanded a supplement: a state with the capacity and will to use coercive force against its own citizens.

Without "peace and harmony between classes," claimed Godkin, "no great advance in civilization" was possible. In the mid-1860s, Godkin had argued that cooperative enterprise would eliminate the root cause of class conflict. By 1871, however, cooperation was a distant prospect. Certainly the French Communards' inversion of cooperation into socialism had something to do with Godkin's shift. Workingmen would require many decades of education before they acquired the virtues of thrift, foresight, and self-restraint essential for the success of cooperation. Godkin thus concluded that until that time the burden of responsibility for maintaining social peace would rest with capitalists. "The rich men of all countries will have to be coerced by public opinion into a deeper sense of the responsibility which wealth imposes on them than the mass of them as yet show."[102] Godkin exalted the capitalist as a type, yet living capitalists, with their moral hypocrisy and consumerist excesses, distressed him. He would thenceforth write as the conscience of the capitalist class, praising it for its dynamism, upbraiding it for its shortcomings, and laying down maxims of political, social, and economic manners. These economic men needed educating as well.

Thus, in 1871, Godkin presented a coherent political project to meet the labor question, which he had honed out of his experiences and observations of class conflict and the assumptions derived from English political economy and political philosophy he had brought to the matter. Cooperation and the education of the working classes into economic men remained part of the project, but in an increasingly pessimistic mood, Godkin asserted that the benefits from these means would not accrue for generations and that civilization could be secured only through a laissez-faire state and the training of the bourgeoisie in their social duties.

The new emphasis testified to how disenchanted with democracy Godkin had become. As the enfranchised but propertyless majority became ever more eager to seek its social goals through political means, Godkin's hopes for democracy faded. If, as he argued, the masses detested individual liberty, then how could politics be maintained as a forum for individuals to protect their self-interest and liberty through political competition? His solution to the practical defeat of the individualistic conception of democracy was to magnify the importance of activity in various sites in a newly depoliticized civil society—the family, the church, the workplace, the school, the press—and to delimit political activity and condemn collective political action. In civil society would be created economic men, instrumentally rational, self-interested, and well versed in the science of political economy—the laws of which they would obey. State action could only foil this evolution in civil society, on which the progress of civilization depended. Even as democracy marched victorious on the world stage, virtuous economic man directed the campaign to extinguish his superannuated ancestor, the republican citizen, political man. Invoking the laws of political economy, Godkin preached that the division between the economic and the political was a fact of nature. The model citizen of a democracy was the economic man; real men who engaged in politics and attempted to eliminate this divide with social legislation gave proof that they had not yet developed the mind and the character requisite for competent citizenship.

Godkin's political economy of democracy was a virtual point-for-point antithesis to Phillips's, and underlying their differences were alternative conceptions of human nature. The democratic state, in Phillips's view, had become enthralled to large capital—"the money power." Without a democratic upsurge, the people would be defrauded of their rights and the moral order of democracy vanquished. To Phillips, equality and rationality were postulates of human nature, and individual freedom entailed the right of all individuals to develop their capacities fully. In addition, because all human beings (and Phillips was one of the few of his generation who truly meant *all* persons) were inherently equal, the conditions of social life for each must remain roughly equal to ensure that all had the means for self-development. Rationality, for Phillips, meant above all the potential for human beings to use their reason to shape, govern, and master the natural and social world to create an order that would allow for the self-development of each and all. He hallowed political activity as the supreme expression of human free will and rationality. Consequently, Phillips charted a path away from atomistic individualism, which was growing in prestige among many of his former Radical allies, and toward an ideal of the social nature of humankind. Politics was inherently and legitimately the arena in which citizens collectively struggled, in accord with their social nature, to achieve justice and equality. In the last two decades of his life, Phillips was traversing the bridge from free labor democratic producerism toward the American variant of democratic socialism.[103]

For Godkin, in contrast, the democratic state under the sway of the masses had become an obstacle to rational, scientific progress. More and more it impinged on individual liberty, undermining the conditions for legitimate capital accumulation. Therefore, its power to interfere in social and economic relations must be curtailed. Sharing Phillips's Enlightenment conception of human nature, Godkin nevertheless understood freedom, equality, and rationality differently. He conceived the essence of freedom to be free contract or market freedom; the essence of equality to be equal opportunity; and the essence of rationality to be the market-oriented instrumental rationality of the economic man of classical political economy. These definitions rested on the premise of atomistic individualism. To Godkin, man was from the first an autonomous being, who derived none of his talents, attributes, possessions, or rights to society, even though he had duties to society. The nature of freedom, equality, and rationality determined that some individuals, endowed with higher capacities, would gain more property and exercise authority over others. Therefore, society created institutions of authority, political institutions, only to protect the liberty of the individual against the encroachment of other individuals. Politics was a narrow strait where individuals defended their precious liberty.

Godkin's ideas were rooted in English liberalism, the locus classicus being John Locke's *Second Treatise*. The logical tensions within classical liberal theory and the political conflicts experienced by liberal regimes over three centuries had issued in a number of offshoots and revisions of classical liberalism. For Godkin, the most influential had been John Stuart Mill's synthesis of utilitarianism, classical political economy, and classical political liberalism.[104] Godkin's flexible approach to state power in the 1860s had been justified theoretically through Mill's theory, which sought to bring the liberal principle of individual liberty into concordance with the utilitarian greatest happiness principle. Mill, late in life, had perceived the difficulties of this balancing act. After concluding that the protection of the liberty of some, most especially market liberty, had become a powerful impediment to the greatest happiness of all, he had begun to call himself a socialist. Godkin charted the opposite course. Damning Mill, the intellectual idol of his youth, he instead scrapped the greatest happiness principle and consecrated individual liberty as the one, supreme object of politics.

In subsequent years, Godkin nonetheless regularly violated the political dogma, the "let alone principle," that he believed individualism demanded. In part, inconsistencies were inevitable as he struggled to maintain his footing on social ground that was shifting with the rise of organized capital, organized labor, and the long crisis of international capitalism in the late nineteenth century. But it is also necessary to insist that by the early 1870s Godkin had become a reactionary in the strict sense: his strident demands for laissez-faire in the labor market and for an unsparing use of the police power of the state against workers were both directed to a preservation of capitalist property rights. He was a reactionary, but one who still adduced liberal principles to legitimate his calls for order to be imposed from above.[105]

When the race of life in free labor civilization could no longer be so easily won, harmony gave way to conflict, and each side was forced to clarify its values. Future liberal reformers, confronting the political movement of workingmen that began in 1865, had been compelled to state explicitly their differences with the adherents of a producerist vision of free labor ideology. To avert state action, the Massachusetts Commissions on the Hours of Labor had elaborated the free contract variant of free labor ideology and had begun to emphasize the superior importance of capital in the progress of civilization and to look skeptically on political activism. An acknowledgment of a real problem was the first step in laying out a viable solution, and on this the Massachusetts commissions had failed miserably. In the midst of the Chicago eight-hour strike, White had introduced a modern and pragmatic recognition of the conflict inherent in industrial life. Cooperation and education in political economy, he argued, would at once preserve individualism, defend capitalist property, promote social mobility, preserve the conditions for the progress of civilization, and reconstitute social harmony. The success of the program depended, however, on the direction in which workingmen and their union movement evolved. Godkin, who from his editorial chair cast a broader net over the international development of the labor movement, shared White's premises to a large degree, but with an important exception. Godkin brought to the issue not only the liberal market presuppositions evident in White's thought but also a strong grounding in English political economy and political theory, which had themselves been forged in an earlier experience of industrial revolution, class formation, and class conflict.

As American workingmen became more politically and economically assertive of their own collective interests in the years before the 1873 panic, Godkin's answer to the labor question became conventional among the liberal reformers. Optimism about a harmonious future gave way to hysterical warnings of the coming of the new barbarians; gradual reformism, both to eliminate the regime of wages and to strengthen individual property rights, became displaced by incessant reminders about the inexorability of natural economic laws. In short, Godkin reminded his main audience of professionals, businessmen, and gentlemen that the American labor movement demonstrated that democracy did indeed pose a threat to capitalist property. With universal male suffrage an accomplished fact, salvation would be found only if politicians were made to understand that the government must stay out of the labor market and if he and his fellows applied themselves to the education of American economic men.

Having launched his American career in the antislavery milieu, Godkin, in his disillusionment with proletarian democracy, arrived at conclusions in which the proslavery conservatives had preceded him. Although he was the most outspoken and one of the most reactionary, he was not alone. Many onetime abolitionists, antislavery men, and their sons joined Godkin in his turn at the right fork in the road. There they met up with some of their former political antagonists, together to chart a movement hostile to the Radical Republican quest to expand American democracy. The ramifications of their journey for the freedmen, the newly minted proletarian citizens of the South, were dire.

A CIVILIZER'S ERRAND

SOUTHERN MAN, THE POLITICS OF FREE LABOR,

AND THE "RACE QUESTION"

In the fall of 1865, George William Curtis, the editor of *Harper's Weekly*, one-time abolitionist circuit speaker, and perennial Republican candidate, made a tour of New York State to promote the Radical plan of Reconstruction. Curtis informed his audiences that America's part in "the Good Fight," the central drama of human history, was "the total overthrow of the spirit of caste." In a democracy, no man was truly free unless he had the right to vote. Americans had rightfully suffered for allowing a system of racial exclusion to flourish. "The breath of our national nostrils was equal rights. The jewel of our soul was fair play for all men. But selecting one class of our population, we denied to them every natural right and sought to extinguish their humanity." Not only was it absurd to claim that the Republic was " 'a white man's government,' " but the notion itself violated the basic principle of liberal, representative government. "Government of the United States was made by men of all races and all colors, not for white men, but for the refuge and defence of *man*. If it does not rest upon the natural rights of man it rests nowhere. If it does not exist by the consent of the governed then any exclusion is possible, and it is a shorter step from an exclusively white man's government to an exclusively *rich* white man's government, than it is from a system for mankind to one for white men." But, Curtis urged his listeners, if they pushed ahead in the Good Fight and eliminated caste discrimination, "our America shall be the Sinai of the nations, and from the terrible thunders and lightnings of its great struggle shall proceed the divine law of liberty that shall subdue and harmonize the world."[1]

Curtis expressed the most noble quality of Radical Republicanism, its rejection of racialist thinking and its racist consequences and its defense of democratic universalism. His fellow Radical colleague Frederick Douglass also underscored that true nationalism rested on the respect of "human rights," which could be secured only through the enfranchisement of African Americans. This was in the early years of Reconstruction. In 1881, in the formerly Radical journal the *North American Review*, which two years earlier had published a debate questioning the wisdom of having enfranchised black men, Douglass wrote a damning article on the intransigence of racism in the United States. His confidence of 1866 had vanished; the conviction that history was on the side of those who believed in the universal principles of equality, liberty, and democracy had been supplanted by the sensibility of a secular prophet testifying against his time. According to Douglass, "the color line" had been redrawn in the brutish world of post-Reconstruction America. "They are Negroes—and that is enough, in the eye of this unreasoning prejudice, to justify indignity and violence. . . . Without crime or offense against law or gospel, the colored man is the Jean Valjean of American society. . . . He has ceased to be the slave of an individual, but has in some sense become the slave of society. He may not now be bought and sold like a beast in the market, but he is the trammeled victim of a prejudice, well calculated to repress his manly ambition, paralyze his energies, and make him a dejected and spiritless man, if not a sullen enemy to society, fit to prey upon life and property and to make trouble generally."[2]

Douglass's indictment was the measure of hopes for freedom and democracy betrayed. The betrayal of the more than four million African Americans in the United States, and of democracy itself, was hastened along by Douglass's former political allies, Radical Republican publicists who, by the early 1870s, had refashioned themselves as liberal reformers. By the beginning of the 1870s, these onetime propagandists for black suffrage were disavowing its consequences. The explosion of the Northern "labor question," combined with its Southern variant, the creation of a free labor system, had pushed them to this point. The enfranchisement of former slave men had produced unexpected results. Viewing the Reconstruction governments as they were refracted through their perception of the Northern labor movement and Northern democracy, liberal reformers began to perceive the freedmen as a less sophisticated, but more potent, body of proletarian voters.[3] As they came to measure the legitimacy of freedpeople's political activity by the gauge of economic rationality, liberal reformers found former slaves wanting in the basic qualities of the democratic citizen. Ambiguities in Radicals' rejection of racism would provide an explanation of the freedman's perceived divergence from norms of human nature. In their abandonment of the freedmen to Southern "home rule" and their opposition to the Reconstruction they had once demanded, liberal reformers articulated a new principle for justifying hierarchies of citizenship in a liberal democracy. It was one that could appear logically consonant with their scientific worldview, even as it aided in achieving the limitation of democratic practices they desired.

At the end of the war, almost all Radical Republicans favored and expected a sweeping economic reconstruction of the former slave South. They disagreed, however, on the methods that would be legitimate to force such a revolutionary transformation. Only a few Radicals followed the logic of their own political economy. If capital was accumulated labor—the savings laborers kept from their earnings—and the value of the slave's labor had been stolen from him by the laws of a barbaric civilization and an idle class, then the true laws of property would return the stolen goods to the slave. It was simply "naked justice to the former slave," Wendell Phillips pointed out, to distribute land to him and provide "a share of his inheritance" that his labor had created.[4] On the left wing of the Radical alliance, some abolitionists, congressmen, and Union army officers supported the freedmen's quest for independent landownership and called for a general confiscation of the land of slave owners and its redistribution to freed men and propertyless white Southern men. To many of these Radicals, such a policy would forge a class of industrious and independent farmers that was considered to be the bulwark of republican government.[5]

By far the majority of Radicals, however, resisted such a radical incursion against property rights, even as they hoped for a gradual diffusion of land-ownership among the freedmen. On this subject, they had much in common with the other factions of their party: many Republicans projected that a comprehensive economic transformation would gradually and naturally ensue in the South, once slavery and its degenerative influence had been rooted out. For these Radicals and many other Republicans, the labor contract, underwritten by the principles of free contract and legal equality, served as a legitimate means to begin the transformation to a free labor system. They insisted that the agencies of the national government in the South, the army and the Freedmen's Bureau, ensure the implementation of free contractual relations between former slave owners and freed men and women and prevent slavery from continuing under a different guise. According to this theory, unlike Northern workers, slaves had never had an incentive to work efficiently and rationally, for they were denied the rewards of their labor. The labor contract would introduce both ex-slaves and ex-masters to the market, where all individuals were equal and free, and each received rewards based on the value of his contribution to production. In the market the former antagonists would learn that their interests were truly in harmony. That both parties had to be coerced into entering the contract did not trouble its Northern proponents; it was merely evidence of the poor habits inculcated by slavery. Like Northern workers, freed men and women would now be able to calculate the link between labor and property, and they would learn to save their earnings and buy land. The opportunity to become independent through hard work and thrift was offered to the former slaves as freedom. Freed men and women gave ample testimony that they viewed such a vision as a cramped one. Nonetheless, these Radicals came forth with exuberant rhetoric about the virtues of free contract and equal opportunity—free labor would work a rapid transformation of the freedmen's character, after which they would stand on level ground with the Northern producer.[6]

Political economy provided the paradigm for evaluating each man's character. As applied to the South, it diagnosed an entire region out of step with modern civilization. The venerable abolitionist and Radical Edmund Quincy sermonized, "The laws of political economy have always been fighting against slavery. They have now compelled it to surrender, and they will not suffer their victory to be a barren one. . . . If there be not a reconstruction of Southern society through its repentance and voluntary return to obedience to those divine laws, there certainly will follow, and in no long time, its reconstruction through bankruptcy."[7] Slavery had thoroughly scourged Southern society, fostering a disdain for honest labor, killing incentive for enterprise and innovation, encouraging inefficient and wasteful use of resources, and begetting a host of moral vices. No one was immune. The degraded Southern white poor was another base product of slave society. One Northern traveler, known for his journalistic attacks on the working classes of New York City, had kind things to say of the freedmen in the low country of South Carolina. They were managing their lives well, while the white people of the state could not feed and shelter themselves, because they had been accustomed to the "aristocracy" taking care of their affairs and did not know how to make it on their own.[8] Indeed, the assertion by antebellum Northern observers that the nonslaveholding white farmers of the South were lazy, ignorant, and backward had been one of the stock indictments against slave society.

The South was full of men in need of education in the rudiments of Yankee pluck. The inability of common white men to take care of themselves was matched by the haughty resistance of the planter class to the ways of civilization. This backward land, according to Radicals, needed the mission of the North. Edward Atkinson, one of the few antislavery textile manufacturers, imagined that the institution of free labor in the South would turn the region into a magnet for industrious Yankees and their fruitful capital, which together would transform the region into a new New England.[9] Quincy asserted that the "true prosperity and power" of a society rested on "the moral and physical well-being" of "the labouring class." He warned that white Southerners resisted the free labor system at their peril. "Capital must either be created anew by cheerful and well-paid labor, or it must be transfused from without. . . . The necessity of the case must compel the present race at the South to work themselves, and to make it worth the while of blacks to work, or they must give way to a peaceful incursion of Northern hordes that will bring civilization, and prosperity, and Christianity in their train."[10] The mentality of the colonizing missionary revealed itself in the vision of a civilization born of Northern capital and upright Northern emigrants. The economic interests of the colonizer, as well, were on display in the swarm of Northerners who descended on the South after the war, looking to capitalize on the ruins of the plantation economy.[11] The colonialist character of the Northern project reached its most refined development among Radicals who opposed land redistribution. Economic transformation, accomplished through political and military domination, would remake the people of the South, and civilization would thus be implanted in the dark corner of the nation.

When disorder persisted in the South after the end of the war, all signs pointed to the institution of slavery and the corrupted social mores it had bred among white people as the cause of the trouble. This idea flowed naturally from the Radicals' diagnosis of the existing power relations, in which many white Confederates continued to defy federal authority and former slave owners attempted to keep freed men and women in virtual slavery. But there was also something else at work shaping their apprehension—and misapprehension—of the situation. Antislavery ideology had taught that slavery degraded all labor—white and black alike—encouraged unrepublican and tyrannical natures in slaveholders, and perpetuated the economic backwardness of the South. Radicals attributed the difficulties of instituting free labor and the conflicts among former slave owners, former slaves, and Northern representatives to the inferiority of Southerners. And the Southerners Radicals most regularly condemned were not the freed men and women, who were the most dependable Unionists in the region, but the idle and disloyal whites—planter and yeoman alike—whose natures had been deformed by the slave system.[12] Principles converged with the politics of securing a free Union to tailor the interpretation of Southern character; those who had been traitors resisted free civilization, while loyal ex-slaves energetically embraced it.

Thus, when Radicals received reports of widespread disorder in Southern agriculture from the representatives of the government, from their business agents, and from the journalists they dispatched to the South, they tended to avoid publicly attributing the trouble to the behavior of former slaves. Not only did their nationalism and antislavery convictions predispose them to suspect ex-slaveholding Confederates of conspiring to undermine Reconstruction; just as important, for Radicals to make their case for the civil and political equality of African Americans, they had to portray former slaves as competent to exercise the duties of citizenship. Given the pervasiveness among Radicals of the norm of economic man—that is, that market-oriented productive labor demonstrated one's rationality and provided the justification for democratic citizenship—their commendations were bound to be phrased in the terms of economic rationality. Since former slaves had entered the free labor system with no property and the government was not going to provide it for them, they would have to work for landowners and support themselves with the wages earned in staple crop production. How would people who had never experienced the peculiar incentives of the free market adjust? Slaveholders had always insisted that black people were inherently idle and that only force compelled them to work. To Northerners, particularly Radicals, their entire program of Reconstruction rested on the validity of the proposition that free labor was universally more natural, efficient, and just.[13]

As Radicals had argued that alleged racial differences were irrelevant to citizenship, so too they tried to resist the temptation to interpret the difficult transition from slavery to free labor as evidence of racial predispositions. Freedmen lacked the traits of fully formed economic men not because they were, as their former oppressors had it, a childlike race but because they had been systematically deprived of education and responsibility for their own lives. W. F. Allen, sent to the South by an association of Northern businessmen to assess conditions in agriculture, recommended in the *Nation* that former slaves be paid by the piece for each task, for the system appealed to the desire to work more to acquire more money—and would stimulate production. But he worried that this innate human characteristic had been suppressed in the former slaves. "The great danger to the negro will be that such will be the competition for his labor as to cause his wages to increase faster than his wants, and thus cause him to become idle." The "cure" was "education to raise his standard of life." Fortunately there was evidence that such progress would be rapid, as "the demand of the stores established upon the Sea Islands" proved that a change "from the coarse and simple requirements of a slave population to a demand nearly like that of a New England village" was already under way.[14] Unlike their Southern counterparts, the paternalistic Northern missionaries imagined that the former slaves possessed the capacity for improvement. The apprenticeship in consumer desire was expected to be of brief duration. Should freedmen learn the lessons of civilization well and begin to develop mental cultivation and economic rationality, racial differences would effectively vanish. Moreover, political rights were fundamental to the creation of economic men out of freed men. Quincy, arguing that an element of humanity's progress was the growing ability of different nationalities to live together, predicted that once "absolute political justice" for the freedmen had been won, the South would achieve an ideal state "of whites and blacks living together in political, industrial unity, and enjoying the prosperity and happiness which spring from impartial justice."[15]

While Radicals labored to be in the vanguard of a nonracial justice, they could not wholly escape the racialism through which the contradiction of slavery and freedom in American society became manifest.[16] For the most part, they conceived of race as differences rooted in cultural and historical experience, not biological nature. But when they pondered how deep down in the soul this conditioning penetrated and thus how malleable the newly freed men and women would be, biology reared its head. Was slavery the sole cause of the differences observed between black and white people in the United States, or did the distant heritage of the African past continue to exert a power over the black American's essential nature? How quickly could the former slaves shed the behavior and values developed in two centuries of enslavement? To many, not just Radical Republicans, the answers to these questions were fundamental to the former slaves' prospects in the United States. Curtis, for example, believed that slavery had blunted the character of the enslaved, but in praising the political interest displayed by freedmen in 1868, he asked, "Does any man seriously doubt whether it is better for this population to be sinking deeper and deeper in ignorance and servility, or rising into general intelligence and self-respect? They can not be pariahs; they can not be peons; they must be slaves or citizens."[17]

The tendency to think that human beings were shaped by their environment, combined with the ambivalence arising from advocating full legal and political equality for a body of people few Radical Republicans believed fit yet for such responsibilities, led most Radical intellectuals toward a convenient evasion concerning the capacities of former slaves. Under the tutelage of Northerners—ideally, cultured New Englanders—the former slaves would be released from the slave owners' prison of perpetual adolescence. Northern teachers, missionaries, and agents of the Freedmen's Bureau would outfit the freedmen for freedom by cultivating in them the attributes needed for success in free labor civilization. Experience was the best teacher, as long as it was supervised by the right sort. Allen observed that freedmen tended to avoid entering into labor contracts, for cotton and slavery were inextricably bound in their minds. Rather than condemning this behavior as an example of economic irrationality, he praised freedmen for their self-assertion. "The fact is, that while we are debating what amount of capacity the black man possesses he has gone beyond the anticipations of his warmest friends—he not only realizes that he is free, but he is not at all disposed to accept any restrictions on his perfect freedom. Those who have been flattering themselves that he would have to pass through a transition state will be disappointed." Yet Allen's freedom was a narrow strait. How easily it could be subverted by false conceptions. "The only trouble now is to prevent him from mistaking license for liberty: to inculcate the doctrine of responsibility among the blacks now should be the aim of every Northern man at the South to-day. For it is only from Northern men the blacks will stoop to learn." But some Northerners were ill suited for such profound responsibilities. Allen chastised white soldiers for deceiving the freedmen "with ridiculous and outrageous" stories about the government giving them land and blamed black soldiers for fostering all the "bad habits" displayed by freedmen. The manly self-assertion of former slaves, when expressed outside the channels sanctioned by the refined class of Northerners, revealed an immature, irresponsible notion of freedom—license.[18]

Thus did those Radicals who would become liberal reformers rationalize that they saw rational market men in the making when they scrutinized the economic activities of freedmen. Through the spring of 1867, however, their attention to economic reconstruction was subordinated to the political questions of Reconstruction. When freedmen gained their first opportunity to vote, through the provisions of the Reconstruction Acts of 1867, Radical publicists uniformly reported the men's behavior favorably. But the undercurrents in their reports testified to the opening divide in the Radical Republican alliance.[19]

What alerted Radical publicists anew to economic questions was the reintroduction of "confiscation" in Congress. In March 1867, Thaddeus Stevens and Charles Sumner, the leading congressional Radicals, introduced bills in both chambers to provide forty acres and agricultural supplies to freedmen from land confiscated from Confederates.[20] Stevens believed land to be more fundamental to the freedmen than the ballot, and although he had raised the issue of confiscation in 1865 and 1866, he had waited to press the matter until he believed that the Northern public was ready. There had never been much support for land redistribution among Republican politicians, not even among Radicals, and there was probably no time after the close of the war at which a measure as radical as the one Stevens proposed could have passed.[21] But the spring of 1867 turned out to be a particularly inauspicious time to agitate the issue, for it coincided with the passage of eight-hour laws in several states and a burst of strikes in the North. Confiscation only intensified a reaction against Radicalism already under way.

Radical publicists such as E. L. Godkin, Curtis, and Horace White had always rejected wholesale redistribution of land in the South. But, at least in 1865, the policy had been within the bounds of acceptable debate. The *Atlantic Monthly* had published an article by Thomas Wentworth Higginson—a former commander of a black regiment and a future liberal reformer—advocating land redistribution. In 1867, the magazine joined almost all other Radical papers in denouncing Stevens's extremism. The proposition clearly unnerved some. Godkin wrote Charles E. Norton about a talk he had had with Curtis and Charles Nordhoff. Norton wrote back: "Of course I agree with you entirely as regards the danger which would attend a policy of Confiscation. It would be unmistakably evil. But I do not share your anxiety in regard to the probability of its adoption. On such a matter Curtis is a very unsafe judge. He is, as we have often said, so susceptible to the currents of popular opinion, that he feels a momentary and passing breath as strongly as if it were the settled tradewind of resolve."[22]

The world outside Norton's Cambridge window may have made him an unsafe judge of Curtis's assessment of popular forces. The town of Cambridge was virtually untouched by labor conflict, and the Massachusetts legislature had apparently already rebuffed the eight-hour movement in the state. In contrast, Curtis edited the most widely read national middle-class weekly from a city wracked by labor struggles. White, one of the most politically savvy of the doubting Radicals, apparently shared Curtis's appraisal of the danger and likewise saw a relationship between Reconstruction politics and the labor movement. During the Chicago eight-hour strike, he proclaimed that there was no need for more congressional legislation on the Reconstruction of the South.[23]

While Radical publicists intimated in subtle and not so subtle ways the link they perceived between labor conflict in the North and renewed proposals for confiscation in the South, the *Nation* bluntly spelled out the lesson to be learned. "There is no question—and this eight-hour agitation, the Fenian agitation, and the negro confiscation agitation at the South prove it—that the mental and moral condition of the laboring classes is rapidly becoming in America what it is in Europe, the great social and political question of the day."[24] In July 1867, two weeks after the Senate passed an eight-hour law for federal employees, Godkin's magazine issued a declaration of independence from the left-wing congressional Radicals, while nonetheless appropriating the cachet of Radicalism in the new departure. Offering advice to troubled Radicals, the *Nation* proposed that the work of Reconstruction had been virtually completed and that it was time for reformers to turn their attention to problems that had been ignored in the long struggle against slavery.[25]

The new demands Godkin and his fellow *Nation* editorialists had in mind raised the age-old problem of democracy: Was property safe when the propertyless masses could vote? The left-wing Radicals had more than gone astray when they advocated land confiscation, "repudiation of the debt," and eight-hour-day legislation; they had betrayed fundamental principles. "All the propositions which are made by demagogues, looking toward special favors for special classes of people, are simply schemes of robbery which will, if carried out, despoil the majority of the very classes intended to be favored." Demagogues had lately been the exclusive property of the Democratic Party, but no informed Northerner could fail to see that this devastating charge was directed at Republicans such as Thaddeus Stevens, Ben Butler, and William D. "Pig Iron" Kelley. "It is not the mission of true radicalism to enter upon such schemes. . . . In the sphere of politics it has long been the maxim of radicals that nothing can or should be done except to secure to every man the free use of his powers and a fair and equal opportunity for his development." The purpose of democratic government was to secure free competition and negotiation between individuals. The liberal form of democracy was the only legitimate one.[26]

What impelled the *Nation* to renounce its Radical Republican allies? The significant issues of the day were being ignored by the political parties and elected officials. "But who cannot see that there are many other great questions which have been lying in abeyance during this great struggle, and which will give ample scope to the powers of the most radical reformer?" By 1867 it had become clear to the "true" Radicals at the *Nation* that the democracy that had triumphed in 1865 was diseased. "With a system of taxation which demoralizes a large part of the community, with rotten legislatures, municipalities, and judges, with systems of education grossly defective, with extravagance and inefficiency the rule in government rather than the exception, it is clear that no one need fear that the work of reform is at an end."[27] New conflicts had emerged that struck the Radical alliance at its most vulnerable point: whether it was legitimate to use state power to achieve economic and social change. Workers' demands for a legislated eight-hour day, and freedmen's willingness to use their new political power to try to gain land, bombarded the Radical Republicans with the weapons of state activism they had fashioned.

Thus, in 1867, with much of the basic Radical program effectively instituted—though, it must be emphasized, tenuously so—many of its onetime leaders hastily pronounced the end of Reconstruction and the passing of Radicalism. The poor showing of the Republicans in the fall elections only solidified their conviction that their allies had gone too far by their support for the "better distribution of landed property at the South, and the production of a general rise in wages combined with the shortening of the hours of labor, and finally, for the cheating of the public creditors," and that it was time for a turn toward the center.[28] By early 1868, the most important Radical forums—the *Nation*, the *North American Review*, the *Atlantic Monthly*, *Harper's Weekly*, and the *Chicago Tribune*—had all signaled their favor for the presidential candidacy of the distinctively unradical cipher, Ulysses S. Grant, and refrained from describing themselves as Radicals.[29]

Questions of economic reconstruction, however, would not disappear simply because the Radical Republicans had faded from power, for before they lost power, they had achieved their main political goal: the enfranchisement of the freedmen of the former Confederate states. And once former slaves had the ballot, their ideas of freedom would perforce be asserted in the formal arenas of political life. Freed men and women understood freedom to be a state of independence, to be secured through access to productive resources—land, livestock, and other agricultural necessities. And they understandably believed that the theft of their labor and the denial of basic human rights for more than two centuries entitled them to freedom dues. Just as English indentured servants in seventeenth-century Virginia had received land upon the end of their bondage, and just as soldiers who fought in the Revolutionary War had been rewarded in the same fashion for their service to the new nation, former slaves thought they should be compensated by the government upon emancipation. But these ideas clashed with the assumptions of free contract held by liberal reformers. After emancipation, freed men and women maneuvered and negotiated to win some concessions to their vision. Nevertheless, the Freedmen's Bureau, the most powerful of the parties contending to shape the postemancipation order in the South, had successfully resurrected staple crop production in 1866 and 1867 on the basis of the labor contract between former slaves and former slaveholding planters. The contract, for all its coercive provisions, did institutionalize principles of legal equality and due process of law and in theory established the means for free workers to accumulate property from their earnings as wage laborers. Those who predicted that the wages earned could be used to establish independence were projecting rather unrealistic dreams—for anyone who examined the Northern economy could see that the old promise of opportunity was vanishing. But conditions in Southern agriculture rendered the projection wholly unreal. The destruction by war of the infrastructure of agricultural production, the shortage of capital and cash (exacerbated by the structure of the national banking system), and two years of alternating droughts and floods left Southern agriculture a wreck. No amount of industry, thrift, and foresight by workers in these depressed conditions would have enabled a substantial number of former slaves to purchase land. Even when some were able to accumulate money out of scanty wages, most white landowners refused to sell land to black people, even preferring the state to foreclose land for nonpayment of taxes than to sell to former slaves.[30]

In this dismal economic environment, enfranchisement in 1867 rekindled freedmen's hopes that their vision of independence could be fulfilled, this time through political mobilization.[31] While Northern wage workers were lobbying for eight-hour legislation in the North, the Reconstruction Acts of 1867 created a million new landless, laboring voters in ten of the former Confederate states, endowing these men with the power to impress their vision of political economy on the state just as Northern workers were attempting to do. Anxious onetime Radical publicists, already wary of extreme tendencies within the Republican Party and the Northern working class, applauded the victory of their program but closely scrutinized the progress of Southern politics for acts beyond the bounds of acceptable political action. Even as the *Nation* commended South Carolina freedmen for their common sense in voting for loyalist whites, it warned that if Southern Republicans "resort to oppressive and unfair legislation, they will injure themselves by driving away capital."[32]

In the year between the opening of Grant's presidential campaign in January 1868 and the congressional adoption of the Fifteenth Amendment in February 1869, the leaders of the nascent liberal reform movement expressed a subtle change in their perception of freedmen. All that could be done for the former slaves had been done: the bureau had supervised the transition to free labor for several years, and freedmen now had the ballot to protect themselves. It was time to see how the former slaves would acquit themselves in the new world of freedom and political equality. Would they develop the traits of economic rationality that signaled their incorporation into civilization? If not, how would liberal reformers explain their failure to conform to a normative standard of behavior? Given the peculiar history of ideas of race in the United States, the question of the significance of race lay dormant as the evaluations began.

In the fall of 1868, the *Atlantic Monthly* published the reflections of a Freed-men's Bureau officer in South Carolina, John W. De Forest. The journal had been a consistent partisan for the nonracial Radical principles and had provided a forum for leading critics of American racism, such as Frederick Douglass and Charles Sumner. But De Forest indulged in a racialism that a year earlier would have been beyond the pale of acceptable Radical debate.[33] And in his presentation, the hierarchy of races and the norm of economic rationality thoroughly interpenetrated each other. "First savages, then slaves," De Forest wrote, the freedmen were a mentally and morally inferior "race," as their imperfect adaptation to agricultural wage labor proved. Freed men and women were both averse to steady labor, he claimed. (De Forest, whose later novels demonstrate that he well understood the etiquette of gender, did not explain why freed women should do agricultural labor instead of guarding the "domestic sphere" for their families.) Former slaves had taken real opportunities to amass capital and squandered the money on trifles and amusements; they were spendthrift and overly generous with their extended families and friends. But De Forest was a difficult man to please, for he was equally piqued by those who saved money, moved to town, set themselves up independently, and engaged in sharp business practices. De Forest neither admired generosity nor appreciated such exemplary display of economic rationality. To him, the freedmen's behavior illustrated that they had received "an imperfect moral education as to the distinction between *meum* and *teum*."[34]

One of the disconcerting "amusements" that distracted freedmen from steady labor was political activity. The freedmen's "zeal for political gatherings" ultimately resulted in "no great harm," given that his district produced more than enough food despite a political mobilization of great vitality. Still, De Forest exposed his assumption that African Americans had to demonstrate their capacity for economic rationality before their political organizing could be seen as credible in its own right, not just an expedient policy of Reconstruction.[35]

De Forest presented his theories as the realistic observations and experiences of a loyal Republican working in the South. Drawing the moral from his narrative, he concluded that "the higher civilization of the Caucasian is gripping the race in many ways, and bringing it to a sharp trial before its time.... It is doubtless well for his chances of existence that his color keeps him a plebeian, so that, like the European peasant held down by caste, he is less tempted to destroy himself in the struggle to become a patrician."[36] Speaking earlier of races of "Chinamen," "semi-civilized Syrians," "Anglo-Saxon," and "Negroes," as well as of "natural selection," De Forest displayed how preexisting environmentalist conceptions of races as distinct, hierarchically ordered civilizations could be overlaid with the new catchphrases of Darwinian biology. The persistence of environmentalist conceptions accorded with his wait-and-see approach: the nature of the "Negro" had been shaped by the backward civilizations he had lived in, but now that he had been ushered into the highest form of civilization, free society, he had the opportunity to develop. Pessimism about success could be explained through the possibility that more fundamental biological laws were at work.

The *Nation* defined the terms of the coming test of the freedmen more explicitly, broadcasting its impatience to get on with the new work. Reflecting on the passage of the Fifteenth Amendment, Arthur G. Sedgwick, one of the weekly's main political writers, explained that it was the final measure that could be justified by liberal principles of democracy. "But *the ballot is no panacea for political ills*. . . . Very little good will come to [the freedman] from laws or constitutional amendments unless supplemented by what in other cases has given newly-enfranchised classes influence among the communities which gave them the suffrage." Sedgwick proceeded to provide a telling comparison in support of his thesis. The German immigrant in the United States educated himself, saved his wages, made self-interested bargains in the market, and used "the ballot intelligently as a weapon against all who would trifle with his liberties." The Irishman in New York City, in contrast, "has no rights which his governors are bound to respect, and this merely for the reason that he is ignorant, and neither industrious, sober, nor thrifty." The Irish wrought his own shackles by electing his own oppressors. Which would the newly enfranchised freed men emulate, German economic man and liberal democrat, or Irish political man? "If the negro will work and earn money, if he will put it away in banks and not squander it in riotous living, if he learns to make as sharp a bargain as his white neighbor, then the ballot will be of some use to him, but not otherwise. Every deposit in a savings-bank is worth ten votes to him. His color will be forgotten as soon as he is 'respectable,' and to be 'respectable' in modern times means to exhibit the faculty of acquiring independent wealth." Color once signified a menial class position, and that in itself was the clue to deficient character. As soon as the connection was sundered, race in effect would vanish, and the freedman would exit the national stage.[37]

Clearly the political activity of freedmen resonated with the disturbances in the North animating liberal reformers. By 1869, liberal reformers explicitly feared the redistributive tendencies in the "class legislation" of the labor movement. Southern Reconstruction governments appeared headed down the same road to ruin. As Southern Republicans gained power, they recast the traditional weak Southern state along the activist lines pioneered by Radicals. Some of their programs merely took on responsibilities long assumed by Northern states, such as public education and road building, or copied the North in the encouragement of development projects. But others reversed the traditional balance of class power. Between 1870 and 1873, Reconstruction governments enacted measures to favor the landless, the laborer, and the debtor. Southern planters for the first time found themselves shut off from the privileges that flowed from control of the state and, even more galling to them, paying taxes to support the measures they opposed.[38]

The promise of the free labor civilization heralded by Radicals lay not only in the elevation of freedmen into free men but, just as important, in the transformation of the South into a rich commercial civilization.[39] By 1870, however, liberal reformers had begun to discern a connection between Republican Reconstruction governments and lagging economic recovery in the South and, consequently, to manifest remarkable sympathy for their former enemies, the ex-slaveholding planters of the South. James Parton, onetime Radical, a regular contributor to the *Atlantic Monthly*, and the author of several exposés of corruption in Northern government, penned an ode to Virginia's entry into civilization via a projected railroad between New York and Virginia. "We feel more than a sentimental interest in the completion of this road. . . . It is reassuring, to see New York and Virginia uniting in a public work after a period of estrangement and contention." With its coal deposits, Virginia would now be able to provide heat more cheaply than the Pennsylvania fields. On Virginia's James River a modern commercial port could be built; New York City's government was too corrupt to undertake the measures needed to make it into a cheap transshipment point. Parton did not mention that the New York port and the Pennsylvania coal fields were scenes of intensive labor conflict. His readers would not, however, have needed to be reminded.[40]

But Virginia was unique among the states subjected to Congressional Reconstruction. It had as yet averted a Republican regime. Things looked different where Southern Republicans were in control, particularly where large black majorities could give the impression that freedmen played an active, even determining, role in government. Godkin conveyed to his readers the reports he had received from two reliable Republican businessmen, who had traveled to the South to assess investment opportunities. "Of course, one of the very first things to which their attention was turned was the government, for government means taxation, and on the manner and amount and application of taxation depend the rate of profits, the prospects of immigration, and the probability of internal improvements. No man will willingly invest much capital in a State whose revenues he has reason to believe will be squandered, or credit destroyed, or whose legislation cannot be depended on for a reasonable degree of uniformity and honesty." The situation was as bad as could be imagined. Stating that the cause was not government by the "colored people" but rather by the "ignorant," he nevertheless reserved his criticism for the freedmen. "The effect on the freedman of the spectacle of large bodies of his fellows in a state of grossest ignorance put suddenly in possession of the government of great, civilized, and wealthy communities, is of course as de-moralizing as the sudden discovery of a parcel of diamonds, and just as likely to turn his mind away from steady industry, and to destroy his faith in the political value of knowledge." Even worse, "Their management of the State funds has been such, and is such, as to endanger American credit everywhere, to frighten away capital, and make general bankruptcy at some not very distant day by no means improbable." The solution was to let the Southern states find their way back into the hands of their natural leaders, none other than erst-while Confederates and slave owners, who were now believed to be the mid-wives of the anticipated commercial order.[41]

Whereas the national government had been goaded back into the defense of the political rights of freedmen by the outrages of the Ku Klux Klan, liberal reformers attempted to draw attention to worse evils. In July, the *Atlantic Monthly* published an article by Nathan S. Shaler that put flesh and blood into the evolving indictment against Reconstruction governments and formulated the problem in explicitly racial terms. Shaler was one of America's leading natural scientists. He had been born in the South but served as an officer in the Union army and was a member of the Republican Party. Recounting his trip to South Carolina, he denounced the bankrupt utopianism of Radical Recon-struction. The natural order had been turned upside down in this state, where a black majority and a large mulatto population had usurped leadership from what had been the wealthiest, most refined class of Southerners. Shaler envi-sioned that the regeneration of the region would come through a diversified economy, created by the old ruling class newly awakened to "the business spirit." But Republican policy stunted the evolution of the new world. Its fundamental mistake lay in its disregard for the limitations of former slaves, which derived from their essential racial characteristics. "Until one has had the good fortune to see how thoroughly exotic the negro is, one cannot appreciate the difficulties of making him a part of the social system which fits us."[42]

Shaler's personal history is relevant to the interpretation of South Carolina's disorder he offered the *Atlantic Monthly*'s readers. Shaler had been a disciple of Louis Agassiz, the leading American theorist of polygenesis, which asserted that the human races had separate origins. Agassiz, holding firm to polygenism, rejected Darwinian evolutionary theory; Shaler broke with his mentor to confirm the scientific validity of evolutionary theory.[43] Although Darwin was a committed monogenesist, evolutionary theory was capacious enough to allow a scientist such as Shaler to hold fast to most of the assumptions of polygenism while still being a Darwinian. Overlaid with Darwinism, the old tropes of polygenism, discredited by the apparent scientific credence it gave to proslavery ideology—even if most Southerners rejected it as inconsistent with biblical teachings—could be revivified. The wide, unbridgeable chasm between races of separate origins posited by polygenism could be reconceived by the Darwinian as the wide divergence over millennia of separate evolution.[44] And all of this could then be assimilated into the familiar Western belief in hierarchically ordered civilizations. Shaler framed the problem as one of racial capacities: "The all-important question is, What should we do to secure to this people the highest cultivation of which they are capable? Should we begin by trying to force upon them the last product of our civilization,—intellectual culture,—or should we first try and create in them the conditions of this intellectual culture?" To him, it was quixotic of the Republicans to give formal education to the freedmen: "Now the fact is, we have almost as much to do in order to change the average negro into an intelligent citizen in a white society as we should have if we tried to embody the Indian into our government; and we have begun by teaching him English grammar. . . . Unless he is trained in thrift, unless his conception of life is enlarged, unless he is freed from the instincts which the savage life of a hundred generations have planted in his blood, this education can do nothing for him." Given that the most promising race trait of "the negro" lay "in his strong imitative faculties," Shaler proposed that an "industrious foreign population" of "the higher race" be encouraged to immigrate to the South to serve as exemplars.[45] A long industrial education would be required before this "race as foreign to us in every trait as the negroes" would be fit to participate in the activities of higher civilization: intellectual culture and, by implication, political democracy.

A new, insidious racism, with a provenance in the most up-to-date scientific theory, was gaining influence among those who had once advocated Radical Reconstruction on the grounds that a "caste system" was inconsistent with the American creed of equal rights.[46] The erstwhile Radicals' contacts with disaffected Northern planters in the South surely nudged them along in their about-face. Most Northerners failed at their ventures, and their experience with freedmen as workers encouraged them to place the blame on their employees and to seek something in their workers' nature to rationalize their own failure.[47] The *Nation* affirmed Shaler's argument with explicit reference to the Darwinian struggle for existence; nevertheless, it corrected, "There is manifestly but one road to avoid the danger, and that is to educate, in the broadest sense of that work, each and all to the highest possible point, and to associate as intimately as possible each of these races in all the avocations for which their capacities may fit them."[48] Even education, the liberal cure-all, could be enlisted in the new desire to fix class hierarchies.

Talk of ineradicable racial traits raised doubt as to the wisdom of Congressional Reconstruction. Not only had black men been enfranchised, but the federal government was committed to protecting the governments created by them in fair elections, no matter how well they governed. And who should lead the governments of the South was one of the most potent questions in national politics. Organized terrorism against freedmen and white Republicans, under the aegis of the Ku Klux Klan and similar organizations, had sparked a crisis of legitimacy in many Southern states and rekindled debate about the federal government's role in defending the legacy of the war. In 1870 and 1871, the Republican Congress passed the Enforcement Acts, which enhanced the power of the federal government to punish the individual perpetrators of political violence in order to protect the rights of citizenship created by the postwar amendments. Just as Republican liberal reformers were looking to let the South alone so it could "be governed through the part of the community that embodies the intelligence and the capital," their own party pursued the opposite course.[49] Deploying their well-honed talents at publicity, liberal reformers proceeded to reverse their assessments of the classes in the South. Through the new liberal alchemy, uncivilized slaveholders were transmuted into eager entrepreneurs, reconstructed patriots, and the best friends of the black man. The natural leaders of the South, liberal reformers suggested, promised to respect the freedmen's rights even as they would reassume the role of tutor in the habits of civilization. In this context, the effort by the national government to enforce Reconstruction laws were "Force Acts."

Godkin bluntly characterized the issue during the weeks of the Paris Commune. Regardless of the admittedly disgusting outrages of the Ku Klux Klan, the governments of "trashy whites and ignorant negroes" in the South were among the worst ever seen in civilized society.[50] Like Northern workers, freedmen were not up to the task of governing, and their attempts to do so had impoverished the region and undermined civilization. He assigned the *Nation*'s resident constitutional expert the task of editorializing against the so-called Force Bill. John N. Pomeroy, the author of an 1868 legal treatise asserting the doctrine of national supremacy, rehabilitated federalism to argue that the

Enforcement and Ku Klux Klan Acts were unconstitutional.[51] The logic was akin to the liberal reformers' proclamation of the doctrine of laissez-faire in 1871. But more than a commitment to a theory of government joined laissez-faire to "home rule." In the North and the South, propertyless, uneducated workers had attained unprecedented influence over the state. Therefore, the link between majority influence and state action would have to be severed, and the practical route was to limit the powers of the state, in this case, the power of the federal government. The battles of Reconstruction were still too fresh to jettison the principle of universal male suffrage that had legitimated the Radical innovation of the enfranchisement of black men.

As liberal reformers worried about the extreme measures issuing from Northern workers and Southern freedmen, the corruption of Southern Republican governments and Northern city governments, and the financial policies and scandals of the Grant administration, they began to forge the Liberal Republican campaign out of their existing network of "Independents."[52] Designed to force the Republicans to nominate a reformer for their presidential candidate, the Liberal Republicans ended up allying with the Democrats in support of their nemesis, the erratic Horace Greeley. Greeley's campaign focused on the injustice and failure of Reconstruction and the need to return the South to local rule—the only point on which the odd alliance of independents, disappointed Republican office seekers, and Democrats could agree. Grant won by a landslide, but he did so by acceding to much of the Democratic critique in his campaign. For the Liberal Republicans, the campaign of 1872 was a fiasco. All reform issues except Reconstruction were ignored, and several prominent liberal reformers, including Godkin, Curtis, and Edward Atkinson, supported Grant as the lesser of two evils.[53]

The failure of the Liberal Republican electoral strategy encouraged a turn toward other tactics to end Reconstruction. Liberal reformers accelerated their publicity campaigns and made greater efforts to promote their political ambitions through the former rulers of the South. The Supreme Court became an unexpected ally in April 1873 when it reversed its earlier support of federal power in Reconstruction in the *Slaughterhouse* decision. Louisiana butchers challenged a state law, claiming that the creation of a slaughterhouse monopoly violated their rights under the Fourteenth Amendment. The majority of the Court in a 5–4 decision upheld the law as a legitimate exercise of the state's police powers. Although the case had nothing to do with the civil rights of African Americans, Justice Samuel Miller, writing for the majority, based the argument on a novel and not wholly plausible reading of the Fourteenth Amendment. Making a sharp distinction between state and national citizenship, he invoked federalism to radically narrow the rights pertaining to national citizenship. Furthermore, he argued, the Fourteenth Amendment only applied to African Americans, not to white citizens. The decision, one of the most significant in American constitutional history, is full of ironies. Whereas it defended the Reconstruction legacy to the extent of supporting the national guarantee of African Americans' civil rights, it rendered those rights meaningless by narrowly defining the rights of national citizenship. The dissenters, especially in the opinions of Justices Joseph P. Bradley and Stephen J. Field, upheld the broader definition of national citizenship and national supremacy, but their arguments became the basis of substantive due process, a doctrine that would transmute the Fourteenth Amendment from a defense of the rights of citizens to the bulwark of corporate privilege. In any event, *Slaughterhouse* set the precedent for the continuing erosion by the Supreme Court of national authority in the former slave states. Federalism, a narrow reading of the Thirteenth and Fifteenth Amendments, and a scholastic interpretation of the Enforcement Acts in *United States v. Cruikshank* (1874) and *United States v. Reese* (1876) eviscerated the acts taken by Congress to protect black voters against organized white terrorism.[54]

A resurgent federalism provided a convenient constitutional defense of the liberal reformers' retreat, but their appeals to the people were aimed more to flatter their prejudices than to persuade their intellects. Despite their history of crusading for civil rights and denouncing racism, they grasped onto ideas of racial inferiority as a useful weapon in the attack against Southern Republican governments. The freedman's alleged failure as an economic man and his propensity and talent for politics opened a window for the old proslavery theory of the childlike African to reenter in new-fashioned Darwinian dress. The natural sciences lit the path for the social science of governance, as liberal reformers moved from criticism of black political influence to outright rejection of black political participation. From their supposedly empirical, scientifically grounded observation of Southern politics, they trumpeted regrets for their onetime utopianism. Order, efficiency, rationality, progress, intelligence, and culture, they apologized, had been sacrificed to their misguided experiment in government by "negro rule," and they were prepared to undo the damage they had done to their unfortunate Southern brethren, the "best men" of the white South.

In this, the liberal reformers of the North and the "Redeemers" of the South paced each other—at times the reformers justified victories of the "new" Democratic Party over Republican governments; at times they prepared their audiences to cheer the imminent defeat of another Republican government. By early 1873, Democrats had won power in Tennessee, Georgia, and Virginia. They controlled the legislatures of Alabama, Florida, North Carolina, and Texas against embattled Republican governors, who most often substituted impotence for cooperation with the Democratic "Redeemers." Republicans remained in power in only four states—not surprisingly, in three of these states African Americans constituted the majority of the population.[55] Therefore, the efforts of Southern Democrats, and the publicity of Northern liberal reformers, were directed at the four surviving Republican governments in Mississippi, Louisiana, Arkansas, and South Carolina.

Whatever the theoretical chances for the survival of Republican governments that respected the political rights of black Southerners, created a space for their political participation, and enacted policies for their economic and social advancement, the 1870s proved to be the worst of times to test the possibility. The depression of the 1870s, beginning with the panic of September 1873, was a calamity for the Southern economy. The market price for Southern staple crops plunged. Considering that economic reconstruction had already ensured that the Southern economy would continue to be dominated by the production of agricultural raw materials, property owners, tenants, sharecroppers, and agricultural laborers were all devastated by plummeting prices. In addition to the economic hardship, black and white Southern Republicans found themselves at the mercy of the shifting fortunes of the Grant administration. New scandals within the administration seemed to be revealed every few months, which contributed to Grant's—and the Republicans'—loss of support among Northern voters and kept Grant preoccupied with his own house, with little capacity to protect Southern Republican governments. And even when Grant attempted to use federal power on the side of black Republicans against a White League attempt at a coup d'état in Louisiana, Northerners—especially liberal reformers—opposed his act with such vehemence that he became much more cautious about taking sides in Southern political battles.[56]

The onset of depression in late 1873 made liberal reformers ever more committed to the end of Reconstruction. The most mundane economic interests reinforced and coincided with the political reversal already in the works. The depression exacerbated the fiscal crisis of cash-strapped Republican governments, and Northern reformers had tender feelings for the oppressed taxpayers of the South—that is, the white property owners, both old Confederates and their old Northern friends who had packed themselves off to the South to become a modern breed of planter. The depression, in pushing many landowners into default and Southern railroads into bankruptcy, also created opportunities on which Northern capitalists wished to capitalize. Southern property was selling for a song—and liberal reformers were pleased to be the chorus for the Yankee leads.[57]

Liberal reformers, however, had for several years insisted that there were two preconditions to economic stability and growth: proper state fiscal policies and a quiescent labor force. De Forest, Shaler, and various writers in the *Nation* had reported that freed men and women made poor workers wherever they could be distracted by politics and that Southern Republican governments enacted atrocious fiscal and taxation policies. In 1873, liberal reformers intensified their publicity campaign against the remaining Republican governments. Magazines and newspapers, such as *Harper's Weekly* and *Scribner's*, that had not initially participated in the *Nation's* and the *Atlantic Monthly's* new racist departure joined in the campaign.[58]

The two seminal publications of the reformers' campaign to delegitimate Southern Republican rule were James S. Pike's *The Prostrate State* (1874) and Charles Nordhoff's *The Cotton States in the Spring and Summer of 1875* (1876). Pike had been an antislavery activist since the 1840s, but one of the many who had combined opposition to slavery with virulently racist views. His book allegedly collected and elaborated firsthand reports he had written for the *New York Tribune* in the spring of 1873 from South Carolina. It has been proven, however, that virtually every point in the book had been published by Pike before he ever visited the South. Pike had several axes to grind. He had worked as a Liberal Republican on Horace Greeley's disastrous 1872 campaign against Grant, and his book revealed his eagerness to hold the Grant administration responsible for every act of corruption in South Carolina. He also had a number of Northern friends who were planters, including Whitelaw Reid, the editor of the *Tribune*, and from them he determined that the stagnation of Southern business was the fault of unruly black laborers. Nordhoff, a New York Republican with no taste for the Radicalism of many of his personal friends, also published his reports in a New York newspaper, the *Herald*. More measured in his appraisal, and also less venomous in his racism, Nordhoff made it clear that the main issue was that a democracy of the propertyless was undermining the great potential of the Southern states for economic development. Both books won widespread praise in the Northern press, and Pike's book was even cited in an 1876 congressional investigation into a riot in the South to prove that any disturbance originated in the illegitimate and corrupt rule of black Republicans.[59]

Despite the subtle differences in interpretation, and in style and tone, Nordhoff's and Pike's motives were the same. They wished to see Southern staple crop production revived on terms favorable to Northern capital. And they both argued that the labor problem in the South impeded this objective and that the roots of the labor problem lay in the premature incorporation of freedmen into the political sphere. After the experience of Northern liberal reformers and capitalists with the Northern labor movement of the late 1860s and 1870s, compounded by the more spontaneous but even more threatening actions by the unemployed and nonunionized workers in 1873, 1874, and 1875, Pike's and Nordhoff's analysis of the Southern politics of labor made perfect sense to their audience. The internal contradictions in their books, the shameful license Pike took with journalistic standards (surely noted by his editors and one so vigilant as Godkin), made no difference when the books could be so useful.

Pointing to governments in which black participation was highest, Nordhoff and Pike clarified the basic problem: the freedmen had been wrenched past a necessary evolutionary stage by being thrust into politics. Not having previously developed the traits of economic rationality that were preconditions to legitimate political behavior, they were caught in limbo. They neither labored diligently nor governed intelligently. A consensus among liberal reformers was emerging that it had been foolhardy to endow freedmen with full political rights. It ruined Southern governments and, moreover, had set back the glorious cause of free labor. Still, it was too early to demand disfranchisement, but removing federal protection from Republican governments would go a long way toward dampening the political enthusiasm of communities of former slaves. Once proper political relationships between the "best men" of the South and the untutored laboring mass had been restored, the principal task of creating a compliant "free" labor force could get a fresh start. Again, with some differences, Pike and Nordhoff assured prospectors that freed men and women had the capacity to be efficient and diligent agricultural laborers if several conditions were met. First, the freedmen's illusions of political salvation had to be dispelled. Second, they must be treated with the formalities of free contract. Third, employers held a special responsibility—a trusteeship—to inculcate the behavior and values of economic rationality in their charges.

In effect, Pike and Nordhoff deferred payment on the dues of free labor. Former slaves, because of biological racial predispositions, would be in but not of the world of free contract. Hence, a racialized and hybrid ideology of free labor rejuvenated the paternalist rationale for slavery for a peculiar kind of freedom. Both Pike and Nordhoff agreed that a long apprenticeship as agricultural laborers would do the best good for the freed person's chance at evolution. Both waffled, however, on whether the old Southern planters or a new breed of superior Northerners would make the best trustees. This ambiguity marked the contradiction of forging a colonial model of development for a region within the territory of a liberal nation-state.

The portrayal of freed laborers by Pike and Nordhoff resonated with ongoing debates about the Northern labor question. But there were political considerations that impelled liberal reformers to cast their criticisms of the two working classes in different accents. In the North, they had charged workers with violating the basic principle of individual equality undergirding free contract. Liberals had enough sense, however, to realize that they would not endear themselves to Northern producers by announcing that workers should allow employers to train them in basic habits of thought. To trumpet the virtue of rising to the level of a capitalist through individual self-exertion was a very different thing than recommending an indefinite personal apprenticeship to one's employer. The taming of Northern labor proceeded along a different route, at least as long as most Northern laborers were still native-born Americans. The majority of producers, judging by liberal reform rhetoric, remained within the fold of manly independence. To attack the political claims of Northern workers, liberal reformers chose instead to discredit their leaders as wily, duplicitous, and un-American communists. The political cost of portraying Northern producers as inherently inferior was too high for them to risk, if they had any hope of influencing public opinion and political policy. Certain things were unspeakable in Northern democracy. When it came to Southern laborers, the new Darwinian racialism, given the rapidly changing balance of power in the South, rationalized the great disjuncture in the image of the two laboring classes. The new silence about the once scorned poor white of the South also marked the distance traveled.

Nevertheless, the political diagnosis of and the solution to the two labor questions were similar. At the end of the Civil War, the future leaders of liberal reform had expressed an expansive vision of democracy, rooted in an individualistic model of democratic political relations. But in the decade following victory, in both the North and the South, propertyless workers banded together collectively, attempting to shape state policy according to their interests and their alternative vision of democracy. By doing so, they challenged the institutional framework—fiscal policy, the law of contract, and such—that served to maintain capitalist property and market relations, the material bulwarks of individual liberty. As liberal reformers believed property to be the foundation of civilization, the new democratic activism threatened not only to undermine personal interests but also to endanger civilized life itself. The doctrine of laissez-faire could become pretext, principle, and rationalization for the calls to remove federal protection from Reconstruction governments—for the reformers' antidemocratic program to confine the genie of universal suffrage. Leaving the South to "home rule" would set the stage for a new class of political leaders to enter office, and Northern liberal reformers were confident that the "best men" of the white South would curtail the fiscal largess and personal corruption that so annoyed them. (Incidentally, their predictions were wrong.)[60] Once the political settlement was reached, Southern property owners and Northern entrepreneurs could work together to reconstitute the material foundation of the New South civilization. In the same decade in which liberal reformers reneged on their commitments to black Southerners, they discovered new allies in the emerging corps of "New South" ideologists such as Henry W. Grady.

As it turned out, Northern liberal reformers offered the South secondhand goods: rudimentary industrial development, a railroad system constructed for the export of raw materials, and the opportunity to scour the land of all its valuable raw materials. All this was sold through the stock images of entrepreneurial individualism. Remove the strong arm of federal power, and the best men would naturally rise to the top to rescue the land with their business genius. In the North, however, property was undergoing a transmutation and thereby calling into question the moral vision of individual opportunity and entrepreneurial individualism. The emergent forms of property, moreover, did not lend themselves so nicely to doctrinaire laissez-faire. As liberal reformers observed and interpreted the economic transformation, they would formulate new ideas about the role of the state. Their proposals shared the antidemocratic logic underlying their proclamations of laissez-faire and home rule, but the policies betrayed the let-alone principle for which they purportedly stood.

PROGRESS AND PROPERTY

ECONOMIC DEVELOPMENT AND THE

COLLAPSE OF ENTREPRENEURIAL INDIVIDUALISM

During the four decades after the Civil War the U.S. economy underwent the transition from proprietary to corporate capitalism.[1] The question for contemporaries, who certainly could not foresee the end of this process, was how to make sense of the material growth, economic swings, and changes in the instruments of property holding and government fiscal policy that characterized these years.

Liberal reformers were in the vanguard in exploring the political and ethical implications of the economic tendencies of the age—the increasing integration of the international market, the emergence of large-scale capitalist property, the unprecedented productive capacity of industry, and the innovations in instruments of credit and property holding. On the one hand, large-scale capitalist property unsettled the moral order, in which property anchored individual selfhood and individual proprietors, through morally responsible personal management of their own enterprises, transmuted the potential overweening power accruing to the propertied into legitimate authority.[2] On the other hand, progress marked a society as civilized or not, and material improvement underwrote all other forms of progress, even those dearest to the genteel tradition—cultural, intellectual, artistic, and moral progress.

The dual commitment to entrepreneurial individualism and to progress turned out to be a divided one, which unfolded as a portentous ambivalence about the new economic world aborning. Ultimately, most liberal reformers acceded to the seeming inevitability of economic "consolidation" and succumbed to the allure of the material progress that would follow in its wake. First tentatively, then boldly, they defended the most advanced forms of capitalist property and market relations. In doing so, they effectively renounced the moral economy of producerism, which valued economic independence above all and held that democracy would fail without a foundation in an economically independent citizenry.

Liberal reform political intellectuals were not unaware of the fundamental challenge the new economy posed to liberalism as a foundational system of values. Individualism was their most highly vaunted ideal—from it flowed the practical defense of individual liberty. But how could individualism survive the massing of capital and the depersonalization of property when American individualism was so deeply rooted in the right to property and the exemplary individual was cast in the image of the property owner and entrepreneur? In their initial reconception of property rights, liberal reform intellectuals mapped one possible route for the reconciliation of economic consolidation with an individualism philosophically derived from the premises about human nature enshrined in classical political economy and institutionalized in economic liberalism. As the economic transformation gained momentum, they and their liberal successors would scrap the fragile structure and engineer a more durable one, firmly moored in the bedrock of late-nineteenth-century corporate and consumer capitalism. Liberal reformers invented a new moral economy for the new economy, legitimating economic relations, forms of property, and state fiscal policies that would secure corporate capital in a democratic polity. And, for most liberal reformers and their successors, the politics of economic liberalism, or laissez-faire, came to be seen as inadequate for the task of administering the bold new world.

The most important nexus between the emergent economy and the state was the federal government's fiscal policies, transformed by the exigencies of civil war, and it was on this topic that liberal reformers first elaborated the emerging revision of liberalism. The Union government had used three methods to pay for the war: the issuance of government securities of various terms and duration; taxation; and inflation of the money supply. (The last, in contemporary usage, was known as a "depreciated currency," for the value of a paper dollar was less than the value of the gold dollar). The main innovations arising from wartime fiscal policy were the creation of a national banking system in place of the former subtreasury system; the enactment of high protective tariffs and the income tax; and the abandonment of the gold standard as Congress made U.S. paper, popularly known as "greenbacks," legal tender for all market transactions. The policies had far-reaching effects, revolutionizing private as well as public capital markets in the North, thus playing a crucial role after the war in reshaping economic relations throughout the country.[3]

The war had thus laid one of the elementary bulwarks for the advance of corporate capitalism: a financial system able to mobilize large sums of capital. But it had also deeply involved the federal government in financial markets, thus rendering private capital particularly subject to government policies. It was David Ames Wells, the man appointed to analyze the government's fiscal health and its effect on general prosperity, who contributed most to the reconceptualization of economic activity by liberal reformers and who gave them the language with which to contemplate the prospects of economic development and the deepening of the state's involvement in the market. Over the next three decades, Wells would act as a tireless organizer of a host of liberal reform causes and emerge as the leading economic writer among them.

Wells's personal history well suited him to fashion the bridge from the old to the new moral economy for the rapidly developing United States. On his father's side, he was descended from a Puritan governor of Connecticut. By marriage, which he explained he undertook "on cool, careful, and economic considerations," he continued the line of the Puritan divine Jonathan Edwards. By paternal inheritance and marital privilege, he was intimately connected to traditions of Puritan rectitude and individualism—the social order of self-controlled individuals. From his mother's side, he was equally immersed in the social world of the pioneering Yankee industrialists. His maternal grandfather was a paper manufacturer and the patriarch of one of the wealthiest families in the Connecticut Valley. After David's father failed in the dry goods business and abandoned the family, his mother moved the children to her father's household, where David was raised. After graduating first in his class from Williams College, and then from the Lawrence Scientific School at Harvard, Wells followed in his grandfather's path, becoming an inventor of machinery and techniques in printing and textile manufacturing. From 1850 to 1866 he was the publisher of *The Annual of Scientific Discovery*. In 1864, he gave the first sign of a shift in interest from applied natural science to economic science. Desiring to contribute to the patriotic cause but blind in one eye and excluded from the army, he volunteered to write a pamphlet to persuade European bondholders that their investments in the Union government were sound. Issued by the Loyal Publication Society in 1864, Wells's *Our Burden and Our Strength* assured that the government would succeed in repaying its debt, for the dynamic nature of Northern economic life, with its rapid accumulation of capital and its constant improvements in technology, created a solid foundation for fiscal stability. The success of the pamphlet gained Wells the attention of influential Republicans, and on Horace White's recommendation, President

Abraham Lincoln appointed Wells to the national revenue commission in 1865. In 1866, the post of special commissioner for the revenue was created for him.[4]

During his tenure as special commissioner of the revenue, Wells emerged as the authoritative commentator on the most contested fiscal and taxation matters confronting the nation: the national debt, the currency, domestic taxation, the tariff on imports, and the impact of domestic production and trade on the government's source of revenue. Politically, Wells was identified with moderate Republicans, but personally he was close to many Radicals through his early editorship on the *Springfield Republican*, his work on the wartime Sanitary Commission, and his membership in the American Social Science Association.[5] His first two reports (for 1865 and 1866) won him praise from the liberal Radical Republican press, primarily for the model of nonpartisan expert investigation he set and for his calls to reform the civil service in the financial agencies of the government.[6] The 1868 presidential campaign, revolving in large part around the issues of the national debt and "people's money," inevitably magnified the importance of Wells's analysis of government fiscal policy, and the publication in early 1869 of his 1868 report gained wide circulation in the liberal reform press.[7]

In 1868, while many erstwhile Radicals were focusing on the day-to-day conflicts between labor and capital, Wells was more interested in questions about the nation's prospects in the international political economy. He was one of the first observers to perceive that the U.S. economy had outgrown its antebellum bounds. The people of the country could no longer consume the enormously enlarged produce of domestic agriculture and industry. In the midst of a campaign by Westerners to inflate the greenback currency, Wells countered that only a vibrant export trade could sustain Western prosperity and that unsound national fiscal policies would ruin them. With his analysis of the relationship between the new abundance and international trade and his recognition that Europeans' decisions to invest in the United States depended on their appraisal of the nation's fiscal soundness, Wells tentatively began to lay out a sophisticated program of modern economic development, albeit one that was still buttressed by the orthodoxies of Manchester. The *Nation* praised Wells's work as one of the most effective pieces of economic writing ever done in the United States, while Edward Atkinson recycled Wells's conclusions in a broadside for the Boston Reform League, an organization established in April 1869 to win popular support for fiscal reform and free trade.[8]

Developments in the politics of the labor question and in the world of finance in 1869 produced a marked change in tone in Wells's report for the year.[9] 1869 was an unsettled and, to some people, unsettling year. Most disturbing to Wells were two scandals engineered by the new capitalists. The struggle for control over the Erie Railroad between Cornelius Vanderbilt, James Fisk, and Jay Gould revealed that certain state legislatures were subservient to the new railroad magnates and their financiers; Fisk and Gould's attempted corner of the gold market revealed that all "legitimate business" was vulnerable to the most egregious kinds of speculation and profiteering. The "Erie Raid" and the "Gold Corner" have rightfully gone down in history as two of the most infamous deeds of the Gilded Age "robber barons," in no small part because two liberal reformers, Charles and Henry Adams, gave their contemporaries a detailed accounting of the depredations.[10] Wells's report dealt specifically with the dangers of speculation and also registered with alarm the increased frequency of strikes and the rise of labor parties. Wells's powerful critique, articulating the new politics of liberal reform, evidently captured a spirit widespread among the urban middle class. Twelve papers reprinted his report verbatim, including the *New York Times*, *Harper's Weekly*, the *Chicago Tribune*, and some Democratic papers.[11]

Apprehension about slowing economic growth and widening economic inequality led Wells to direct most of his ire against unscrupulous "speculators." Critiques of this sort have earned Wells and his liberal reform colleagues their historical reputations as the opponents of "plutocracy," and by extension, as opponents of the centralizing economic tendencies of the Gilded Age. But to condemn the behavior of some capitalists was by no means to reject the emergent consolidated economy. Liberal reformers, even in their apotheosis of the market, had always been suspicious of the extreme individualism encouraged in the marketplace. In any social order, some would fail to be swayed by the prevailing means of winning moral order, and certainly a system that placed so much importance on the cultivation of self-control, in lieu of established authority, gave especial license to immorality. But the new mechanisms of finance and ownership were elevating the rascality of speculation into a new moral standard.

Nevertheless, Wells had no desire to turn the clock back on industrial progress. What he worried about was the eclipse of the moral order of proprietary capitalism. In condemning "the spirit of trading and speculation" and praising the "spirit of production," Wells drew on the ideal conception of the self-directed, autonomous property owner, one who contributed to real material growth and dealt responsibly and fairly in his business.[12] The ideal derived from the classical theory of capital as the reward for diligent labor and payment for risk. Abstinence from consuming the fruits of the original labor legitimated the earnings of capital. The discipline of savings fostered the responsibility expected of the individual entrepreneur and thereby grounded the moral order not only within the market but also beyond into the other realms of civil, private, and political society. To Wells, if economic activity could be rechanneled into its natural course, opportunities for laborers to gain property would be restored, and the world of autonomous individuals, their individualism anchored in private property, could be re-created. And this society best guaranteed moral order, justice, and general prosperity.

Wells, on the one hand, seemed to defend an economic ideal of the individual entrepreneur that was already clearly outdated in post–Civil War America. Yet at the same time, Wells believed that general prosperity in the modern world depended on the continuous increase of industrial production, and his lingering fascination with the responsible individual entrepreneur combined with his commitment to national progress and prosperity to make his views confused and contradictory. Prosperity, Wells made abundantly clear, required sustained economic growth, which necessarily entailed qualitative technological improvements and an increase in mass consumption. Wells was a great admirer of the dynamism of capitalism and the bountiful natural and social resources of the United States. He worried that the unnatural preponderance of speculation over production was grinding down the laborer and preventing him from accumulating capital, while also corrupting the propertied. The "deflated currency" increased the cost of capital and led to the "concentration" of business and "the utter annihilation of thousands of little separate industries." But, at the same moment, Wells lauded industrial consolidation, which, "by promoting method, system and division of labor, and thereby reducing the cost of product, is undoubtedly beneficial." He tentatively and temporarily averted facing the contradiction between his dual appreciation for widespread individual proprietorship and for efficient, advanced, and large enterprise with an unsustainable distinction between voluntary and involuntary economic development: "When the growth of such a system is unnaturally fostered through the necessities rather than the free will of the laborer, the result cannot be otherwise than to render the many dependent for all the elements of their livelihood upon the will of a few rather than upon their own."[13] Although his point was consistent with the liberal idea of free contract, it is difficult to see how, even if under the doubtful assumption that the free will of the laborer had been enlisted in "concentration," he would be any less dependent for his livelihood on the few as consolidation proceeded.

Wells was undoubtedly correct that government fiscal policies played a large role in shaping class relations and that the dual currency fostered speculative trading. But his vision was limited in several ways. First, he did not take into account that all the Western countries engaged in the capitalist market were caught up in a speculative mania and an inflationary era, until everything came crashing down in 1873.[14] As in any boom, unscrupulous adventurers played the markets along with respectable investors, and some transactions were wholly removed from any material production of goods. But Wells also failed to acknowledge that the economic development he desired was in practice stimulated by the speculation he deplored. The bulk of speculative investment was in railroad securities, and although many railroad corporations were overcapitalized and some run corruptly, the nation's railroad network grew immensely in these years.[15] The international trade Wells wanted to recapture depended entirely on an advanced railroad network to link domestic production in all regions to the Eastern ports, and he was well aware of this. Though Wells attempted to demarcate speculative from productive investment objectively, in practice it was impossible to distinguish whether one railroad bond was for a speculative project and another was for a productive one—that is, until a stronger state administrative apparatus could evaluate projects and publicize reliable information on corporate accounts. Wells hearkened back to the familiar order of individual entrepreneurship, but his desire for an increase in national production and capital accumulation propelled him toward championing the new world of international capital flows based in abstract property claims and international trade in commodities produced under technologically advanced, capital-intensive enterprise.

More consistently, Wells's evolving understanding of the American political economy had forced a revision in his practical politics, most significantly on the issue of free trade versus protectionism. (He earned a dismissal from the Grant administration for his apostasy from Republican protectionism.) As a free trader directly inspired by the paragons of classical liberalism, the English Cobdenites, Wells was seen by some of his contemporaries and by many later historians as a thinker stuck in the outmoded ways of a bygone era.[16] What these observers miss is the distinctive historical character of the postbellum free trade movement. In England, where the enemy had been the mercantilist state, the free trade movement had been the defining crusade of economic liberalism. The American free traders took their model of political agitation from the English, but the context and their motives were different. In the United States, the problem was not a too powerful state but the obstacle that mass democracy, based in highly competitive party politics, posed to capitalist economic development. "Protectionism" made American goods uncompetitive in the world market, and industrial lobbies taught workers lessons in "class legislation."

Wells's economic analysis of the effect of protectionism was particularly prescient and innovative. He insisted that a pragmatic reform of the tariff to achieve free trade was "coextensive with the present most important economical requirement of the country, which, embodied in a single brief expression, may be defined to be *cheaper production*, and as a necessary consequence, *larger consumption and more extended markets, domestic and foreign*." His earlier sketch of an integrated economic developmental policy had matured into a consistent theory of how the United States could stave off social crisis and reap rewards in the international capitalist market. Continental development itself made foreign trade essential to stable economic growth and class harmony. The nation's surplus could be absorbed only if the whole world was its market, and Wells pointedly noted that the nation would remain at a disadvantage unless it began to reorient its export trade from agricultural raw materials to industrial commodities produced in all regions of the country.[17]

Wells was an astute analyst of the structural developments of international capitalism. Although he still conceived of economic disruptions and instability in the terms of classical political economy, he perceived that the economic revolution under way in the United States required a revision of the moral foundation of the old. Accordingly, the moral simplicities of entrepreneurial individualism gave way to a vision of opportunity through consumption, founded in a sophisticated and new analysis of the relationship between mass-productive capacity, the limits of domestic consumption, and international trade.

By 1871, Wells was a leader of the "Independent" movement against the Grant administration, and his efforts to publicize his analysis of American economic life were closely tied to his political quests. Some account of popular sentiments therefore had to be taken. Yet, even as Wells pitched his campaign as a defense of the producer and the consumer—the broadly defined working and middle classes—it was evident that he was cutting free from both strands of the old free labor ideology. In the conception of the widely popular producerist ethic, the individual man created value out of the capacities of his personhood—his skills, his mind, his creativity. The stature of the individual proprietor, likewise, grew from the fruits of one's labor. But in Wells's tale of industrial progress, there was a significant erasure of the concrete individual producer from the category of labor. Creatures of body and soul had effectively vanished from the site of production, where the truly miraculous power was that of "labor-saving machinery." (Wells, it is worth remembering, had spent his young adulthood inventing machines and disseminating knowledge about practical technology.) Laborers had become abstract embodiments of labor power, as mobile as units of capital; when displaced from one industry, they glided almost effortlessly into another.[18]

To Wells, the "labor-saving machine," tended by fewer and fewer men, provided the promise of continuous material progress. Technology, and by implication the inventors and capitalists who paid for machines, were the creators of value for all intents and purposes. The labor theory of value and the promise of individual advancement were not abandoned yet, just extremely attenuated in this notion. Technological innovation and the tremendous increase in production consequent upon it, to Wells, were inevitable by-products of the dynamism of American economic life. But problems arose, because production of all types of goods (agricultural, capital goods, and consumer goods) tended to outpace population growth and the capacity to consume the increased product. Wells perceived that the very power of the new technology-based order created the conditions of its own crisis: an unmarketable surplus would be produced, to which the market would adjust through depressed prices and the cessation of production. Even before the ruinous panic of 1873, Wells was moving toward a theory of capitalist cycles of boom and bust, but in accord with orthodox political economy, he insisted that overproduction was not possible. Markets existed, but a debauched currency system, overtaxation, and an irrational protective system prevented their harvesting.[19]

Still, Wells celebrated the increasing scale and scope of production. In doing so, he laid the empirical and ideological foundation for the liberal embrace of economic progress through technological innovation and economic consolidation. As he acknowledged that individual opportunity vanished—the main chance was now to change industries rather than to accumulate property—he did not yet foresee the implications of his analysis for proprietary capitalism. No nation has ever achieved the industrial development Wells desired and at the same time preserved "thousands of little separate industries." If there was a tendency for constant improvement in technology and the replacement of laborers by machinery, where would the large sums of capital to pay for the machines come from, and how would this large-scale property be held and managed? The question was whether small business could survive and whether the new forms of abstract property holding could be construed to be simply an extension of individual proprietorship and compatible with the familiar world of entrepreneurial individualism.

As Wells instructed his colleagues about the significance of economic consolidation in a grand vision of national wealth and progress, others among his political circle would perform a similar duty in revising ideas about property. And just as the fiscal policies of the state impelled liberal reformers to examine the implications of the fiscal revolution for economic development, so too did the extension of railroad networks and the increasing centrality of railroads to the American economy force a reexamination of ownership, entrepreneurship, and responsibility. If one could ask an American man living in the 1860s to name the forces most responsible for the country's progress, after boasting of the American character and republican government, he probably would have answered, the railroad. Since the 1830s, communities in the North and West had tumbled over one another in a race to get one of their own, on the theory that prosperity rode the tracks into town. Americans were culturally fascinated with the machine, and there was no machine that could rival the railroad as a symbol of the power of man over the forces of nature and the awesome material energy Americans had harnessed to impress their civilization over a vast and wild continental landscape and put its resources at their disposal.[20]

Liberal reformers expressed an ambivalence about the implications of railroad development similar to that they displayed in the face of the fiscal revolution, as they were pulled between the promise of progress and the attenuation of the moral economy of entrepreneurial individualism. Railroads were the quintessential modern enterprise: they required unprecedented sums of capital for building and operational expenses; they served as the linchpin of the continental transportation system, creating the conditions for a national market and hence for the nation to participate in the international market; and they served as the experimental ground for innovations in technology and new managerial techniques.[21] When all these elements are taken into consideration, for those most in favor of economic progress, an effective railroad system equaled in importance a sound national fiscal policy—American prosperity ultimately depended on these two central institutions.

Yet both the fiscal policies of the Republican-dominated Civil War state and the extensive development of railroads represented a departure from the forms of property typical of the small-scale capitalist economy of prewar Northern society. Waging a modern war and constructing continental railway systems each required that immense amounts of capital be mobilized. These projects drew on the capital of thousands of individuals, who received interest income on bonds or dividends on stock, but unlike the typical entrepreneur or proprietor, these bondholders had no direct responsibility for the direction or management of their property. Rather, salaried managers, in the case of railroad securities, or political officials (elected and appointed), in the case of government bonds, supervised the use of aggregated capital and thus in effect became the intermediaries between owners qua rentiers and the enormously enlarged enterprises they legally and theoretically owned. Both developments tended to concentrate capital as well as to loosen the direct link between the property owner and the property owned.[22]

Thus the history of the railroad is inextricably bound to the transformation of capitalist property and the rise of corporate capitalism. Railroads were first built under the traditional Anglo-American common law of corporations. Traditional doctrine held that a corporate charter was a grant from the state, a public creation for a public service that remained under the regulatory power of the state. Railroads later revolutionized corporate practice, and inevitably, corporate economic, legal, and political theory. By the end of the nineteenth century, the modern definition of the corporation as a "natural entity" or "real entity" had triumphed. (The new legal doctrine would become known as the "theory of corporate personality.")[23] And with the "Great Merger Movement" of 1898 to 1902, corporately organized industry accounted for the vast proportion of U.S. production and private wealth.[24] From once being a quasi-public enterprise, the corporation by the end of the century had been redefined in law as a particular form of private property, which was accorded the newly articulated constitutional protections of private property. Even as new forms of regulation were devised, such as the Interstate Commerce Act of 1887, regulatory practice had to conform, or abdicate, to the principle that corporate holdings were constitutionally protected under the rights of private property.

The transformation of corporate theory in the United States is usually treated as a matter of constitutional law. But, as recently demonstrated by the legal historian Morton Horwitz, the theory of "corporate personality" did not emerge until the late 1890s, much later than previously believed.[25] The new business corporation and the regime of corporate capital did not, however, have to wait on constitutional law to gain legitimacy. The ideological revision began with other thinkers, especially liberal reform political intellectuals and allied political economists.

It was not that the legal structure was not available for use. While Wells was gaining recognition for his explanation and defense of economic consolidation, part of the legal theory that would later be employed to secure corporate dominance was being forged. In 1868, Thomas McIntyre Cooley, an elected Republican judge on the Michigan state supreme court, published *A Treatise on the Constitutional Limitations Which Rest Upon the Legislative Power of the States of the American Union*. Cooley's was the first legal treatise to articulate the doctrines of substantive due process and the vested rights of property, the principles on which the late-nineteenth-century courts would void most of the economic regulation passed by Congress. The right to property specified in the Fifth Amendment, Cooley argued, was not only a procedural right but a substantive, fundamental right, which could not be abridged without due process. Furthermore, vested rights included not only tangible property but also abstract claims in the existing value of one's property. As one could not be deprived of a fundamental right without due process of law, legislation that either deprived a person of property or lessened the value of the property was an unconstitutional encroachment on the fundamental right of property.[26]

Ironically, at least from the perspective of generations of legal historians who have credited Cooley as the architect of judicial laissez-faire and a leading apologist for corporate power, Cooley's treatise went unreviewed by the alleged dogmatists of laissez-faire, the liberal reformers.[27] Why? Cooley's treatise was, after all, about the limitations on state regulation, and the doctrine of substantive due process would later serve as a strong bulwark against any form of regulation that might impede the market activities of corporations. In 1868, national supremacy remained a conviction for the liberal former Radicals, and perhaps this is why Cooley was ignored. The *Nation*, for example, sought its legal opinions elsewhere. John Norton Pomeroy, whose interpretation of constitutional law strongly defending national supremacy over the states was reviewed positively in the *Nation*, argued in 1868 that the interstate commerce clause of the U.S. Constitution endowed Congress with the authority to regulate railroads.[28] Indeed, when liberal reformers first confronted Cooley's doctrines, in response to their incorporation in the circuit court ruling on the slaughterhouse cases, they were disturbed at the implications. Justice Bradley had ruled that the creation of a municipal slaughterhouse monopoly in New Orleans violated the Fourteenth Amendment guarantee of due process by depriving butchers of "their sacred right of labor." A. S. Sedgwick warned in the *Nation*, "If the decision is sustained, every moneyed corporation in the country is in danger of destruction. Whenever a court can be satisfied that the exclusive privilege granted by the State of the United States inures rather to private than to public advantage, the franchise will be set aside as in violation of the Fourteenth Amendment. Very few corporations will be able to stand this test."[29] It was not until the mid-seventies that liberal reformers decided that the doctrine would defend, not destroy, corporations.[30]

The discordance between legal theory and liberal political economy and ideology on the subject of the corporation would persist through the Progressive Era, as we shall have some occasion to see below.[31] In the 1860s, liberal reform political intellectuals looked to other sources to understand the nature and significance of corporate enterprise. In doing so, their contribution to analyzing the new economy would outweigh that of the legal theorists of the limited state, especially in resolving the potential conflicts between liberal political theory and corporate economic dominance.

Before examining the transformation of corporate theory and the role liberal reformers played in the reconception, it is necessary to review the legal theory of the corporation in the first half of the nineteenth century. In legal theory and political practice, a corporation was an artificial entity created by the state and subordinate to the state under the terms of its charter. Under this grant theory, the corporation was legally subject to the principle of ultra vires, which specified that if a corporation acted in ways "beyond the powers" designated by its charter of incorporation or the laws of the state of incorporation, the state could intervene to revise the rights of the corporation or rescind its charter altogether. In short, the state retained strong powers over the basic activities of a corporation. Corporate charters tended to be created by acts of special legislation, characteristically for projects considered beyond the means of an individual to capitalize or for publicly desired services that appeared to require special incentives. Corporate entities often had monopoly privileges, either because the project itself was considered a natural monopoly (for example, a water company) or because the project was considered of such importance to the community that the incorporators were ceded rights of monopoly as an incentive to enter a capital-intensive enterprise that could be ruined by competition (for example, a ferry). Traditional Anglo-American antimonopoly sentiments complemented and buttressed the legal doctrine of ultra vires: with the potential corruption lurking in any monopoly enterprise went public scrutiny and control that did not apply to exclusively private property, deemed to be sufficiently controlled by the market and the morality of individual proprietors.[32]

Twin pressures eroded the grant theory of the corporation in the antebellum decades. First, courts increasingly defined the corporation in terms of its private, rather than public, purposes. Second, emergent political forces—on one side, Jacksonian attacks on special corporate privileges and, on the other, the lobbying of entrepreneurs and corporations—led to a reaction against special incorporation acts and resulted in a shift to general-purpose charters and general incorporation laws, which made incorporation available to any group of capitalists who sought it. Even though general incorporation laws retained regulatory powers over corporations, the combined force of legal, political, and economic developments gradually transformed the corporation into a private business entity.[33]

Accompanying the legal and practical development of the corporation, a new theory of the nature and legitimacy of the business corporation arose in opposition to the grant theory. This was the "trust" theory of the corporation, evolved through numerous specific civil court cases and concurrently legitimated by legal theorists and political analysts. A corporation was still deemed to be an artificial entity, but it was no longer the creation of the state. Rather, the trust theory posited an individualistic market model of the corporation, in which the contracts of individuals created corporations that were thus subject to their will and regulated under the law of contract. Managers were accordingly "trustees" of the shareholders' property and ultimately subordinate to the aggregate of individual shareholders: managers theoretically ran the corporation as a " 'trust fund' for its creditors."[34] As the new and the old conceptions coexisted, legislators set ambiguous precedents. Even as they abdicated the fundamental principle of the grant theory with general incorporation laws, most of these laws reserved rights of regulation for the legislature.

By the end of the Civil War, the trust theory had replaced the grant theory as conventional legal doctrine regarding corporations, and it was also considered practical wisdom among those seeking profitable capital investments and their allies among commentators on political economy. But the decade after the Civil War was pivotal in the growth and transformation of railroad corporations and instruments of corporate ownership, and this seemed to put even the relatively novel trust theory into question. It was also the decade when Americans took notice of the profound impact of these changes in property on both the market and the political system. Eventually some Americans, particularly Western farmers organized in the Granger movement in the 1870s and in the Populist movement in the 1880s and 1890s, would reassert traditional grant theory to insist that the corporation should remain subordinate to the democratic state that brought it to life. Because corporations were an exceptional form of enterprise, the people had the right to politically limit the powers, size, and activities of the corporations. To check the overweening power of the railroad corporation, these groups of Americans looked to the grant theory and its supporting antimonopoly ideology. In contrast, liberal reformers tended to look positively on economic development, and they understood the pivotal role that larger enterprises were coming to play. They sought not only to understand the rapidly changing realities of modern economic enterprise but also to fend off the political challenge of the antimonopolists. Liberal reformers did not, nevertheless, blind themselves to the novelty of consolidated property; by confronting this issue, they also pointed the way toward a new method of state regulation.

"The civil war in America, with its enormous issues of depreciating currency, and its reckless waste of money and credit by the government, created a speculative mania such as the United States, with all its experience in this respect, had never before known," Henry Adams wrote during his few brief years as a professional political journalist. "Some lost everything; many lost still more than they had, and there are few families of ordinary connection and standing in the United States which cannot tell, if they choose, some dark story of embezzlement, or breach of trust, committed in these days."[35] The audience of the liberal reform press was made up of the professional and businessmen of such families, and as Adams's characteristically precise observation suggests, the security of their investments was of more than ordinary interest to this stratum. The corporation, along with the exact meaning of the trust theory, was not simply an abstract question of political economy.

In the *Nation*, it was left primarily to a New York broker, James B. Hodgskin, to perform the public service of explaining these developments. He began to write about railroad corporations in May 1868, while the daily press was covering the struggle of Vanderbilt against Gould and Fisk for control of the Erie Railroad, one of the major trunklines in the country. The struggle over the Erie Railroad sensationally revealed the old dangers of corruption and tyranny lurking in the new monopolies. Starting from the trust theory of the corporation, that the managers of corporate property were the trustees of the individual stockholders, Hodgskin detailed how new forms of finance, which allowed managers to manipulate the bonds and stocks of the corporation, had severed the formal relationship that was intended to subordinate managers to stockholders. Into this by now well-established idea of the corporation as a trust Hodgskin imported some of the substance of the old grant theory of the corporation. Because of the overriding public interest in the "freedom of locomotion," and considering that railroads were a monopoly currently abusing their grant, state intervention to regulate the corporation was legitimate.[36]

Hodgskin justified state interference because the railroads had freed themselves from the discipline and order of entrepreneurial individualism. The tendency of managers to treat railroad stocks as temporary investments to be traded at the slightest rise or fall in the stock market left the railroads bereft of responsible owners, long-term investors whose personal vested interest and evolved sense of the duties of the property owner would see to it that railroads ran efficiently, profitably, and safely. Speculators had thus supplanted stock-holders as effective owners of railroads. As Hodgskin traced the abuses of railroad management to new mechanisms of finance, particularly mortgage indentures, he proposed that the government regulate the types of securities issued on railroad property. "If the object of the proposed legislation were merely to influence investments, the legislation itself would be an unwarrant-able interference with individual rights. The change is not intended to influ-ence investments at all, nor to restrict private rights. It may do so incidentally, but its object is solely and exclusively to protect the public against the evils of railroad companies without responsible owners."[37] Hodgskin's solution was paradoxical. Regulation of railroad investments, an exception to the general validity of laissez-faire, must be pursued in order to subject the industry to the rule of its individual property holders, thus bringing it once again into the moral order of entrepreneurial individualism properly governed by a mini-mal state.

Whereas Hodgskin focused on the classic problem of the oppression of the public by monopolies, James Parton attended to the problem of political cor-ruption that flourished once the corporations had become unhitched from the moral, individual proprietor. Parton observed the "Lobby" in Washington and foretold that Americans would one day wish they had constructed the Pacific railroad entirely through public money as a public road. "We have to contem-plate the time, not distant, when all our towns will be Lowells, all industry a mill, all land model farms ploughed by steam, and all the resources of the country wielded by presidents and boards. With us it is the inevitable DIREC-TOR who looms up formidable and menacing." The "check-drawing magnates" had surmised that it was more profitable to prey on the public than on one another, and from the unions they formed with one another the corporations had become "omnipotent."[38]

A sharp indictment of the new "plutocrats"? Absolutely. But Parton was stuck with the familiar dilemma. What gave the "director" power was the consolidated capital that he controlled, yet according to Parton himself, "this massing tendency is a law of nature, which the steam-engine has only stimu-lated and aggravated."[39] Parton regretted the consequences, as did Hodgskin, but by the early 1870s it was evident they were in a minority among liberal reformers when they reminded the urban middle classes of the dangers of corporate power.

The dominant line of reasoning that emerged among liberal reformers was most forcefully articulated by Charles Francis Adams Jr., descendant of two presidents, John and John Quincy Adams. Like many young men of his class, after the war Adams was in search of a meaningful—and remunerative—professional career that, in his case, could be construed as following in the family tradition of public service. He had set up a law office in the late 1850s but had few clients and despised the work. Defying his father's desires, he enlisted in the Union army in late 1861—he was the only one of Charles Francis Adams's four sons to do so. (As his father pragmatically put it, the family's venerable devotion to country had never involved actually fighting in the wars the Adams family had led.) Charles enlisted in the elite cavalry corps; at the end of the war he was an officer of the Massachusetts Fifth Regiment, composed of free blacks from Massachusetts and Canada. He resigned from the army in August 1865 in extremely poor health, quickly married Mary Hone Ogden, the daughter of a well-descended and wealthy New York businessman, and went on the requisite European tour for a honeymoon.[40]

Adams and his wife returned to the United States in 1866, and he began to plot his future. His ambition was to combine literature, politics, and business to carve out a public role for himself. He had enough sense to realize that he had none of the political talents of his forefathers and had little aptitude for electoral politics in a populist age. Instead, he wrote later in life, "I endeavored to strike out a new path, and fastened myself, not, as Mr. Emerson recommends, to a star but to the locomotive-engine. I made for myself what might be called a specialty in connection with the development of the railroad system."[41] His first articles on the railroad appeared in 1867 in the *American Law Review* and the *North American Review*, and he soon fashioned himself into the leading national railroad reformer. His railroad journalism—and his cultivation of influential contacts—won him a position on the Massachusetts Railroad Commission in 1869, the first effective state regulatory commission of its kind. Until 1890 he was active in the railroad business: first as the chairman of the Massachusetts commission until 1878; then as a member of Albert Fink's abortive pooling experiment in the late 1870s; and finally as the president of the Union Pacific Railroad from 1883 to 1890, during which he engaged in many of the practices he had excoriated as a "railroad reformer" while on the Massachusetts commission.[42]

Adams, like Hodgskin and Parton, premised his analysis of the railroad on the legal doctrine of the corporation as a trust, incorporated traditional Anglo-American doctrines on the regulation of monopoly in order to endorse pragmatic forms of regulation, and was equally disturbed by the separation of ownership and control and its consequences for the "public" and the real property owners. Although Adams displayed ambivalence about several key issues—the appropriate form of regulation, the potent political power of corporations that derived their being from the state but could dictate terms to politicians, the moral status of speculation—there was one point on which he was unambiguous. The railroad was a major force of progress, plain and simple. Adams appreciated the railroad's role in creating an integrated national economy and consequently its incalculable contribution to economic growth. He very early insisted that the tendency toward consolidation and expansion was determined by natural economic law that could not and should not be stopped. Therefore, adjustments in the relations between the three main parties in the incipient conflict, stockholders, trustees who managed the corporations, and the public, would have to be deduced from scientific analysis of the facts of railroad operation and be designed in accord with incontrovertible natural laws.[43]

Not only did Adams see economic growth and consolidation as inevitable, natural, and beneficial for the community, but he also asserted that such benefits derived principally from the effectiveness of the profit motive. The problem was that the existing system of state regulation, a relic from the origins of railroads, thwarted the operation of the profit motive and hence economic development. Legislatures typically set maximum rates of profit that railroad lines could earn, in an effort to keep costs to travelers and shippers low. Under this policy, Adams argued, expansion would not produce any benefit for the owners, and hence they would not bother to expand business or improve service. The community thus suffered by the loss of increased business activity and the indifference of the corporation to the community it served once it had reached its legislated maximum of profit. Adams turned the old theory of monopoly on its head, while following the trust theory of the corporation to its logical conclusion: legislation did not protect the public but brought the community and corporation into antagonism. Recounting the decision of stockholders of one corporation to reject a project to expand their line because they could not reap the profits that would accrue from it, he concluded, "The time-honored and carefully guarded legislation intended to protect the interests of the community, was used as a powerful weapon against a natural business development, from which the community could derive good alone, and which was a part of the natural growth of that system on which the prosperity of that community depended."[44] This was not simply a conflation of the interests of stockholders and the community. Rather, Adams saw the community as entirely dependent for its well-being on property owners spurred on by the profit motive to expand business.

This was no argument, however, for laissez-faire. Instead, Adams advocated state-supported economic development, and that required a rational form of state regulation. According to Adams, advances in the social sciences enabled rationality to prevail. Accurate statistics on railroad costs would provide for "a substantial, philosophical, basis of railroad legislation,—a basis of explicit, binding, individual contract" free of excessive "legislative meddling": maximum charges, not maximum profits, should be established, and hence stockholders would choose to expand, knowing that the additional profits would be theirs to keep if they pursued efficiency.[45] Implicit in the argument was a plan to shift the locus of regulation from legislatures to administrative bureaus, staffed by experts capable of understanding the complexity of railroad financing and management.

In a two-part article in the *North American Review*, "Boston," written the same year, the developmental imperative was even more pronounced, as was the antidemocratic sensibility underlying the pragmatic argument for a transfer of regulatory power. Once the capital of the Atlantic trade, Boston had become a backwater, supplanted by the vital Chicago–New York–London axis of commerce. Adams was a local booster with concrete plans. Modern transportation facilities were crucial to local wealth in the new world economy. Boston could, "by some comprehensive scheme, by some well-organized system . . . make herself . . . a cheaper and more convenient centre of certain trades than any of her rivals."[46]

How could a proposal for managed development be reconciled with his philosophical belief in the natural laws of political economy? Equivocation easily dispensed with the discipline imposed by the law of natural advantage, by which Boston held its preordained status as a secondary commercial center. A more serious practical difficulty, in Adams's view, was how to accomplish the right kind of managed development under democratic governance. "To establish such a system amid the ebbs and flows of a democratic form of government is not easy."[47] Legislatures and their committees talked too much and knew too little. On the other hand, "commissions" of "scientific men" could investigate the complex issues and intelligently design the solution to the community's problem. In many cases, Adams warned, "scientific direction can alone save the day."[48] Adams waxed euphoric over his plan for modernizing representative government: commissions were "the germs of a new system, springing out of a great necessity,—a new phase of representative government. Work hitherto badly done, spasmodically done, superficially done, ignorantly done, and too often corruptly done, by temporary and irresponsible legislative committees, is in future to be reduced to order and science by the labors of permanent bureaus, and placed by them before legislatures for intelligent action."[49] Practically, commissions were a step removed from the conflicts and debates of legislatures and took important decisions out of the hands of the unqualified. Efficiency, science, and intelligence would reign under the new administrative order. Plan would triumph over politics, and commissioners would be neutral and disinterested, in contrast to legislators. Public money disbursed by the dictates of an informed and neutral commission must, by definition, serve the public good.

Adams's encomiums to neutrality, science, and system were grounded in an unexamined assumption: the necessity of capital accumulation and economic development to the progress of civilization. He imagined his cherished commissions examining every factor contributing to development and then encouraging it along. In Boston, "internal improvements" were needed to create a welcoming environment for development, and Adams distinguished between those that would be privately developed because they would be profitable and those that were "unremunerative . . . upon which perhaps the success of the whole may depend, [and] must either ever be uncared for, or be a source of constant care of the government." In plainer language, the state should provide those facilities necessary for capitalists' use that capitalists would not invest in themselves. As the community's prosperity depended on capitalist development, it would naturally commit its resources—such as tax moneys and state-supported bonds—to the grand plan.[50] Adams had thus universalized a class interest, notably soon after the Massachusetts legislature rejected eight-hour-day legislation for workers as an unwarranted interference in the free market and illegitimate "class legislation."

Clearly, a degree of vested interest and old prejudices shaped Adams's vision of Boston's political economy. To the workingmen's claim that their labor created all value, Adams retorted that capital was the source of value, and as such, the public interest rested on capital's nurturance. And that crucial task was beyond the limited competence of democratically elected legislators.

Understandably, the world of modern enterprise and its material improvements had its champions. Adams was one of them, but he was not wholly uncritical. Indeed, he is remembered by many historians as one of the most eloquent scourges of the new "plutocrats"—a word Adams was searching for in 1869. He earned the reputation chiefly through his 1869 exposure of the "Erie Ring" involving the outrageous, even farcical, struggle for control over the rail lines between New York and Chicago by some of the most infamous capitalists of the Gilded Age, Vanderbilt, Gould, and Fisk.[51]

At first appearance, there is a tone of dissonance between Adams's piously sensational narrative of the Erie peculations and his other laconically technical analyses of the railroad system. The voice of the modern resounds from most of his railroad articles; the rhetoric of classical republicanism suffuses the account of the Erie scandal. The tensions and conflicts of personal experience announce themselves through the discordance in his writings. Adams's biographer makes it abundantly clear that the scion of the Adams dynasty was addicted to personal enrichment through financial speculation. When he wrote the "Boston" articles, he had significant investments in the Massachusetts railroads that were the subject of the articles and, by his own admission, competitors of the New York railroad lines to Chicago. Respectable speculation, of course, ran in the Adams family, particularly from his mother's line. But so did the classical republican condemnation of luxury and the political corruption resulting from it—and this from the imposing, notoriously cold and exacting patriarchs of the family. We can imagine that the revelations of the Erie machinations touched off something of a personal crisis in Charles. The intense animus Adams expressed toward the new capitalists does appear to have been psychologically bound up with his own ventures and his feelings of turmoil (expressed in his diaries) over them.[52]

Nevertheless, there remains a logic linking his exposé of Erie to his other analyses of the railroad system. Underneath the classical republican rhetoric are nagging misgivings concerning the separation of ownership and control in the modern corporation. The struggle for control over the Erie Railroad was waged through financial scheming. To Adams, the director of a corporation was properly a "trustee" for its real owners, the many stockholders. But now, "a directorship in certain great corporations has come to be regarded as a situation in which to make a fortune, the possession of which is no longer dishonorable. The method of accumulation is both simple and safe."[53] With the help of unscrupulous financiers and corrupt politicians, the new breed of corporate managers had taken millions in profits and left the stockholders' property effectively valueless. Financial ruin was not Adams's only fear. Just as significant, the whole moral order of capitalist proprietorship was collapsing like a house of cards. In the process, it was raising serious problems of legitimacy for the engine of economic progress, the business of railroads.

Over the next two decades, Adams contemplated how a corporation in an industry crucial to the public interest, with natural tendencies to monopoly, could be brought within the moral regime of entrepreneurial individualism, when, with his astute and celebratory analyses of concentration, he revealed that he entertained few illusions but that the old forms of individual proprietorship were being historically superseded. Even though many corporate managers behaved reprehensibly, Adams did not conclude—as others would— that a return to a past order of smaller, individually controlled enterprise and competition was the solution. As he reiterated in every article on railroads, consolidation and centralization were natural and inevitable.[54] The solution was not to turn the corporations over to public ownership, or to leave them alone, but to devise rational regulation that would arrest their power to do evil without impairing their contribution to progressive economic development. Adams earned the opportunity to be the prime innovator of such regulation when the Massachusetts legislature passed a bill to create a railroad commission in 1869 modeled on his plan and then nominated him to the commission in June 1869.[55]

Thrust into the politics of the railroad question, Adams quickly established himself as the leader of the commission, and from 1869 until he resigned in 1878, he would use his official position to mediate conflicts among competing railroad corporations, between investors and corporate managers, between capitalists and railroad workers, and between the corporations and the public. In this official government role, he became nationally recognized as one of the leading experts on railroads in the country, and his official reports and related writings were widely disseminated in the liberal reform press.[56] Adams was remarkably successful in implementing his ideals in Massachusetts and in winning imitators in other states. Personal prestige and competence aided him in his success. But the allure of his program ultimately derived from something more profound. Adams's administrative model of regulation pointed a way to reestablishing order and progress under the new conditions of dispersed ownership. It also served practically, and expressly, as a counterweight to democracy as democracies began to challenge the power of capital.

Wells and Adams, both of whom emerged in the 1870s as national leaders in the liberal reform movement, faced the quandary that the new industrial economy presented to like-thinking men in an exemplary fashion. For liberal reformers, entrepreneurial individualism had guaranteed material and cultural progress, as well as the moral autonomy of the individual. Capital was the fount of civilization; those who owned and controlled capital, endowed with such autonomy, were thus grounded in a way that would ensure responsible social rule. This was a vision of a self-regulating society, in which individuals would take care of themselves and the government would let them alone in their private endeavors. And for these men, such an individualistic model still applied to relations between capital and labor, for they did not yet perceive that the consolidation of industry, which massed hundreds or even thousands of laborers in one enterprise, had upset equally the theory of social harmony premised on the personal relationship between owners and workers. In a social order of entrepreneurial capitalism, in which enterprises were managed by the individuals who owned them, progress and autonomy could appear to be in harmony.

When economic growth accelerated, however, and with it the scale of enterprise and the aggregates of capital necessary for large-scale production, the direct bond between the individual capitalist and the specific productive property became attenuated and finally sundered. The security of property, now investments, was a minor matter when considered with the destruction of the social order rooted in an ideal of the self-controlled proprietor. The two core values of entrepreneurial individualism—individual autonomy and material progress—emerged as a perplexing antinomy during the transition from entrepreneurial to corporate capitalism. Liberal reformers puzzled over the dilemma. It was exactly the economic progress of their age that diminished the autonomy of the individual property owner and undermined the social order governed by individualistic principles, and their attacks on corporate managers, illegitimate speculation, and the like testified to their oblique perception of the connection. A few rejected the materialism of the age of progress and sought haven outside the market and the political sphere—even outside the country. But most followed the path of progress, which required that they accede to and justify the mechanisms through which economic development proceeded, even at the cost of abandoning the moral economy of entrepreneurial individualism.

Liberal reformers, recognizing that economic development had fragmented the former identity of owner and leader, leaving economic enterprise under the control of those freed from the old moral order, were thus forced to reexamine their ideas about the state. Committed to the benefits amassing from the new economy, they understood that it was in need of discipline if the recklessness, corruption, and greed of its new leaders were not to wreck the social order. Consequently, they looked to government to provide direction and thus justified endowing the state with powers to sustain an advanced capitalist economy and to promote national economic power. Despite this striking change, they refused to acknowledge the effective death of the old order of competitive individualism. For the liberal reformers of the late 1860s and early 1870s, the issue of autonomy, of liberty and individualism, was occluded by unconvincing assertions that no qualitative change separated the individual who ran his own factory and the individual who owned stock in a limited liability corporation or the bonds of the government.

The depression of the 1870s and the following two decades of economic instability, stalemate, and restructuring rendered this notion, as well as a host of others, untenable. New social forces and new intellectual influences would force liberal reformers to face more directly the logical inconsistencies of their theory and the social contradictions of their world. Ultimately, a new conception of individualism would emerge from the political and intellectual clash between them and their challengers. And with it, a new theory of the state emerged, one that accorded the new individualism its pride of place in liberalism yet allowed for extensive governmental regulation of the ostensibly free market—regulation in practice divorced from democratic processes and accountability but in ideology defended as consistent with the protection of liberty. To place limits on the once vaunted arena for the play of individual liberty, the free market, was a small price to pay in exchange for reconstituting social order and progress. And even as liberal reformers continued to trumpet the cause of liberty and little government, they themselves sketched the lineaments of the administrative mandate.

THE STATE VERSUS MAN

LIBERAL REFORM POLITICS AND THE

ADMINISTRATIVE MANDATE

Liberal reformers hailed economic progress, even as they felt apprehensive about the disintegration of the world of entrepreneurial individualism and were disturbed by the chaos of ungrounded materialism and the moral and political corruption that seemed to be arising from the ruins. Fraught with dangers as this new world was, a "let-alone" posture was clearly insufficient. As they faced both backward and forward, they began to forge a political program out of their examination of fiscal policy, international trade and investment, and new corporate practices. Active administration and regulation were called for in the more complex spheres of the new economy, but democratically controlled government had not displayed much talent in maintaining an environment favorable to economic development. As a counter to a disruptive democracy in which workers agitated for shorter hours and farmers lobbied for inflation, liberal reformers elaborated new principles and mechanisms for state *action*: a complex, national economy, fully integrated into an ever growing world market, required expert administration of its state. The new economy, in short, mandated an administrative form of governance, with a logic and objective distinct from the laissez-faire doctrine that former Radicals had turned to in order to foil labor's eight-hour movement and to discontinue federal support for Reconstruction governments.

The dual nature of the liberal reform movement, its championing of laissez-faire even as it sought to augment the bureaucratic capacities of a state with expanded administrative powers, was revealed in one of its founding documents. In 1871, William Dean Howells offered a kind of manifesto for the movement in the short-lived "Politics" column in the *Atlantic Monthly*. It deserves to be quoted extensively, for it lists the particular reforms liberal reformers sought as well as succinctly encapsulates their administrative designs and the somewhat contradictory rationale supporting them.[1]

> There is a movement—it is yet too early to call it a party—of large numbers in different parts of the country whose aims, desires, and intentions the Republicans will do well to consider earnestly. They are commonly said to be to reform the civil service, to abolish the protective system, to return to specie payments; the new movement also includes those who desire in the various States to introduce minority representation, to abolish the elective judiciary system, greatly to reduce the number of other elective offices, and to lengthen official tenures to such an extent as to secure responsibility, and to prevent, at least for the present, any extension of the elective franchise to women. To those who are given to retrospective politics, there may seem in this list of principles no common bond of sympathy; no doubt it appears to many wise politicians that the new movement merely represents the local and personal discontent always ready to array itself against the party in power.

The list of reforms itself is familiar to historians of Gilded Age liberal reform. What is particularly revealing in the passage is that an attack on democratic procedures—elective offices, majority rule, universal suffrage—unifies the reforms, despite Howells's disingenuous claim that there appears to be no "common bond." This assertion prefaces his own explanation of what held the disparate projects together.

> But there is a feeling common to all those interested in the reforms we have mentioned, that the course of administration in this country during the last forty years has been in the direction, not of good government, but of anarchy. The method of selecting judicial officers, the tenure of office, representation, the circulating medium, the civil service, the collection of revenue, the limits of the franchise, *all questions relating to these subjects belong to the department of administration. They have little to do with the form of government; they do not touch upon natural rights; they are questions of administration, pure and simple. The new movement, then, is to effect reforms in the machinery of politics and in administration, it is to evolve order out of chaos, government out of anarchy.*

Howells severed "administration" from underlying principles—of democracy and rights—as if virtually every Western political theorist had not taken the problem between the form of government and the principles underlying it as one of the central questions of political organization. Although Howells could not have been more direct about the practical object of the movement—administrative reform—he concluded with a quite different gloss on its essential character: "The political ideal of the Anglo-Saxon is liberty. With Englishmen and Americans the most perfect government is that which governs least; the most perfect state is that in which moral self-control is substituted for the sanctions of government." This passage immediately follows the one above, but a logical step appears to be missing from the argument. Howells had bluntly stated his movement's political design: administration as a counterforce against democracy. Instead of allowing this controversial declaration to stand on its own, Howells invoked a lofty principle to assert a coherence that appears—at best—at some remove from the very obvious coherence of an administrative solution to democratic "anarchy." The keywords "liberty" and "self-control," Howells knew, would resonate with core values of Americans' political and religious heritage and simultaneously evoke the idea of the "let-alone" theory of government.

It is evident, notwithstanding the veiling effort served by the proclamation for liberty, that unifying these measures was the conviction that incompetence and inefficiency pervaded the legislatures, the elected judiciary, and the patronage-staffed executive agencies. Some of the liberal reformers' proposals fit squarely in the laissez-faire approach to government. In part, it was necessary to accomplish a preliminary clearing—to insulate the government against the excessively democratic inclinations of American voters. Only then, they believed, could a state with rational, efficient, and scientific administrative capabilities to support a complex capitalist economy be constructed. Although liberal reformers continued to be ambivalent about the moral value of specific types of economic changes, they were much less troubled by professional bureaucracy as a political solution to the new conflicts of the postwar world. The challenge for them was twofold: to design a means to insert bureaucratic procedures into the unique constitutional structure of the nation, and to explain why such procedures were consonant with liberty and violated neither the procedural requirements nor the substantive promise of democracy to which many Northerners appeared to be particularly attached.

Although liberal reformers did not achieve all their goals, their influence in the transformation of American liberal democracy should not be gainsaid. The administrative mandate that liberal reformers divined marked a real departure not only from antebellum traditions of limited government but also from experiments with an active democratic state, which had been directed by Radical Republicans and subsequently had been taken up by a number of the postbellum social movements.[2] Moreover, liberals laid the critical practical and ideological groundwork for the creation of a modern liberal democratic state with powers to regulate and intervene in social life—through means almost wholly removed from democratic participation or accountability. In deed, the liberal reform movement of the Gilded Age was both precursor and progenitor of the Progressive Era's administered democracy.

In reaction against the postwar labor movement, as we have seen, many Radicals had rejected the state activism they had once endorsed, and they had declared themselves liberal reformers devoted to laissez-faire. But at the same time they were making the transition to laissez-faire about matters in the labor market, they were promoting a very different method of statecraft on other subjects. Drawing on the social ties and cultural knowledge they were developing in the American Social Science Association, liberals hoped to establish a new kind of nonpolitical, expert administration of many of the government's powers. In doing so, they would simultaneously create an efficient modern state that could be trusted to act appropriately in sensitive matters and would insulate the government from the pressures of democratic politics. Just as they had been disappointed by Northern workingmen and Southern freedmen who would not follow the correct liberal path, so too they became frustrated by their inability to overcome the lock of party politics, the influence of social movements over legislators, and the incompetence of the patronage-staffed agencies of the government.

The administrative designs of liberal reformers were most evident in areas in which government policy affected the development of the nation's economy. The new complexity of the economy, as a practical matter, made irrelevant the old strictures of economic liberalism that the government should stay out of private economic activity. For example, liberal reformers commonly favored pragmatic governmental regulation of railroad corporations, because they understood that the tasks of financing and managing the complex industry had endowed corporate managers with an expertise that left the individual owners of corporate securities helpless to assert their theoretical prerogatives of control. They were among the first to propose transferring regulatory authority from the states to the national government.[3] Similarly, once the scope and scale of enterprise extended to involve large-scale investment, abstract property holding, and substantial international capital and commodity flows, private enterprise became inextricably linked with government fiscal and monetary policies.

The hopes and frustrations raised in the liberal reform quest for administrative governance were most evident on the subject of federal fiscal policy. Financing the Union war effort had intertwined the national debt, taxation policies, the greenback currency, and the private national banking system.[4] When and how would the debt be paid off? Would the country return to a hard money—a specie—standard? If so, what should be the means to bring the depreciated greenbacks up to par with the gold value of the dollar and enable redemption? How should the widespread desire for abatement of the income, licensing, and excise taxes be balanced with the need to pay down the debt? Should the high protectionist tariffs passed during the war to raise revenue be continued for the protection of domestic industries? How could the national banking system, concentrated in the Northeast, direct sufficient currency and capital to the outlying regions of the West and South?

A revision of fiscal policy would affect different segments of capital and different types of producers differently. Among businessmen and their middle-class associates, several distinct positions emerged in the two years following the war, which nonetheless rested on a shared vision.[5] National progress required that a favorable environment for capital investment be maintained, that foreign trade be reconstituted on more secure grounds, and that the nation attract capital investment from overseas. To achieve these goals, a stable currency and "good faith" toward the nation's creditors were essential. Whatever the government did regarding the national debt, it must not impair the security of investments or predictability in capital markets, even as reasonable men could disagree about appropriate methods to achieve the goal.

The debates, conducted in the business and middle-class press, revealed certain assumptions about the capitalist mainspring of the nation's economic progress. It was not, however, until the fall of 1867, when technical questions of fiscal policy became the subject of partisan political competition, that concerns about the government's capacities arose. Almost half of the national debt still outstanding in 1867 was composed of tax-exempt bonds known as the 5–20s. Congress had legislated that the interest and principal on all other wartime bond issues were to be paid in gold. But the act issuing the 5–20s neglected to specify that the principal as well as the interest was to be paid in gold, even though, like all the other bonds, these were marketed with the promise and expectation that the principal would be paid in coin. (Key figures in the act's passage in Congress disagreed about whether this was indeed their intent.) With Western farmers particularly strapped by the shortage of money and urban workers converting to greenback doctrines, some Democrats soon decided that they could make political hay out of paper money. In particular, they could stake out their differences from the Republicans by portraying the national debt as Republican-supported privilege for bondholders and a burden on producers. Taking up an idea originated by Radical Republican Thaddeus Stevens but rejected by his party, Democratic senator George H. Pendleton proposed in 1867 that the principal on the 5–20s be paid in greenbacks, and the Democratic Party soon took this up as the "Ohio Idea."[6]

Once Democrats asserted that bondholders should be forced to accept reduced profits in the interest of the people—the producers—and that payment of the principal in greenbacks could accomplish this while respecting the letter of the laws creating the public debt, George W. Curtis, Godkin, Horace White, and their cohorts countered with the charge of debt repudiation. By the fall of 1867, with a presidential campaign soon to be under way, the leading publicists in the Radical alliance had already been sorely tried by the eight-hour movement, proposals for land confiscation, and other unsavory radicalisms. Although "repudiation" was a Democratic Party scheme, the congressional "extreme Radicals" such as Benjamin Butler and Stevens endorsed greenback principles, and the attack on the national debt compounded their irritation and disillusionment with Radicalism.[7]

The future standing of public credit, and its importance to the security of both private and public investments in the United States, most concerned the reluctant Radicals. The issue of the national debt seemed likely to become one of the major dividing lines in the 1868 presidential election, and in order to win popular support, they phrased their protests in the language of democratic patriotism. Taking on the Democrats' charge that paying off the 5–20s in coin would enrich a class of bloated bondholders and speculators, Godkin insisted that the bonds were in fact held "on a democratic basis." To pay off the debt in depreciated paper amounted to repudiation, and no one could fail to see, he charged, that this was a devious pro-Southern stratagem to undermine the nation. "Without credit, nationality, in fact, is not possible."[8]

As it became clear that their admonitions had scant influence over the voters, the agitation over the national debt helped propelled an official break with Radical Republicans. Months before the impeachment of President Andrew Johnson, erstwhile Radical publicists began to speak as the most ardent proponents of new priorities and new leadership for the Republican Party, and Ulysses S. Grant seemed to be the ideal man to effect the turn. As the *Nation* cynically hoped, "It would be an excellent thing to have a president *without a policy.*"[9] No small part of their support for Grant was due to his image as an economic liberal with sound fiscal views. And, fortunately, they believed he was a sufficiently sympathetic public defender of the civil and political equality of African Americans.[10] White was one of Grant's earliest and most influential backers. White, with his friends in Chicago and the senators that had voted for Johnson's acquittal, dominated the platform committee of the 1868 Republican convention, which denounced debt repudiation as a "national crime."[11]

As the debt issue helped to force a realignment in the Republican Party that removed the Radicals from dominance, so too did it seem that it might effect a shift in the balance of power in the Democratic Party. The party's base included large numbers of working-class and farmer Greenbackers, and Democrats had the opportunity to remove the stigma of disloyalty from the party by, first, making greenbackism the center of their campaign to attract the producers of the North and, second, by nominating Pendleton, who was willing to endorse the political and civil rights of black people in order to focus on what to him was the more important currency issue. But the party did not lack for respectable businessmen who had little patience for financial experiments. In a hard-fought convention battle, the 1868 Democratic platform conceded to Green-backers Pendleton's "Ohio Idea," but the presidential candidate, Horatio Seymour—put forward as the favored son of the Eastern capitalists of the Bourbon Democracy—refused to campaign on the plank to repay the federal bonds in greenbacks. Having jettisoned the opportunity to chart a new path and increase the party's popular base, the Democracy was left to campaign on its old reactionary line—white supremacy and opposition to Reconstruction. The Democrats' vice presidential candidate, Frank Blair, set the tone of the campaign with his lurid racist fantasies of Republican rule in the South.[12]

The election of 1868 hinged on Reconstruction, but as Grant took office, he revealed the shift that had occurred in the priorities of the Republican Party. His first act was to proclaim that every dollar of the national debt would be paid in coin. Congress passed the Public Credit Act, which declared that the United States "solemnly pledges its faith to make provision, at the earliest practicable period, for the redemption of the United States notes in coin."[13] Such a rapid and exemplary resolution of the question confirmed for budding liberals that their break with Radical Republicans had been sensible and seemed to promise that they would continue to have political influence. As the *Nation* had observed in 1867, there were a host of new issues that demanded their civic intervention.[14] The national debt had been placed beyond the reach of popular politics, but there were still many other areas of federal fiscal policy dangerously exposed to what they considered irrational political tinkering.

Liberal reformers had cause to be sanguine about their potential power over fiscal issues, as one of their own, David A. Wells, held the position of commissioner of the revenue. Wells, who had gained his government post by the usual means in the patronage system of midcentury America, was the leading expositor and practitioner of the model of the expert social scientist above the fray of democratic politics. As the *Nation* recommended before Grant took office, "The men whose hands the public should now strengthen are the hands of the working practical reformers, like the Jenckeses and Garfields and Wellses, whose aim it is to bring the real products of 'advanced thinking' to the poor man's home, and to give the weak some better protection for their rights than platform oratory."[15] Wells's widely touted revenue commission report for 1868, published in the months between Grant's victory and inauguration, laid out the case for more extensive fiscal reforms in anticipation of Grant's defense of the national debt.[16]

Wells advocated reforms in managing the currency and taxation, in order to make American industry competitive in the international market. He believed that the influence wielded by legislators and party appointees over the debt, currency, and taxation was disastrous for the nation's economic development. At the end of 1869, after observing numerous strikes, mounting agitation by Westerners for legislated inflation, and new lows of corruption by speculators, Wells pronounced the Grant administration a failure. Behind the new pessimism was his disapproval of the entanglement of politics in economic policymaking. The poor quality of the patronage appointees in the treasury, customhouse, and post office exacerbated less than ideal revenue policies.[17] Even as Wells tried to compel the administration to act responsibly, Congress, by virtue of the power over the nation's currency it had acquired in wartime legislation, offered an additional channel for greenback movements and other financial heresies to wreck the nation's fiscal superstructure. In 1869, a bill expanding the greenbacks in circulation gained substantial initial support; in 1870, Congress passed the National Bank Currency Act, widely condemned by financiers and their attendants as inflationary.[18]

Liberal reformers, thwarted in their efforts to convert the administration and Congress to sound finance, sought relief elsewhere. Perceiving that they had come up short because of the too intimate bond between the people and uninformed politicians who owed their jobs to elections or party service, they rediscovered the virtues of the Supreme Court and looked to it to fortify the nation's vault against the tempests of democratic governance. The desire to seek redress through judicial review was itself a sign of an important change in ideas of the state. To Republicans, the Supreme Court had lost legitimacy in its proslavery *Dred Scott* decision of 1857, and during Congressional Reconstruction, Republicans had warned against any resort to the courts. But now Congress and the president had proved incompetent and had demonstrated that they would not yield power to the experts. As the legislative fiat of the Legal Tender Act (1863) had given the country a depreciated paper currency, so would court fiat restore a specie standard without the inconvenience of legislation. Godkin, who was often ahead of his comrades in reform, had discerned the utility of the Court even before Grant took office. Analyzing the Supreme Court's review of an elected state court ruling in *Texas v. White* (1869), Godkin gloated that the "decision acted like a bucket of water on a drunken man's head. One or two more in the same direction will completely sober most of the currency madcaps and put the greenbacks before us in their real character—as a makeshift which it was excusable to resort to at the outbreak of the war, but which is the source of incalculable evils, and whose disturbing influence on trade and on private and public morals should, now that the war is over, be kept within the narrowest possible limits till we finally get rid of them." The Supreme Court could serve as an arbiter of legislative acts; elected state judges, too attuned to popular opinion, had shown themselves incapable of doing so. When Chief Justice Chase issued the narrow majority opinion in *Hepburn v. Griswold* (1870), declaring part of the Legal Tender Act unconstitutional, Godkin praised the practical benefits of the decision.[19] Although the liberal reform and financial press phrased their attack on governmental powers over the currency in principled language about the natural laws of trade, the politics of money weighed more heavily in their consideration. Likewise, the liberal reformers' assent to the decision reflected their belief that monetary policy was currently too subject to democratic influence, rather than that the principle of laissez-faire should apply.

A fleeting victory on the currency was, however, paralleled by a more disturbing defeat in their assay to lay the groundwork for a new type of governmental administration. Wells's disregard for the niceties of partisan politics won for him only the enmity of Republican Stalwarts. Yet Wells himself was appointed by the president and, like all other appointees, held his job on the pleasure of his boss and his party. As he continued to agitate for free trade and tariff reform, Republican congressmen persuaded Grant to end the annual annoyances issued by Wells. In 1870, Wells lost his job.

Liberal reformers nevertheless continued to defend the model of nonpolitical, scientific administration that Wells had helped forge, even in the face of defeat. Considering that the legislative and executive branches still retained extensive powers over the currency, and thus indirectly over industrial production, liberals proposed that financial experts be given broad powers to advise both Congress and the president. The idea drew inspiration from an idealized model of economic efficiency and was ratified by a commitment to the procedures of neutral social science. Francis Amasa Walker, who had served as Wells's assistant on the revenue commission, argued that the United States could benefit from "a finance minister."[20] The *Nation* defended governance by commission against charges that the practice was antidemocratic, while presenting a theoretical and historical analysis of the superior efficiency of nonelective commissions. Godkin's journal likewise proposed that a single congressional committee specializing in financial legislation be created, in which expertise would incubate. All financial legislation should originate in the special committee and not be subject to amendment by the less knowledgeable members.[21] If the institutional mechanisms of fiscal management could be reformed in such ways, then, liberals suggested, the state had an active role to play in managing the supply of currency to foster stable economic growth.

In 1870, the prospects for administrative reform in a number of areas looked mixed. To advance their designs for a new type of scientific administrative governance, liberals believed they needed the present Grant administration to commit to reform. But Grant was clearly leaning toward the Stalwarts and in that year ousted two other liberal reformers from important positions; Attorney General Ebenezer R. Hoar was fired, and Senator Charles Sumner was stripped of his chairmanship of the Committee on Foreign Relations, both for their opposition to Grant's scheme to annex Santo Domingo. Yet, in the same year, Grant and the Stalwarts created the Civil Service Commission and appointed Curtis chairman, and at the state level, Charles F. Adams was gaining renown for the new methods of railroad regulation he pioneered on the Massachusetts Railroad Commission. On balance, though, it was plain that Grant did not highly value the support of liberal reformers. Consequently, a number of them, including Wells, Godkin, C. F. Adams, White, Atkinson, and Missouri senator Carl Schurz, met after the elections of 1870 under the auspices of the Free Trade League and declared that henceforth they would act as "Independents" in politics.[22] This was the first national meeting of the group that would fashion the Liberal Republican movement against Grant in 1872.

The 1870 meeting focused on "revenue reform." The timing of the movement, its roots in the Free Trade League, and the rationales for independence issued by the participants suggest that economic and fiscal issues were the critical ones in their break with Grant (even though they were also angered by other matters—such as Grant's Santo Domingo annexation plan and the subsequent attack on Charles Sumner by the administration, Grant's renewed efforts to enforce Reconstruction, and increasing evidence of political corruption in the administration). In 1871, Wells wrote in the *North American Review* (then under the editorial hand of Henry Adams) that "revenue reform" was now the highest priority of national politics.[23] A financial policy designed by men ignorant of economic science and implemented by none too intelligent and often corrupt government employees was to blame for the continuing stagnation of the national economy. First, the tax system needed reform. It was not necessarily that taxes were too high but that waste, inefficiency, and outright theft in the collection of taxes "takes far more from the people than the treasury ever receives or needs, and . . . blights a harvest it cannot gather."[24] Tax reform hence entailed civil service reform, as well as a brake on congressional meddling.

The horrendous fiscal policies of the government, however, were exposed most graphically by the many problems of the protective tariff. A number of converging theories of the need for tariff reform were circulating among liberal reformers at this time. Godkin, Atkinson, and Charles F. Adams all had exposed the connection between manufacturers' success in gaining special tariff legislation and the labor movement's political assertiveness. They had therefore concluded that protectionism must end if labor's claims were to be rebuffed without arousing charges of class favoritism.[25] Wells concurred with these political objections to the tariff and indeed provided one of the more powerful cases against protectionism in his detailed exposition of the irrationality and injustice of a system designed to reward the most persistent industry lobbies and corrupt the Congress.[26]

Wells, for whom the disagreements about policy with the administration were sharpened by an arrogant certitude in the superiority of his scientifically derived opinions as well as by the personal slight he had suffered, nonetheless revealed that the essential objection of the "Independents" was that Grant's administration had failed in its administration of the economy. The "Independents" declared, he wrote, that "at the present time, there is neither good sense nor sound judgment displayed in the management of our national fiscal affairs: and further, that, under the present administration, all attempts to insure progress through investigation have been studiously repressed and forbidden, rather than encouraged and stimulated."[27] Similar indignation was evident in the *Nation*. At the end of the crisis-ridden year of 1871, the magazine went beyond its demand of the previous year and called for a nonelective commission to be formed to dictate financial legislation to Congress. "That such a Commission ought to form a permanent part of our administrative system, no thinking man can doubt. That congress should ever attempt one particle of legislation affecting directly or indirectly the industrial system of the country, without having before it such reports as such a Commission would furnish, is greatly to be regretted."[28]

As it became apparent to liberal reformers that the Republican Party under Grant would never accept their counsel to place government economic policies under the rule of science and its practitioners, they first had to confront the question of where they could act politically. It was not a light matter. Most of the "Independents" had once been prominent Radical Republican publicists, and they still believed that the party was the home of most of the respectable men in the country. In 1872, the "Independents" tried first to foment an anti-Grant movement within the Republican Party; when they failed, they then organized to nominate their own candidate. But the Liberal Republicans were bested at their own convention. They found themselves as co-conspirators with a barely reconstructed Democratic Party and saddled with Horace Greeley, a man many had denounced for his flirtation with the radical schemes that had originally soured them on the Republicans.

The Liberal Republican movement is often viewed by historians as, if not the pivotal, at least a defining moment of Gilded Age liberal reform. In this interpretation, the twin goals of liberal reformers were the restoration of uncorrupted government through the rule of the "best men" and the erection of laissez-faire as a first principle of government. The argument presented here challenges these conclusions. The liberal reform movement of the Gilded Age was much broader than the Liberal Republican movement, and I would argue that the campaign of 1872 does not reveal very much about the deeper currents of liberal reform. Likewise, historians have been too uncritical in accepting the "Independents'" self-designation as a party of liberty and have overlooked their equally powerful quest to develop an activist, administrative state. It was indeed their failure to win much support for this administrative vision that turned many to a more extreme classical liberalism. But even this was honored more in rhetoric than in practice.

Just as the Liberal Republicans' character as dogmatic classical liberals has been exaggerated, so too has been the role of corruption in their political shift.[29] The prime objection liberal reformers raised against the Grant administration centered not on its political corruption but rather on its incompetence and inefficiency, especially in policies that affected the national economy. The main focus of early discussions of corruption concerned municipal corruption, and these were inextricable from the labor question. They complained that urban "bosses" overtaxed property owners, in order to pay for the redistributive programs that would keep the working-class voters loyal to the machine, and gave too much encouragement to the class politics of labor. The issue of national corruption itself was linked closely to liberals' deeper concerns with the government's maladministration of the economy; corruption at the national level was first identified in 1866 by Wells as a problem of inefficient tax collection, resulting from staffing customs and internal revenue collection through patronage rather than merit. Although it is clear that the liberal reformers' attacks on corruption mounted in the late 1860s, it is important to understand their revulsion against it as a projection, in part, of personal slights that often stemmed from their failed administrative designs. By the time of the Liberal Republican movement, three reformers, Wells, Curtis, and Hoar, had all been expelled from the administration. Liberal reformers were obviously appalled that their beneficent and disinterested contributions to the nation could be so shockingly disregarded by the crass and uncultivated officeholders and influence peddlers surrounding Grant. But they were more concerned that their policies were not being implemented, and corruption was a lesser obstacle than the ignorance and inefficiency of the untrained politicos.[30]

The Liberal Republican electoral campaign of 1872 was an utter disaster for the "Independents," and as John G. Sproat, one of its ablest chroniclers, has pointedly argued, it was of doubtful importance in American political history.[31] It can be added that the botched political campaign did not noticeably influence the ideological journey of American liberal reformers in the Gilded Age. Indeed, it would soon appear that their success at shaping opinion and influencing statecraft had little to do with their fortunes in the electoral arena.

A few minutes after 11 A.M. on September 17, 1873, Jay Cooke and Company, the largest bank in the United States, closed its doors and went under. Cooke wept, while the rest of the bankers and brokers scrambled to salvage what they could in the aftermath of the financial shock. Few could rescue themselves. On the news of Cooke's failure, railroad stocks started to lose up to half their value on the stock exchange; all day long, news of business suspensions fed the frenzy. The panic continued for another ten days, with hundreds of individual brokers and five thousand commercial banks declaring bankruptcy before the market steadied on September 29.[32]

The United States had experienced ruinous panics before, but the one of 1873 would prove to be the most devastating yet. It initiated the depression of 1873 to 1879: lasting five years and five months, it still stands as the longest economic contraction in the history of the United States. During these years, fifty-four thousand businesses defaulted on more than $1.3 billion worth of assets, leaving their employees jobless and their owners bankrupt. Half of the railways of the nation fell into receivership, as holders of railroad stocks and bonds watched their investments disappear, and receivers attempted to manage their way back to solvency by draconian wage cuts and layoffs. Production and revenues plummeted in all the major industries. The deep contraction of business spawned mass unemployment for the first time in American history. Perhaps up to a third of the nation's workforce lost their jobs.[33] Farmers shared the sufferings of industrial workers, businessmen, and urban residents, as prices for the raw commodities they produced plunged. Small farmers sank deeper into debt, often losing their land and their treasured independence. In the South, the already dwindling postemancipation hopes of freedmen were crushed, as the sharecropping system in the cotton belt became firmly entrenched.[34]

In June 1878, fifty-seven months into the depression, the House of Representatives resolved that it was its "solemn duty" to inquire into its causes and to devise remedies. In the rhetoric of producerism, Congress declared: "Whereas our real and permanent prosperity is founded and dependent upon labor, as the source of all wealth; that when labor suffers from any cause which may be removed, or its rigor mitigated, our national harmony and property are thereby imperiled." Representative Abram S. Hewitt, a wealthy capitalist from New York City who had helped finance the Democratic Party back to life, chaired the investigative committee chartered by the House. The committeemen listened to testimony from labor leaders, businessmen, liberal reform economists and editors, Southern planters, Western farmers, and just about any other man with a theory of his own about the depression. The committee published a thick volume of testimony in 1879. The diversity of opinion the volume revealed is remarkable; even more telling, however, is that the congressional committee published no authoritative conclusion and recommended no legislation.[35]

By the time the House committee published its report in 1879, business had begun to revive. Therefore, one might say that the absence of conclusions or positive legislation reveals nothing more than that Congress moved slowly and that the moment for action had passed. But in 1882, following a wave of strikes and at the beginning of a downturn that would lead to another brief depression, the Senate Committee on Education and Labor took up an investigation of the same issues of "capital and labor." This time, the Senate committee convened hearings in every region of the country. The Senate committee, however, never completed its assigned task. Four volumes of testimony were published in 1885, but the chairman explained that the volume that was to contain the committee's conclusions and recommendations could not be published because of "obstacles and opposition."[36]

Certainly, democratic legislatures are renowned for a tendency to talk much and do little. Nonetheless, the inaction of the national Congresses after 1874 signifies a more historically specific phenomenon. The Republicans' failure to respond to the initial suffering of the early depression and the "Redemption" of Southern states from Reconstruction Republican government enabled the Democratic Party to recover legitimacy and competitiveness. In the fall elections of 1874, the Democratic Party won control of the House of Representatives for the first time since the election of 1858, gained a substantial number of Senate seats, and won control of key Northern states. Between 1874 and 1896, the year when the Republicans won the presidency and both houses of Congress by a landslide, the two main political parties competed fiercely with each other, but neither could establish or sustain its dominance. In only a few years during these two decades did one party control the presidency and working majorities in the Senate and House.

Thus, for more than two decades, the executive and legislative branches of the federal government were mired in a political stalemate. Whatever ideological differences continued to exist between the Democratic and Republican parties, neither could hope to enact a program in accord with its principles or have any confidence that if it took the risk to do so it would survive the next session of Congress. Since the first party system, American elections had been very competitive; the close balance of power between the parties in the third party system of the Gilded Age intensified this historical competition. Throughout the period, seven to eight out of every ten men eligible to vote turned out for every election, and these men demonstrated that the pull of traditional party loyalties remained strong. Intense competition encouraged politicians to minimize the divisions within their own parties by propounding nebulous or superficial programs and by appealing to seemingly incontestable values among their constituents. The notorious scandals of the era also had their origins, in part, in this competitive environment: election campaigns became more expensive to conduct even as the outcome became more unpredictable and politicians became more dependent on elective office as their sole career. Historians have long indicted the now forgotten politicians of the age: they were corrupt; they failed to react positively and creatively to the palpable social problems of the industrial age; they engaged in a disingenuous non-ideological politics divorced from any concern for the public welfare. All these charges insinuate that national politicians made themselves irrelevant, and there is some truth in all these counts. But first it must be recognized that this political order had its origins in a seemingly intractable political stalemate that rendered the federal government nearly impotent to enact new policies. The two congressional investigations into depression and class conflict give oblique but compelling testimony to the effects of the standoff. They evince a new approach to active governance on the federal level. (When a program could be presented vaguely enough as to appear to satisfy all sides and political fortunes were at stake, innovative policies were enacted, as when Congress created the national Bureau of Labor in 1884.) But in the final analysis, stalemate between the parties left the committees able to do little more than provide a forum for others to comment on the social disarray and misery in the nation.[37]

The difficulty of sustained policymaking by elected politicians in the formal institutions of government shaped the balance of political power in civil society in complex and profound ways. During the depression of the 1870s, a conjuncture of economic and political developments provided an unanticipated boon to self-identified liberal reformers. Soon after their apparent setback in the election of 1872, the depression provided a fresh opportunity and enabled them to amass the greatest degree of influence that they would ever attain.

Chance alone did not bolster the liberal reform vanguard to prominence in the 1870s. They consciously exploited the economic and political conditions of the decade to advance their cause actively. And the first order of business was to discredit those who, during the flush years before 1873, had posed the greatest challenge to their broad political program: organized labor and organized farmers, or, as they called themselves, the "producing classes." The severe economic crisis split the ground under the feet of those organizing collectively to make demands on the state. Liberal reform publicists took advantage of the social conflicts ignited by the labor and farmer movements to persuade a broader public that measures must be taken to permanently remove the threat of "class legislation."

The economic crisis quickly devastated the formal organizations and institutions of labor—trade unions, labor newspapers, and federations of unions—which were entirely dependent on financing from within their own ranks. When the panic struck, hundreds of thousands lost their jobs or suffered severe wage cuts. With them went many unions and labor papers into perpetual oblivion; others felt the full brunt of organized capital's power and were crushed; some scraped by until the recovery in 1878 allowed them to begin anew. Workers engaged in new methods of agitation, made new alliances, and issued novel demands, but these all proved ephemeral. The most notable were the movements of the unemployed. Throughout the industrial Northeast, skilled and unskilled workers demonstrated together to demand from local and state governments "work or bread," explaining that public employment could serve not only to aid the unemployed in legitimate ways but also to improve the quality of urban life. But within a few months of the panic, the movements had disappeared, hastened along by urban police forces.[38]

The demise of most labor unions and the defeat of the fledgling organizations of the unemployed left workers and the poor more vulnerable to their better-organized opponents. Traditional labor actions were met in ways that cast their participants as criminals. State and local governments called out the militia to break strikes or won court orders sending workers back to work, and throughout the industrial Northeast and Midwest vagrancy laws were reactivated, making criminals and "tramps" out of the unemployed. A new and decidedly nasty ideology of separate classes developed, much of it drawn from the earlier musings of the vanguard liberal reform intellectuals. Nativism resurfaced, this time casting immigrant workers as anti-American communists.[39] Simultaneously, the scientific charity movement that had arisen in the 1860s successfully wrested public relief from the state by arguing that its organizations had the money and the expertise to dole out charity efficiently. In practice, these organizations administered aid in a niggardly and punitive manner. Private administrators provided aid only to those who demonstrated their submission to the dictates of natural economic law through industrious, individual effort—and stayed out of the company of their vice-ridden neighbors and relatives.[40]

Even considering these tight-fisted and closed spirited developments, it was in response to the protests and strikes of workers that liberal reformers most betrayed the liberal values of tolerance and state neutrality. Time and again, ignoring distinctions between peaceful demonstration and anarchic riot, they urged the state authorities to use physical force to repress labor actions. In one of the first signs of the new militancy, Curtis praised the newly professionalized New York City police for their bloody repression of the unemployed at a Tompkins Square demonstration. The police had correctly taught laborers that the "follies and ferocities of the Commune are alien to American thought and methods." Similar constructions of Americanism and communism, honed in liberal circles, shaped the interpretation of the so-called Molly Maguire conspiracy. Godkin's inflamed musings about the Paris Commune suddenly appeared to be simple common sense, as the respectable classes throughout the country consumed the sensational news coming out of the Pennsylvania coal fields and applauded the execution of the foreign menaces. Whereas all semblance of due process had been abandoned in the Molly Maguire trials, railroad commissioner C. F. Adams tried to translate the cultural criminalization of labor into the regular channels of law. Responding to a strike by railroad engineers in February 1877—a prelude to the Great Strike of that year—Adams's Massachusetts Railroad Commission invoked the "public interest" to recommend amending the state penal code in order to criminalize most of the actions taken by workers in the midst of a strike. Their recommendations had the virtue of making police actions less arbitrary and less politicized—henceforth the police would be acting in accordance with specific statutes, rather than waiting for orders from the governor or mayor to proceed. The logic was the same nonetheless: "The railroads of Massachusetts are its arteries. If, to secure some trivial and private end, either party to a conflict undertakes to wantonly stop the flow through those arteries, it becomes a question, not between private parties, but between the Commonwealth and a public enemy." Once in the fold of the all-American producing classes, industrial labor was becoming a special interest, and one disturbingly alien.[41]

But if liberal reformers and their associates among the men of business and government hoped to redefine Americanism and the status of labor in the nation, the most dramatic confrontation of the decade—the Great Strike of 1877—suggested that the liberal reform consensus among the respectable classes had very shallow roots in the citizenry as a whole. Railroad enthusiasts liked to speak of the national railroad system as the arteries of the national body, and they were none too happy to learn that strikes traveled as rapidly as locomotives over the lines. Beginning on the Baltimore and Ohio Railroad in Martinsburg, West Virginia, on July 16, 1877, the strike spread to all four major trunklines and many of their subsidiaries within a week, thus initiating the first nationwide strike in the history of the United States.[42]

Scruples about "home rule" and the use of the federal military against American citizens, which had played so prominently in the rhetoric to end Reconstruction, were junked when the menace was to Northern property and commerce. Denouncing the strike as a "riot" led by un-American communists, anarchists, and other undesirables, the voices of respectability applauded the use of armed force to put an end to the treasonous rebellion of workers. President Rutherford Hayes and most governors hardly needed the encouragement. Enough of a consensus existed between the politically and economically powerful and the elite shapers of public opinion that a threat to an essential economic function was not just a matter of market relations between labor and capital, but rather a political insurrection, that the use of the full coercive might of the democratic state against its citizens sparked no pang of conscience. By July 29, the superior power of the state, directly serving capital with state militias and the U.S. Army, had done the trick, and the strike had been crushed. The vogue of constructing city armories in the wake of the strike revealed the traditional liberal night-watchman state renovated to meet the new menace of communism among its laboring population.

Theoretically, liberalism is opposed to coercion, the use of force to impose particularistic interests, and militaristic actions by the state. From this perspective, liberal reformers' ready endorsement of coercion appears to contradict their professed values. Nevertheless, liberalism has also been concerned with social order, proposing that order issued from the free play of individual competitiveness. American liberals, like their compatriots past and present, condemned collective action, believing that it violated the basic maxim of individual liberty as well as threatened to disrupt society. In pursuing collective means to improve their standard of living or seek government action, workers violated—in liberals' opinion—the fundamental law of individual liberty and thus called down on themselves the sanction of rightful authority. Nevertheless, liberal reformers' phrasing of the conflict suggests that they were uneasy with state coercion. Military action could be justified more readily if striking workers were portrayed as "communist" revolutionaries bent on destroying the social order. To use force against citizens who were simply protesting against their employers or petitioning their elected officials would smack too much of tyranny.

In the ideological censure of industrial workers, liberal reformers redrew the boundaries of citizenship, banishing industrial workers from the category of noble producers, so central to the antebellum imagination of democratic nationhood. Producerism also came under attack in the farmlands, as American farmers found themselves vilified in hitherto unimaginable ways—even if state violence against them was as yet unthinkable.

Liberal reformers' suspicion of farmers dated to the prepanic years. In the late 1860s, Midwestern farmers and their allies, decrying "monopoly," had organized to pressure state legislatures to regulate the railroad and grain elevator corporations that they believed were responsible for their declining fortunes. The "Granger movement" achieved one of its first successes in 1870, when the new Illinois constitution boldly asserted legislative supremacy over corporations. The constitution of Illinois deeded regulatory power to the popularly elected legislature and reasserted the traditional powers of the legislature in a way that recast them as powerful levers over the corporations. Community interests and demands were to guide regulation.[43]

Adams, the liberal reformers' resident expert on railroads, had provided direction for them in this political moment. In 1869 he had begun his tenure on the Massachusetts Railroad Commission and in that capacity attempted to modernize railroad regulation and governmental administration in much the same way that Wells was doing on the national revenue commission. A state commission, Adams thought, should be directed by neutral experts and remain independent of the legislature. Commissioners should take the economic development of the railway system as their mission, and they should first devote themselves to scientific analysis of the railroad system before they presumed to act. But Adams was not quite as neutral as he thought himself to be, for his particular vision of economic development made him partial to only one of many possibilities for regulation. As the national railroad network was the linchpin of national economic development, and as the profit motive was the only sure spur to its continued growth, the first consideration for regulators must be to safeguard profits, even as they limited the abuses of the railroad corporations.[44]

Adams recognized the popularity of the new steps taken by Illinois, and pragmatically he sought to appease popular opinion by staking out an ostensibly moderate position. After all, he was not only a budding expert on the business of railroads but also a savvy, and anxious, observer of the political scene.[45] Aware that several European governments were turning to public ownership of railroads to solve similar problems between corporations and the public in their own countries, he perceived that Illinois had let in through the back door the possibility of state ownership. Appearing to coolly entertain the idea, he quickly forecast failure. In principle, he reasoned, public and private should be kept separate. In practice, the low quality of government employees, absent civil service reform, ensured that if such men were placed in charge of complex enterprises such as railroads, the result could only be "increased corruption and commercial disaster." As if trying to preempt any radical action by the Illinois legislature—and to instruct it to interpret its constitutional mandate narrowly—he proposed a distinction between state ownership under legislative control, which was certain to fail, and regulation by independent, powerful commissions. Thus, while citizens continued to look to legislatures as their protectors against monopoly power, Adams ingeniously shifted the ground of debate. He conceded the need for regulation and public control over corporations that had a natural tendency to monopoly. But his proposal sought to remove effective power from popularly elected legislatures, for Adams saw in the popular movements an imminent threat to private property.[46]

The legislature and citizens of Illinois had declined to take Adams's advice, even though it had been broadcast widely in the national press. As his confidence in his ability to steer the public on the right path waned, he began to vent his spleen against democracy. The legislative actions in Illinois confirmed that "the passage of a statute-law is the natural remedy to which every American has recourse in the presence of any matter calling for reform," wrote Adams, the tribune of expert, neutral tribunals. "It is a species of popular political pill,—a panacea good for all social disorders. As a general rule the remedy is found to rather aggravate the disorder than to remove its cause; but faith is strong, and the nine failures out of ten trials do not in this case greatly shake it." Such was Adams's lamentation that haphazard legislation was going to over-awe scientific administration. But he did not, as might be expected, conclude that laissez-faire was the solution. Instead, he proposed a bold "experiment" in administrative governance, which would avoid the mismanagement and cor-ruption that resulted from legislative regulation. First, it was desirable to allow the ongoing corporate consolidation to proceed. It would be much easier to compel a few large companies to act responsibly, for a "group of small corporations . . . is always irresponsible." Then the state should assume owner-ship and management of one of the remaining large corporations, and, as in the Belgian case of mixed ownership, achieve an efficient regulation of the whole railroad system through the competition created by the well-managed government-owned line.[47]

After the panic, the Granger movement had pushed ahead, and in the four Western states of the upper Mississippi Valley it had continued to pass new legislation regulating corporations. Legislation that, to liberal reformers, had seemed ill conceived now appeared truly threatening, as economic recovery depended on renewed growth in Western commercial agriculture. Importing the vitriolic language of industrial class conflict into their campaign, liberals such as Adams, Godkin, Wells, and A. G. Sedgwick insisted that the Grange laws amounted to the confiscation of property and that all forms of property were endangered by the deluded political theories on which the Grange state legislatures had acted. Godkin informed Westerners that, in good faith to all good people, "in the present moral condition of the politician, all schemes of this kind mean robbery at some stage or other; and as long as they are talked of, we mean to do our share towards putting investors on their guard against all borrowers and all enterprises of whatever kind in the States in which they are talked of."[48] Business papers echoed the charge, and the *Nation* and the busi-ness press were read in Europe. With this news about legislated communism in mind, as well as simple calculations about the poor returns to be had from American railroads, investors shunned the Western "Granger states."

The rhetoric of damnation had escalated in response to the passage in Wisconsin in 1874 of the Potter Law, which legislatively set rates for the grain elevators of Chicago. For Adams, it served as the occasion for his rejection of a significant role for the state and a turn toward a wholly voluntaristic approach to the solution of the railroad problem. "For years to come, the reaction sure to follow upon the fantastic excesses of Grangerism will bring even judicious railroad legislation into contempt," he wrote in the *Nation*.

> The great railroad system is to be allowed to develop, subject only to its now natural laws—to combine, to consolidate, to monopolize. Meanwhile, in so doing it must necessarily draw itself together under one or a few heads, and those finally responsible in the full face of public opinion, with the strong arm of the law in the background. Such a system at least has one merit—it is thoroughly American in theory, and in this respect wholly unlike those weak intimations of French communism which, under the name of railroad laws, have recently disgraced the statute-books of the Granger States.

The Grangers had taught Adams that, no matter how hard he might try to win acceptance of a rational politics, it was no use. In 1879, he resigned from the Massachusetts railroad board to join Albert Fink's experiment in business self-regulation through cartelization. In the following decades, he would become the most prominent exponent of limiting the power of governmental regulatory commissions to investigation and publicity. He only reached this position, however, after failing to achieve his more expansive administrative design.[49]

From the standpoint of the corporations, the Potter Law was the most onerous of the Grange laws, and it prompted them to take their case to the courts. As the lawsuits proceeded, Wells injected a new principle into the debate. Echoing the arguments made by the corporations, and perhaps drawing from the writings of Thomas McIntyre Cooley, a prominent Midwestern jurist and liberal reformer, Wells argued that the due process clause of the Fourteenth Amendment rendered the Grange regulations unconstitutional, as they deprived the corporations of property without due process of law. The Supreme Court took up the Granger cases as a body in 1876, after state courts affirmed the legislation. A year after arguments, on March 1, 1877, the Court issued the landmark decision *Munn v. Illinois*, affirming the right of states to regulate property "clothed with a public interest" and ruling that such legislation did not violate "any of the constitutional prohibitions against interference with private property." Although *Munn* has been correctly viewed as evidence that the courts were not yet ready to condone the dogmas of economic liberalism and the unfettered rights of corporations, two points suggest that the perspective of liberal reformers had nonetheless made significant headway. First, Justice Stephen J. Field rested his dissent on the principle of substantive due process, and he shared the same fears as the liberal reformers. As he wrote

Wells, forwarding along his dissenting opinion in the case, "I think that the doctrine announced by the majority of the Court practically destroys the guaranties of the Constitution intended for the protection of the rights of private property." Second, it is often overlooked that most states had already revised or revoked the most offensive elements of their regulatory statutes under the indirect but forceful pressure of chary investors.[50]

At the same time that liberal reformers did ideological battle against those groups that would organize collectively to enact their interests through politics, they also worked to achieve the structural changes in the state that would help advance their administrative mandate. Both the collective actions of labor and the Grange movement raised particular questions about legislative power. Clearly, the state and national legislatures were the branches of government most attuned to popular agitations, and it was evident that social movements had warmed to active state intervention. Consequently, liberal reformers moved to constrain legislatures, and they met with substantial success. In some cases, pressure on the executive branches of government was sufficient to win the reversal of the oppressive legislative acts. The governor of Wisconsin, persuaded by the decline in the state's credit standing, sought the repeal of the Potter Law. President Grant, under pressure from liberal editors, Northeastern businessmen, and European investors, vetoed a congressional bill to expand the volume of greenbacks in circulation.[51]

The veto was an uncertain method of victory, but fortunately for liberal reformers, the years of criticism of state legislatures and municipal governance found an audience in the seventies that could give them more permanent results. A wave of state constitutional revisions occurred, imposing numerous limitations on state legislatures and transferring traditional legislative powers to the jurisdiction of state courts or the executive branch. The new constitutions gave relief to taxpayers, especially by curtailing the distributive functions of the legislatures and, in many cases, eliminating altogether the right to pass special incorporation acts. Some new state constitutions also denied municipalities the power to incur debt and created appointed commissions to manage basic municipal services.[52] Even though the causes and politics of constitutional revision were quite complicated, liberal reformers interpreted it as an endorsement of their position. Sedgwick condensed the liberal critique of legislatures, underscoring that reformers had articulated "a moral which the proceedings of many constitutional conventions show is becoming well understood: that the legislatures are bodies which need to be hedged in and fenced about with every sort of restraint and prohibition that can be devised, that they constitute a part of the Government which we can best afford to abridge in its prerogative without at the same time having much fear that in doing so we are striking at the root of popular liberty."[53] The historical veracity of such a statement was open to question, but the satisfaction exuded was palpable.

The handiwork of liberal reform political intellectuals and the diffusion of their ideas of legislative power were, however, quite clear in the new relationship between state governments and municipalities that emerged in the seventies. For years, liberals had argued that cities should be classified as corporations and managed according to principles of economic efficiency, rather than as political communities governed by the standards of representative government. The redefinition of municipalities as corporations had been auditioned first in the liberal reform press, where it then became a popular staple of local political commentary.[54] The boldest attempt to put their idea to a real test took place in New York City. New York Democratic governor Samuel Tilden, flush with a victory over Tammany Hall, appointed a commission to report on an appropriate restructuring of municipal government in 1875. Tilden appointed nine commissioners, including the prominent liberal reformers Godkin, Simon Sterne, and William M. Evarts. Coauthored by Godkin, the Tilden Commission report reiterated the ideas of municipal governance that had been parried in the liberal press for close to a decade, and in its most radical moment, it recommended that the vote in large cities be restricted to taxpayers. This audacious attempt to turn back universal suffrage was widely supported in the business community of New York City and endorsed by the liberal reform press. It came stunningly close to passage.[55] The very attempt to disfranchise thousands of working-class men itself reveals the self-assurance liberal reform intellectuals had acquired in their quest to turn their moral influence over public opinion into actual policy.

The attack on legislative power might be taken to confirm the interpretation that liberal reformers were, above all, exponents of a rigid laissez-faire program. Undoubtedly, laissez-faire was one component of their political agenda, but if the limitation of legislatures is considered with their movement for civil service reform, their administrative designs also become manifest. The success of their new model of expert-dominated administrative governance depended practically and essentially on the elimination of the patronage civil service. The civil service reform movement advocated that the staffs of government agencies be hired and promoted according to competitive exams and performance in office. The standards of social science and the efficient business should reign. As the movement's leader, George W. Curtis, explained, "The Civil-Service Reform therefore begins with the assertion that there is no reason in the nature of things or of our form of government that the United States should not manage its affairs with the same economy, ability, and honesty that the best private business is managed."[56]

Of all the multifarious reforms liberals sought, the movement to professionalize the civil service posed the greatest challenge to the existing political parties, for it struck at congressional patronage powers, which had become the crucial means by which elected politicians rewarded those who had rallied the vote for them. In this way, the civil service reform movement appears to be simply a continuation of antebellum Whig attacks against the Jacksonian "spoils system." But after the war, questions of rational administration had overtaken those of republican virtue in setting the direction of the movement. As has been shown, Wells and others first broached civil service reform as a solution to the maladministration of financial and taxation powers by municipal and federal patronage appointees. The close link between civil service reform and concerns about the management of a complex economy can be found as well in Francis Amasa Walker's seminal critique of census methods and his call to establish the new science of statistics and rationalize the procedures for census surveys. Walker thought an accurate manufacturing census was imperative to adjudicate the conflicts raised by the labor question, and only when census employees were selected by merit could this occur. The common complaints about inefficiency and lack of rational procedure, and recommendations about how to get qualified and educated men into the civil service, suggest that liberal reformers were not trying to eliminate state power. Rather, against the dual perils of excessive democracy and incompetent officials, they sought to redesign state institutions to regulate or supervise new market forces more efficiently, in order to maintain an environment conducive to capitalist development.[57]

Not surprisingly, every victory liberal reformers won on civil service reform seemed quickly to be reversed by congressmen wise to the power struggle they faced. The effective control that legislators wielded over the executive branch administrative agencies no doubt made liberal reformers all the more determined to constrain legislatures. The stakes were high for both sides, and Congress had the superior resources in this battle. Nevertheless, by the late seventies, the prospects for reform had advanced, even though the leading civil service reformers, Curtis and Dorman Eaton, had suffered personal setbacks. (During the 1872 campaign, in the hope of defusing the Liberal Republican movement, Grant had opportunistically accepted Curtis's plan for merit staffing, but after his election he proceeded to ignore it. Curtis resigned in protest, and Dorman Eaton, the most highly regarded expert on a professional civil service, replaced Curtis. In late 1873, he was able to institute merit examinations in the most troublesome and influential federal agency, the Treasury Department. Congressional opposition to the abolition of patronage, however, increased in response, and Congress cut off funding for Eaton's commission. Grant followed Congress's lead and officially abandoned Curtis's and Eaton's civil service rules in 1875. Liberal reformers, once again, were infuriated by Grant.) The election of 1876 pitted two proponents of civil service reform, Samuel J. Tilden and Rutherford Hayes, against each other. Because of his work against Tammany, some liberals initially and privately leaned toward the Democrat Tilden, but after extracting satisfactory pledges from Hayes on civil service reform and other reform issues, most backed the Republican.[58] Under Hayes's administration, liberal reformers were extremely satisfied with the progress made in reforming the civil service. Even if each small step proceeded hostage to struggles within the political parties, the effort by most politicians to appear publicly to support civil service reform indicates how far liberal reform political intellectuals had directed political opinion onto favorable terrain.[59]

From the period in the late sixties, when reformers had coalesced as the party of "liberty" and political "independence," they had sought both laissez-faire and the increase of the administrative capacities of the state. To defeat the political projects of the producing classes, liberal reformers sounded the tocsin of liberty and laissez-faire; to remove democratic influence over state actions, they publicized and lobbied for various administrative reforms that would put their own kind in charge of critical state policies such as finance, taxation, and policing.

Considering their fear over the growing "communistic" tendencies of the American citizenry, it is not surprising that liberal reformers questioned anew the validity of universal suffrage. Yet to do so required a delicate balancing act, for it was nearly impossible in America to claim the moral high ground when depriving any individual of the vote. Likewise, there is no principle more fundamental to liberal democracy than the right of individual suffrage, and American liberals had to stand by this principle to be true to their creed. But as the most influential liberal democrat of the nineteenth century, John Stuart Mill, observed, there appeared to be an irreconcilable conflict between universal suffrage and efficient governmental administration.[60] In America, limits on universal suffrage had to be broached subtly, almost by indirection, and aimed at the margins of the citizenry. Their task was especially tricky in the Northern cities, which to liberal reformers harbored the largest body of ill-suited voters, but ones that were male and white and had long held the right of suffrage in the United States. Rather than explicitly calling for the vote to be taken away, liberal reformers attempted to nullify universal suffrage in the cities by a series of indirect maneuvers. One, literacy tests would disfranchise many working-men and recent immigrants who kept the "machines" and the "bosses" in power. Two, redefining cities as nonpolitical units served to remove many decisions and state activities from the realm of politics, again loosening the grip of the machines. Three, by providing an enhanced suffrage for taxpayers under the guise of "minority representation," the working class majority could be outvoted.[61] Each method sought to circumvent the fundamental liberal democratic tenet: one man, one vote. It is hardly surprising that in this en-deavor they had little success.

Matters were simpler where universal suffrage had not been fulfilled, namely, in the vote for women. Many Radical Republicans had once favored woman suffrage, but as some advocates of the vote for women endorsed other radical causes, such as labor reform or free love, a liberal reform consensus emerged in the seventies that the enfranchisement of women was ill advised. Godkin, once a proponent of woman suffrage, decided that with one of the pillars of civiliza-tion—property—already under attack, it was perilous to undermine the other—the family. J. M. McKim, one of the Radicals who had founded the *Nation*, expressed the question of women suffrage in a metaphor sure to turn a few stomachs: "For, while it has been admitted that our 'body politic can take in and digest and assimilate an immeasurable amount of raw material,' it ought also to be submitted that, after the meal of freedmen and coolies, with the extra large dessert of European foreigners, which has just passed through the political gullet, the body politic ought to be allowed to breathe awhile before bolting another of still greater dimensions. The gastric solvents of a democratic body are powerful, but they should not be presumed to be miraculous."[62]

More complicated for liberal reformers was the question of black suffrage, for many of them had been Radical Republican publicists when the party decided to use the votes of freedmen as the means to transform the South and subdue the Rebel spirit. "Ought the Negro to Be Disfranchised? Ought He to Have Been Enfranchised?" was the title of a symposium conducted by the *North American Review* in 1879. Only Wendell Phillips defended enfranchise-ment as an act of morality and justice, and all respectable men knew that Phillips had become a crank, with his naive support for labor reform. The *Nation* had nothing better to say about black suffrage than that it was an accomplished fact, even as it made it abundantly clear that the act had been foolish. Of the former Radical organs, only Curtis's *Harper's Weekly* unequivo-cally upheld the old Radical principle of equal suffrage, defending the voting rights of both African Americans and women.[63] Whether it was municipal rule, minority representation, or the vote of women or freedmen, liberal reformers couched all their recommendations for limiting suffrage as special cases. But even if it was conducted through evasion and circumspection, it spelled a retreat from *universal* suffrage.

The liberal reformers of the Gilded Age earned a reputation as doctrinaire classical liberals from their critics of the time and from later historians. The reputation was only partly deserved. Indeed, their theory of state action and their program for reform was significantly more complex than the classical nomenclature allows. What Howells termed "administrative reforms" in fact contained a logic of bureaucratization and increasing state regulation that derived from the conclusions liberal reform political intellectuals reached after ruminating on the relationship between the changing nature of property and democratic governance.

Liberal reformers turned to administrative governance, in part, because they perceived that the new practices of corporate management had escaped the bounds of the moral order of entrepreneurial individualism, thus rendering obsolete the old politics founded on a belief in a self-regulating market. Howells had claimed that the common bond for reformers was the defense of "liberty" as the constitutive foundation for Anglo-American political institutions. Despite the appearance that laissez-faire and administrative "reform" were antithetical, they were compatible. Simply put, both made incursions against the practices and procedures of democracy. The branches and institutions of government in which democratic influence was most pervasive incurred the greatest condemnation for incompetence, inefficiency, and corruption. Even basic principles that erstwhile Radicals had proclaimed to be fundamental—universal suffrage, majority rule—were quietly discarded under euphemisms such as "minority representation" or dramatically recanted with appeals to evolutionary racism and exaggerated fantasies about the destruction of the family should women gain the vote. It all added up to a straightforward point. Whenever really important political business arose, it should be removed from the purview of elected legislators, elected judges, and administrators appointed by political parties. If possible, the power to act should be transferred to a newly created realm of nonpolitical administration—if not, it should simply not be done.

In this reformulation of liberal democratic ideas of the state, what was the fate of "liberty" and "democracy"? In 1865, liberty and democracy appeared to liberal Radical Republicans to have been wedded together. George W. Curtis's "divine law of liberty" legislated worldwide democracy, after all. A normative vision of individualistic democracy had been ratified, for these men, by the victory of Northern free civilization in the Civil War. For a moment, the age-old opposition between liberty and democracy had been transcended in a new synthesis of liberal, individualistic democracy, in which the traditional fear of state power dissolved in a near utopian optimism about the natural progress of liberal democracy. But subsequent developments would again reveal how closely the opposition between liberty and democracy was bound up with the also classic opposition between property and democracy. The problem for liberal reformers, however, was that since the end of the Civil War, other Americans had demonstrated that they held different normative visions of democracy, specifically about the relations among citizens acting collectively and about how their democratic state should act to preserve their cherished producers' democracy. Even as liberal reformers became more explicitly anti-democratic among themselves—and in public when the targets were not white, native-born American men—democracy was the unalterable terrain in which they operated. Their political challenge was to define incipient bureaucratization in areas concerning the maintenance of a complex, internationally oriented capitalist economy, laissez-faire in matters of relations between labor and capital, and localism in relations between black and white Southerners as consistent with the procedures of democracy and the political ideals of the United States.

In practice, their politics contained many contradictory elements. As we saw in the previous chapter, liberal reformers felt quite anxious about the power of corporations, yet they upheld the modern corporation—when properly managed—as a model for progressive state administration, in which scientifically informed experts would seek maximum efficiency. Likewise, they tended to see national progress as dependent on the success and prosperity of the new consolidated industries. They presented themselves as principled laissez-faire liberals whenever they responded to the demands of workers or farmers for intervention by statute, arguing that the market must rule. Yet when labor ratcheted up the stakes in the market by strikes, self-proclaimed liberals were in the front row applauding the newly ferocious night-watchman state marching into action. They longed for a professionalized and efficient bureaucracy to override ignorant legislation, yet the programs they hoped to see enacted by this bureaucracy were, for the most part, those of economic liberalism—international free trade, virtually unregulated and untaxed domestic production and commerce, and the gold standard as a discipline for currency heresies. Liberal reformers were publicists and analysts, and some of their inconsistency was a product of a transitional age, in which change ruled and the future was unclear. But they were also political actors, and their contradictions were no greater nor less than those of their opponents.

Perhaps the clearest portrait of liberal reformers in this period, of their practical success and their intellectual and political debility, can be drawn by reflecting on the two most momentous historical events of the decade: the Great Strike of 1877 and the Compromise of 1877, which ended Reconstruction. Both actions were justified in language that had been honed in liberal reform circles, and they looked at both as personal victories. Each event, nonetheless, revealed the fragility of the liberal reform consensus and boded ill for liberal reformers' long-term prospects of success.

The racialism through which liberal reformers had justified "home rule" for the white South dovetailed with the pervasive racism in the North, and it enabled most Northerners and Westerners to ignore the patently illegitimate practices of Southern political life. The violence-ridden, fraudulent elections between 1877 and the end of the century created a crisis in Southern governance. But when Southern governments were placed under scrutiny about their democratic legitimacy, Northerners rationalized away all the disquieting evidence of fraud by reference to their racist definition of "the Negro Problem." When the next moment of truth arrived, all the rest of the nation could do was sit back and condone disfranchisement, Jim Crow laws, and segregation with tired repetitions of the problem of black inferiority. At least the semblance of order after disfranchisement gave a better appearance than had the body counts of many previous Southern elections. Nevertheless, the favor given to planters and the propertied in the South by the terms through which Reconstruction was ended would create internal conflicts and breed one of the most powerful movements to threaten the late-nineteenth-century settlement liberal reformers had helped to forge. Had those surviving into the 1890s had sufficient historical imagination, they might have reflected that the Populist movement they decried was the bastard child born of their own betrayal of the values of liberal democracy.

Nevertheless, it would take another decade and a half for this betrayal of liberal democracy to be fully played out. More immediately, the rapid growth and consolidation of American industry and its consequent transformation of relations between labor and capital threatened the producers' democracy. As we have observed, despite liberal reform political intellectuals' perceptive accounts of the transformation of enterprise, they refused to credit that relations in the labor market had also changed, as so many striking workers and labor leaders insisted. Blinkered by dogmas of free contract, they failed to perceive that the human suffering of the depression was itself wrought by economic consolidation and the systemic crises of capitalism. The Great Strike of 1877 demonstrated that a vast body of the American people identified themselves with workers, against those miraculous agents of progress, capital and the railroad. Repression by the U.S. military could only reinforce for many Americans that the corruption of American democracy derived not from such problems as bad finance, "sentimentalism," or an inept civil service but rather from a pervasive "money power" that had usurped the people's democracy. The 1877 strike was a spontaneous one; but when an organized labor movement arose in the 1880s and 1890s, its members would remember the strike as a pivotal moment when the conflict between the "moneyed interests" and the "virtuous producers" was revealed.

Most significant, liberal reformers were blind to the crisis of legitimacy engendered by the state's clear bias for capital. While they only saw principles of the sanctity of property and the necessity of public order when they applauded the state's repression of its citizens, others spotted a class state aborning. The plain inadequacy of liberal reformers' explanation of the conflict between labor and capital—and, it must be said, their hardly liberal inhumanity to suffering workers and their families—begat a predictable reaction against its tribunes and their shibboleths. What was surprising was that one such reaction occurred within the family and that the rebellious sons would aim their attack at the system of belief that sanctioned and sanctified their fathers' politics: the science of political economy.

II

FORGING A
NEW LIBERALISM

THE AMERICAN
SCHOLAR REVISITED
DEMOCRACY, EXPERTISE, AND THE
NEW POLITICAL ECONOMY

When Henry George titled what would become a best-selling classic of economic protest literature, *Progress and Poverty*, he was inverting conventional wisdom. With its publication in 1879, at the end of the most severe economic crisis the Western capitalist nations had ever experienced, George found a large popular audience for his explanation of an entirely novel phenomenon: unemployment, hunger, homelessness, and poverty in the midst of a material abundance greater than the world had ever known. Part of the bite of *Progress and Poverty* was its debunking of Anglo-American common sense, first codified by Adam Smith in *The Wealth of Nations*, that progress and national wealth, grounded in individual private property, marched hand in hand. George's readers would have anticipated a jeremiad from the moment they learned of the book's existence, simply from the jarring, provocative assertion of its title, the censorious couplet progress and *poverty*.[1]

But what sort of prophet was he, an Elijah or a Jonah? Liberal reformers did not at first know what to make of *Progress and Poverty*. Who was this Henry George? He announced himself as an authority on the science of political economy, but most of the liberal guardians of the universities and the American Social Science Association had never heard of this man. Edward Atkinson and David A. Wells dashed off letters to each other and like-minded friends. Had they read the book yet? How should they answer him? Indeed, was he on their side, or was he another dangerous radical to be vanquished by their publicity networks?[2] Even though George had announced his polemical stance at the start, by 1879, the domain of political economy had become vastly more complicated, as the depression of the seventies had triggered doubts about accepted axioms and spawned new forays in economic theory. So it had become somewhat difficult to sort friend from foe, particularly when one introduced himself as George did, as a scientific soldier who did battle against "the leadership of charlatans and demagogues" by elaborating and diffusing the truths of political economy to "the great masses of men."[3]

George had set himself to the rigors of political economy in order to comprehend what seemed to him unwelcome economic changes that endangered the American way of life. Like George, many Americans were disturbed by the rapidly permutating economic relationships. The many different movements of laborers and farmers in the three decades after the Civil War disclose how acutely the new mechanisms of advancing capitalism impinged on their daily lives and violated their sense of the appropriate ordering of economic relations.

In a nation that officially celebrated change and progress, however, it was not surprising that there would be many who welcomed the economic developments, which, even if they brought temporary troubles, promised future benefits. It was not only the notorious "robber barons" who happily exploited the new opportunities to amass unprecedented fortunes, regardless of what principles of sound business might have to be flung aside.[4] As we have seen, others believed that the new economic forces and institutions promised to advance civilization, even if they were uneasy about the sordid or unconventional practices accompanying them. In the 1860s and 1870s, liberal political intellectuals had pioneered an examination of the meaning and implications of capitalist economic development from this vantage point of approving skepticism.

As it developed, the hard times of the seventies were only the opening chapter in a nearly quarter-century-long worldwide economic crisis that would become known as the "Great Depression," until the far more devastating one of the 1930s won the title away.[5] The changes and instability wrought in the daily lives of Americans by the depression generated enormous social and political conflict. To an unprecedented degree, differing ideologies of the just political economy framed the rancorous debates of these years. As we have observed, the legacy of antebellum ideologies of political economy had exerted a powerful cultural influence after the Civil War. In the last two decades of the century, political economy gained an even greater prominence, as Americans argued with one another about the problem of democracy during the transformation of capitalism primarily through languages of political economy. They fought over the justice of the wage contract, abolishing rent on land, legislating consolidated industry out of business, rescuing debtors through inflation, and even the possibility of nationalizing essential industries.

In this environment, the social science of political economy acquired a notoriety and importance that it had not held in antebellum America, when constitutionalism had dominated political debate. For those who approved of or benefited from the expansion of industry, English classical political economy became the preeminent means of justification for market liberty as the highest social and political good. The Manchester mentality, additionally, escaped the bounds of the institutions of high culture and formal higher education and flowed over into once dominant languages of theorizing about social life. With many of the landmark constitutional cases of the era centering on economic disputes, lawyers and judges invoked the laws of the market to erect the law of the land.[6] Protestant preachers, such as Henry Ward Beecher, married political economy according to Manchester to the gospels in a sacred union, divining the laws of the market in God's providential design.

By the same token, alternative and oppositional renderings of political economy dominated the rhetoric of those who opposed or suffered from the postbellum economic transformation. One need only survey a list of the most popular protest literature of the era to appreciate this. Henry George turned Ricardo on his head in the fantastically popular international best-seller *Progress and Poverty*. Edward Bellamy made a new organization of industry the centerpiece of his utopia in *Looking Backward*. *Coin's Financial School*, a primer on currency theory, sold a thousand copies a week in the farmlands. The distopian novels of the age, Mark Twain's *A Connecticut Yankee in King Arthur's Court* and Ignatius Donnelly's *Caesar's Column*, unmasked the dark side of industrialization and modernity. In urban churches attended by working families, dissenting Protestant preachers pronounced that "the principles of political economy, as ordinarily understood . . . justify men in acting unsocially. . . . The kind of conduct which is assumed by certain economists in their scientific discussions, is, then, a kind of conduct which makes society impossible; which tends to destroy society." They interpreted Christian ethics to condemn the gulf between rich and poor and proselytized for Christian socialism to heal the divide.[7]

The revival of the "labor question" was even more important in propelling debates about political economy into the forefront of social discourse. The "labor question" resurfaced in the 1880s, as wage workers, small producers, and farmers organized anew with the return of prosperity. For the first time in the nation's history, the working classes formed and sustained national organizations, capable of coordinating protests and strikes on a national scale. Additionally, workingmen's national organizations, the Knights of Labor and the Federation of Trade Labor Unions (the predecessor to the American Federation of Labor), could give voice to the cause of producers throughout the country and thus finally compete in the public arena with the long-established national institutions of their elite opponents. Not only did the vibrancy of the labor movement make the "labor question" a practical matter of political economy, but the newspapers and speeches of "producers" (wage workers and farmers) were filled with technical and practical discussions of economics as well.

Today we might say that economic questions dominated the political discourse of the Gilded Age. This would not necessarily be inaccurate, but it would be anachronistic. In our time, the liberal bifurcation of the economic sphere from the political sphere has triumphed as common sense. This had not always been so. When Gilded Age Americans spoke of "political economy," they did not conceive that the political and the economic could be practically or analytically disassociated. They believed that when they argued about labor, monopoly, and money, they were confronting the basic question of how the development of capitalism influenced the foundation, character, and future of their political democracy. Did democracy sanction capitalism? Did capitalism sustain democracy? Or, rather, was it exactly the opposite? Their preoccupation with political economy was at once political, ethical, and cultural.

Against the background of a boisterous and contentious national discussion of the political economy of democracy, those who had relied on the science of political economy to justify existing practices and those who viewed themselves as the real political economists were forced to take stock of their old verities. It was not difficult to dismiss most of the untutored popular theorists. But within the discipline of political economy, the pioneering social science discipline in the modernizing university, a new generation of academically trained intellectuals came to maturity in the late 1870s, individuals who were skeptical about the intellectual dimensions and the political implications of classical political economy and the politics it buttressed.[8]

For two distinct yet intertwined reasons, the debate in political economy carried serious implications for the political fortunes of liberal reformers and the future of liberalism as a foundational system of political values and principles. First, the debate touched on central issues of theory and the political conclusions drawn from it. Second, the conflict between liberal reformers and younger social scientists raised very practical matters concerning the implementation of the liberals' dual program of laissez-faire and administrative governance. Within and beyond the sanctified cultural institutions of universities, respectable publishing houses and journals, and professional organizations and their publications, the "old school" or "classical liberals" and the "new school" or "ethical economists," as they were variously known, understood that they were engaged in a constitutive political struggle to define the character of American democracy.[9]

Liberal reform political intellectuals had legitimated the developing capitalist market on the ground of classical political economy, which they claimed was deduced from scientific and universally valid observations of human nature. The upstart social scientists entered the public stage attacking liberalism. Not only did they refute specific theses of classical political economy, but, more important, they assailed their elders on the validity of the ideas on which their system of liberalism rested: the universality of the instrumentally rational economic man, the teleological assumption that a society of primarily self-interested individuals enjoying market liberty constituted the highest stage of human progress, and the conception of politics as an analogue to market competition.

Liberal reform intellectuals had staked out their own authority on the claim that the possession of social scientific knowledge was a prerequisite for just and efficient governance. The program of nonpolitical administrative governance depended on the cultivation of a cadre of new experts that would provide the staff for administrative bureaus of the reformed civil service. And liberal reformers had to acknowledge that the new generation of university-trained social scientists would be the ones to inaugurate the era of expertise, as well as to carry on the tradition of critical and politically engaged intellectual production through which they defined themselves. What liberal reformers did not foresee in the promotion of social science was that the specialized study to achieve the level of expertise demanded might lead some of their heirs to reach contrary conclusions.[10]

The debate between the two generations of intellectuals took place against the backdrop of broader, more popular, and more divisive political conflicts over economic questions, and it gained its significance from this conjuncture. The movements of producers were assaulted through many means—ruthless employers and oppressive monopolies, Pinkerton spies and private police forces, and the military power of the local and national state. In a democracy, however, the battle for public opinion is also critical. The liberal reformers had waged a long campaign to whittle away at the identity of interest between middling and producing classes that had been at the heart of free labor ideology. They were very conscious of the cultural shift they sought to engineer. The young political economists threatened to derail this project by establishing relationships with popular movements, especially labor, and providing them with legitimation that could meet the increasingly positivistic standards of the age. There was also the potential for a direct alliance between left intellectuals and the labor movement, as European labor, radical, socialist, and social democratic parties were beginning to demonstrate. Although the relationship between the working-class majority and middle-class intellectuals in European leftist parties was fraught with tension, the role of intellectuals on the left surely had something to do with the prominence of leftist parties. One has only to look at the history of the Dreyfus Affair, the British Independent Labor Party, or the German Social Democratic Party to appreciate this.[11]

Despite the abstraction with which the argument between the two generations of American intellectuals was frequently carried on, the conflict thus had broader and more portentous political ramifications. It was more than an academic matter of methods and more than an internal matter of the universities. The younger generation of social scientists did successfully redirect the main current of social theory, especially in political economy. But the older generation of liberal reformers wielded sufficient power to steer their challengers back onto terrain more favorable to the survival of core liberal values. In the struggle for cultural hegemony between the two, the social scientists won the battle but lost the war.[12] Not only did popular movements lose a valuable resource in a nationwide struggle for political power and cultural influence when they lost their allies in the preeminent cultural and political institutions of the nation, but they also lost potential soldiers in their cause and found their claims elegantly discredited. In no area did the liberal reformers exert more pressure, with greater effect, than in the drive to stifle the democratic enthusiasm of their critics. Once this milepost had been passed, liberal reformers became more willing to reexamine their ideas about state action and economic liberalism.

"Factoryism, bankism, collegism, capitalism, insuranceism and the presence of such lump-headed malignants as Professor William Graham Sumner," according to one workingman, were the sources of labor's oppression.[13] Though William Graham Sumner would have mocked the politics underpinning the statement, he might have relished such testimony to his importance. Sumner's career was emblematic of the trends in liberalism in the 1870s and 1880s. As a professor of social science, he represented the rise of a new type of intellectual, one who gained his authority from his possession of specialized knowledge and his occupancy of a professor's chair. He also displayed, to an excessive degree, the least admirable trait of the Gilded Age liberal reformers: a smug certainty in his own superiority. His avid and successful popularization of liberalism conveyed a particularly dogmatic version of it to opponents. When the upcoming generation of intellectuals launched their rebellion in the mid-

1880s, Sumner was the individual they identified as the most influential ideologue to be reckoned with.

Sumner had been born into a less fortunate situation than most of his liberal reform associates. His family was middle class, Yankee, and Protestant, to be sure, but his father failed at virtually every venture he tried, leaving the family relatively poor. A contemporary of the Adams brothers, he entered Yale College at age nineteen in 1859. While most of his college mates throughout New England rushed to enlist in the Union army, and despite the antislavery sentiment of his family, Sumner remained in school until the draft compelled him to act. With money borrowed from a wealthy, conservative friend, he bought a draft substitute and went to Europe to continue his education at Oxford and Göttingen. His brother thought him "coppery" in sentiment and kept his distance from him.[14]

Sumner's novel path in young adulthood well situated him to take advantage of changes in American intellectual life. His European education equipped him to become an accomplished professor at a time when this traditional profession of modest prestige was being transformed in modernizing universities into the premier position for one who aspired to make his public mark through the products of the mind. At age thirty-two, he left his Episcopalian rectorship to take a professorship at Yale. He was elected to the chair in political and social science and held the position for the remainder of his life. The men of Yale College adored and admired him, and Sumner likewise viewed them as his conduit to educate Americans in right thinking. As one of his biographers aptly observed, he taught the rich and believed his theories would then "trickle down" to the masses.[15] His efforts to shape public opinion did not stop at the university gates; Sumner wrote numerous popular essays for magazines such as *Scribner's Monthly* and the *North American Review*, published several books of his collected popular essays, and lectured regularly to business groups and social clubs. Even his more theoretical works, such as *History of the American Currency* or his articles in the *Journal of Social Science*, tended to be pitched toward contemporary debates and a popular audience.

The popularization worked so well that from the 1870s until now, Sumner has been considered both the paragon and representative of Gilded Age liberalism. For this reason, even though the judgment rests on a misapprehension of the intellectual trajectory of liberalism, it is important to briefly survey his theories. At the foundation of Sumner's philosophy was an extreme atomistic individualism. Nature created man as an isolated being, and in a conventionally teleological argument, Sumner asserted that man would reach the social state that sanctioned the absolute liberty his nature demanded. The building blocks of his social theory were Calvinism and classical political economy, with a commitment to Protestant rectitude and the work ethic surviving his rejection of organized religion and adoption of agnosticism. He derived his sociology from Harriet Martineau's popularization of the Manchester school, Sir Henry Maine's historical analysis of the social development from status to contract, Herbert Spencer's deductive analysis of the evolution to contract as progress, and Charles Darwin's empirical studies of natural selection. To Sumner, these authorities confirmed the scientific, political, and moral inevitability of the regime of liberty.[16] If liberty was duly respected, he asserted, "we can count on a general and steady growth of civilization and advancement of society by and through its best members. In the prosecution of these chances we all owe to each other good-will, mutual respect, and mutual guarantees of liberty and security." What was duty? "Beyond this nothing can be affirmed as a duty of one group to another in a free state."[17]

Sumner's extreme brand of liberalism, however, was not hatched in a cloistered study. His attention to politics and his attempt to reach a popular audience with a total social philosophy began, rather, in his powerful reaction to the Great Strike of 1877. Before this date, Sumner had focused on narrower policy questions, especially the currency, on the rare occasions that he had addressed a public beyond the lecture rooms of Yale College. From 1877 on, Sumner stalked his political quarry: the extermination of socialist ideas and movements in America. An 1878 essay in *Scribner's Monthly* reveals his view of the harrowing power of socialism. Under socialism and communism, he asserted, there "would then be equality,—the equality of swine,—and no other equality is realizable in the material circumstances of man on earth." What was to be done? "The new task is to devise institutions which shall protect civil liberty against popular majorities. . . . That task lies next before us in the development of the art of government, and it appears that the great civilized nations will have to execute it before the end of this century, if they do not intend to give up all that has been won in five thousand years of history."[18] Just as his predecessors had identified the role of the state in an expansive democracy as the central problem of the postbellum order, so too did this problem underlie every question Sumner approached. He presumed that any action by the state must derive from malevolent socialistic designs against civil liberty, and he concluded by articulating the most dogmatic statement of laissez-faire. "At bottom, there are two chief things with which government has to deal. They are the property of men and the honor of women."[19]

Sumner's conception of civilization and progress must have seemed to compel such a position. Because capitalism and material progress undergirded civilization, there could be no dissent from his point that all government could do was protect "the property of men." Darwinism compelled the exception: as innately weaker individuals, women could not be forced unaided into the struggle for survival without catastrophic consequences for the family, the institution that made progress into civilization possible. As we have seen, the inextricable bond between capitalism and civilization had become axiomatic to most liberal reformers by the early 1870s. Sumner had a knack for consuming the ideas of others, but he preferred his fare unadulterated by qualifications. He took from Wells and Adams the idea that economic consolidation and growth were natural, particularly Adams's understanding of this economic process in evolutionary terms. Yet Sumner simplified and recast evolution in explicitly Darwinian terms of the individual's struggle for survival and concluded that wealth gave evidence of superiority in the scale of evolution, or, in the words of his chapter titles, "That we must have few men, if we want strong men" and "That it is not wicked to be rich; nay, even, that it is not wicked to be richer than one's neighbor."[20] With such statements, Sumner earned a reputation as the most renowned polemicist for the virtue of capitalism and the inalienable rights of capitalists.

Importantly, Sumner enlisted the discipline of political economy as his main proof that the social order of capitalism was natural. In an era when science had attained such prestige, if the leading professor of the *science* of political economy pronounced that natural laws rendered all efforts to intervene in the market futile at best, then all right-thinking men should know that, although progress might be hard, one must be strong and let it take its course. Sympathy for those who had failed at the competitive struggle might swell the breast, but true humanitarianism dictated that they be left to whatever fate nature deigned necessary. It was a cold and rigid dispensation the agnostic economist divined.

It was Sumner's pronouncements that came to be seen by opponents as the quintessence of Gilded Age liberalism. His talent for popularization gained him perhaps undue attention for his derivative ideas, and the extreme quality of his pronouncements earned him many enemies. With the possible exception of his work in sociology that began in the late 1880s, Sumner's intellectual production was unoriginal. It was not only that he was the American Spencer. Indeed, many of the notions for which he became known had appeared in Godkin's writings in the mid-sixties. But even Godkin was less dogmatic than he—at least initially. The Manchesterian side of Gilded Age liberalism, so exaggerated by Sumner, would not survive the 1880s. Although challenges from radical thinkers and political movements would play a large role in its demise, the more determining overthrow of its premises and justifications would be launched from within the small circle of elite intellectuals that had always formed its core constituency. And when the attack came, it began with the subject on which Sumner had laid his case for civilization: the role and significance of capital as disclosed by English classical political economy.

The first and most devastating challenge came from one of the young stars among liberal reformers, Francis Amasa Walker. Walker was the son of the businessman-turned-abolitionist and economist Amasa Walker. Francis appeared to be following in his father's footsteps and, if anything, gave promise of becoming an even more illustrious representative of the "best men." He commanded a black regiment during the Civil War, fulfilling a duty at once to his family and the abolitionist and Radical Republican causes. After the war, he served in several midlevel national appointive offices: he was chosen by Wells to be the chief of the Bureau of Statistics on the revenue commission, which he reorganized along scientific lines, and in 1870, after supervising the national census, he established himself as the leading authority on census rationalization. His economic writings before the mid-1870s read almost as homages to his father, who was the most widely read political economist in America.[21]

Walker's experiences as a young man pulled him in two directions. Family ties introduced him into the privileged world of New England high culture dominated by liberal reformers; family bonds and loyalty likely predisposed him to respect the ideas of his eminently respectable father. Yet his entry into the world of liberal reformers provided him with opportunities that led him to question its conventional truths. Most important, his participation in an organized war effort, his work in government bureaucracies during a period when their tasks had increased enormously, combined with his commitment to social scientific and statistical investigation, exposed him to the practical problems of governance and impelled him to admit the inadequacy of old economic dogmas to explain the changing U.S. economy. Humanitarian convictions, likewise inherited from his family, made him recoil from the conclusions his liberal reform colleagues were drawing from their unexamined social science.[22]

In 1875, the year his father died, Walker launched an attack on one of the fundamental doctrines of classical political economy, the wage-fund doctrine, with an article in the *North American Review*, which was followed by an economic treatise published the next year, entitled *The Wages Question*.[23] The wage-fund doctrine, asserting that nothing could alter the existing distribution of income between labor and capital, had become the main intellectual bulwark of those who justified the untrammeled rights of capital, economic inequality, and governmental noninterference in the labor market.

The wage-fund doctrine was Manchester's legitimation of capital's profit, even as it rested on a version of the labor theory of value. (Capital grew from its owner's "abstinence" in consuming the fruits of his labor.) The doctrine asserted that the costs of production were paid in advance out of the fixed fund of capital that had been saved from the product of the last production period, and only with a return to capital could production be renewed. Competition determined the cost of all factors of production (machinery, profit and interest, rent, and wages); thus the capitalist faced fixed costs at every point and had to divide up into parts the fund of previously saved capital with which he began in order to pay for each factor. Wages were paid out of the fixed quantity available after all other costs had been paid. The total wage fund of a society was the aggregate of the wage fund of all capitalists. Therefore, the rate of wages was arithmetically and irrevocably determined by the amount of the wage fund divided by the number of laborers. Several implications for relations between laborers and capitalists issued from this doctrine. As the quantity of the wage fund was fixed, higher wages for any worker would lessen the number of workers hired, and vice versa. The irrefutable conclusion to this fact was that if some workers agitated successfully for higher wages, they might receive more themselves, but at the price of denying employment to their fellow workers.

As Walker quipped, "A most comfortable doctrine surely, and one which made it a positive pleasure to conduct a quarterly review in times when the laboring classes were discontented or mutinous."[24] To refute the theory, Walker demonstrated that laborers' wages were determined by the product of their own labor, not by a preexisting "fund" of capital set aside for wages. Capitalists, Walker further observed, calculated wage rates on the basis of the quantity of goods they expected to produce and the price for which they expected to sell it. In short, the only people who took the wage fund seriously as a matter of practical business were deductive political economists so wedded to dogma that they overlooked the abundant evidence of American industrial production.[25]

By the mid-1870s, academic political economists throughout Europe and the United States were examining the once accepted axioms of English political economy.[26] New paradigms were in the making, and in this international community of scholars, Walker's book was well received as an additional, particularly compelling, and, to some, final judgment on the wage-fund doctrine. Not to the American keepers of orthodoxy, however, and particularly not to Walker's colleague at Yale, Sumner.[27] In the United States, Walker's book was at once controversial and influential. The reason is suggested by the apt review of the book by the English philosopher and political economist Henry Sidgwick, who was himself engaged in the critical intellectual project of revising English liberalism. Walker's argument was so devastating to the wage-fund doctrine, Sidgwick observed, that it left a gaping vacuum in the science of political economy. Namely, what was capital's contribution to production? Sidgwick predicted that this would become one of the fundamental questions for examination in the coming years. His prediction was accurate.[28]

The role of capital in production was not simply an abstract theoretical question in the social sciences, particularly in the United States in the midst of a severe industrial depression punctuated by frequent strikes. In all the countries of the industrialized world, the revision in political economy was closely related to the emergence of working-class movements.[29] Nevertheless, the longer history of political democracy in the United States, conceived by many as a democracy of producers, gave the debates a particular charge and particular accent. American capitalists had always categorized themselves with laborers among the producers of wealth: the abstinence theory legitimated their wealth by announcing that their past labor had created their fund of capital, and the wage-fund doctrine and other associated "natural laws" gave them an argument to resist claims by their workers for a larger share of the product of industry while making it clear that labor depended on them in the first place. To the contrary, as Walker demonstrated, if labor's productivity could raise or lower the product available for distribution, then what did capital contribute to the production process that would give it a claim on a portion of the product?[30] As the majority of Americans believed that one's political rights and one's claims to a share of "the fruits of labor" were legitimated only in and through active production, Walker seemed to leave capitalists exposed as nonproducing parasites feasting on the labor of honest workingmen.[31]

Walker did, however, provide a route out of the dilemma of capital's share of production and found a means to legitimize it on a new basis. His theory of the superiority of the "entrepreneurial class" demonstrated the limits of Walker's break with his colleagues.[32] Nevertheless, in his attack on the wage fund, Walker signaled a willingness among liberal reformers to move beyond a rigid adherence to received wisdom. He met his peers on their own terms—classical political economy, the insufficiency of ethical arguments uninformed by science—to dethrone their dogmas. For his efforts, Sumner had him driven out of Yale. Nevertheless, the reverberations of Walker's *The Wages Question* could not be quelled. Intellectually, Walker's refutation of the wage-fund doctrine endured. Politically, it served as the opening parry in a contentious debate among intellectuals over the justice of capitalism. Walker had cracked the edifice of classical political economy at the point where it ratified the contemporary capitalist order with the authority of science.

Liberal reformers, in order to educate Americans into proper economic men, had attempted to diffuse the truths of English classical political economy throughout American culture. They had tried to extend instruction of political economy into secondary schools and to modernize college education to give preeminence to the social sciences—political economy above all. They had formed societies to publish and distribute popular pamphlets on free trade, currency reform, and the harmony of labor and capital, and they had taken to the lecture circuit to inform workingmen and businessmen about the verities of economic science.[33] Scientific truth was on their side. The effort they devoted to these various publicity campaigns suggests that they believed they could persuade Americans that political practice should follow the principles that were impartially presented to them.

Liberal reformers might find it easy to explain why some men, especially those in trade unions or farmer organizations, disregarded their lessons: ignorance, demagogic leaders, or the inherently deficient character of some immigrant groups deafened the irredeemable to the siren of truth.[34] The case was different with their presumed heirs. In the late 1870s, a group of young intellectuals pursued careers in political economy and took up with zeal the work of critical revision that Walker had begun.

Henry Carter Adams would become one of the most renowned of the young social scientists, and his early life and career are suggestive of the forces and motivations underlying the personal and professional paths taken by his future colleagues and representative of their intellectual influences. The extensive personal papers he left also reveal much about the connections between them and the older liberal reformers. Adams was born in Iowa in 1851, the son of an evangelical Congregationalist family that had moved west on an abolitionist mission. His father was a leading minister in the new state and a founder of Grinnell College. His parents sent Henry to Andover Seminary for a theological education, for they keenly hoped he would follow his father's calling and become a minister. But Adams struggled with his faith and was unable to have the conversion experience necessary for membership in the Congregationalist Church.[35]

As Adams agonized over his crisis of faith, he began to channel his enthusiasm and ingrained sense of duty to social questions, and in the mid-1870s, he thought of starting a serious political magazine. He wrote of his desires to Godkin and asked him for advice. Adams did not receive the reply Godkin claimed to have sent, but Adams met with Godkin in 1876 during a visit to Cambridge and was overawed by his encounter with the man he judged "the first political writer in our country, but a most kind and considerate gentleman." Godkin advised him that if he wanted to become a great editor, he must avoid writing for the newspapers, pursue a broad liberal education, and learn to write clearly—and that he should get out of the study of theology. Encouraged, Adams reflected that "this prince of writers—this most severe man—if judged by his writings did not say at once that the plan was absurd."[36]

With such an endorsement of his ambition and advice to get an education, Adams accepted a fellowship to study social science at the new Johns Hopkins University, led by Godkin's friend and fellow liberal reformer Daniel Coit Gilman. To allay his mother's fears that he was slipping away from his faith and the duty to society that it dictated, he explained to her—and to himself in his diary—that his secular education was an addition to, not a substitution for, his religious devotion. But privately, at Hopkins, he was experiencing serious doubts about the dogmas of his religion and searching for a new field of endeavor. He studied political economy with Walker, who had been hired after being forced out of Yale by Sumner. Adams began to imagine political economy in quasi-religious terms. Torn between the pessimistic Calvinist strains of his Congregationalism, the optimistic ones of his evangelicism, and his increasing doubts about religious dogma, he chastised himself in his diary that it was a "*duty* to see to it that I am not a dead weight." To avoid this horror, he explained that he was studying political economy. "This world must learn to think. It takes no prophet to discern that we are on the eve of a great religious upheaval. Not by enthusiasts is it to be wrought but by those who study religion comparatively. The world will depend on Economy for its motive to right actions—upon religions for the feeling of adoration and praise."[37]

Adams's later prominence as one of the ethical economists might lead us to read his personal reflections at Hopkins as proof that he had already rebelled against unsentimental classical political economy. But Walker kept him to the straight and narrow, and although Adams chafed under his direction, Adams did not translate his sense of the mission of "Economy" into a challenge to Manchester orthodoxy.[38] (Although Walker had rejected the wage-fund doctrine, he still propounded most of the other laws of English political economy.) Indeed, Adams disagreed hardly at all with the liberal reformers on political matters during his time at Hopkins. In October 1877 he wrote his mother that public policy was not based on sound principles of economy and that "people were complaining of hard times." Echoing the interpretation of the depression proposed by Sumner and popularized by Wells and Edward Atkinson in many venues that would have been available to him at Hopkins, he informed his mother that unemployment and low wages were caused by paper money.[39] One can hear a young Godkin in the making in his uncharacteristically didactic tone to his mother.

Nevertheless, Adams's searching temperament, his deeply held reformist beliefs, and his fundamental intellectual honesty prepared him to abandon inherited dogmas once he was exposed to new influences. At Hopkins, Adams wavered between continuing his pursuit of an editorial career and starting anew as a professor of political economy. But in the late 1870s, jobs in both fields were scarce, even though Adams earned Hopkins's first doctorate in the social sciences. President Gilman and Professor Walker encouraged Adams to go to Germany to study in the superior German universities, pointing out that with this training he would have a much better chance of finding a position as a professor.[40] In the summer of 1878, Adams left for Europe, and after a summer tour of the continent he began his studies in Berlin.

Historicism was the dominant intellectual movement in Germany in the 1870s, and Adams took his courses in political economy and political philosophy from the leading scholars of the German historical school of political economy. The German historical economists, derisively labeled "Socialists of the Chair" by their opponents, rejected the deductive methods of English classical political economy. Many refuted the very notion of natural economic laws, universally applicable and beyond the control of human will. Although there were significant theoretical differences among the leading scholars of the German school, they agreed on several basic propositions. Their distinctive contribution to the study of political economy was to insist that the appropriate method of analysis was inductive and historical. As a corollary, because any economic order was the product of the particular history of a particular nation, there was no governmental policy inevitably dictated by the study of political economy. All the historical economists rejected the laissez-faire doctrines of English classical political economy as inappropriate for other nations, and most, following in a long tradition of German philosophy, strongly supported statist policies to develop and regulate the national economy. Among the German professors, political affinities ranged from sympathy with right-wing Bismarckians to association with left-wing socialists; nevertheless, the common denominator for the German historical economists was statism.

Those among them who tended to the left believed that socialism would be the historical result of industrial society and that economics was an ethical as well as historical science.[41] It was this tendency that captured the enthusiasm of Adams.

Adams's life in Germany quickly jolted him out of his own national folkways, and within months he was forging a new system of political and ethical beliefs for himself. He had felt constrained by his professors at Hopkins, but his German mentors encouraged him to tackle the large questions of history, economy, and ethics that he had desired to pursue for years. He was also strongly affected by German politics. Berlin was a beautiful city, he wrote his mother, but "my hatred to the system grows in intensity the more I see of it. It is one great military despotism." Particularly appalling to him was Bismarck's antisocialist law, which, to Adams, violated fundamental freedoms of association and speech. He was sure that it would not be tolerated in the United States, just as he was convinced that the huge standing army of Germany left the people helpless to challenge tyranny.[42] His patriotic sentiments for the United States and his devotion to democracy sharpened as he lived amid the repression of Bismarckian Germany.

At the same time, his professors taught him that the state could act as a positive force to ameliorate the social misery of industrialism. Soon, Adams was derisively mocking Sumner and other orthodox laissez-faire economists and carefully studying the theory of socialism and the practice of the German socialist trade unions and politicians. (He hid the socialists' literature in a trunk in his room to avoid Bismarck's censors.) Two months after beginning his studies in Berlin, he had completed an essay on socialism, and his faith in the "efficacy" of political economy had been rekindled. He sent the article to his professors at Hopkins and confided to his diary, "I hope it does not sound too socialistic. I am a socialist—to tell the truth—with the very characteristic exception of accepting their plan of reconstruction—and the study of the question has given me a foothold again on Political Economy."[43] The project had revived the moral fervor that was his most powerful family inheritance and provided him with a route out of the "darkness" he had felt in his crisis of religious faith. "I only know that English Economy has served & is serving as an opiate to the consciences of men who are trampling their fellow men in the dirt—The slavery question is not yet worked out."[44] Although Adams would not admit until 1882—and then, only privately—that he was an "agnostic," during his first months in Germany he found a new secular faith in the power of political economy to mete out true justice in the new day of proletarians and massed capital.[45]

Adams returned to the United States in the summer of 1879. Cornell, like Hopkins a modern university modeled on the German system and founded after the war, extended a job offer to him, mistakenly thinking he was the historian Herbert Baxter Adams. (They made good the offer even after they realized their mistake.) His first published article, he confessed, contained "one or two things slightly socialistic," and the second vigorously attacked the narrow English conception of liberty.[46] Imagine how Godkin might have reacted to these essays. Would he have connected the author to the adoring youth who so obviously wanted to emulate the great editor? We can speculate with confidence that when Godkin met with Adams, he believed that he was aiding one of the next generation of "best men" and that he would have been reassured that a man of Adams's background and character would carry on the tradition of critical and liberal journalism that Godkin believed he had founded in the United States. If Godkin had followed Adams's career at Hopkins (and it is highly likely he did, as President Gilman was one of his friends, and Adams received Hopkins's first doctorate in the social sciences), he would have no reason to doubt that Adams would mature into an illustrious member of the liberal reform movement. And undoubtedly, as one of the most ardent promoters of reforming American universities, Godkin believed that the new modern universities founded after the war, especially Hopkins and Cornell, would produce a corps of sober social scientists to carry on the cause of liberal reform. Once Godkin and company realized their mistake, they would set their publicity mills churning against the heretics they had unwittingly birthed.

Adams became one of the leading figures in the movement of the "ethical economists" to revise American political economy and to win public assent to the overthrow of the politics of economic liberalism. Adams's compatriots in this endeavor, John Bates Clark, Richard T. Ely, Edmund J. James, Edward Bemis, Simon Patten, Edwin R. A. Seligman, Richmond Mayo-Smith, and others, shared much with one another. They had all been children during the Civil War. They were raised in evangelical Protestant families oriented toward service to the community, and they projected for themselves a life following in the family tradition. (For Seligman, reform Judaism provided a similar seedbed for the cultivation of social reform and community service.) They came of age witnessing the social conflict and economic misery of the 1870s, and their reactions to the troubles of American society turned them from diverse pursuits toward the profession of political economy. All of them studied in Germany with the scholars of the German historical school of economics.[47]

The ethical economists pursued an idea that was bound to bring them into conflict with the liberal reformers: the superiority of socialism to individualism.[48] The title of Adams's second published essay suggests what motivated them to turn toward a system abhorred by liberal reformers. It was "Democracy."[49] The ethical economists believed that the theoretical system of classical political economy, central to the liberals' justification of their positions, sanctioned injustice and betrayed democracy. In the language of the Gilded Age, the "labor question" asked whether the "distribution" of the product of industry between labor and capital was just. If the liberal reform intellectuals were correct about unchanging human nature and natural scientific laws, which together rendered economic relations impervious to any human intervention, there would be no foundation for criticizing the fruits of the capitalist order or the politics that sustained it. The young new school economists set to work to prove that the so-called laws and axioms of classical political economy were not universal but rather the products of particular national histories. They saw their work as an act of political intervention, a step toward transforming the present economic order into one more ethical, harmonious, and democratic.

Clark, inspired equally by his reading of Henry George as by his study with the German historical economists, was the first of the group to publish dissenting views. "How to Deal with Communism" was Clark's response to the 1877 strikes and the ideology of anticommunism that emerged from respectable opinion in their wake. He sought to define a middle ground between the forces of "communism" and the forces of reaction. Accepting the dominant characterization of the strikes as communistic, Clark condemned violence and condoned state repression of the strikes. But he refused to follow respectable opinion, especially that of the classical political economists, any further. Although it was necessary to repress the criminal elements of communism, Clark argued, it was a moral and practical imperative to recognize that the underlying causes of communist agitation resided in poverty, the unequal distribution of wealth, and industrialism itself. Forthrightly acknowledging the class conflict that emerged out of the conditions of industrial production, Clark set out to delegitimize the two extreme positions—violent communism and dogmatic economic liberalism—while suggesting that there was a different way.[50]

Although Clark had found it possible and necessary to challenge the economic theory of his elders, he had not yet questioned the antidemocratic sensibility that accompanied their social science. He desired fundamental changes in economic relations yet had no faith that those who suffered—the working classes—had the capacity to devise rational solutions. So deeply ensconced in respectable intellectual circles were elitist sentiments that it seems Clark hardly noticed that his assumption that suffering people only had "demagogues and criminals" to whom to turn implied that the working class was bereft of the capacity to act rationally. It also revealed a theoretical lacuna in his idea of reform: Who would be the agents of reform? The general intellectual climate of antidemocratic prejudice at once excluded the possibility that participants in popular movements could contribute to the cause and flattered the assumption that experts would engineer the new order. Clark's personal heritage of evangelicism and Whig-Republican politics, with the latter's notions of moral stewardship and the power of moral suasion to right social evils, reinforced his faith in expert leadership.

The following year, Clark began to ponder what his third way might be, and in so doing, he started to push at the limits of inherited ideas concerning individualism and market competition. As he diagnosed unrestrained competition as the root cause of economic injustice, he began to discern a positive role for the state.[51] "The Nature and Progress of True Socialism" represented Clark's greatest departure from conventional opinion, as well as a more coherent theory of the object, method, and agency of economic transformation. He proposed that individualism had reached its apex in the age of Adam Smith and since that time had been progressing in "a socialistic direction." He then proceeded to distinguish true socialism from illegitimate communism, insisting that those who viewed them as the same were mistaken. Socialism was not a violent, revolutionary program for the abolition of property. It was, rather, "a practical movement, tending not to abolish the right of property, but to vest the ownership of it in social organizations, rather than in individuals." Many forms of organization could accomplish this, "provided only that working men be represented in them." He favorably counterposed socialism's principle of distribution, one "founded on justice" derived from ethical criteria, to the amoral distribution "determined by the actual results of the struggle of competition."[52]

Clark concluded that "true socialism"—previously "unknown to social theorists"—was simply "economic republicanism," the evolutionary development of the American ideal of personal independence. Clark revealed nostalgia for the old individualism based on personal proprietorship, but he clearly insisted that the natural tendency toward economic consolidation would soon eliminate the social conditions that had provided ample opportunity for the fulfillment of independence. On this point, Clark was elaborating on the analyses of Wells, Charles F. Adams, and others from the late 1860s, but he was reaching toward a theory in which the transcendence of entrepreneurial individualism might hold promise for a cooperative future. In place of the former individualism, a new organization of social relations would evolve—laws of history and divine Providence assured that the "true socialism" would gradually emerge in its proper time and form. Ethics and evolution dictated that individualism and competition be left behind.[53]

Clark emphasized *true* socialism because he was as concerned to discredit "false political socialism." False socialists not only frequently resorted to violence but also illegitimately tried to smuggle socialism in through the methods of political democracy. "Political socialism" sought to achieve complete state ownership of industry, a program Clark considered disastrous as a practical matter. Yet corporate consolidation was creating private entities with power to control the state, and it appeared that the day would soon be reached when it would be preferable for the state to assume management of corporations rather than to continue to allow corrupt corporate managers and lobbyists to abuse their political power. In the end, when it came to deciding what economic functions the state might assume in the present, Clark oscillated between hearty endorsements of state ownership of industry and warnings about rash action, "untrustworthy" civil servants and government officials, and suggestions that individual independence would be undermined.[54]

Clark, however, failed to take into consideration how difficult it might be to suppress false socialisms and, when the question emerged in the political arena, how difficult it would be for "social philosophers" to channel demands on the state into reasonable form, particularly when Clark himself was so ambiguous about what exactly the state should do. Clark's desire for Christian ethical judgments to replace the struggle of competition was heartfelt, but his endorsement of "economic republicanism" and a democratic means to an ethical economics was bedeviled by ambivalence. The ambivalence would have important ramifications as Clark refined his economic theory in the social world of America in the eighties.

Adams's 1881 essay "Democracy" was an even more devastating attack on the philosophical foundations of American liberalism. Adams had deeply imbibed the historicist teaching of his German professors that national differences had enormous import for the historical evolution of a nation's political economy, and "Democracy" was an exemplary scholarly exercise in the comparative historical method. It was nonetheless principally a political brief against "the excess of individualism" in America and a call to strive for the substantive promise of democracy.[55]

Adams defined democracy as "the expression of political individualism"; he explained that it had multiple meanings but that nonetheless all conceptions of democracy originated in individualism.[56] Within the many varieties of democracy, there were two main types: the English and the French. The English valued an extreme liberty that defined freedom as the individual's right to be left alone, only partially applied the principle of popular sovereignty, and repudiated equality. The French version of democracy, in contrast, placed the highest value on equality and popular sovereignty and conceived "liberty to require that society be defended from the encroachments of individuals."[57] In sum, democracy in the two traditions rested on opposite notions of the relationship between the individual and society. The educated readers of the *New Englander* would have readily discerned that Adams's description of the English variety bore a striking resemblance to the social theory of the illustrious Sumner.

The purpose of Adams's historical genealogy was to analyze the nature of American democracy. The United States was unique in its "commingling" of the two varieties of democracy. From the French the nation drew a deep commitment to political equality, yet American equality fell short of the French version because it was alloyed with the narrow English idea of liberty. Adams particularly objected to the economic relationships fostered by this peculiar version of democracy. Lacking both a sense of the duties individuals owed to one another in society and a sentiment of social equality, Americans allowed class inequalities to flourish and had left themselves no resource to combat them. With the evolution of economic inequality, the "extreme individualism" of the English variety left most men and women without "practical liberty" in the industrial order. Abstract legal freedom and equality no longer provided true freedom to most people. And without true freedom there was no real democracy. "Harsh class relations are out of harmony with democratic conceptions, and contradict what is demanded in the name of both equality and liberty." Adams refused to cede the national devotion to liberty to the propagators of "extreme individualism." Rather, achieving "that liberty promised by democracy" required "the abandonment of the wages system and the establishment of industries upon the coöperative basis." Adams desired socialism, and he said so explicitly: "The guiding principle of the industrial reformation here proposed must be to realize socialistic aims by individualistic means." A substantive democracy must be founded on economic democracy and a broader conception of individualism than that known to the Anglo-American spirit.[58]

The essay, nevertheless, was not without its contradictions on precisely the question of democracy. Adams's claim that people choose to place themselves in "servitude" to "Caesarism," his confidence that the educated would guide the masses to discover the proper goals, and his theory of history that attributed progress to the action of great men together made for a rather equivocal appraisal of democracy. In Adams's age, many had recommended that the solution to the eternal danger in democracy lay in enhancing the power of experts in social science. Even though Adams displayed uncertainty about democracy, he was no less sincerely its defender. Nevertheless, notions that were hostile to self-government by the people would leave him vulnerable when put on the spot to defend his democratic inclinations. Ideas about stewardship and expertise bred in his bones would offer a haven. Adams would always feel more at home among fellow scholars than he would among the men in the workshops and streets.[59]

The early writings of Clark and Adams, the two most theoretically innovative of the young ethical economists, hinted at the detrimental social consequences of the liberal reformers' politics. The young, socialistically inclined social scientists believed that their elders held an excessively individualistic model of society, narrowly defined the individual as the economic man of classical political economy, and conceived of individualism as the absolute right of the individual to be let alone by society. Absolutely free market competition was the practical corollary of individualism defined in this sense. In this way, liberal reformers sanctioned the political tenets of economic liberalism by presenting them as consonant with the historical American valuation of liberty and democracy. Trained to question the philosophical foundation and the methods of classical political economy and the political program it claimed to ratify scientifically, Clark and Adams had registered their dissent from the intertwined foundation of liberal reform: the individualistic, instrumental conception of human nature and free market competition.

Despite the profound intellectual challenge to liberalism issued by Clark and Adams, the young critic that ultimately drew the wrath of the liberal reformers was Ely—by any standard, a thinker inferior to both Clark and Adams. As if replaying the conflicts of the Gilded Age, historians have also tended to pay greater attention to Ely and to call him to stand in as the representative for the ethical economists. Ely won his notoriety, then and now, through his brash style and relentless self-promotion. In 1884, Ely declared that classical political economy, and with it, laissez-faire, had met their death in the inexorable march of history. Historical economics was the method of the future and positive state action the policy for the present.[60] Godkin, who had been attacking the German historical school since 1875 for "strengthening and diffusing amongst the vast mass of ignorant and unreflecting men who are now coming into possession of political power all over the world, the notion that wonderful changes may be effected in the conditions of human existence by the vigorous use of governmental machinery," was alert to Ely's importation of the suspect theories. The review he solicited of Ely admonished, "The doctrine of laissez-faire is completely misunderstood [by Ely], as well as that of the influence of self-interest," and concluded that the German school of economics was as worthless as that of " 'our own Carey.' "[61] That Godkin ensured that the magazine responded editorially to Ely's article revealed that Ely was not the only one who considered the status of the "English system" of economy primarily a matter of politics.

As Ely became bolder, linking the new method of historical economics to a positive evaluation of socialism and indirectly praising striking workers, Sumner came forward to lead the classical economists' opposition. Sumner countered Ely with a reassertion that natural laws had been firmly established by the science of political economy. Not content to attack Ely's method of analysis, Sumner subsumed socialists and "sentimentalists"—that is, social scientists who imported ethical criteria into science—under one indistinguishable category of ignorant, dangerous, and false social prophets.[62]

In reaction, Ely decided to create a new professional social science organization that would explicitly reject economic individualism and laissez-faire and commit its members to solving "the conflict of labor and capital." Ely looked to his fellow young economists to join in the enterprise. As he wrote to one prospective member, their professional organization should "combat the influence of the Sumner crowd."[63] When the organization met in September 1885, its main order of business was to review Ely's draft platform for the organization: "We regard the state as an educational and ethical agency whose positive aid is an indispensable condition of human progress. While we recognize the necessity of individual initiative in industrial life, we hold that the doctrine of *laissez-faire* is unsafe in politics and unsound in morals; and that it suggests an inadequate explanation of the relations between the state and the citizens." In discussion, Ely lambasted certain unnamed orthodox economists for the unseemly and unscientific defense of social injustice. "The respect for political economy, as it has been hitherto taught, is very slight. I think it has been kept alive largely by ignorance on the one hand—on the other by the cloak it affords to wrong-doing and the balm it offers to still the voice of outraged conscience."[64]

Even among the sympathetic ethical economists attending the meeting, Ely's audacious declaration of a new age in economic science and his program of extensive state intervention to solve the labor question could not win approval. Adams and James were closest to Ely in sentiment, but both warned of the dangers of excessive statism and the overly radical impression they might give to the public with Ely's language in their platform. Clark and Seligman played the role of compromisers. Clark recommended that the platform be modified and that it not be binding on members. The language Clark substituted for the crucial first plank was wonderfully vague: "We regard the state as an agency whose positive assistance is one of the indispensable conditions of human progress."[65] With a few like-minded changes, the delegates voted for the platform, and the American Economic Association (AEA) was created.[66] Initially, it was the vehicle for the ethical economists' challenge to the classical political economists and liberal reformers who dominated American high culture.

The process of forming the American Economic Association helped to clarify the differences between the "new school" and "old school" political economists. Both sides understood that the pivotal theoretical questions concerned wages and profits—the "distribution" of the product of industry between labor and capital—and the role of the state in the evolving industrial order. Ely had declared the irrelevance of classical political economy to the foremost ethical and political question facing the nation—the "labor question"—and had reproached the old school for its apologetics for capitalist privilege. By rejecting the established natural laws of English political economy, the new school economists hoped to delegitimate the "wages system" by demonstrating that competition and individualism were historical products whose time had passed.[67]

It all might have amounted to nothing more than a scholastic debate if it had not occurred during the largest mobilization of labor yet in the history of the United States and if the new school economists had not placed themselves on the side of industrial workers. Discussing Ely's *French and German Socialism in Modern Times* with his mother, who had admired the book, Adams acknowledged: "These socialists are the earnest men of the day:—the trades unions are I think the great movers of the present, or rather through their organizations it appears to me that the next step toward a nearer realization of Liberty and Brotherhood is to be taken. Yet the great numbers of *respectable people* look upon unionists as enemies of society, disturbers of the peace. . . . Do you want to know what I am? I am a socialist of the general Philosophy of Karl Marx. [Ely's] book doesn't give any good account of him, nor do I think he has the true method of work and agitation but his criticisms upon our present society are just and true."[68]

The mid-1880s were years of fierce conflict between labor and capital. Strikes were frequent, and membership in local unions and national organizations grew to unprecedented levels. In contrast to the 1870s, labor was able to meet organized capital with its own increasingly effective organizations. The

Knights of Labor, founded in 1879, joined all types of "producers" in the first significant industrial-type union in U.S. history. The American Federation of Labor, begun in 1881 (under a different name), brought together trade union locals in a national organization, and after many job actions and much political lobbying in the first years of the decade, in 1886 the organization renewed the national campaign for the eight-hour day. In 1886, at the peak of the mobilization of the producing classes, about 840,000 men and women were formal members in one of the two national organizations of labor. In the same year, more than 400,000 working people went on strike in 1,432 separate actions.[69]

The upsurge of labor was prompted not solely by economic hardship but also by particular values that seemed under siege in the new economic order. Workers linked the promise of democracy to their political economy, and in their view, large industrial enterprises and distant banks seemed to be overpowering the people's democracy. As the constitution of the Knights of Labor asserted, "aggregated wealth" was degrading and pauperizing "the toiling masses." Therefore, "to enjoy the blessings of life . . . a check should be placed upon its power and upon unjust accumulation, and a system adopted which will secure to the laborer the fruits of his toil, and this much-desired object can only be accomplished by the thorough unification of labor, and the united efforts of those who obey the divine injunction that 'In the sweat of thy brow shalt thou eat bread.' "[70]

While advancing a vision of the future, a "cooperative commonwealth," workers and farmers also exerted efforts to make economic and political changes within the existing system. Trade unionists attacked the mythology of free contract in their efforts to repeal conspiracy laws that stymied their organizing drives. The Knights of Labor attacked the institutional bases of consolidated capital by calling for the abolition of national banks, the regulation of corporations into extinction, and the establishment of cooperative institutions. Labor organizations lobbied for the regulation of working conditions and continued to promote legislation for the eight-hour day. Local third-party initiatives of producers were common throughout the decade, and the labor vote exerted tremendous leverage on both established political parties. Indeed, the most innovative national legislation of the era, the creation of the U.S. Bureau of Labor Statistics in 1884, was passed because both parties hoped to buy off workers' discontent before they felt it at the polls.[71]

At a time when an active and growing labor movement put forward ideas of the virtue of "producers," the oppression of labor, the unjust accumulation of capitalist wealth, and the partiality of the democratic state to capital, the ethical economists' public refutation of the science that sanctioned this allegedly unjust economic order was dangerous indeed. At least, so thought liberal reformers. The younger economists effectively joined labor in their protest against the inequality of the new industrial order and its betrayal of the promise of American democracy. Their positive appraisal of socialism and an activist state likewise seemed to underscore the significance of labor's collective orientation and its political demands for specific state policies.

Since the time Ely had taken the ethical economists' concern public with the formation of the AEA, the elder liberal reformers had worked to discredit the intellectual credentials of the younger economists. The stakes were raised substantially in the wake of the Haymarket Affair. On May 4, 1886, several days into the renewed campaign to win an eight-hour day, a bomb exploded during a rally at Haymarket Square in Chicago. The deed was laid at the feet of anarchists, one of whom was speaking at the time of the explosion. In the days following, the police arrested hundreds of Chicago workers on a wild and ultimately futile hunt for the bomb thrower, while the respectable press cried that an anarchist revolution threatened the nation and called for the full wrath of the state to come down upon the perpetrators. Some commentators insisted that there was no meaningful distinction between the activities of the Knights of Labor, trade unionists, and the anarchist bomb throwers. Others, such as the generally broad-minded but inveterately xenophobic George W. Curtis, claimed that the episode dramatized the difference between honest American workers and revolutionary immigrants who endangered the Republic.[72] In either case, the ranks of the virtuous producer were being winnowed more and more. The Haymarket Affair was a watershed in American history: it profoundly weakened the labor movement of the 1880s, crystallized opinion in the middle classes in a distinctly antilabor direction, and helped to briefly shift the balance of power—economically, ideologically, and politically—in capital's favor.

For intellectuals who had shown support for the labor movement, everything they had said or written was reevaluated in the wake of Haymarket. Ely was the first to feel the heat, in part for his well-publicized leadership of the AEA, in which he attempted to align the organization with radical movements.[73] But his main embarrassment arose from his own publications, especially *The Labor Movement in America*. The book praised the Knights of Labor and, more broadly, argued that it was the collective and political organization of the mass of working people that promised the greatest hope of social and moral progress. That advances in civilization should come from the bottom up was anathema to liberal reformers, who viewed themselves as the defenders of civilization against the "new barbarians." Ely, moreover, suffered from bad timing. Though written and put in print before the bombing at Haymarket, the book came out soon afterward and allowed hostile readers to interpret Ely's advocacy of labor activism as an approbation of revolution. In July, the *Nation* published a vitriolic book review by Simon Newcomb concluding, "Dr. Ely seems to us to be seriously out of place in a university chair." As the article appeared after Haymarket, Newcomb did not need to tax his audience's belief when he asserted that Ely's "worst defect is an intensity of bias, and a bitterness toward all classes of society except one, to which it would be hard to find a parallel elsewhere than in the ravings of an Anarchist or the dreams of a Socialist." Godkin, meanwhile, began organizing his friends to have Ely ousted from Johns Hopkins University. Ely marshaled his allies, and despite reservations some of them had with Ely's scholarship, they discerned the seriousness of the struggle. As Adams wrote Clark, "Plutocracy is in the saddle and is bound to unhorse every body who does not ride behind." For the time being, Ely held on to his position and gained promotion to associate professor.[74]

Ely had a penchant for the limelight, but in the hysterical atmosphere of 1886, Adams uncharacteristically found himself as vulnerable as Ely. Like Ely, Adams had an intense longing to turn his talents to public account, transforming the role of professor into a missionary of social reform. "The task," he wrote, "for one who has avowed himself a defender of democracy, is to present a purpose worth the striving of a great people."[75] Democracy had to evolve through the self-activity of the sovereign people, but the intellectual could fulfill his own life's purpose by presenting to them the true trajectory of history. In 1884, Adams had directly addressed the social responsibility of the intellectual. Adams's "On The Education of Statesmen" was written in a familiar vein: What were the responsibilities of the American public intellectual in a democracy? Much that Adams wrote would have been heartily endorsed in 1830 by Whigs, in 1860 by Republicans, and in 1884, by the liberal reformers. The scholar had a civic responsibility to educate men in order that they might exercise their citizenship responsibly. In modern times, this required a knowledge of political science, for governance rested on proper principles established in the disciplines of the social sciences. Adams advocated the reform of university curricula to emphasize the modern sciences, and civil service reform to encourage the best-trained men to enter public service. In some passages there is little sign that the writer was Henry Carter Adams and not Charles Francis Adams. But then Henry Carter Adams parted company with the liberal reformers. He criticized them in sharp terms for the antidemocratic sentiments pervading American higher education. He repudiated the technocratic tendency of social science and instead insisted that the main purpose of education should be to bring students into sympathy with the modern spirit of democracy and the necessity of a strengthened state. Attacking laissez-faire and righteously mocking the social scientists who hid behind alleged natural laws to conserve an unjust social order, Adams praised the native genius of the people for rebuffing the leadership proffered by these virtual aristocrats. The essay, despite its censure, remained temperate and civil in tone. And evidently, in that year, no one noticed that Adams had frontally attacked the authority of the majority of university professors in the country.[76]

Adams would not have such luck once his intentions became better known. His trouble came after he participated in a forum in March 1886 on the labor question before a Cornell University engineering school audience. He soon confronted personally the power of the "plutocracy" and the nexus of influence between the new capitalists and the prominent liberal reformers. The forum took place in the midst of the Knights of Labor's second massive strike on the Gould railroad system, and Adams was informed shortly before the forum that the other speakers were opponents of the labor movement and would present the case that the strikes violated basic principles of free contract and the liberty of property owners. Adams, to the contrary, decided to give a speech forcefully supporting the Knights of Labor and the principles that appeared to underlie the current strike. Two propositions he made in his speech were guaranteed to offend the defenders of capitalist prerogatives. First, he pronounced that historical tendencies and ethical considerations demanded that the quintessential American values, individual freedom and self-government, find expression in industrial relations. Only a little "imagination" was required to see how industrial relations could be "brought into harmony with the idea of equal rights realized in our political institutions." Legal and economic theory on capital contravened the true idea of Anglo-Saxon liberty—that with every right went a duty—and propounded an inaccurate definition of capital as a personal attribute. "The great power of the nineteenth century is capital. He who controls capital controls men." This was an observable fact, but because of the prevailing false definition of capital, few restrictions on its personal use could be achieved. Adams asserted that capital was in reality a "social product" and that therefore "it follows that the use of this social product should be granted to individuals only on conditions of strict responsibility to society. There is no more reason for granting irresponsible control over this, the greatest social force of the day, than for permitting irresponsible control over the exercise of the coercive powers of government." Considering that liberal reformers had enshrined market liberty, "free contract," as the sine qua non of freedom, Adams's political economy was subversive indeed.[77]

Adams committed an even greater heresy when he claimed to have discovered the basis for reform in the actions of striking workers and that the reform would transcend the current industrial system. Privately, Adams believed that the demands of the Knights of Labor pointed to a partial solution to the problem he had been grappling with: how to achieve socialistic goals by individualistic means. He publicly suggested that the Knights had laid out the means for realizing substantive liberty for the laborer and democratic control of industrial production. The specific demands of the Knights, as Adams interpreted them, amounted to a claim for the worker to have a property right in his job and hence the company for which he worked. Even as legal ownership of property would remain basically untouched, in practice, if workers had a "proprietary right" to their job in a particular company, directors would have to consult with them about the basic economic decisions of management and distribution. To Adams, even if the Knights did not comprehend the implications of their specific proposals, this "new proprietary right" for laborers was "in full harmony with the further development of Anglo-Saxon liberty," and it could usher in a form of cooperation, which many agreed was the solution to the labor question.[78]

Adams had been an "apprentice" lecturer in political economy at Cornell and the University of Michigan for several years and anxiously awaited a permanent appointment as a professor.[79] The lecture he gave in March initiated a year-long test of his political fitness to teach in a university; it ended with his effective dismissal from Cornell and an embarrassing protestation of political conformity to the president of the University of Michigan before he could be elected for tenure. When Adams gave his lecture at Cornell, the capitalist Henry W. Sage was in the audience. Sage was on the Cornell board of trustees, and his will included a bequest of one million dollars to the university. Sage went to work immediately to railroad Adams out of the university, and communications between the presidents of Cornell and Michigan put Adams in jeopardy at the latter as well. The basic charge was that Adams was either a "socialist" or a "communist" and that a man with such views was not qualified to teach in a university. James B. Angell, the president of Michigan and a liberal reformer himself, wrote Adams that the board would probe him about Adams's views if he were to recommend him for a full professorship. Angell therefore examined Adams about whether he believed in "the right of private property" or, rather, advocated "State Socialism." Adams promptly responded, explaining his views on state regulation and the proprietary rights of labor, and assured Angell, "In answer to the question if I am a socialist, I say no." He mildly protested the nature of the inquiry—after he elaborately explained his ideas.

It was bad enough to be viewed as a socialist in March 1886 during a major railroad strike. Adams surely understood that the events at Haymarket in May put him in a more precarious position, and he acted to ensure that his views would not be misunderstood. He wrote an article for the *Forum*, a new middle-class magazine on politics and culture, condemning the Haymarket anarchists and defending their repression by the government. He did so as a proponent of democracy and liberty. The anarchists, he wrote, "place themselves outside the law by refusing to carry on their agitation according to the law; and the law is not to be blamed if it accepts the sentence which such men pronounce against themselves and treats them as outlaws." Adams was fully aware that the anarchists charged had been proven to have done nothing more than make inflammatory speeches; this was for him sufficient proof of their guilt.[80]

Thus far, his efforts to win some security in his profession were to no avail. Cornell let him go, and one year later, in March 1887, Angell again interrogated Adams, this time in blunter terms. Explaining that he might be "embarrassed" before the board of trustees if he nominated Adams, Angell asked him if "he could help him any more." Specifically, Angell informed the errant political economist: "I do not think you have worked out with clear & definite shape the ideas to which you are inclining on the relations of labor w/ capital & on Socialism in some of its various phases." Adams protested more strongly this time such a violation of academic freedom, but he made sure that Angell would be convinced that he held views that the trustees would find acceptable. He confessed he had been confused over the years, starting out as "an individualist," then finding himself persuaded by socialist criticism of industrial society, but coming back to "the fundamental principle of English political philosophy, in which I still believed." He admitted that his comments on the Knights of Labor in 1886 "were as unwise as they were unpremeditated" and proceeded to explain that he had realized too late that he had been duped by the labor movement. "The result of this unfortunate venture is, that I believe more strongly than ever in the necessity of scholarship as an element in the solution of this terrible question that is upon us." His imminent contribution to the "terrible question" was a tome entitled *Public Debts*—hardly a subject that was driving the American masses to the barricades. Adams's capitulation had its desired effect: in June the trustees of the University of Michigan elected him to a full professorship.

Put under formidable pressure by the power of capitalists and their liberal reformer allies in the universities, Adams retreated into the realm of experts and the philosophy of individualism and was rewarded with a professorship. Ely's ordeal would be more drawn out and more public. Because he was well connected and popular with Christian factions, in 1886 he was able to preserve his job at Hopkins. But moderate and more classically inclined members of the American Economic Association worked behind the scenes to lessen his influence.[81] While he was able to escape from the overt cultural power used against Adams, Ely continued to speak publicly for radical reform and the labor movement. But in 1892, he lost his national platform when the other members of the American Economic Association finally found a sufficient cause to oust him from the secretaryship. Ely had overstepped the new boundaries being drawn behind his back when he scheduled the association's annual meeting to convene jointly with a Christian socialist reform association. Then in 1894, while the country was in a new state of alarm over the Pullman boycott, a trustee's accusations against Ely at the University of Wisconsin, claiming that he was aiding a socialistic labor movement, led to a public trial by the university regents. Ely won acquittal, but he did so only by admitting that if he were a socialist, the university would be justified in dismissing him.[82]

The conflict in political economy between the ethical economists and the liberal reformers about "individualism" and "socialism" was as much about who would politically direct the reform of the economy as it was a question about private property and individual liberty. For the classical economists and liberal reformers, a democracy agitated around issues of the injustice being done to "producers" threatened the survival of the right to private property and the supreme principle of individual liberty. The age-old opposition between democracy and property had reemerged in an extreme form, for never had there been such material abundance, so unequally distributed, and never had there been a democratic polity on such a large scale. But some form of democracy was inevitable in the United States—and increasingly, in the Western world. The fundamental challenge for the liberal reformers had therefore been to contain and limit democracy, without appearing to reject it. They had emerged from the Civil War with an individualistic and universalistic conception of democracy, modeled on the competitive free market and founded on assumptions that citizens would behave as classical economic men. In reaction against social conflict, they lost their affection for democracy and turned toward the dogma of laissez-faire and the practice of bureaucracy. Despite the seeming contradiction between these stances, both nevertheless sanctioned the authority of experts and delegitimated collective political action. When the untrained populace united to make political demands on the state or to pressure their employers, liberal reformers described them as too ignorant and impetuous, accused them of illegal coercion, and, finally, called on the state to repress revolutionary and un-American behavior.

The relationship of liberal reformers with the young social scientists was more complicated. Why did liberal reform political intellectuals, the self-professed champions of tolerance and freedom of thought and action, as well as the leading proponents of the new modern university, exert so much power to rein in their unorthodox successors? The answer has much to do with their earlier projections about intellectuals and the new realities of intellectual activity and influence. If expertise was to be the means to resolve the crisis of governance and social order in the new consolidating economy, then what the rising generation of experts thought and did was of critical importance. The liberal reformers had hardly cultivated social science education and modern universities in order to raise rebels bent on subverting the values in which they believed. But their own role in this educational modernizing movement, as well as more important changes in government and the economy, had created conditions for the rise of a new kind of political intellectual. The new school economists were trained scientists, experts in a particular field, professionals working in universities or government bureaucracies and publishing their most important work in specialist journals read by their peers. Already the generalist, who like Godkin or Curtis felt as confident pronouncing on literature, economic theory, or current politics, was becoming a relic of a simpler world. No doubt Sumner's rise to prominence over his nemesis Godkin had something to do with this cultural shift. Sumner was a leading economist, pioneered the study of sociology, and directed a social science department in one of the most prestigious modernizing universities, while in 1881 Godkin added the tasks of publishing a daily newspaper (the *New York Evening Post*) to those of his duties for the *Nation*.[83] Even though an honest comparison of the two would show Godkin to have been the more original thinker and formidable opponent, the ethical economists singled out Sumner as the representative of an outmoded liberalism for good reason. The battle for cultural and political influence had moved onto a different terrain; the engagement and persuasion of the middle-class public in a multifaceted public sphere had become less important than the deployment of specialized, scientific expertise in business and government administration and practically oriented research. Likewise, the education of the middle class was no longer a matter of patriotic school primers and lyceum tours. Those middle-class men who wished to attain authority, influence, and a decent salary now had to enter the doors of the academy, where experts ruled and the rest of the populace need not be privy to the instruction.

The ethical economists had been animated by a substantive vision of democracy, one that reckoned a more equal economic distribution of wealth and self-government in the workplace necessary to fulfill the national ideal of democracy and freedom. As they said in many different ways, socialism was merely economic democracy. They had also attempted to refine an alternative conception of the social science expert as a public servant to a democratic people, rather than an authority over them. Their positive appraisal of the labor movement stemmed from an ideal that public participation was an essential feature of democratic institutions and government, and their criticism of distribution under the wages system derived from an ideal of positive freedom that the individual, in order to reach his or her highest potential, required freedom to be grounded in economic independence and material well-being. Linking an understanding of the consolidating tendency of modern industry to a vision of the virtue of an organic society and cooperative endeavor, they initially assessed the collective action of laborers and producers positively, as legitimate political activity undertaken for democratic ideals.

Thus the conflict involving the new school and old school economists was in essence a contest to define and shape democracy. And on this point the liberal reformers won, and they did so by exerting substantial cultural and economic power over their younger opponents. Every academic freedom case in the 1880s and 1890s was directed against a social scientist who had expressed some economic heresy, such as criticizing economic inequality or sympathizing with labor. In the most renowned cases, Adams and Ely both repented their public declarations of sympathy with collective action and prospered in elite cultural institutions. In 1887, the year he received tenure, Adams was appointed to be chief statistician of the new Interstate Commerce Commission—an experiment in national regulation under nonpartisan expert administration. His associate at Michigan, Thomas M. Cooley, had recommended him for the position. Other ethical economists did not recant or failed to convince the guardians of orthodoxy that they had changed; these men lost their jobs in universities and their access to the publications of high culture. Edward Bemis, of the University of Chicago, for example, lost his battle over political beliefs. He was dismissed, and afterward he devoted himself to the popular movements for which he had been censured.[84] At the heart of the matter, the loyalty test for individualism taken by the ethical economists was intended primarily to define their relationship to popular, democratic activism. Once this issue was settled, all who had acceded were able to pursue means for industrial reform under the shelter of the university, government agencies, and commissions of the enlightened.

The public debate between the two generations had been triggered by Ely's pronouncements on the death of laissez-faire, and for a while the argument seemed to express fundamental differences about the role of the state. But, in the end, state intervention in the economy was less the issue than how the state was to be controlled—democratically or bureaucratically. The liberal reformers, as we have seen, were never such "classical" liberals as either their young challengers or later historians have made them out to be. Examining the new complexity of the international economy, they had discerned a positive role for the state yet had retreated from the administrative mandate while the government was still subject to the whims of an untutored democracy. The young social scientists were certainly more enthusiastic about state activism than their still reluctant forebears, but their more significant dissent from the values of the liberal reformers had consisted of their endorsement of democratic means and their articulation of a substantive democracy grounded in economic cooperation and equality. Just as the liberal reformers had been ambivalent about the role of the state, so too did the ethical economists waver in their defense of democracy as they contemplated, on one side, their own ruin or, on the other, the alluring prospect of the essential service they might perform as intellectuals. When they abandoned their advocacy of democracy for expertise, the way was cleared for a reconciliation with the liberal reformers whom they had initially challenged. Together the two groups would work to conceptualize the principles and methods of new kinds of state activism. The work proceeded under the tacit assumption that the tasks of decision making and execution should be carried out by experts shielded from democratically controlled processes. The conflict between the two generations of intellectuals in the 1880s set the boundaries of acceptable debate, especially about socialism, collectivism, and democratic collective action, on the cusp of the era when new liberalism, progressivism, and socialism were about to sweep transatlantic politics. In the United States, the liberal reformers and the once dissenting social scientists would collaborate to craft America's modern liberalism.

LOOKING FORWARD

THE CRISIS OF THE 1890S AND THE

INVENTION OF MODERN LIBERALISM

The social conflicts that consumed the United States during the "crisis of the 1890s" were, at heart, not only protests against the distribution of the nation's wealth but also struggles for the power to determine the meaning and practice of American democracy. To the intellectual and business elites of the nation, it appeared that democracy was showing its true face of "anarchy" and "spoliation." To those who participated in the decade's unions and Farmers' Alliances, the dividing line appeared to be the one that had been defined succinctly in the Knights of Labor constitution: the "producing classes" versus the "moneyed interests." Only in the Civil War had the country been so divided, and to contemporaries—at least with the comforting aid of historical distance from the sectional conflict—the cleavage of class seemed far more potent.

After Haymarket, despite the chilling effects of state repression and ideological censure emanating from the arbiters of respectable opinion, the protest of the "producing classes" did not abate. Wage workers, especially skilled workers in consolidating industries, continued to organize unions and initiate strikes and boycotts. Farmers in the West and South formed cooperatives and united in Farmers' Alliances and the People's Party to thwart the economic and political power of the merchants and corporations that controlled the financing and distribution of their crops. The flashpoints of social crisis followed rapidly on one another. In 1892, there was the bloody and violent Homestead strike, prompted by the desire of Andrew Carnegie, the author of the *Gospel of Wealth* and the corporate innovator in steel, to crush the powerful union in that industry. Also in 1892, Populists won election throughout the South and West and gained control of several states. In February 1893, the bankruptcy of the Philadelphia and Reading Railroad triggered a major panic. The depression that followed proved to be the most severe phase of the economic disturbances from 1873 to 1897, and the devastation it wreaked was a direct or contributing cause of many of the struggles that occurred in these years. In 1894, there were the coal strikes, the Pullman Strike, and the march of Coxey's Army of the unemployed to Washington. The crisis reached its apex in the 1896 election, after Populists, free-silverites, and labor reformers captured control at the Democratic Party convention and nominated William Jennings Bryan.

Each instance of social contest had its own particular causes and distinctive tone that helped to shape the specific result, but at bottom, most were the consequence of the difficult transition to corporate capitalism. For workers and farmers, historical traditions of "equal rights" and "free labor" defined the promise of America as the opportunity for all to achieve economic independence and to participate in a democratic republic. Defending these values, workers and farmers insisted that the consolidation of industrial enterprise and the misery generated by depression eliminated the material conditions for their producers' democracy. To capitalists and their allies, the producers' upsurge dallied irresponsibly with property rights. But, just as important, many were worried about the deeper implications.

Between 1886 and 1890, the social scientists, who had launched the challenge to liberal reform, and the liberal reformers, who had attacked them, reached a personal, political, and intellectual reconciliation. In the process, they formulated a new dominant theory of economics and new principles for economic regulation. The importance of their work was to provide a sounder theoretical foundation for interventionist policies of a still liberal democratic state and to legitimate the consolidating economy and administrative state as consistent with historical traditions of liberty, individualism, and democracy. And, just as the mobilization of labor in the 1880s had shaped the struggle for cultural power, so too did the crisis of the 1890s turn the theoretical debates to practical political service. Ultimately, members of both generations of liberal political intellectuals played a critical role in interpreting and legitimating the victory of the consolidators.

Once the cultural conflict between the liberal reformers and the ethical economists was settled, space opened for amicable theoretical explorations to be undertaken together. Through the more technical questions raised in the debate, classical political economy in its American incarnation had been fatally undermined. But three primary theoretical questions remained undetermined, and how they would be answered would have far-reaching political ramifications. First, considering the prolonged economic crisis, what were the laws and tendency of economic development? Second, given the apparent failure of the unregulated free market to provide economic stability and contain social conflict, what was the proper role of the state and on what principles could state economic intervention rest without opening the floodgates to socialism? And finally, in the face of widespread criticism of the unequal distribution of wealth between capital and labor, would it be possible to restore capital's claims to profit and disprove theories of exploitation that were surging up from the enfranchised producing masses?

Many theorists were involved in the project to revise political economy. Francis A. Walker, associate and gadfly to the liberal reformers and mentor to Henry Carter Adams and other younger economists, was personally instrumental in reconciling the two groups. For ethical economists he held the reputation as the pioneer of the attack on classical economy, whereas for liberal reformers his drift to a more conservative position in the 1880s probably enhanced his credibility. He replaced Richard T. Ely as the president of the American Economic Association in 1889. From the side of liberal reform, most joined the common dialogue; David A. Wells, Edward Atkinson, Horace White, and Charles F. Dunbar actively participated in the reformulation of applied and theoretical economics, while Thomas M. Cooley contributed to a revision of state policy in economic regulation. The younger generation of classically inclined economists, who had initially sided with the older classical economists, played a large role in the reconciliation. Among the most influential of this group were Arthur T. Hadley, Frank W. Taussig, and Franklin H. Giddings. From the ranks of those who had first sparked the revision by their challenge to the dogmas of the English school, almost all participated avidly, even if some ultimately would not assent to the new theory of economics. The most important theorists on the new economics among the erstwhile ethical economists were Adams, John Bates Clark, Simon Patten, Edwin R. A. Seligman, Edmund J. James, and Richard Mayo-Smith, while Ely, resisting and vacillating, was nudged out of his positions of power. The American Economic Association provided the main forum for the airing of differences and the work of reconciliation. Discoveries were tested and codified in new professional journals, such as the *Political Science Quarterly*, the *Quarterly Journal of Economics*, and those of the AEA, which superseded the religious monthlies and the middle-class journals and quarterlies as the place where serious intellectual dialogue would be convened. The most notable holdouts against the new political economy were E. L. Godkin and William Graham Sumner. Godkin continued to preach that none of the changes in political economy could be sustained, because the science had to be founded on the basic fact of human nature, Manchester's "Economic Man." Sumner refused to join the American Economic Association, continued to hold to classical dogmas, but, marginalized in the discipline in which he once ruled, turned to sociology and sought to devise a total theory of society.[1]

The most important innovations came from Adams, Wells, and Clark. Adams continued to draw inspiration from historical methods and was the first to formulate a specific theory of state regulation of a market economy undergoing economic consolidation that preserved basic liberal institutions and values. Wells developed the empirical side of classical political economy to explain the relationship between economic crisis and structural change. Despite Wells's reputation as one of the most rigid economic liberals on the scene, his work was critical in legitimating corporate consolidation, he discarded a number of the central laws of the Manchester school, and he adopted a pragmatic stance toward state intervention in the economy. Clark became the most nationally and internationally renowned of all American economists. He did nothing less than redefine the "labor question" with his new theory of value and original theory of distribution between the factors of production.

As Adams confronted the attacks against him in 1886, he began to channel his enduring commitment to democracy into a narrower but more specific examination of the possibilities for economic regulation by the state. The results were significant, as many of the scholars investigating the history of liberal state economic intervention have noted. In 1886 and 1887, he made three signal theoretical contributions to formulating state regulatory practice, all of which would influence his colleagues and would be adopted in altered form in twentieth-century liberal statecraft.[2] *Public Debts* (1887) and *The Science of Finance* (1898) established Adams as the pioneer of the subject of public finance in the United States, a field that, as he defined it, covered the financing and the organization of the state's enlarged administrative capacities. Necessity beckoned, and Adams had consciously decided that he needed to establish himself as an expert in one subspecialty in order to attain broader influence. It is telling that he chose to undertake this at the juncture where the science of political economy and the administrative mandate met.[3] Yet closer to his heart were his ideas of controlling monopoly and regulating competition, first presented in 1886, in which he drew on his two most important philosophical influences, German statism and Anglo-American individualism.[4]

In "Relation of the State to Industrial Action," Adams grappled with the question that would occupy many as business in America continued to consolidate. For the antimonopoly farmers and laborers, the matter was relatively straightforward: size equaled monopoly, and monopolies were unrepublican.

But for those who credited economic consolidation with propelling the nation in a progressive direction, there remained a problem of how to distinguish between legitimate and beneficial consolidation and that which infringed on public well-being. Adams was one of the first to perceive that those who favored consolidation would need to determine a way to distinguish which consolidations were legitimate, if public assent to the change was to be gained. The collapse of a faith in laissez-faire had "left the present generation without principles adequate for the guidance of public affairs. . . . Principles of action we must have, for nothing is so mischievous as the attempted solution of great questions on the basis of immediate interests alone."[5]

In seeking to demonstrate the mistaken theory and baneful consequences of laissez-faire, Adams articulated two distinct principles on which it would be legitimate for the government to regulate economic activity in a manner consonant with a proper understanding of individualism.[6] Examining the tendency of business to consolidate into larger units, Adams largely agreed with the probusiness liberal reformers that consolidation was natural, inevitable, and ultimately beneficial for the public. He did, however, seek to accommodate the antimonopoly critics by acknowledging that all businesses able to acquire monopoly power should be controlled by the government. Adams argued that the only businesses that could acquire monopoly power were those falling into the class of "industries of increasing returns," in which it was easier and more profitable for an existing business to expand than for a new enterprise to enter the field. These "natural monopolies" could prevent competition, charge higher prices, and win excess profit. Because in such cases competition was ineffective as a regulator and could not harmonize the interests of the business and the public, industries of this class should be subject to government regulation.[7] Railroads, telegraph companies, and municipal gas and water works were some of the industries in which monopoly was the natural tendency.

On the "labor question," Adams also found the middle ground. The problem with labor market competition was that the sharp practices of the tradesmen with the lowest ethics forced the rest down to that level, effectively lowering the ethical plane of the whole society. For example, if nine out of ten manufacturers refused to employ children but one of their competitors did, the rest would be forced to do so as well just to stay in business. Adams argued that "society should be secured in the benefits while secured against the evils of competitive action" by the state enacting laws to "raise the legal plane of competition." Significantly, Adams asserted that state regulation of working hours would be justified under this principle.[8]

Adams was proposing that laissez-faire was incidental, not essential, to liberalism, and none of the benefits of a competitive society would be lost to certain modifications of current practices. He formulated two distinct amendments to the prevailing axiom that competition was the most just and efficient regulator, while crediting the superiority of competition in most circumstances. Explicitly discussing governmental regulation in the context of a criticism of laissez-faire and an endorsement of competition and individualism, Adams charted a way toward a new liberalism that could incorporate reform, intervention, and regulation, while neither abandoning the core values of liberalism nor challenging the fundamental institutions of the market. Just as important, he repudiated socialism—a matter of personal importance to him, as we have seen.[9]

The crux of socialism in the United States in the 1880s was the "labor question." What Adams conceded and what he refused were the most telling aspects of his theory of state interference, for they demonstrated the distance he had traveled as well as the new terrain of debate. When Adams had first broached these ideas on regulation in a lecture in January 1886—two months before his speech at Cornell on labor, for which he was called down for his excessively radical stance—he received sharp criticism from the *Nation* and the *Independent*. At that time, he had forthrightly challenged the reigning orthodoxy of free contract with his analysis of the social power exercised by capital, and he had praised the strikes of the Knights of Labor as a move toward the effective transcendence of the wages system. Several months later, however, he concluded his published monograph with an assertion of the essentially conservative spirit in which it was written. And as proof of his good word, he assured his readers that the "theory of industrial responsibility" laid out drew "a clear line between the labor question and the monopoly question." The latter concerned the relationship between business—employers and workers considered as one—and the public. The labor question, on the other hand, was an internal one that "must be adjusted on the basis of free contracts; for to settle them in any other way would result in the destruction of legal liberty." The state might act indirectly to raise the plane of competition, yet it was clear that the concept of setting the moral plane of competition was a retreat from Adams's more encompassing idea of the social power that inhered in capitalist property. Thus having divorced the labor question from a conception of power, Adams asserted that the relation between labor and capital "is not, and from its nature can never become, a political question, and they deceive themselves who suppose a well-crystallized political party may be erected upon the interest which it represents." The first version of the essay for which he received criticism did not include this demurral on the labor question. The published work, which did, was not criticized. Indeed, at the behest of Cooley, Adams was soon after appointed to be the chief statistician of the new Interstate Commerce Commission (ICC).[10]

It was exactly the prospects raised by the politics of the labor question and the appearance of political parties of the "producing classes" that had agitated liberal reformers so much. Since the 1870s, their reflex had been to depict almost any state action for industrial reform as an opening wedge for socialism, even as most conceded—at least in private—that the newly complex and evidently unstable economy demanded an enhanced role for the state. Adams provided a route out of the dilemma. His was the most sustained analysis of the principles underlying state regulation that attempted to define a middle ground of true liberalism between socialism and laissez-faire liberalism, while placing the labor question off-limits. By distinguishing what was political from what was not, he signaled that he had learned his own lesson even as he provided new terms on which liberals could proceed to expand state powers.

In his final argument against laissez-faire, Adams again provided evidence of his essential agreement with all those interested in administrative regulation, while suggesting an approach that would enable a way around a serious obstacle. Addressing the concerns of civil service reformers, he posited, given the inefficiency and corruption of government, would not matters be worse if the state were to intervene? Adams agreed that government officials were incompetent but, in a somewhat subversive twist, proceeded to attribute bad government to little government. Because the state was weak, officials had few serious duties and, accordingly, were paid poorly. Lacking status, responsibility, and salaries commensurate with private enterprise, the respectable and able refused to enter government positions, leaving the work to the incompetent, uneducated, and corrupt. Furthermore, he argued, it was excessive individualism that spawned overlegislation, as individuals had little understanding of the proper boundary between private and public and looked to legislatures to enact their private interests. Adams concluded that enhancing the "administrative duties" of the state would dampen legislative excesses as well as attract more qualified, honest, and independent experts into service. In other words, the agenda of the civil service reformers could be accomplished only with the extension of the administrative power of the state.[11] While Adams's private communications and later writings indicate that he desired a more active state than most, they could all agree that experts would decide how the state should intervene in industrial life. And if experts such as Adams could agree that the labor question was beyond the scope of their power, and retreated from the more radical conception that capital exercised unjust social power, no one need fear that regulation was one step toward socialism.

Just as the conflicts of the 1880s raised questions about the role of the state, so too did they open up debates about the political economy of democracy. The latter question was further underscored by the panics and depressions of the era. By late 1887, virtually every active economist acknowledged that the period since the panic of 1873 constituted a sustained economic crisis, representing some fundamental transformation in America's industrial economy and social relations. They recognized that the labor movement, farmer unrest, and antimonopoly parties arose, in part, because of economic distress. More important, economists observed an ongoing transformation in the organization of industrial production that failed to produce sustained growth and profitability.[12]

In 1889, Wells published the book *Recent Economic Changes*, immediately praised by economists trained in different theoretical traditions.[13] Wells provided abundant empirical evidence that, since the panic of 1873, the international capitalist market had been beset by "overproduction." Overproduction, however, held a very specific meaning for Wells. It was not that there was too much produced in absolute terms; rather, "overproduction" meant that there was "an amount of production in excess of demand at remunerative prices," or, in blunter terms, that profits from industrial production had nearly vanished because too much was produced by too many competing enterprises.[14] In the course of the analysis of economic change, Wells statistically demonstrated that, because prices had fallen drastically while wages had not, real wages had increased substantially since 1873. Taking the three main observations as a whole—falling prices, falling rates of profit, and an increase of real wages—Wells described a situation in which there had been a transfer of national income from capital to labor.[15]

As workers criticized the tyrannical control of large industrial employers and farmers protested the exploitative practices of "monopolies," Wells instructed that consolidation was to be the nation's only salvation. He argued that excessive competition among enterprises caused profits to disappear, and he identified small capitalists as the main culprits behind downward competitive pressures. Easy credit allowed too many individuals to enter a business; they then produced too much and put their goods in the market at low prices just to cut their losses. He proposed that the crisis of "overproduction" could be overcome through economic consolidation—that is, the elimination of small business through absorption—and agreement among large producers to regulate their supply. Willfully ignoring the sentiments of most Americans on the status of the large corporation, he declared, "Up to this point of procedure no exception on the part of society can well be taken." Invoking the familiar equation of civilization and material plenty, he observed, "Society has practically abandoned—and from the very necessity of the case has got to abandon, unless it proposes to war against progress and civilization—the prohibition of industrial concentrations and combinations. The world demands abundance of commodities, and demands them 'cheaply' and experience shows that it can have them only by the employment of great capital upon the most extensive scale."[16] Industrial consolidation and continuous increase in production would provide relief from economic troubles that provoked hostilities between labor and capital, farmers and corporations, small business and large business. It would do so by rescuing capitalists and providing the rest of the people with unimaginable material plenty. Profits for capitalists and consumption by the mass would place salve on the wounds inflicted by the class conflict that issued from overproduction.

The greater part of Wells's *Recent Economic Changes* detailed the statistical evidence for his principal argument about the problem of profits and the promise of material plenty. It was not written as a political treatise, but it was still very much in the tradition of *political* economy. Wells was explicit about only one side of his political position: economic liberalism. He invoked natural economic laws on a number of occasions, devoted several chapters to the advocacy of a gold standard and free trade, and concluded with what on face value was a brief for laissez-faire. But if one reads these sections in tandem with his advocacy of economic consolidation and a corporate-administered market, we see both faces of Gilded Age liberal reform—its retreat to minimal government in the face of democratic pressures and its faith in an administrative resolution of the strains created by the development of the capitalist market. When Wells attacked interference in the market, he specifically repudiated ideas that "the new conditions of abundance should be further equalized by some other methods than intelligent individual effort, self-denial, and a natural progressive material and social development."[17] Such a notion was simply rank socialism, as it implied that the state must redistribute property. State intervention of this sort was both illegitimate and counterproductive. We can also surmise that Wells worried about the origins of such ideas in collective movements and their lack of technical knowledge about the workings of the international market. Nevertheless, Wells acknowledged that when large enterprises dominated the economy, they could wield excessive power that would be economically and politically unjust. From this view, a carefully designed state regulatory apparatus would have to accompany the natural evolution of capitalist enterprise. The inevitability of consolidation demanded mechanisms for state administrative regulation. The starting point for regulation was these questions posed by Wells: "To the producer [capitalists] the question of importance is, How can competition be restricted to an extent sufficient to prevent its injurious excesses? To the consumer, How can combination be restricted so as to secure its advantages and at the same time curb its abuses?"[18] As a practical matter, Wells devoted himself to pursuing an administrative solution through his leadership in the currency reform movement, which sought to stabilize industry through enhancing the government's role in managing the currency.[19]

On the final balance sheet, however, the credit accrued by economic consolidation and a restoration of harmony through a consumer's utopia—itself called into being by the inevitable consolidation of enterprise—overwhelmed Wells's onetime ambivalence about economic development. Wells must have thought it pointless to mourn the passing of the moral order of the entrepreneur by this late date; extinction, after all, was natural in a world governed by the laws of evolution. Most revealing, Wells reconstituted the American people as consumers. He mentioned no more the historical link between the moral status of the producer and the basis for democratic citizenship. Consumer fulfillment, apparently, constituted the apex of social life.[20]

Whereas Wells focused on economic consolidation and crisis and charted a path away from the small-scale competitive society of nineteenth-century America, Clark addressed the problem of value and distribution that had emerged from the labor question. Clark believed that the existing basis of economic science itself was inadequate to the demands of explanation and legitimation of the emergent form of capitalism. Its primary weakness, he thought, was that the labor theory of value encouraged class conflict.

By 1887, Clark had abandoned his onetime advocacy of economic republicanism, Christian socialism, and the transcendence of the competitive struggle, and had instead discovered a new moral economy. From this year until his death, he became the foremost apologist for capital in the United States. Indeed, he was such an enthusiastic booster that many of his successors, including his son (a respected twentieth-century economist), were simply embarrassed by his penchant for finding moral meaning in his Panglossian capitalist world.[21]

His parting of ways with the ethical economists became evident in early

1886, in his first and widely circulated book, *The Philosophy of Wealth*, a collection of previously published essays that had been revised to reflect his changed opinions. Observing that the United States was in the midst of a transition to a fundamentally new economic order, Clark's suggestive but internally contradictory essays reveal that he himself was betwixt and between. What had happened to Clark? He was genuinely frightened by a mobilized working class. Unlike the other ethical economists who were reined in after Haymarket, Clark made his about-face on his own and did so earlier, during the months when the Knights of Labor was at its height. Although the "consolidation of labor" followed naturally and legitimately from the consolidation of capital, the evolution of industrial relations threatened "to introduce into the industrial system an element of strife . . . and which, for possible brutality, may perhaps be accurately likened to a club contest of two cave-dwelling men."[22] The Knights of Labor spoke of the "cooperative commonwealth," a notion that surely bore a resemblance to Clark's economic republicanism. But if their strikes and boycotts were the means by which Clark's fleeting ideal was to be created, he wanted no part of it. The book marked a turning point in Clark's intellectual development, signaling his final rejection of democratic economic practices and radical causes. In its place, his personal fear of social conflict prompted him to seek a harmonious resolution of industrial conflict through the only means he knew—economic theory and the authority of experts. He struck a sympathetic chord among his peers who had been leery of the direction in which social science had been heading. Franklin H. Giddings wrote him, "After all the wash and swash and fog of recent historical economics it is delightful to read the pages of a thinker who is bold enough to name his book the *Philosophy* of wealth and show by his clear definitions and logical coherence that he means just that. There are a dozen pages in one of your chapters that are worth more than all the padded books and monographs that Ely has produced put together." Woodrow Wilson read the book while he was writing his own book *The State*. He thanked Clark and explained, "I feel that it has fertilized my own thought not only in the field of economics but also in the field of practical politics in which my special studies lie. . . . A sane, well-balanced sympathizer with organized labour is very dear to my esteem; and one who finds all the necessary stimulations of hope, not in chimeras or in hastened reformation, but in the slow processes of conversative endeavor is sure of my whole respect."[23]

As the reviews suggest, the adaptations Clark made in his theoretical work had political implications. Clark was never reticent about his political motives.

In "Profits under Modern Conditions," an essay of 1887 that introduced his evolving theory of the role of capital, he notified his readers of the stakes involved:

> We are drifting toward industrial war for lack of mental analysis. Classes in society are at variance over a ratio of division, and have no clear conception of the thing to be divided. If the profits of business constitute a limitless fund, they furnish a corresponding incentive to strife; and if this sum is virtual plunder, if it consists of wealth wrested by a social arrangement from the men whose labor creates it, the discontented class ought to include every member of society, and will include most members. It needs to be definitely known what profits are, and who earns them; and again how large they are, and who actually gets them. The nature of the prize of the social contest and the equities of the case need to be made far clearer than they have been.[24]

Virtually every address, paper, or book Clark wrote over the next three decades included a similar observation about the political and ethical significance of the problem of profit.

To prove that the distribution of income between capital and labor was determined by natural law and hence just in its own terms, Clark applied the new and internationally dominant economic theory of marginalism to an analysis of "distribution" within production. In doing so, he became the most influential theorist among American economists and an original contributor to the "neoclassical" synthesis of marginalism.[25]

Of primary importance in Clark's version of marginalism was the way in which it superseded the terms of social dialogue that took classical political economy and the labor theory of value as its reference point. Classical political economy began with an analysis of the social relations of production: How did capitalists, laborers, and owners of land coordinate productive activities to produce commodities and income for each participant? Whether in its bourgeois or socialist variant, laws inherent in the conditions of production enabled the production of commodities for sale at a value higher than the cost of production, and particular laws within production determined the share of income each would receive in rent, wages, interest, or profit. Hence "distribution" among the different classes resulted from laws of production, and the share of income each class earned constituted the amount of money each would have to purchase commodities.

In contrast, marginalism shifted the focus of economic analysis from relations of production to the sphere of exchange and demand; focusing on the nature of consumption, it concluded that the desires of consumers determined the value of goods in the market. The value of a commodity, as Clark put it, was its ability to satisfy an individual's desire, and price directly expressed this value. The labor theory of value, which found the essential value of a good in the amount of labor that had gone into its production, was wholly repudiated by the marginalist definition of value. And, indeed, the "marginalist revolution" originated in those countries in which the "labor question" had been an issue of intensive social contest.[26]

A hedonistic psychological theory was the philosophical underpinning of marginalism, and it was this that made the new economics something more than just a new technique of social science. Human beings had a wide range of desires of varying intensities. Individuals rationally allocated their income to satisfy their desires, and they had to make choices between their desires, and the way they did so set market demand for a product. Crucially, every desire was capable of satisfaction, at which point the individual would not choose to consume any more of that particular object of desire. By the late 1890s, most economists of this school had settled on a theory and terminology of "marginal utility." Value was set at the margin of consumption: for any commodity, a certain level of consumption sated the desire for it, and at that point, consumers would use their income to satisfy a different desire, rather than spend money to buy more of the same good. The final unit of a commodity demanded therefore set the value and price of it and determined how much should be produced. The demands of consumers created a new kind of competition and self-regulation of the market, and a state of equilibrium was achieved by gearing production to consumers' demands.[27] The theory represented, among other things, a radically new stance toward desire and rationality. Rationality, as conceived by marginalism, concerned the ability to perceive, calculate, and adjudicate among manifold desires in order to enjoy the full range of one's personal desires. The contrast with the rationality of the classical economic man, whose abstention and self-control in the service of production assured social order and the progress of civilization, could hardly have been more dramatic.

Even as marginalism redirected economic analysis toward the sphere of consumption, it still had to take account of the sphere of production.[28] It was the American economists who devised the most compelling application of marginalism to the sphere of production, and Clark was the pioneer in this field of economic theory. In 1881 Clark's fledgling theory of utility was still wedded to a vague notion of labor as the source of all wealth.[29] In 1886, the producer-as-laborer had disappeared, and the idea of utility was harnessed to a draft plan for how economic evolution would result in a transcendence of competition. In 1887, Clark published his first installment in his mature utility theory: competition, revised, was restored to its position as the basis of economic relations; the entire structure of value inherited from classical political economy was abandoned; and an explanation of the indispensable contribution made by capital to production was sketched. The synthesis of this project, comprising revised articles written in the 1880s and 1890s, was *The Distribution of Wealth* (1899). In it Clark proposed to "show that the distribution of the income of society is controlled by a natural law, and that this law, if it worked without friction, would give to every agent of production the amount of wealth which that agent creates." Clark had accomplished a crucial theoretical feat. He had refuted the scientific validity of any version of the labor theory of value and had reconstituted capital's right to income on the foundation of the new paradigm of economic theory.[30]

Clark's theory of distribution, to summarize, generalized the Ricardian law of rent to provide a formula for the return to each agent of production. The Ricardian law of rent asserted that the rate of rent was determined by the productivity of land at the last margin of cultivation. Clark argued that each agent of production received what it actually contributed to production and that its return was determined by the "final productivity" of the last unit (of land, labor, or capital) that would add more value to the product. Except in conditions of monopoly or unfair competition, no agent—not the landowner, nor the capitalist, nor the laborer—could gain a "surplus" over what it had actually contributed to the act of production.[31]

Whether Clark's theory, which survives in revised form in mainstream economic capital theory, is scientifically valid is not the issue here. What is of importance is the influence of Clark's work on other theoreticians, its adoption as a practical tool by businessmen, and its political significance. By the mid-1890s, marginalism had displaced both classical political economy and historicism as the dominant paradigm of economic science. No more would political economists have to defend the heartless wage-fund theory or fend off popular interpretations of the labor theory of value. The adoption of marginalism was intimately connected to desires to legitimate the capitalist market, and its foremost expositor in the United States was at pains to make the link explicitly.[32] Additionally, marginalism was readily adopted by business. With corporate consolidation, firms no longer were at the mercy of competition but rather could engage in economic planning to control their supply to meet effective demand. The method of calculating marginal or final productivity, now known as opportunity cost, provided a practical means for business managers to coordinate their level of production, as well as to calculate the relative cost and benefit of substituting one "input" (capital or labor) for another. Clark's theory of marginal productivity was part of the solution to "overproduction" as Wells and others had defined it.[33]

Considering both Clark's understanding of his work's political significance and the practical use to which marginalism was put, Clark's theoretical practice was ideological in the full sense of the term—it offered a realistic interpretation of social reality, while at the same time it was infused by particular social interests and bore the marks of engagement in a social dialogue with opponents. But Clark did not just rationalize any form of property—this is why it is not sufficient to conclude with the observation that he was a champion of the liberal capitalist market. Rather, he elaborated a portrait of a complex economic order that was coming into being, justified why it would provide universal benefits, explained how its routines of daily life operated, and explained why certain accepted political and social norms would have to be abandoned for the promise of the new world to be realized.

However much Americans cherished independence and small business, Clark repeated again and again that consolidation was a matter of natural economic law, and nothing could reverse the evolutionary trend. Whereas small businessmen, farmers, and producers denounced the new large businesses as "monopolies" and, hence, illegitimate forces of tyranny, Clark argued that with few and transitory exceptions, large-scale business could not acquire monopoly power, and competition remained the fundamental motive force of economic activity. Whereas laborers argued that consolidation made a mockery out of notions of individual free contract, Clark explained that the former justice of contract persisted, only now operating through the collective bargaining of consolidated capital and consolidated labor. Competition among large firms and contract between organized capital and organized labor ensured a just distribution between capital and labor and low prices for consumers. Competition and individualism lived on, only now on a new plane of organization and consolidation.[34] Still, there was work to be done. Writing his most important work during a period when large businesses were experimenting with various forms of "combination," such as "pools" and "trusts," Clark acknowledged that the problem of monopoly had not disappeared and that government regulation would be necessary to police any unfair practices of the new consolidated industries. He also intimated that a rational policy of regulation would take the wind out of the sails of the radicals: "If the natural law of wages is an honest and beneficent law, and if it works fairly well and can be made to work better, then we know, at least, at what we should aim in all civil law making. . . . The study that assures us of this, incidentally shows how the work is to be done. It reveals a line of public policy that is sage and efficient, and that offers an outlet for the reformatory energy that, with a zeal that is not according to knowledge, is now trying to undermine society."[35]

The theoretical debates between the liberal reform political intellectuals and the formerly radical economists went far toward resolving the politically charged questions of the role of the state, the nature and validity of economic change, and the distribution of income between labor and capital. Just as the political and social struggles in the broader society had informed the debate, so too did their conclusions begin to take on practical significance as the nation entered the "crisis of the nineties." The two most significant conflicts of the decade, the Pullman Strike and the election of 1896, illustrate both the struggle for practical victory and the contest over public opinion.

The Pullman Strike, more commonly known to contemporaries as the "Chicago strike" presented two contrary images of the approaching age of consolidation. What one saw was in the eye of the beholder. One image was of a powerful national union pitted against powerful corporations, with business brought to a stop, affecting Americans in all parts of the country, no matter with whom they sympathized. The second image was of the federal government using military force to break a strike in order to restore a vital service, yet against the will of the state's elected officials and a majority of the citizens of the local communities, and doing so on terms favorable to the reviled railroad monopolies. Neither prospect could have pleased many Americans.

The strike that pitted thousands of railroad workers against the united power of the railroad corporations began as a local dispute at the Pullman railroad car company. Sharp wage cuts imposed in the wake of the 1893 panic had aggravated the workers' existing resentment of the autocratic practices of management. When an additional wage cut was unilaterally imposed in the spring and George Pullman refused to talk with the workers' union representatives, Pullman workers decided to strike. They convinced the fledgling American Railway Union, a new industrial union of railway workers led by Eugene V. Debs, to support their strike by boycotting all trains carrying Pullman cars. When other Midwestern railroad companies banded together in the General Managers Association, sided with Pullman, and designed a strategy to crush the union in all their own companies, the threatened boycott developed into a nationwide strike.[36]

As the union boycott commenced, President Grover Cleveland's administration greeted it as tantamount to civil insurrection. Attorney General Richard Olney, a former railroad corporation lawyer, announced that the nation had reached "the ragged edge of anarchy and it is time to see whether the law is sufficiently strong to prevent this condition of affairs. If not, the sooner we know it the better that it may be changed."[37] It was, in other words, to be a test case. The government's strategy sought to defeat the strike through the government's military power and thus, not incidentally, to destroy the militant new union. On the pretext that the strikers were preventing the delivery of the federal mail, the government went to the federal courts demanding injunctions against virtually all union activities. The judges, as they had already done many times in the preceding years, willingly complied. With injunctions in hand, Cleveland then dispatched federal troops to Illinois, the locus of the strike, to enforce the injunctions. Debs and other leaders of the union were imprisoned for violating the injunctions, while federal troops attempted to defend company property and strikebreakers against union workers and their allies in the community. The deployment of federal power defeated the strike, and not long after, the Supreme Court upheld the injunctions and the government use of military power in *In re Debs*.

The spectrum of middle-class, professional, and business opinion on the Chicago strike was represented in the new leading journal of opinion, the *Forum*, started in 1886 by Issac Rice, lawyer, corporate innovator, and quasi-professional political scientist. The *Forum* had displaced the *Nation* as the most influential American political journal, as the latter lost touch with the new sensibilities of its readers. As Henry Carter Adams observed to his friend and fellow economist Seligman, "The New York Nation is a decided Bourbon. Its editors have learned nothing during the last twenty-five years and I doubt if they are capable of learning anything. Perhaps in the general shifting of social forces it is necessary to have a classical expression of incompetent ideas but I must say I weary of the reiteration of major premises which are found in the columns of this paper."[38] In contrast, the *Forum* more accurately gauged the interests of its audience—the same men and women who had once relied on the *Nation*—devising its editorial policy in accord with changes in the sociology of intellectual production. Under the editorship in the early 1890s of Walter Hines Page, on his way to becoming one of the leading editors and literary figures of his generation, the magazine refined a policy of soliciting articles from experts on the leading contemporary issues and presenting various points of view in a symposium format.[39] In this way, the *Forum* became exactly that, a forum for airing conflicting perspectives as the nation struggled through a period of wrenching transformation. In addition, unlike the previous leading journals such as the *Nation*, *North American Review*, and even

Harper's Weekly and *Atlantic Monthly*, the *Forum* was not exclusively a New England–New York affair. The authors in the *Forum* came from all over the country and displayed a lively awareness of being mutually engaged in creating and articulating a national consciousness.

As with so many other forums, however, there were limits to the range of debate. Occasionally, the editors would solicit an article by a bona fide radical—Henry George, Edward Bellamy, or "Coin" Harvey—but usually as an educational service to readers presumed to be opposed to such extremes and rarely in the midst of a true crisis such as the Chicago strike, when the spectrum of opinion to be presented narrowed. On the right, but respectable, end of this spectrum were those who viewed the Pullman boycott as a crisis of law and order and an anarchical insurrection. "It is probably safe to say that in no civilized country in this century, not actually in the throes of war or open insurrection, has society been so disorganized as it was in the United States during the first half of 1894," wrote one commentator. "During the period of suspense the situation was more critical and more menacing than anything which has been seen in the United States since the close of the Civil War. It is not surprising that the events of those days should have awakened in many quarters grave misgivings as to the stability of our form of government, and serious doubts as to the adequacy to our present political conditions of that instrument on which our Government is founded."[40] Such hysteria was quite common. It was exactly that of Supreme Court justice Stephen Field, who heartily approved the use of force against "the monstrous strikes." As one of the justices who ruled the government's military intervention constitutional, he reflected on Cleveland's resolve that "no battle of the century will reflect upon the winner greater honor."[41]

These reactions were not very different from those that had been typical of elite opinion during the Great Railroad Strike of 1877. But from other quarters in the middle class a different interpretation emerged, that it would be possible to avoid these monumental conflicts between capital and labor by augmenting governmental intervention in the railroad industry. Straddling the boundary of acceptable opinion, Ely cautiously endorsed a fully compensated nationalization of the railroads. His view was published by the *Forum*, but perceptions of his prolabor stance during the Pullman Strike helped precipitate his prosecution by the University of Wisconsin.[42]

Nationalization was further than most would go, but many favored an expanded role for the government in recognition of the special nature of the railroad industry. Cooley, renowned as the architect of judicial laissez-faire, had by the late 1880s become a major critic of the federal judiciary's interpretation of his doctrines. As chairman of the Interstate Commerce Commission from 1887 to 1892, he had tried, unsuccessfully, to cultivate a new form of administrative law, in which nonpartisan bureaus, free of legislative and judicial meddling, could develop a model of positive and conciliatory government intervention. Arbitration and conciliation between organized labor and organized capital, supervised by the ICC, was the solution, not the anachronistic competition and individualism enforced by the courts in tortured readings of congressional acts.[43] Clark, in his presidential address to the American Economic Association five months after the Pullman boycott, proposed a comparatively limited extension of governmental administrative regulation, which nevertheless called for the legal recognition of responsible unionism and the right to strike in consolidating industries. In a formulation that might have mystified traditionally inclined listeners, he insisted, "Natural law works through labor unions."[44]

The most influential interpretation of the Pullman Strike was presented in the report of the official investigation of the strike, authored by Carroll D. Wright, U.S. commissioner of labor. Wright, born the same year as Francis A. Walker, had gotten his start in government administration in Massachusetts in the bitter political battles over the labor question. In 1873, the Massachusetts legislature had created a state labor bureau as a concession to labor reformers after refusing a charter for the Shoemakers' Union, the Knights of St. Crispin. The move was widely considered a sop to labor; nevertheless, labor reformers had been appointed to lead the bureau, in recognition of the political realities under which the state legislature had acted. But when the prolabor commissioners refused to leave off their exposures of the injustices committed by Massachusetts industrialists, the governor replaced them with Wright, a Republican politician with a reputation as a liberal reformer and no experience in either labor issues or industry. In the late 1860s, Wright had been first and foremost an aspiring politician, and even as he had preserved his viability as a regular Republican, he had aligned himself with liberal reform elements: he had been a member of the American Social Science Association; as a state senator he had favored civil service reform and had voted against hours legislation; and when he ran (unsuccessfully) in a three-way race against Benjamin Butler, the local papers had identified him as the reform candidate.[45] Offered the position of commissioner of the bureau of labor in 1873, Wright had turned to Walker for advice. Walker, who had already made a reputation for himself in similar administrative positions, instructed, "Your office has only to prove itself superior alike to partisan dictation and to the seductions of theory, in order to command the cordial support of the press and of the body of citizens. . . . I have strong hopes that you will distinctly and decisively disconnect the . . . Bureau . . . from politics." In accord with Walker's charge, Wright had set out to establish the bureau as a neutral agency, whose main role would be investigation, not advocacy. He devoted himself primarily to labor statistics and the institutional development of state labor bureaus and gradually built a national and international reputation for himself.[46]

Wright's promotion in 1884 to the head of the newly created U.S. Bureau of Labor Statistics was born of similar co-optive strategies by labor's opponents. From 1868 on, labor organizations had demanded a cabinet-level post to represent the interests of labor within the national government. On the eve of the hotly contested election of 1884, Congress created the Bureau of Labor Statistics, placing it within the Department of the Interior (instead of giving it cabinet status). Labor leaders expected that one of their own would be placed in charge, but just as Congress had diluted the power of the labor bureau by placing it within the Interior Department, President Chester Arthur resisted labor's lobbying and appointed Wright instead. Wright was the first and leading national administrative expert on the labor question.[47]

On the authority of a federal railroad arbitration act of 1888, President Cleveland authorized a three-man commission to investigate the Chicago strike, and as commissioner of labor, Wright served as its head. After issuing the strike commission's report, Wright took his findings to more accessible and influential arenas, including the *Forum* and the annual meeting of the American Economic Association.[48] Wright's report helped redefine the issues at stake in the conflict and thus set the stage for a new approach to labor conflicts in consolidated industries. Just as significant, his interpretation crystallized and clarified a new ideology of the social meaning of property and labor that had been gradually emerging in intellectual debates, economic practice, and legal rulings.

The commission's investigation in large part was an effort to provide public opinion with an assessment of responsibility for the monumental strike. Wright and the commissioners' conclusions revealed a shift from the reflexively procapital stance typical of the federal government. They assigned the Pullman company and the General Managers' Association the lion's share of the blame for the economic losses and violence of the strike, for the companies had "closed the door to all attempts at conciliation and settlement of differences." The officers of the American Railway Union were exonerated of blame for directly instigating violence, most of which the commission believed had been the work of "mobs" of "hoodlums, women, a low class of foreigners, and recruits from the criminal classes." Nevertheless, the union leaders knew that strikes bred mob violence, and thus in a more profound sense, responsibility for the loss of property and life ultimately rested equally with them. Although labor had legitimate grievances, in the modern world strikes were "barbarisms," and capital and labor needed to learn how to avoid them.[49]

Wright espied the solution to destructive and barbarous labor conflict in the growth of responsible unionism. In the heat of battle, the leaders of the American Federation of Labor had shown admirable restraint in resisting the entreaties of the railroad workers. To Wright, their behavior "indicate[d] clearer views by labor as to its responsibilities, the futility of strikes, and the appropriate remedies in this country for labor wrongs."[50] But the U.S. courts, with their injunctions and conspiracy rulings against labor unions, placed an insuperable obstacle against the very force that might resolve the endemic and costly conflict between labor and capital. Ultimately, the most enduring solution to the labor question would be to acknowledge the fact of consolidation and provide governmental recognition to responsible and conservative unionism. "The growth of corporate power and wealth has been the marvel of the past fifty years. Corporations have undoubtedly benefited the country and brought its resources to our doors. It will not be surprising if the marvel of the next fifty years be the advancement of labor to a position of like power and responsibility. . . . Does not wisdom demand that each be encouraged to prosper legitimately and to grow into harmonious relations of equal standing and responsibility before the law? This involves nothing hostile to the true interests and rights of either."[51]

These conclusions about trade unions extended beyond the railroad industry. In the railroad industry specifically, government intervention would be needed as a supplement to responsible unionism. Wright understood that the Chicago strike was not a singular incident but a symptom of more general problems in the railroad industry. Since the passage of the Interstate Commerce Act in 1887, railroad industry managers and procorporate business analysts had been lobbying for a revision of government policy. Attempting to capitalize on the widely held belief that railroads were the linchpin of national prosperity, they argued that the troubles of the industry resulted from "ruinous competition" that eliminated profits and sent many corporations into bankruptcy. (At the time of the Pullman boycott, one-quarter of the country's railroads were in receivership.)[52] The only solution, they insisted, was more consolidation, and the main way to accomplish this was through "pooling" the receipts of all companies and hence eliminating the motive for cutthroat pricing. In deference to antimonopoly constituents, however, Congress had specifically outlawed pooling in the Interstate Commerce Act of 1887. The industry lobby was approaching triumph at the time Wright's report was issued: a bill to allow pooling, which would have given the ICC the power to increase rates and enforce compliance, had already passed the House by a large majority.[53]

It appeared that the railroad corporations would thus be able to revive their sagging fortunes through a government-aided consolidation. Whereas some analysts viewed the pooling bill as unproblematic and others attacked any extension of government intervention, Wright argued that fairness dictated that government control should be extended further, but not simply to favor the interests of only one of the parties. Framing the issue explicitly in the terms of "*laissez faire*" and "socialism" that had dominated the debate about government economic intervention since the 1870s, he observed that the pro-shipper rate regulation clause in the Interstate Commerce Act "was emphatically state-socialistic," and so was the pending pooling bill, which would provide "for a great trust, with the government of the United States as the trustee."[54] Despite the socialistic associations, Wright insisted that such measures in the United States were eminently conservative and that the only point left to complete the "revolution" and guarantee justice was to bring labor under the regulatory purview of the federal government by legislation establishing "that *all wages paid as well as charges* for any service rendered . . . shall be reasonable and just." Wright explained that this declaration, "backed by the machinery of the government to carry it into effect, would give to railroad employés the status of quasi-public servants."[55] Merging the logic of recent judicial rulings, derived from common-law doctrines that railroads were "quasi-public" enterprises, with newer notions of the nation's dependence on prosperity won through the vitality of industry, Wright drew sanction for increasing state control. Relations between capital and labor in the railroad industry would no longer be left only to the market, because "the prosperity of our railroads is a necessity upon which depends largely business stability, and every reasonable means which can prevent disaster should be considered."[56] The commission also recommended that a system of investigation, mediation, and compulsory arbitration be adopted in the special circumstances of the railroad industry. There would be three permanent appointed members, and during disputes, representatives from labor and capital would be included, as a means to promote conciliation. In accord with the new approach to labor unions, the statutes on trade union incorporation should be revised; unions would achieve legal recognition, and likewise, the statutes could be used to discipline workers.[57]

Even though organized labor as a rule opposed compulsory arbitration and looked askance at the repressive possibilities contained within Wright's notion of union incorporation, the commission's report was considered quite pro-labor, and for this the commissioners received some sharp abuse.[58] The true object of Wright's solicitude, however, was not labor but the "public interest," a familiar notion that was gaining new meaning in the changing economy. The debate triggered by the Pullman Strike, Wright observed, "is dissipating a good deal of the haze which has hung before the eyes of both labor and capital; it is teaching the public the necessity of placing labor and capital on a strong business basis of reciprocal interests, but interests which recognize the public as their chief master."[59] Wright could not be disputed that the public, in a literal sense, was greatly affected by the strike: the business paper *Bradstreet's* estimated that eighty million dollars had been lost in the strike, and in a nationally integrated market, an effective strike on the single transportation system did paralyze trade. But Wright endowed the public with a grander cultural importance than such a neutral definition of numerical majorities necessarily entailed. The crucial issue, as Wright, who had spent most of his adult life on commissions whose power depended on publicity, surely understood, was how public opinion would assign blame in the strike. Relatively speaking, Wright displayed a neutrality rare among federal officials, but still, the "barbarism" of strikes had to cease. In a nationally integrated, complex economy, Americans depended on railroads to transport the commodities that sustained them. Therefore the parties involved in the strike had to be controlled in order to prevent disruption of the public's service, and hence the commission's practical recommendations concentrated on designating and treating railroad workers as "quasi-public servants."[60] In recognition of the "quasi-public" nature of the railroad industry, the federal government would act as a neutral administrator through a nonpartisan expert commission; capital and labor would be treated as legitimate but particularistic interests, whose collective organization would be sanctioned by the government and then regulated—if need be, compelled—according to the "dictates of lofty patriotism."[61]

Wright's language revealed more than he probably intended. Like many Americans, Wright had adapted the French word "employé" in order to evade the historical negative connotations of the terminology of hired labor, but in this case railroad workers became "servants." Wright's formulation of the "public" and the "dictates of lofty patriotism" against "quasi-public servants" upended historical conceptions of the citizenry as a body of producers. Even though the formulation drew on existing legal doctrines of the quasi-public nature of the railroad corporation, Wright was pouring new wine into old bottles. What gave the railroads their public character was the essential role they played in the new economy: every American, as a consumer, depended on railroads. The fact that railroads originated through state incorporation certainly helped Wright skirt the thorny constitutional issues raised by his regulatory designs, and, strictly speaking, his notion of the public interest was not new. But his conception of what interests animated the public was. Americans worked in all sorts of distinct occupations, but, Wright implied, all were consumers in the national market, and thus the common or public interest derived from this shared identity. The Pullman Strike, however, demonstrated that many Americans still held to producerist ideas, as the communities in which the strikers lived supported the striking workers and refused to lend their hand to its suppression. Indeed, it was the strength of the Western labor unions and the public support they enjoyed that had convinced Cleveland and Olney to dispatch federal troops to Chicago before any significant violence had occurred.[62] Wright, against the evidence of a more complex alignment, equated the "public interest" with the majority's interest as consumers. On this point, it is worth observing that Wright, in his position as commissioner of labor, pioneered the statistical study of living standards and was one of the first to shift attention from unequal income distribution deriving from production to unequal opportunities to consume.[63] The social crisis created by the Pullman boycott had brought to light a redefinition of the relationship between labor, capital, and the commonweal. The republic of citizen-workers was being transmuted into the public of consumers.

It is reasonable to conjecture that, despite Wright's effective revision of key terms in American democratic ideology, he believed he was advancing the cause of democracy. Wright never viewed himself as a labor reformer, nor did he have personal relationships with workers or labor unionists, but in the context of the procapital stance of the federal government, Wright stood for a reformist alternative. While the judiciary ruled virtually every collective action by workers illegal and presidents lent the U.S. military force to private employers, Wright used his official position to bring before public opinion an accurate and scientific portrait of the dismal and inhumane conditions in many industries. Even when he seemed most like the liberal reformers, he never endorsed the harsher views of the social Darwinists or the rigidity of some of the Manchesterians. By the nineties, he had rejected his former antiunion sentiments and had become a prominent advocate of the legal recognition of labor unions. He did not shy away from reproaching capitalists or from challenging the faulty truisms of orthodox political economy.[64] He thought that his proposals for government intervention in railroad labor relations would inevitably bring higher wages, and he welcomed the improvements in the lives of working people the policy would achieve.

Thus, to Wright, subjecting the railroad industry to public accountability in a way that would provide social benefits to workers was a democratic advance. However, in many other ways, his solution could undermine democracy. The encouragement of responsible unionism was the centerpiece of his reform. He obviously hoped to subvert the prevailing judicial policy of issuing injunctions against virtually every collective act. But, in his call to subject unions to strong government oversight, to a far greater degree than other new liberal intellectuals who were also beginning to see a positive role for unions, he set severe limits on what would be considered legitimate. His model was certainly a far cry from the expansive vision of the industrially organized American Railway Union, and even the more appreciative conservative craft Brotherhoods balked at Wright's predilection for discipline and compulsion. Likewise, Wright's administrative proposals—a permanent, expert strike commission; the setting of wages by the ICC; federal incorporation of trade unions; compulsory arbitration—rejected democratic procedures in two areas that had been significant to the producers' movements and their allies. First, the submission of the interests of workers to the dictates of the public necessarily contravened workers' efforts to control the conditions of their work and participate in the management of their industry—the central demands of unionists' struggle for "worker's control."[65] If Wright's motive was to forward economic democracy, it was a democracy of material results, in which the matter of self-government in the workplace was null. Second, the bureaucratic technique of regulation Wright advocated, while recognizing consolidated labor and capital and providing for each to *present* its position in the councils of administrative bureaus, deprived labor and capital—and indeed, the public—of substantive *representation* in democratic governance. Should such a solution gain wide acceptance, it would inexorably lead to a conception of workers as a particularistic, special interest, thus wisely removed from direct participation in decision making involving the larger public interest. Wright, in an important sense, had a great faith in the workings of democracy—public opinion, enlightened by expert investigation "to intelligently sustain the side of right and justice," would resolve many conflicts before strikes could wreak their toll on society.[66] Yet, even though he was quite specific about the mechanisms for administrative governance, his nostrums on the harmonizing force of public opinion were vexingly vague. Despite his sincere desire to further democracy, he nonetheless promoted the administrative counterweight that weakened it.

Wright's interpretation of the Pullman Strike had incorporated many of the ideas that had been formulated in the liberal reform and social science circles in which he moved. Progress would be won through economic development, while, to the contrary, "state socialism meant the destruction of industry and the retrogression of society."[67] There were great public benefits to be won from consolidated industry and consolidated labor, if only each could be molded into responsible civic actors. The problems of the new economy would be eased by the partnership of conservative trade unions and broad-minded corporate managers and managed through an emboldened federal government, acting through administrative bureaus dominated by experts. The public interest was constituted by the majority's principal interest as consumers. It was in the wake of the Pullman Strike that many of these ideas were gradually diffused more widely in public debate and came to set the parameters of government policy. When the turn-of-the-century corporate merger movement occurred, creating many industries that now looked more like the quasi-public railroad than the dispersed private enterprises of the nineteenth century, the questions raised by the Pullman Strike about labor and capital, state and citizenship, would seem to have broader application. As Wright's model became one of those characteristic of the progressive approach to the problem of the relationship between democracy and corporate capitalism, the ambiguity of Wright's conception of democracy would also persist.

The defining moment of the decade—indeed, of the era coming to a close—was the 1896 presidential election. In the "Battle of the Standards" between the free-silver forces and the advocates of a gold standard, the badly fractured agrarian Populist movement met the enthusiasts of economic progress in the electoral arena and lost grandly. William Jennings Bryan's failure to attract the broad spectrum of producers among farmers and wage workers spelled the demise of the producers' movements and coalitions that had been so prominent in nineteenth-century America.

The cause of the dramatic election and the subsequent electoral realignment was the rise of the Populist movement, first embodied in the formation of the Farmers' Alliances in the South and West and culminating in the founding of the People's Party in 1892. The Populist movement was one of the largest social protest movements ever in U.S. history and the Populist Party the most successful third party since the Civil War, yet its showing as a national force never lived up to the expectations of its supporters or the anxieties of its opponents. Indeed, the pivotal election of 1896—the "Battle of the Standards"—has been dismissed by some historians as so much sound and fury, a symbolic, hypocritical, and hysterical exaggeration of a single issue, that in the end meant little, except for its disastrous impact on the farmers' movement.[68]

Yet it was precisely the silver agitation that inspired the Populists' most vocal and powerful opponents with dread. When populism was strongest locally in the Western and Southern states, it attracted relatively little attention from the national politicians, businessmen, and intellectuals who opposed radicalism in all forms. In those years, industrial labor conflicts, tariff and pension legislation, U.S. international relations, and the small but well-organized silver lobby concerned them far more. To be sure, the Populists' business, urban, and professional critics disliked their various radical schemes—a national income tax, the subtreasury plan, and the nationalization of the railroads and telegraph and telephone systems—but they sensed that these programs were supported by a minority of farmers, and they witnessed with pleasure the rapid collapse of the more radically oriented Populist administrations.[69] When Populists had been identified with this radical and broad antimonopoly platform, they had drawn ridicule but little passion.

The movement for free silver was a different matter, for it threatened key institutions of the developing economy, raised the specter of democratic rule over the state's critical fiscal policies, and attracted a broader constituency in the South and West than had been drawn to radical agrarian populism. It was only after the farmers' movement turned to agitating for free silver as its key demand that the mobilization of Western and Southern farmers became one of the leading subjects of national political debate. The encounter between the "silverites" and their "gold-bug" opponents, culminating in the 1896 election, would be crucial to creating the political conditions for the triumph of a new political economy.

The opposition to the free-silver forces in the 1896 election had its roots in the currency and banking reform movement of the early 1870s. What truly concerned the reformers was the threat that the free-silver movement posed to the industrial development of the United States, for monetary inflation was believed to be both a catalyst and an underlying cause of economic depression. As Horace White explained in his influential book *Money and Banking* (1895), uncertainty about the "standard of value," created by the Sherman Silver Purchase Act of 1890, had caused the panic of 1893.[70] The solvency of the government would continue to be in jeopardy while the treasury was legislatively committed to keeping silver in circulation.

More fundamental, the free-silver movement was a new manifestation of greenback and other assorted inflationist movements, and it was this that was most challenging to the long-term economic goals of the reformers, as these had evolved over the years of economic crisis. Any sort of inflation, through greenbacks, silver, or land loans, would perpetuate the most damaging aspect of the current industrial order: low and uncertain profits under conditions of "overproduction." The leaders of the currency reform movement were the intellectuals and businessmen who had concluded that the further consolidation of industry was the solution to ruinous competition and repeated panics and crises. Contrary to the producerist antimonopolists, who attributed economic depressions to the usurpations of corporations and the decline of competition, the publicists for consolidation insisted that small entrepreneurs, given life by easy credit, prevented the large firms from adjusting their supply to demand and thus caused overproduction and the inevitable depressions following in its wake. Stability would return only with a transformation of the investment system to limit credit and thus secure the market dominance of the new large industrial firms. The inflationist free-silverites hoped to do exactly the opposite: to make credit more easily available and to enable debtors to pay off their existing debts with currency worth only the value of the original loans, thus restoring opportunity for individual producers and entrepreneurs.[71]

A crucial foundation for the program of corporate consolidation was banking and currency reform, and in this the corporate innovators shared in the administrative mentality. Congress and the public still exerted too much authority over money and banking. A new system, one that would provide "elasticity" in the currency in order to manage speculative panics and booms, had to be substituted for the ineffective, makeshift banking and currency systems that had evolved since the Civil War. Whatever form the new system might take, and there were many proposals circulating among the reformers, the goal was to create a force capable of countercyclical intervention that would rescue legitimate enterprises during commercial panics. The basis of the currency in a highly developed credit economy had to be a commodity with a stable and predictable value, because profits depended on the ability of investors to calculate rationally the future value of their capital and of corporate managers to calculate the relationship between cost of production and price. The value of silver, because of its abundance, fluctuated wildly, whereas that of gold, a rarer commodity, stayed stable. In addition, gold was the standard of international exchange. For these reasons, not for fetishistic ones, the reformers defended the gold standard.[72]

The reformers had gained an ally with the election of Cleveland in 1892. Like them, Cleveland believed that the panic of 1893 had been caused by uncertainty in the standard, and he was convinced that his primary duty to the nation was to preserve the gold standard by guarding the treasury's gold reserves. He forced the repeal of the Sherman Silver Purchase Act through a hostile Congress and antagonized many free-silverites in his own party. Yet even with repeal in November 1893, the gold reserves kept dwindling, and Cleveland entered into a number of bond deals directed toward boosting the gold reserve, each of which was followed by a new depletion. The gold reserve was finally secured in February 1895, when the Morgan bond syndicate, at a nice profit to itself, effectively bailed out the government. Whereas the reformers lauded Cleveland and the deal with Morgan, the free-silver movement was galvanized by the image of the nation going begging to bankers. The reformers consequently redirected their efforts away from banking reform and embarked on a "sound money" campaign to win legislative affirmation of the gold standard.[73] The evidence of the 1894 midterm elections was that reformers would have to do significant political work themselves if they hoped to achieve their goals. Their main ally in national politics, Cleveland, had been repudiated by many in his own party for his position on silver. In the South, many of these disaffected Democrats voted Populist, and subsequently, the national chairmen of the Populist Party announced that the party would turn its main attention to the "financial question" by endorsing free silver. The conversion of the radical Populists to free silver underscored to financial reformers the menace of public debates about the currency: that democratic majorities, ignorant of the ways of international finance and exchange, would take over the fiscal instruments of the state. Ever since the federal government had gone fully into the business of creating the country's money supply and regulating banking operations during the Civil War, inflationist political movements of great popularity had shaped the outcome of financial and monetary policy. Currency democracy was the worst imaginable democracy of all.

As politicians of both parties, reacting to the election results, avoided taking definitive positions on the standard of value, the reformers took it upon themselves to defeat the free-silver movement politically. To do so they consciously developed a sophisticated campaign of public education about sound currency.[74] The campaign for the gold standard thus began long before the heated campaign between Bryan and McKinley, and in the earlier stages before the conflict became personalized, the economic conceptions of the "gold-bugs" were more explicitly and calmly presented. In venues in which the "sound money" reformers knew they were addressing urban professionals and businessmen, they were forthright about the role the gold standard played in the economic development of the nation.

Wells was one of the leaders of the "sound money" movement, and, as we have seen, he believed that national prosperity depended on industrial consolidation and international trade. In the *Forum* in 1893, he had explained why disaster would befall the United States if it did not settle the silver issue. Gold was "the money of account in the commercial world and of all international trade." All great commercial nations had established the gold standard, and "if the United States proposes to be a commercial nation of the first class, it has got to fall into line with its powerful commercial competitors." The argument was a pragmatic one, which depended neither on natural immutable law nor on a fetish for gold; nothing implied that gold would be the perpetual standard, as later advocates of the gold standard would insist. Nevertheless, Wells at the same time endowed gold with a cultural meaning that made his opponents' charge of idolatry of gold seem apt. Gold was the medium of exchange favored in countries of the "highest civilization," and "by a process of evolution, as natural and inevitable as any occurring in the animal or vegetable kingdom, gold has come to be recognized and demanded as never before in such countries as the best instrumentality for measuring values and effecting exchanges."[75] In plainer terms, Wells meant that the most industrially advanced nations used gold for its greater convenience in exchanges of large value, and these large transactions were the way of the future. If his brazen defense of consolidation were not cause enough, his recourse to the language of civilization and evolution surely antagonized his opponents.

The nomination of Bryan on a free-silver platform by the Democrats in 1896, though frightening to the "sound money" men, ultimately redounded to their benefit. Illinois governor John Altgeld, infamous for his resistance to Cleveland's dispatch of troops during the Pullman boycott and for his pardon of the living Haymarket anarchists, had controlled the Democratic convention. Shortly afterward, in a separate political convention, the People's Party also nominated Bryan but retained almost all the radical planks of the Omaha platform of 1892 and chose a Populist running mate in place of the banker that was on the Democratic ticket. This combination of circumstances marked Bryan, once an ordinary Democratic politician who had lobbied for the silver interests of his home state, as the representative of a sinister force. The campaign became a struggle over something much larger than free silver; it became a struggle over morality itself. The sound currency proponents could claim that Bryan was the stalking horse not only for free silver but for labor radicalism, socialism, and agrarian leveling.

For all the invective unleashed during the election of 1896, the Republicans' successful campaign relied on the quite ordinary appeal to self-interest, and the "sound money" publicists in their work for McKinley did much the same. They consciously pitched their literature to wage earners, commercial farmers, and middle-class men with small investments. They instructed wage earners that the depreciation of the currency would reduce their real wages. They informed the middle classes that they would be defrauded at every turn: as consumers they would be charged higher prices, and as investors—in life insurance policies, trust companies, savings banks, and the like—the value of their property would be cut in half by the fifty-cent silver dollar. In an attempt to set commercial farmers against the small and failing farmer, the "sound money" forces argued that the real price of most farm commodities had increased, and thus the farmer really needed no help from the free-silverites' promised rise in prices. To the contrary: "The prosperity of the farmer has always depended upon the ability of other classes to buy of him and his comfort upon the ability of other classes to furnish him with what he needed and could buy." As producers and consumers of commodities they would be swindled by a depreciated currency. To each class was repeated the adage that only "speculators" and "gamblers" would gain from free silver.[76]

Like any successful ideological appeal, the claims had some grounding in the real conditions of American life and thus appeared plausible. There was more to the "sound money" campaign, however, than an appeal to self-interest, and in this, the broader political concerns of the enthusiasts of economic progress were forwarded. First, within their appeals to self-interest, they effectively redefined the interest of large classes of Americans as consonant with the emerging corporate order. No matter which segment was targeted, their message included an assertion that all were consumers and that all consumers benefited from mass production and the specialization of large industry. Rejecting the ideals of producerism, they assumed that wage earners had permanent interests as wage earners; workers were dependent on the solvency of the company for which they worked, not men on their way to a competency. Farmers, as well, were notified that they were businessmen whose interests were intertwined with those of "the manufacturer, merchant [and] railway man." The competencies these producers once owned were, in the current order, savings invested in the same sorts of abstract property holdings as those of the wealthy, and all would suffer from the debt repudiation of the free-silverites. In this reconfiguration of identities and interests, the "gold-bugs" diffused the new political economy to redefine the terms of debate characteristic of American politics. The campaign for McKinley and sound money was also an education for citizenship in the emerging corporate economy.

A second undercurrent of the "sound money" campaign was its lesson about political action. The various pro-McKinley forces charged the Bryanites with all sorts of sins: anarchism, revolution, socialism, demagoguery, and the like. The presence of laborite radicals and agrarian Populists in Bryan's camp allowed this, yet it is significant that the professed representatives of the producing classes were now seen as a radical and dangerous fringe group. There had been tendencies in this direction since the railroad strike of 1877, but in 1896 the argument was elaborated into an alternative conception of political action. Andrew D. White, president of Cornell and one of the few liberal reformers to participate in the founding of the American Economic Association, used the election campaign to articulate a positive notion of reform against revolution. White had been one of the first of the liberal reformers to endorse state action enthusiastically, and he had always been explicit about the role that the educated—that is, graduates of his university—would play. Explaining his appeal "To Patriotic Democrats," he justified his charges that the leaders of the Democrats were "anarchists" and "socialists" with an extended analogy to the "tragicomedy" of the French Revolution under the Jacobins. In the midst of the usual appeals to the interests, honesty, patriotism, and good sense of the vast majority of American workers and farmers, he worked the analogy to contrast "sterile revolutions" and "rational reform." While he believed that the contest concerned the "continuance of this Republic," he left the question of reform in abeyance, but he returned to it after victory. There had been much "buncombe" in the declamations against trusts, corporations, and monopolies, "but no one can doubt the necessity of wise and vigorous regulation of these combinations." He called on the wealthy to put their fortunes to "patriotic use," for they should know that "revolution can be prevented only by evolution,—the evolution of right reason in obedience to the best knowledge and thought thus far attained by men." How would this be accomplished? "Our leading colleges and universities should be strengthened more and more as fortresses against future outbursts of demagoguism and Jack-Cadeism." The time was coming when "public men will take more and more the character of experts."[77] With the defeat of the revolutionists, the rational reformers could proceed with their administrative solution.

The sense of accomplishment expressed by White and others in the "sound money" campaign was somewhat unwarranted, as Bryan's loss was as much, if not more, a consequence of the weakness of his candidacy. Despite his platform's rhetorical commitment to laborers, Bryan failed to campaign among industrial workers, and in any event, they would have had little objective interest in the free-silver program. Even the Populists could not deliver their vote to Bryan and instead split over the strategy of fusion. Finally, free silver was simply insufficient to address the problems of economy and democracy diagnosed by those who had attempted to unite the broad producing classes in the crisis of the 1890s.

But if the election of November 1896 played out as an anticlimax, its consequences were momentous. Regardless of the insufficiency of the free-silver panacea, the Bryan Democrats and Populists had challenged one of the essential supports of the evolving consolidated economy, the financial system, and had done so explicitly in terms of the danger it posed to democracy. Their defeat was that of a long tradition of struggle to preserve and achieve a producers' democracy, as their foes branded them dangerous radicals. In contradistinction, those on the side of McKinley and sound money had promoted a new form of responsible political reform against the agitations of the "revolutionaries" and had begun to redefine the commonweal as a public of consumers. Their vision of a new social harmony constituted within the order of consolidated industry and material abundance seemed to have carried the day. McKinley's full dinner pail carried something weightier than pot roast and potatoes.

The political and economic defeat of the popular upsurge, consummated in the 1896 presidential election, was only part of the task required to reconstitute social stability and guarantee the prerogatives of private property. The social conflicts of the nineties had demonstrated that the bonds of public unity were frayed. The campaign of 1896 had seen the American political parties split—at least, rhetorically—by class, for one of the first and last times in the nation's history. The victors, as it would quickly become clear, were the prophets of economic progress and the corporate innovators; those who had spoken for a producers' democracy had been trounced. McKinley's victory thus raised fundamental questions about legitimacy in a democratic system. A justification of the new order in the workplace and in the state was required, one that would present a coherent and compelling legitimation of the characteristic new relations, institutions, and practices that emerged victorious in the wake of the crisis of the nineties. The surviving liberal reformers and the pioneering social scientists, who had concentrated their attention on the consolidation of the national economy and its relationship to the practices of the liberal democratic state, were well situated to forge a new legitimating ideology for the very transformations that had been so contested. Their practical and theoretical work had always been ripe with deeper political implications. In the late 1890s, they and others whom they inspired would gravitate to the notions that had emerged in three decades of debate in order to explain and justify corporate capitalism, an activist liberal state with powers to investigate, regulate, and intervene in civil society, and an administered democracy. Their apotheosis of the consumer and empowerment of bureaucracy would be elaborated into a new model of democratic practice, citizenship, and national identity.

Clark, who had pamphleteered for McKinley's campaign, reflected on the implications of both the Pullman Strike and the election of 1896 in a way that reveals much about the new conceptions of state, citizenship, and economy. The profound change during the 1880s in his economic theory, from Christian socialism and cooperation to neoclassical marginalism, had forced him to confront some of the central terms of liberal democratic political ideology: What was liberty? What state actions were legitimate? Did the market dispense justice? Underlying all of these was the problem of individualism: How were individual needs and interests realized and protected in the central social institutions of state and economy?

The Pullman boycott had motivated Clark to address the political implications of the consolidated economy that he celebrated. His reflections on politics in 1894 derived from the vision of material abundance achieved through consolidation that he had been investigating since his turn-about in 1886. Clark well understood that earlier versions of individualism, that of the entrepreneur and that of the independent producer, had been destroyed through a natural economic evolution that consolidated capital, even as it massed and deindividualized labor. How, then, did he present the benefits of the new order, if it so clearly undercut the values of the old? The material plenty yielded by the new, enormously productive consolidated enterprises more than compensated for the bygone entrepreneurial individualism. The utopian promise of individual fulfillment at the heart of individualism would be realized through consumption of a bounty unknown in human history.[78] What was the satisfaction of the individual producer in his skill, his concrete creations, his autonomy, compared with the possibility that every particular individual desire could be sated in the realm of material abundance?

Clark had to do some more fancy footwork to persuade those who had experienced the command of proprietorship that the order of massed capital could offset the blow to their once obvious claims to authority. Certainly providing them with an elegant new claim to rightful expropriation sweetened the bitter pill. Clark also offered a theory of "higher order" desires, in which he included the natural satisfaction the mentally adept experienced from the exercise of management and supervision. Those whose fathers had been the directors of family-owned enterprises could gain similar elevation by performing the "entrepreneurial function" in the new and more complex productive facilities. Indeed, large-scale enterprise, with its complex technology and production for a world market, called for even finer qualities in its "captains of industry."[79]

Clark's redefinition of individualism had implications beyond its reconception of the relationship between the laborer and the capitalist and its transcendence of producerism and entrepreneurial individualism. In the political economy of American democracy, claims to full citizenship had been based on the norm of the free producer and proprietor. The exclusion of women from the franchise and the resistance to enfranchising the recently enslaved had both illuminated this underlying logic of democratic citizenship in the United States. Clark's consuming individualism not only implied a new foundation of political rights and obligations; he proclaimed that democracy itself was transformed and preserved by his discovery of the true character of economic evolution.

"Positive are the claims of that form of society that evolution has secured; yet it is by its possibilities of progress that it is mainly to be judged," Clark informed his audience. Competition was the fundamental action that assured progress and the resolution of social conflicts. Contrary to the unrealistic socialist, political reform grounded in the understanding of the superiority of competition was "of the earth and not of the air." From the vision of infinite material plenty Clark declared the fulfillment of the democratic promise.

> What productive energies will this process unchain! What diffusion of motive power from cheap sources will electricity secure! What deft machinery will it everywhere move; and what forms of utility and beauty will it call out of non-existence at the touch of a button! The crowning gain of all is the irrepressible democracy of it. By processes that others control, and by wealth that others own, the laborer will get, in the end, the most valuable personal gains. Mastership and plutocracy, in a good sense, yield by natural law a democratic result; for it is by the wealth that these ensure that the productive power of labor must rise.[80]

Clark's key intervention was to recast the notion of equality, a central tenet of democratic theory, and, more important, the ideal on which the popular movements of the 1880s and 1890s had indicted the new economic forms of ownership and social relations.[81] If democracy required equality, Clark insisted that the effective equality of consumption created by industrial consolidation constituted the only meaningful sort. With this he subverted the understanding shared by labor radicals and agrarian Populists, in which equality was a matter of the possession of property and only with social ownership or widespread diffusion of small property among the majority of men could all individuals participate fully in social and political life. But to Clark human beings were fundamentally bundles of desires, and if most desires could be satisfied, then justice reigned.

At the same time, Clark circumnavigated another of the most contested points in the conflicting definitions of democracy forwarded by antagonistic groups in the Gilded Age: the question of democratic participation. Liberal reformers had at one time enthusiastically promoted democracy, for they conceived of politics as an arena in which individuals could protect their liberty and self-interest through competition with other individuals. In contrast, workers, farmers, and other reformers had organized collectively and regarded collective political action as natural, practical, and legitimate. In reaction against the "class legislation" proposed by collectively organized producers, liberal reformers devised elaborate means to limit political participation in state institutions. In short, the participants in the social conflicts of the era disagreed over democratic procedures as well as over substantive definitions of democracy. But both sides shared a notion that activity in the political sphere was a fundamental routine of citizenship in a democracy. By transferring fulfillment and participation to the realm of material consumption, Clark appeared to view the debate about political procedures irrelevant to the modern age.

Clark, however, shared more with those who feared the consequences of collective political action. Apparently, the circumstances of the 1896 election impelled him to reflect more deeply on his ideas about state regulation. Whereas Clark had once offered "democratized pleasures" as compensation to the masses for their democratic aspirations, he had much more concrete ideas about the administration of the state.

In 1897, Clark gave a speech to a collegiate association that elegantly wove together his innovations in economic theory with his political ideas. Reminding his audience of the "bitterness" of the recent elections and alerting them that "the contests of the factory and the shop are more and more often fought over again in the larger field of party warfare," he offered a basis for the resolution of conflict. The discoveries of "modern political economy" proved that the amazing law of competition guaranteed that there were no classes of "plunderers and the plundered." Taking on another "count in the indictment against the social state," that "its tendencies are undemocratic," Clark drew on his previously articulated reconception of a rough equality of consumption to limit even more categorically the meaning of democracy to personal pleasure. "We shall democratize the finest pleasures. Withal we shall democratize culture," he pronounced. Enticing the "capitalists of the twentieth century" to forge ahead, he predicted, "Your billions will do something for you; but they will do more for us—the democracy of the future."[82]

Nevertheless, there was a caveat, and on this Clark erected his practical politics. The democratic utopia would arise only if natural laws worked without obstruction, and this was where the "state demands from scholarship" a contribution. "As a first service, scholars are to know and to make known the good forces and tendencies of our social system; as a second, they are to point out and help to remove obstructions, and so to let nature work." Clark called for "positive reform" of the many complex problems the country faced: the "trust problem," "a many-sided labor question," "a railroad problem," a "corporation problem," and many others. "More and yet more will the state demand of the men who are trained to look below the surface. There must be many such men."[83] Clark's onetime zeal for reform had found a new outlet in the conviction that the modern economy would require more and more tender care from experts.

While Clark had dodged the question of democratic participation in earlier public pronouncements, he condescendingly dismissed the possibility that widespread democratic activity could resolve complicated problems. He addressed the issue through metaphor in discussing the trust question, the subject that was currently replacing the labor question as the preeminent topic of political debate. A solution, he asserted, "can be accomplished only by the finest discriminations," such as educated men were trained to make. "A blind rush at the supposed enemy will not do it. . . . Shall we bid our citizens to charge at a trust, wherever they see one, like a herd of bulls at a red cloth? That would be using the amount of intellect that a bull uses."[84] Educated men should do all they could to teach the desiring mass that economic consolidation, operating through natural laws, would democratize society. But they must be on their guard, for the creatures of desire might behave like wild animals. Only the entry of the college educated into the realm of political administration, carrying their tool boxes of social scientific formulas, could keep the nation on the path of progress. Although the people were not privy to the lecture, Clark offered them a new democracy. When he equated democracy with consumption, he suggested that the test of a just society was its ability to maintain material abundance and that participation in consumer culture constituted civic participation. If the promise of democracy lay in the material goods one could acquire, then participation in making decisions about government policy was beside the point, and no one would argue against such matters being left to the experts in social science. Clark's formulation of democracy justified and rationalized removing questions of policy from democratic institutions. To accomplish this revisionary feat, Clark had adduced a new model of citizenship: the consuming individual.

Henry C. Adams also reflected on the relationship between the new economy and the old individualism shortly after the election, in his December 1896 presidential address to the AEA. The contrast between the two economists is instructive, for Adams, who had sympathized with farmers and contemplated voting for Bryan, charted a path not taken.[85] Whereas Clark had effectively jettisoned self-rule, self-realization, and self-control, Adams reasserted the ethical centrality of these fundamental principles and the imperative to develop a new basis for individualism in the conditions of modern industry.[86]

Although Adams recognized the tendencies toward consolidation as inevitable, he dissented strongly from the conclusions most of his colleagues had drawn about the relationship between popular politics and the stability of the new economy. The problem, Adams believed, was not the irrationality of the masses. Rather, the nation faced a true crisis of legitimacy because of the disjuncture between the "evolution of corporations, trusts, and great industries" and the persistence in law of antiquated notions of rights and duties that failed to accord with the new facts of "interdependence" and "social production."[87] Adams observed that corporations were coming to claim for themselves the rights of individuals on an untenable theory of corporate personality. To the contrary, he argued, corporations could exhibit none of the attributes on which the moral order of entrepreneurial individualism had been premised, and thus "the old theory of society which assumes the identity between personal interests and social morality" could no longer provide justice or social harmony. "If it be true that the growth of a corporate enterprise is only limited by the world's demands, that its life is only limited by that of the civilization to which it pertains, and that it is deprived of those restraining influences which work so powerfully upon the individual, is it not clear that a new theory of industrial relations becomes a necessity?"[88]

History demonstrated that new conditions generated new social claims, and the only options for society were repression or reform.[89] Adams implicitly chastised his audience for its ready endorsement of authoritarian practices and warned that social conflict would cease only with the elaboration of rights. Reform lay in the direction of adjusting free contract to accord with the reality of social interdependence and industrial consolidation. Social order in a society organized on rights was enforced not by arbitrary rule but by voluntary contract. The system of voluntary contract, however, required that the contractors be "commercially responsible." The source of the violent struggles between labor and capital, Adams explained, was the fact that workers "have no property, privilege, or advantage that they can place in jeopardy." Workers were "reckless," and employers "appeal[ed] to force" in disputes because workers had nothing to lose.[90]

Adams, linking liberty and democracy, defended the traditional conception of democracy as self-rule and active citizenship. He argued that political democracy derived from the commitment to liberty, "personal independence and self-realization," and that it followed that "in the industrial world the possession of property is essential to industrial liberty."[91] He admitted that he could only speculate about what the content of this new property right would be, but he convincingly argued that the attempt to extend the individualistic model of property to the corporation was as illogical as it was dangerous. The new property right, philosophically, must be premised on the recognition of "social production" and social interdependence. There was "no reason why each individual must be swallowed up in society"; if the new forms of "social service" could be "expressed as a social claim, and made the basis of a personal right," the promises of individualism could be fulfilled.[92] The new "industrial liberty," Adams conjectured, would evolve through voluntary collective bargaining institutionalized in the labor contract. He believed that the collective agreements would provide for fair pay, establish industry boards of arbitration, and "secure to each worker an industrial home"—that is, a proprietary right of each worker to his job. He considered the arbitration boards to be the critical agency toward promoting industrial responsibility; over time, the boards would create a "common law of labor rights," and thus the worker "would be the proprietor of the rights which the board of arbitration defined."[93] Adams did not clarify how workers would attain a role in industrial governance: Would they be represented on the arbitration boards, or would collective bargaining evolve into participation in management? But in whatever way the "labor problem" might be practically resolved, "the test of its solution should be freedom for the individual to realize himself."[94] Though the proposal remained vague and ambiguous, Adams hoped to resurrect the substance of freedom and democracy in the new economic order.

It is notable that two of the most perceptive and influential social scientists turned to the problems of individualism and democracy in the aftermath of the 1896 election. Clark and Adams had once forecast the transcendence of individualism and competition and the realization of democracy in the evolving cooperative order. Their rejection of statism and return to the market economy had forced them to confront the problem that liberal democratic theorists had always faced: the conflict between liberty and equality, between property and democracy. How could the old values survive in the new consolidated economy? Clark's optimism about the benefits of economic abundance left him unconcerned about what might be sacrificed in such complete redefinitions of individualism and democracy. Adams, in his effort to rejuvenate ideas that had been central to free labor ideology and producerism, revealed that he was troubled by what might be lost in the new accord between corporate capitalism and liberal democracy. In his warnings about the dangerous social power of corporations and the need to find new means to guarantee substantive liberty, equality, and self-rule, he was, however, in the minority among his new liberal intellectual peers. Clark's vision of a consumer's democracy, founded on a market economy and administrative political order, emerged victorious in the contest to define a new liberalism.

7

MASTERING PROGRESSIVE DEMOCRACY

THE LEGACY OF THE GILDED AGE RECONSTRUCTION

OF AMERICAN LIBERALISM

In 1898, under the prodding of congressmen who represented antimonopolist small producers, Congress chartered the U.S. Industrial Commission (USIC) to conduct a sweeping investigation of the economic and social questions that had been the cause of so much political conflict. Contrary to the intentions of its congressional sponsors, the McKinley administration stacked the commission with its own procorporate allies, while economists employed simultaneously by the National Civic Federation (NCF), a voluntary business organization, directed its investigations and wrote its final report. The commission's lead economist, Cornell professor Jeremiah W. Jenks, had been a student of Richard T. Ely's, but his thought ran more in the course charted by John Bates Clark. By the time the USIC issued its final and nineteenth-volume report in 1902, the "Great Merger Movement" in the American economy had ended in the corporate dominance of the economy, and Theodore Roosevelt was president.[1]

"The economic advantages of combination, and the apparent success of most of the new companies, have led many of the ablest business men and economists to the conclusion that the combinations have become an established factor in the industrial life of the nation," the USIC observed in its final report. Paying heed to the source of its authority in Congress, where antimonopoly sentiments endured, the commission represented itself as neutral on the question of whether competition or combination was best. Nevertheless, it was evident that the writers' hearts were with the consolidators. "It is assumed that the people desire to preserve and will preserve laws to protect the public from all the dangers of conspiracy and extortion, while at the same time they desire to promote and will promote the most scientific and economical methods of business." The empirical testing of the citizenry's assumptions was to be a later invention, but Americans could be counted on to rally to the cause of progress.[2]

Essentially concluding that "the tendency to consolidate" was inevitable and largely beneficial, the USIC elucidated how a corporate-administered market would provide a better guarantee of economic stability and social peace than had the old competitive order. Social conflict, which many Americans laid at the feet of rapacious monopoly, would be resolved by granting legal recognition to corporate consolidation, not by foolhardy antitrust laws, which restored competition at the expense of the nation's material progress and social stability. To the long-festering labor question, the USIC answered in the new idiom promoted by the American Federation of Labor, whose president, Samuel Gompers, was a member of the NCF and a witness to the USIC investigation. Just as workers would achieve a higher standard of living working for the corporations rather than small businesses and focusing on higher wages rather than the old fruits of labor ethic, so too would the interests of the American public be consummated as consumers in the bounty dispensed by corporate efficiency and class conciliation. There was no whisper of economic republicanism in the USIC report, even though it had heard testimony from dissenters from the new consensus.[3]

The new harmony, however, required the aid and sanction of the state. There remained certain "evils of combination, remedial by regulative legislation," especially the potential for monopoly power and public deception. The procorporate members of the commission looked more favorably on national regulation than they did on the often overzealous efforts of state legislators. Specifically, the USIC proposed a revision of the antitrust laws, to forbid unfair competitive practices rather than consolidation itself. It recommended that the national government supervise and regulate corporate activity through a permanent trade commission modeled on the Interstate Commerce Commission (ICC), which would hold powers to compel the investigation and disclosure of corporate practices. It suggested that federal incorporation of the largest combinations might solve some of the issues of federalism raised by the new assertion of federal regulation of private enterprise and also that progressive taxation of corporations was viable. Likewise, the government could encourage the evolving compromise between labor and capital by promoting voluntary mediation and collective bargaining between organized business and responsible trade unions. State regulation could hasten the reconciliation by adopting many of the labor reform laws widely favored by workers and middle-class social reformers. Recommending that labor relations be largely left to the regime of legal individualism, free contract, and collective bargaining, the USIC nevertheless supported such national laws as a ban on child labor, the eight-hour day for public employees, the regulation of convict labor, and a reform of the courts' use of injunctions. The national government's regulation of economic activity would increase, by historical standards, but industry would remain largely self-governing through the collective organization of business and labor.[4]

The conclusions of the USIC expressed the new liberalism that had emerged out of the debates from 1865 to 1896 among liberal reformers and social scientists and inserted it into public debate and the political arena. In its new conceptions of economy and state, even as a market economy and liberal-democratic political institutions were preserved, the USIC report testified to the changes that had been wrought in liberal values, principles, and programs.

At the close of the Civil War, liberal Radical Republican publicists such as E. L. Godkin, Horace White, and George W. Curtis had proclaimed that the moral triumph over slavery had fulfilled the founding promise of the Declaration of Independence, that the United States could now achieve its destiny as the world's evangel of liberal democratic values. But the democratic enthusiasm of the Radical Republicans was quickly put to the test, as they discovered that the abolition of slavery did not permanently end conflicts over the political economy of democracy. The emergence of the "labor question" in the immediate postwar years rekindled the perennial conflicts between liberty and equality, democracy and property, that have always troubled liberals. The agitation for prolabor economic legislation by Northern workingmen and Southern freedmen reminded liberal Radical publicists that democracies threatened private property and individual liberty, to them the bulwarks of progressive civilization. In response, they refined a notion of citizenship that had been implicit in their notion of individualistic democracy, the norm of economic man, and drew from this several political conclusions. First, they devalued political activity as an arena of self-rule and, in its stead, venerated the individual drive to succeed in the market as the true mark of a man's character. Second, in the face of collective movements for enhancing state power to interfere in the labor market and property relations, they lost their love for the powerful national state and became proponents of laissez-faire. Third, they abandoned the principle of equal and inclusive citizenship and reinvigorated the American tradition of hierarchical categories in their social Darwinian reinvention of race. The classical liberalism and social Darwinism that, to many historians, have seemed to define Gilded Age liberalism were thus a response to the new paramount question of postbellum America, the compatibility of the developing capitalist economy with American democracy. What united these political ideas was not an ideal of limited government that appeared to be expressed in laissez-faire in the Northern labor market and "home rule" in the South. Rather, they shared the motive to limit and constrain the power of propertyless majorities in a polity that had recently erected universal male suffrage as its cardinal political ideal.

Simultaneously, however, newly self-proclaimed liberals examined the development of the nation's economy and concluded that laissez-faire was insufficient for the exigencies of the modern world. The liberal reformers' discovery of economic "consolidation" and the material abundance it created was a pivotal moment in the transformation of liberal ideas about citizenship and the state. The ideal of the minimal state had been rooted in a conception of society as an aggregate of self-controlled individuals, morally grounded by virtue of their self-possession, in which individual proprietors efficiently and justly governed the social order. The new forms of consolidated property and abstract property claims, however, had snapped the link between the entrepreneurial individual and social order. The first to note and examine the consequences of the withering away of entrepreneurial individualism under economic consolidation, liberal political intellectuals discerned that the old forms of independence, as well as the old forms of authority, would have to give way if the promise of progress was to be consummated. They also concluded that the new economy required a new politics. Complicated technical matters of economic development could not be understood by the masses or by their democratically elected representatives, and moreover, it was clear that the American people were overwhelmingly hostile to the very changes so lauded by the prophets of progress. In this impasse, liberal reformers divined an administrative mandate. To regulate the economy and guarantee stability, the power of the state would again be enlarged, but only if it could be insulated from the vagaries of democracy through the creation of nonpartisan bureaus of experts who were not beholden to the voters. The administrative solution had gained impetus as well from several directions: the belief in the complexity of the modern industrial economy, a positivistic faith in the social sciences, an idealized vision of the superior rationality and efficiency of consolidated enterprise, and confidence in the new managerial techniques employed in business. But its taproot was the antidemocratic turning of liberal reformers against their Civil War handiwork as they contemplated the likely consequences of majority rule, once propertyless wage earners and debt-ridden farmers dominated the electorate.

From the late sixties to the late seventies, liberal reformers variously touted laissez-faire, to restore the fundamental principle of individual liberty, or administrative reform, to restore pure and efficient government. If they had been primarily interested in social theory, they would have had to admit that their dual projects, laissez-faire and administrative regulation, were contradictory. Their concern, however, was with actual political practice, and their shifts reflected the state of their fortunes more than the state of their first principles. Furthermore, the two apparently inconsistent principles of political action both served the desire to check the threat democracy posed to capitalist property and economic progress. Laissez-faire deprived the state of effective power in the market; administrative governance insulated the policymaking institutions of the state from the influence of the people.

Within the terms of their endorsement of administrative governance, liberal reformers believed that experts in the social sciences should take over the important business of policymaking from legislators doing the bidding of collectively organized partisans. But even as they sought to train a new generation through institutions such as modern universities, social science and reform clubs, and publications geared to the middle-class public, their solution to the problem of the relationship between democracy and capitalism was unraveling under the pressure of social conflicts, economic change, and internal criticism. Among the young men who came to maturity in the institutions they sponsored, a significant minority repudiated the ideas of the older liberal reformers and charged that they had betrayed American democracy. When the young ethical economists attacked individualism, market competition, and laissez-faire in the name of the higher virtues of cooperation, democracy, and socialism, the liberal reformers deployed their arsenal of cultural power to deprive their young challengers of place and influence. The theoretical conflicts in the discipline of political economy became politicized—in contrast to analogous methodological debates in other disciplines—because of the practical salience of economic theory at the time. Workers and farmers, "the producing classes," had injected questions about economic justice into the heart of American politics. Opposing the politics of producerism, liberal political intellectuals had defended market liberty and competitive individualism by reference to the immutable natural laws disclosed by classical political economy. The challenge by the young thus struck at the ideological foundation of the liberal edifice of social order and national progress, and the struggle for cultural hegemony between the two generations of intellectuals, revolving on the opposition between socialism and individualism, resulted in the relative defeat of the younger social scientists. As the price exacted for the right to continue in university and government positions, they were forced back onto the terrain of liberalism. Their broader conception of collectivism and more expansive vision of democracy had been ruled out of order, eliminated from the acceptable range of debate.

At a time when the pressures of capitalist industrialization were spawning a revision of liberalism and the rise of socialist and social democratic parties throughout the developed economies of the transatlantic world, the conflict between the liberal reformers and the ethical economists had important implications for the course of American politics. The debate had winnowed out the untenable theoretical positions, mostly from classical political economy, and the inadmissible political sentiments—the new school economists' positive appraisal of democracy and socialism. At its conclusion, the conflict turned to dialogue, and a new concord was discovered. On one side, laissez-faire was abandoned; on the other, the cooperative democracy that had been glimpsed in the strivings of the labor movement was renounced.

In the late eighties and nineties, the producers' movements so characteristic of nineteenth-century American protest reached their apex, even as venerable notions of producerism were giving way to modern conceptions of class.[5] While producerist critics mounted what would prove to be their last stand, excoriating the undemocratic nature of large capital, members of the two generations of liberal political intellectuals were analyzing the workings of the emergent corporate political economy and attempting to derive commensurable principles of state regulation. In doing so, they invented a new liberalism. Their theoretical explorations were, in part, intellectual responses to the insufficiency of classical political economy in the face of modern economic life. Yet the theorists were engaged as well in the project of legitimation, as is demonstrated by their participation as publicists in the political contests of the nineties and after.

On the eve of the "Great Merger Movement," which would result in the dominance of corporate capital in the U.S. economy, the new liberalism had already explained and legitimated an economy dominated by large-scale corporate enterprise. Lauding the material prosperity created by consolidated enterprises, new liberals endorsed the means to smooth the path of evolution: tariff revision; the reconstruction of the investment system through banking reform; the legal redefinition of corporate property; the revision of statutes enforcing competition, and so forth. Just as capital had been massed and deindividualized, so too, according to new liberals, did labor inevitably consolidate. In the past, free contract—one of the "inalienable rights of man"—had made impermissible the collective action of workers.[6] In the new order, in which consolidated capital bargained with consolidated labor, new liberals explained that competition and free contract persisted on a higher plane to protect the rights of the individual. The liberal dream of self-realization had been updated, as well, made possible by the emergence of new techniques of mass marketing and new industries of consumer goods and commodified leisure.[7] Equality of opportunity to climb the economic ladder to the position of self-rule, authority, and independence was replaced by the opportunity to fulfill one's desires through consumption. The benefits of consumption accruing to the worker surpassed those that could be obtained by the old promise of individual independence and the right to the full fruits of labor. Corporate enterprise would not only mete out justice, equality, and individual fulfillment but also resolve the nation's social crisis and enact the national interest on the world stage. Uniquely qualified to enter the world market with the nation's surplus, corporations would overcome the vicious cycle of overproduction, panic, depression, bankruptcy, foreclosure, and unemployment that had sowed the social conflicts of the age.

New ideas about the role of the state flowed largely from the analysis of the new consolidated economy. To the limited extent that a politically inspired commitment to laissez-faire had characterized liberalism of the seventies and eighties, the new liberalism dispensed with it altogether. Corporate enterprise had to be defended and preserved, but laissez-faire would not serve in the new circumstances. Justice, social order, and progress demanded a new domestic and international activism by the state. Although corporate capitalism was largely governed by the laws of competition, state regulation would be necessary to guarantee that large enterprises did not engage in unfair uses of their market power and to rationally direct fiscal and monetary policy so as to stabilize the economy and avoid the ruinous depressions that had dominated the era. Similarly, if the national interest depended on the health of American industry, and if the latter required access to the international market, the federal government would have to promote and defend the actions of American companies outside the nation's borders. In the 1890s, after the European industrial nations had turned to formal imperialism, American corporate innovators, economists, and politicians debated how the United States could secure its rights in the international arena. Despite their disagreements over whether it was practical or just for the United States to build up its navy or acquire colonies, imperialists and anti-imperialists agreed that access to the international market was critical to national prosperity. For all the opposition of the liberal anti-imperialists to the Spanish-American War of 1898, the acquisition of colonies was a logical, if not necessary, result of their prescription for the preservation of the new political economy. The Open Door policy, certainly, was the more desirable solution.[8]

It is clear, notwithstanding the claims of a handful of doctrinaire classical liberals (then and now), that nothing fundamental about liberalism was lost in the adoption of state activism. Historical hindsight as well as contemporary commentary confirms that the political and ideological reconstruction of the Gilded Age and Progressive Era conserved, not transcended, liberalism. The preservation of individual liberty, market competition, and private property remained the foundational principles by which to evaluate the legitimacy of any state action. The new in new liberalism could not exceed these bounds.

Liberalism in the United States, in contrast to liberalism in Europe and Latin America, has always been joined to democratic political practice. Modern liberalism was also a form of liberal democracy, but one in which the preexisting values and practices of democracy were attenuated. The administrative mandate at its core proposed that decisions about regulation should be removed from their traditional locus in the legislative and judicial branches and transferred to new expert-staffed administrative agencies, divorced from partisan politics, legislative direction, and popular participation.[9] Despite the claims of its promoters, the vogue for administration that swept government and industry was not simply a technical solution but rather a political one. To new liberals, part of the appeal of the administrative solution was its usefulness in legitimating a political innovation that might not have gone down so well in unadulterated form. Power gained by administrative agencies was unquestionably that surrendered by institutions in which citizens held more direct influence—legislatures, patronage-staffed agencies, political parties, and elected judiciaries. The advantage of the administrative solution to the problem of democratic rule over the consolidating economy was that it could all be done in the name of a truer democracy. To limit democracy required no frontal attack on representative government.

Participants in the social movements of the Gilded Age had demonstrated their belief that political and economic democracy were reciprocal and self-reinforcing: political equality and active citizenship assured them democratic control of their lives as producers and sustained a substantive economic equality among citizens; to accede to extreme economic inequality would be to betray the American promise.[10] The transfer of many state powers to the administrative realm would deprive American citizens of the procedural means through which they had expressed and enforced beliefs in economic equality and self-rule. At the moment when economic change promised to exacerbate the imbalance of power in American society, most Americans lost access to the institutional means through which to assert their ideas about the substance and purpose of democracy. The administrative solution refashioned the institutions in which social and political conflict would unfold in the future.

Because ideas of citizenship in nineteenth-century America had been so firmly planted in the political economy of the competitive market and the boisterous party politics of representative democracy, such profound redefinitions of economy and state inevitably prompted a revision of the rights and benefits of citizenship. For the men of the middle classes, the loss of one's social authority as an individual proprietor was to be offset by the expansion of authoritative administrative positions in government and business. But for the majority of Americans, administrative governance left little space for active political participation, and it was incumbent upon its advocates to describe how, nonetheless, democracy prevailed. For white working men, who had long held full citizenship and the rights of suffrage, the new liberals assured that the democratic promise would be fulfilled in the new marketplace of abundance. Citizenship was reconceived as an attribute of the consuming individual, not of the producer, the model citizen of the various strains of nineteenth-century political ideology. Self-satisfaction had superseded self-rule in the purposes of life, and political participation was no longer a necessity or a good in and of itself. The promise of the fulfillment of all imaginable desires circumvented a debate about the nature of self-government in the new political economy.

Whereas discretion was a virtue when it came to constricting the democratic participation of native-born white American men, widely shared prejudice against other groups abetted the drive to narrow the suffrage. Liberal reformers vociferously opposed Henry Cabot Lodge's 1890 "Force Act," the last effort to defend black civil rights. And neither they nor the social scientists objected when the Supreme Court validated the trend toward the segregation and disfranchisement of African Americans in the South in *Plessy v. Ferguson* (1896) and *Williams v. Mississippi* (1898). As the liberal reformers had established the pseudoscientific terms of the new racism, so too did the allegedly progressive American Economic Association advance its elaboration in the turn-of-the-century debate about the imminent extinction of the "Negro" race.[11] Furthermore, the racial logic first developed in the 1870s was extended to encompass the new immigrants from Asia and southern and eastern Europe and the inhabitants of the territories taken by the United States in the Spanish-American War of 1898. The assertion that these diverse peoples had failed to evolve to the civilized standard of the high-consuming white American male worker merged with prestigious theories of scientific racism to justify depriving them of full citizenship and self-government. The new imperialism showed "the Mississippi Plan as the American Way," as the historian C. Vann Woodward so aptly put it.[12]

By the late nineties, the ideas characteristic of new liberalism had been deployed for political effect and diffused to a wider public. In its acceptance of an active state, its vision of an administered democracy, and its reconception and delimitation of citizenship, the new liberalism offered a practical guide for politics and policymaking. Just as significant, in accommodating corporate capitalism to the traditions of liberal democracy and in redefining individualism, it constituted a legitimating ideology for the new political economy. The union of liberal democracy and corporate capitalism seems commonplace to us in the age of "globalization," but it is worth reminding ourselves that attacks on concentrated economic power have played a pivotal role in American politics. Those who wished to sanction the new order of corporate capitalism that arose on the eve of the twentieth century faced not only opponents mobilized economically and politically but also a nationalist historical narrative that celebrated the revolutionary generation's fight against the tyranny of monopoly, the Jacksonian destruction of the "monster bank," the antislavery and Unionist struggle against "the lords of the loom and the lords of the lash," and the rugged individualism of the frontier. To embrace the corporate economy required new definitions of opportunity, equality, freedom, justice, and order.

The characterization of the new liberalism proposed in this work will appear familiar to historians of twentieth-century American politics. A large body of historical analysis identifies the rise, legitimation, and political institutionalization of corporate capitalism, the articulation of a theory and practice of bureaucratic state activism, and the material and ideological shift from producerism to consumerism as defining innovations and features of the Progressive Era.[13] Because the Progressive Era inaugurated the modern American liberalism that dominated twentieth-century politics, the era has proved a fertile ground for the proliferation of conflicting historical interpretations. One of the recurring questions concerns the origins of "progressivism." Much of the analysis of the Progressive Era has sought to identify why and how progressivism emerged when it did. As Daniel Rodgers observed in his perceptive analysis of progressive historiography, no satisfactory answer had yet been given. Although Rodgers's recent *Atlantic Crossings* demonstrates the critical importance of an international dialogue among social reformers in the adoption and adaptation of American progressivism, I would argue that the problem of origins has not been resolved. I venture that we have been looking not only in the wrong place—as Rodgers insists—but also in the wrong time.[14]

On the eve of the twentieth century, many of the innovations in policy and social thought that are typically identified as the hallmarks of the Progressive Era had already been formulated, explained, and diffused by the two generations of postbellum liberal political intellectuals. It is not simply that the continuities between Gilded Age liberalism and progressivism have been overlooked or denied and that it is necessary to revise the periodization of the origins of modern liberalism. Rather, the Gilded Age liberal political intellectuals exerted a profound influence over the progressives, and their influence brings us to the heart of the debate about the nature of the Progressive Era. As others have noted, progressive reform was unthinkable without the defeat of the producers' movements of the 1880s and 1890s. I would go further, however, by proposing that the political economy of modern liberalism bears the marks of its birth in the social conflict of the Gilded Age, in which the question of the compatibility of democracy and capitalism was preeminent. The reconstruction of American liberalism thus took place during an era in which the alternatives were sharper and the stakes were higher than they would be later. Furthermore, before any progressive politician took office, a number of fateful revisions in the ideology and practice of American liberal democracy had already occurred. Those who aspired to change American society and politics entered a political terrain in which certain limits had already been set by their predecessors. Part of their challenge necessarily involved the question of whether they would accede to or renegotiate the boundaries. Until this is recognized as a critical element of the dialectic of the Progressive Era, our understanding of the origins and nature of modern liberalism will remain incomplete.

Again, the traditional narrative of liberalism after the Civil War holds that dogmatic classical liberals dug in their heels in the Gilded Age and prevented the nation from recognizing that it must come to grips with the ills of industrialism. The (bad) classical liberals were nobly overthrown by the "proto-progressives" who first elaborated "the general welfare state" and who, in every regard, were the antithesis of their predecessors.[15] As this work has demonstrated, the sharp distinction between the so-called classical and progressive liberals cannot be sustained.

Indeed, during the first two decades of the twentieth century, many of the projects of Gilded Age liberal reform won legislative and administrative enactment, even though many of the founding liberal reformers were dead. Tariff legislation enacted in 1913 and 1916 accomplished everything that the liberal free trade movement had sought. The Federal Reserve System, one of the quintessential and most enduring acts of national progressive legislation, had direct roots in the liberal currency reform movement that dated from the 1870s. If we consider how little the antimonopolists and inflationists won in the new banking system, the significance of the long reach of liberal reform becomes even greater.[16] Conversely, some of the relics of the alleged old liberalism, viewed as barriers to progressive reform, were in fact equally rejected by liberal reformers. Thomas M. Cooley, who "supplied . . . a legal ideology" to "laissez faire capitalism" according to one of our classic legal histories, spent the last ten years of his life fighting the federal judiciary's interpretation of his doctrines of substantive due process and vested rights. As the first chairman of the ICC and a proponent of government mediation of labor conflicts, he discerned the need for a more powerful administrative state to address the consequences of economic development. He devoted himself to the elaboration of administrative law, through which the power of economic regulation would be removed from the courts and legislature and placed in executive administrative agencies. In that project, he aided the removal of questions of economic regulation from more direct popular scrutiny and control, even as he promoted a modern active state.[17]

The impact of liberal reform on state-level progressive politics is also evident. In some cities, the reform clubs that had been created by liberals in their quest for efficient, cheap, and uncorrupted government remained in existence, and some of the early members survived to participate in coalitions with progressives. The relative strengths and weaknesses of the different groups determined whose vision of reform would triumph. Nevertheless, many reforms that seemed to some progressives to promise a more expansive democracy, such as the Australian Ballot and the direct primary, were actively supported by surviving liberal reformers, who viewed these measures as devices to limit political participation to the qualified.[18] In other cases, long-standing liberal critiques applied the brake to the more radical impulses of the era. For example, "municipalization" (the public ownership of public utilities) became wildly popular once urban middle-class consumers began to experience the indignities of private monopoly in the provision of public services. But when the old liberal reform canard about the incompetence and corruption of the civil service was trotted out—just as it had been in the parallel debates in the 1880s—the zest for municipal socialism withered. In all but a handful of cities, in lieu of public ownership, progressives chose to preserve private ownership and assign the regulation of public utilities to nonpartisan expert regulatory commissions. The failure of the movement for public ownership not only illustrates the limits of radical reform in the United States but also hints at one of its sources.[19]

In some cases, the influence of postbellum liberal reform in the Progressive Era resulted directly from the work of survivors among the generation of liberal reformers. No one dramatizes better the inadequacy of the conventional distinction between old classical and new progressive liberal than Carroll D. Wright. Wright was the first commissioner of labor in the United States, one of the only fields of social reform in which the United States took the lead internationally. When he retired from his position in 1905, having served for twenty uninterrupted years, in five presidential administrations, there was no one in the country who had done more to establish an administrative solution to the labor question.

Owing to Wright's position in the government and the relative congeniality of his ideas to moderate reform, he was remarkably successful in translating his ideas into reality. The report he wrote for the Pullman Strike commission established new parameters for the federal government's stance toward labor unions. Railroad legislation, from the Erdman Act of 1897 to the Adamson Act of 1916, incorporated a number of his specific proposals and, more generally, gave form to his animating assumptions about the relationship of railroads to the public, the purpose and form of government supervision and regulation, and the role to be played by responsible unions and consolidated industries. Wright served as President Theodore Roosevelt's point man in the anthracite coal strike (1902), the event in which Roosevelt's progressive labor policy of state neutrality, mediation, and the de facto recognition of conservative unionism was inaugurated. More indirectly, Wright's innovative analyses of overproduction and underconsumption helped lay the foundation for the emerging idea of an "American standard of living" that displaced traditional ideas of economic republicanism.[20]

In Wright's mature social thought and political practice, the legitimation of corporate capitalism, administrative governance, and consumerism came together in a profound and influential way.[21] As I suggested in the preceding chapter, his view of democracy was quite ambiguous. Whether Wright's true democratic yearnings fell victim to a naive faith in science and administration or whether his commitment to democracy was intrinsically more ambivalent is a question that is not resolved by his biographer and would require a thorough analysis of his private and published writings. I venture, however, that Wright's career illustrates the power wielded by liberal reformers and the alternatives that were closed off by their victories.

Wright, more than any single individual, defined and shaped national policy on the critical question of postbellum politics, the labor question. He had gained the opportunity to do so because liberal reformers and businessmen had decided that they did not appreciate the course that was being charted by the prolabor leaders of the nation's first labor bureau. The model of a nonpartisan agency, devoted primarily to statistical investigation by experts, that Wright pioneered in Massachusetts and promoted throughout the nation was neither the inevitable nor the only means by which governments could tackle the new issues of industrial labor. To the contrary, labor reformers had originally envisioned governmental labor commissions as an extension and complement to prolabor legislatures; bureaus were bodies in which workers were represented, and their job was to formulate prolabor legislation. Liberal reformers, in contrast, were convinced that legislators were too beholden to their constituents, and they advocated governance by expert administration as the means to win policies suitable to the developing capitalist economy. It is hardly surprising that, in 1884, when President Chester Arthur was required to appoint a commissioner to the new federal Bureau of Labor Statistics, he looked to Wright, who had already put the liberal reform model into practice to wide acclaim. For a brief time, an alternative model of state activism, based on a very different view of the relationship between policymaking and representation, had appeared viable. But ultimately, under the formative leadership of Wright, the liberal model that originated in the quest to constrain the power of labor reformers prevailed.[22]

The form, content, and objective of critical elements of progressive reform thus owe more to Gilded Age liberal reform and its antidemocratic designs than is generally recognized. Likewise, many of the social scientists who had participated in the postbellum reconstruction of liberalism remained active during the Progressive Era. They and their students produced scholarship relevant to contemporary politics and occupied the expert positions burgeoning in new government bureaucracies and private foundations through which modern liberalism was acquiring practical form.

Henry Carter Adams worked at the heart of the juncture of the new corporate economy and emerging regulatory state. From 1887 to 1911, he served as the head of the statistical division of the ICC, the only effective arm of an agency that had been crippled by Supreme Court decisions. He remained an advocate for strong state control of monopoly (short of public ownership) and believed that the rights and power of labor could be enhanced and institutionalized through the use of state power.[23] As I have suggested above, Adams retained his democratic commitments to a far greater degree than many of his colleagues and seems to have chosen the route of working from within to achieve gradual change. His career can be interpreted, nevertheless, as an illustration of the power of the antidemocratic compromise within new liberalism. He had achieved stature and political influence from a Faustian bargain, and the moral compromise took its toll. Whether or not Adams was correct that a more forceful use of state powers would have extended democracy in the workplace, his advice was not heeded. Despite a tremendous loyalty to the institutions of the administrative state, his investment yielded few dividends for the democratic cause. Instead, his lasting contribution to state regulation consisted of his day-to-day work for the ICC, in which he developed the statistical tools that facilitated the regulation of the railroad industry by expert commission. As a number of historians have observed, the knowledge produced by Adams could as easily be turned to rationalizing and stabilizing industry in ways desired by corporate owners and managers, even if that was not Adams's intention. If the new liberalism provided a critic such as Adams with the platform through which to raise a democratic critique, it just as thoroughly bounded a terrain in which even small dreams could not be fulfilled. It is perhaps worth noting as well that Adams took up the cause of business school education in the post-1896 settlement, believing that it could provide a conduit for stimulating democratic thinking and social responsibility in the new configuration of corporate management. It was another field in which he reaped the whirlwind.

John Bates Clark lived a long life, and during the Progressive Era his influence flowed through several channels. His 1899 *Distribution of Wealth* established him as the leading marginalist, neoclassical economic thinker in the nation, and thus his influence during these years resulted most importantly from the diffusion of his theories as the new common sense of economics. The historians of American social science and those of progressive politico-economic legislation agree on the importance of marginalism in progressive politics. On the one hand, it provided a theoretical foundation for the legitimation of corporate capitalism and state regulation. On the other, professional economists—many of them marginalists—played a disproportionately large role in progressive reform in their capacity as advisers, analysts, and regulators in civic and state commissions and agencies.[24]

Clark had always been a bellwether of political trends, so it is not surprising that before the turn of the century his scholarship had already begun to focus on the "trust question." He emerged as one of the most important theorists of corporate enterprise.[25] Clark received the opportunity to put his theories of corporate enterprise into practice in 1911, when the Roosevelt-aligned National Civic Federation appointed him to serve on its committee to draft trust legislation. Clark served with Jenks, the other leading expert on trusts; Seth Low, the president of the NCF; and Talcott Williams, an NCF leader and director of Columbia University's School of Journalism. Negotiating between the dictates of theory and the often conflicting interests of the different businesses within the NCF, Clark and his co-members recommended that Congress pass a corporate licensing act and charter an interstate trade commission with powers to compel publicity, review proposed mergers, and enforce its decisions. In short, Clark believed that the state should assume a strong regulatory power over all large corporations, through which the normal and legitimate market competition and combination of corporations would proceed and any unfair practices would be avidly policed. (In his 1914 *The Control of Trusts* he designated this approach "regulated competition.") It was a position very close to Theodore Roosevelt's ideas about good and bad trusts and the role of government, absent Roosevelt's suspicions of corporate power that had blossomed during the 1907 panic. Clark's view in the teens was perfectly consonant with the theories he had articulated in the nineties. Although the proposal of the NCF committee was not the one eventually chosen, it did exert significant influence during the debates over the Clayton Act and the Federal Trade Commission. Congress ultimately chose a less "statist" route. It is worth observing that the fact that the NCF business-dominated initiative proposed a stronger role for the state calls into question the assumption of Progressive Era antimonopolists and some contemporary historians that the more powerful the state role, the more democratic the result. At least to Clark, an authority we might trust, a strong state and corporate hegemony were compatible.[26]

Lest some raise the objection that Clark was not a progressive, it is important to note that Clark believed himself to be one. In a public lecture, later published as *Social Justice without Socialism*, he endorsed a wide panoply of progressive initiatives, including environmental conservation, the initiative and referendum, factory health and safety legislation, workmen's compensation, the regulation of the labor of women and children, banking reform, and the control of monopoly. Explaining that it was unlikely that socialism could ensure the perpetual increase of industrial productivity that was "the sole condition of a sound hope for the future of the wage-earner," he concluded that the "progressive paradise" must be won through reform without revolution.[27]

Other social scientists, especially economists, lent their services to the progressive state. Edwin R. A. Seligman emerged as the leading theorist of progressive taxation that gradually became incorporated into the income tax rates as the "preparedness" campaign commenced. The more conservative new economists Frank Taussig and Arthur Hadley were instrumental in tariff and railroad regulation, respectively. John Commons, who did more than anyone to link the scholarly analysis of "business unionism" to a new policy on the labor question, had studied with Richard T. Ely but deemed Adams the greatest influence over his thought. The list goes on. In sum, part of the explanation for the similarity between progressive statecraft and the ideas of the new liberalism of the nineties is that many of the intellectuals of the earlier period influenced the formulation of state policy. It is critical to underscore that these men had formed their ideas and opinions in the Gilded Age social struggle, in which certain options were closed off. To the degree that the college-educated, and particularly social scientists, were instrumental in progressive politics and culture, the strengths, weaknesses, and compromises of Gilded Age social thinkers must be acknowledged as the legacy with which their followers had to contend.[28]

Just as ideas that had arisen in the postbellum decades found expression in Progressive Era state policy, so too did ideas formulated during the Gilded Age in modernizing businesses seep into the broader political culture of the Progressive Era. It became commonplace in the Progressive Era to apply business standards of efficiency to government. It was most obvious in the vogue for scientific management that swept through progressive circles after 1910. Close to forty years ago, when the view of the progressives as democratic heroes still prevailed, the historian Stephen Haber made a compelling case that the popularity of scientific management and the related "efficiency craze" revealed important antidemocratic tendencies in the progressive movement. Haber's conclusion retains its force today. "If [equality and rule by the people] could not with ease be attacked frontally, they could be outflanked—and this most successfully when almost inadvertently. 'Let the people rule' is, in part, a rhetorical phrase. Exactly how one lets the people rule is decisive. The progressives who greeted efficiency with enthusiasm were often those who proposed to let the people rule through a program in which the bulk of the people, most of the time, ruled hardly at all."[29]

Scientific management was the brainchild of Frederick Winslow Taylor, an engineer in the steel industry, in which consolidating capital faced a powerful craft union. It burst into public view in 1911, when Harper and Row published Taylor's popularization of the technique, *The Principles of Scientific Management*, and Louis Brandeis lent it practical political weight in the important *Eastern Rate Case* before the Interstate Commerce Commission and a House committee opened investigations into its use and impact in government works.[30] The congruence between Taylor's esoteric system of management and certain tendencies in progressive thought can be seen by looking first at Taylor's writings.

"Taylorism" was a product of the class conflict of the Gilded Age. Taylor's technical studies were suffused with political concerns like those of the professional economists of his generation—who, not incidentally, republished his first paper of 1895 in a special issue of the American Economic Association journal.[31] As a number of historians have argued, one of Taylor's primary objectives was to shift the balance of power in industry from labor to capital by eliminating skilled workers' control of the pace and output of production.[32] Taylor championed his science of "management," however, by promising that it would solve the labor question and restore social harmony. The greater efficiency to be gained once engineers, wielding the methods of science, ruled the factory would usher in the age of plenty, simultaneously fulfilling the yearnings of the public and the true interests of the individual worker. Taylor dangled before his readers the temptation of a world free of conflict and want, should scientific management be adopted. "Think of what this means to the whole country. Think of the increase, both in the necessities and luxuries of life, which becomes available for the whole country, of the possibility of shortening the hours of labor when this is desirable, and of the increased opportunities for education, culture, and recreation which this implies." For employers and "workmen," even more, it would mean "the elimination of almost all causes for dispute and disagreement." Just as the hours question would be transcended as science impartially pronounced what constituted a "fair day's work," so too would the wages question, as rising productivity would lift wages beyond imagination.[33] His main audience of engineers and corporate managers discerned the usefulness of the method in union busting, even if Taylor repeatedly asked them to take a higher view of the matter.

Whether or not we take Taylor's utopian claims at face value, a more explicit claim that social justice and order issued from the rule of experts and the promise of consumerism could hardly be imagined. Taylor, of course, also formulated his program within the large corporation, and his techniques had no relevance outside it. The question remains, How influential was Taylorism or scientific management? During the Progressive Era, employers launched a drive to adopt its practices, and by the 1920s, although many of the specific elements of Taylorism proved unworkable in industry, a broader form of systematic management prevailed in American corporate industry.[34] In that sense, it played a critical role in the corporate reconstruction of American industry. But that was not its only triumph, for scientific management gained prestige in progressive social thought in the teens, when the desires and designs of many middle-class progressives converged on the ideal of "social efficiency." Among the more prominent enthusiasts of scientific management were Louis Brandeis, Herbert Croly, and Walter Lippman.[35]

The attraction some progressives felt toward scientific management suggests that Taylor had helped give form and content to more inchoate sentiments. Since the Gilded Age debate over municipal governance, liberal political intellectuals had held up the efficient business as the model for a properly functioning government. Social questions had been redefined as technical questions, each equally amenable to engineering. Likewise, Taylorism not only drew from and reinforced the "cult of the expert," through which many currents of American thought ran, but also served to embed it in bourgeois culture.[36] Taylor rested his case for expert rule on the superior knowledge of the engineer; it did much to ingrain the obverse notion, that workers were ignorant brutes, incapable of the higher calling of management. Although disdain for manual labor had run deep in antebellum American culture, it had always faced the countervailing force of ideas shared across class divides, such as Jacksonianism and free labor ideology. Taylorism, and its adoption by progressive intellectuals, translated the old hierarchies of mind and body into a modern idiom. Subsequently, the prospects for a robust faith in a "mass" democracy were not promising. It does not, however, require the hindsight of ideological analysis to discern the implications of the appeal of scientific management for American democracy. Workers of the Progressive Era almost universally condemned and resisted it, charging forcefully that larger questions of self-rule were at stake.[37]

Intellectuals engaged in formulating bodies of practical knowledge—policy-oriented social science and business management—thus transmitted the ideas and assumptions of Gilded Age new liberalism to progressive culture and politics. These intellectuals were technical experts, and their prominence during the Progressive Era is indicative of a shift in the sociology of intellectual production. The typical intellectual of mid-nineteenth-century America had been a critic, a publicist, and a man of political influence. Men such as Godkin, George W. Curtis, White, Wells, and Charles F. Adams were cultured gentlemen who often were as at ease in commenting on economic affairs and theory as they were in literary criticism, and they enjoyed a practical political and cultural influence because of their cultural attainments. Until the 1880s, intellectuals could reflect on society in a critical manner as well as pursue the practical implementation of their ideas—and there were few others with the qualifications and stature to challenge their prerogatives. After the 1880s, the social role of the intellectual was split in two: on one side were the experts; on the other, the critics. Various forces—such as the modernization of university education, the specialization and professionalization of the social sciences, and the expansion of white-collar employment—combined to render the new experts a narrower breed than their predecessors. Yet it is also clear that the practical political influence of the expert social scientists increased significantly in the Progressive Era and after, as government bureaus and private research institutions proliferated.

One of the ironies of Progressive Era historiography is that the technical experts who played such a large role in the practical transformation of business and governance have received far less attention than the critical thinkers of progressivism.[38] The fruits of Progressive Era critical social thought were indeed bounteous. Legal realism, the social gospel, the philosophy of pragmatism, cultural modernism, and feminism were but some of the products, and the originality and luster of the ideas surely are reasons why latter-day intellectuals swarm like moths at the source. But it is also true that the critics of the Progressive Era seem to have accomplished something that present-day intellectuals admire and might wish to re-create. Historians generally portray these men and women as people who acted in a principled way and at the same time were able to brew practical influence out of their penetrating perceptions. (A frequently bruited expression, "critically engaged intellectuals," trades on the dual sense of critical: using the faculty of intellect to accomplish important work.) But in the appreciation of the accomplishments of our forebears, interpreters have perhaps avoided some more troubling conclusions. I would argue that by broadening the intellectual history of the Progressive Era to include the technical experts, affinities among the critics and experts are revealed that call into question the greater prominence of the critics in progressive scholarship, as well as the generally accepted portrait of them.

An examination of Herbert Croly and Walter Lippman, the editors of the *New Republic* and two of the most significant progressive social theorists, can illuminate these issues of ideology and influence. In contrast to other progressive thinkers who are typically included in discussions of progressive thought, they acted principally as "critics," not as intellectuals (like John Dewey), activists (like Jane Addams), or policy theorists (like John R. Commons).[39] Croly and Lippman, in addition, hold a distinctive place in the historiography of progressive political thought. They have generally been treated as both innovators and representatives of the most advanced democratic tendencies in progressivism or new liberalism. Specifically, their strong defense of a powerful national state is perceived as a bold social democratic route not taken. The focus on the two men is deserved because, in contrast to many of their counterparts among progressive social reformers and theorists, a case can be made that they had a discernible impact on politics. They were advisers to Roosevelt throughout his "New Nationalism" phase. As the European war and the return of the Republicans to Old Guard conservatism proceeded between 1914 and 1916, the *New Republic* shifted the weight of its growing influence to Wilson. Lippman wrote campaign speeches and hit the stump himself for the politician he had once derided as a narrow and anachronistic thinker.[40] More than any other progressives, they articulated the progressive case for the U.S. entry into World War I and, in its aftermath, the progressives' profound disillusionment. Whether they are seen as models of the democratic public intellectual, visionaries of a postmodern democratic politics, or tragic figures in the barbarous history of nationalism, Croly and Lippman are considered central figures in the history of twentieth-century liberalism.[41] The extent of their democratic commitments and the extent of their practical influence are questions, however, that merit revisiting.

In the way Croly and Lippman sought to join intellectual ambition and political influence, their progressive careers are most parallel to the Gilded Age liberal reform publicists. Croly and Lippman wrote four of the most renowned books of progressive social thought, but they made their mark primarily through the day-to-day shaping of intelligent public opinion. Their *New Republic* was to progressive social reformers what Godkin's *Nation* was to Gilded Age liberal reformers. Like Wells, White, Curtis, and Charles Adams, Croly and Lippman were intimate with the politically powerful, to whom they dispensed practical political advice. But, like Adams, Clark, Ely, and their colleagues, they received their education in modernizing universities from mentors and scholars who sought to overthrow the regnant intellectual systems. The intermediate position they chose had much to do with their conception of the relationship between ideas and politics and something to do with personal temperament and ambition.[42]

Croly and Lippman, who were twenty years apart in age, were both natives of New York City, and each returned to the city after college, attracted by the opportunities for intelligent, ambitious men provided by the nation's capital of publishing and cosmopolitanism. In the first two decades of the century, New York City was a breeding ground of progressive social thought as well as the central station of American radicalism. Lippman at first plunged joyfully into the world of the radicals as a self-proclaimed crusading socialist. After graduating from Harvard, where he had founded the Socialist Club, he served as Lincoln Steffens's assistant in muckraking the financial trust and then parlayed the influence into a position as the assistant to the Socialist mayor of Schenectady. He gave it up after four months, publicly complaining of the tepid reformism of the socialists in office, but, personally, he was more bored than incensed. In the summer of 1912, he nursed his intellectual ambitions and focused his idealism in a cabin in Maine and rode out of the pines with his first book, *A Preface to Politics*. Published in the spring of 1913, it made a splash among Bull Moose Progressives and Greenwich Village Bohemians and earned the twenty-three-year-old Lippman the national and international reputation he craved. In 1913, he immersed himself deeply in the crusades and fascinations of the Village radicals. He marched in protest at the side of Big Bill Haywood and Emma Goldman and rallied the striking textile workers in Paterson. He became the confidante of Mable Dodge, helping her bring rigor and order to her Greenwich Village salon, where anarchists, feminists, socialists, Wobblies, and the avant-garde communed to make revolution and shatter Victorian mores.[43]

In mid-1914, personality, philosophy, and politics converged to bid Lippman to part company with the radicals with whom he had shared many heady evenings. Other prospects beckoned more brightly. In the fall of 1913, Croly had asked Lippman to join him in editing a new magazine, designed to provide a forum for advanced social thought and a platform for Rooseveltian Progressives. Croly himself had come to national attention in 1909 with *The Promise of American Life*, an impassioned theoretical exploration of how the democratic ideal at the heart of the American promise might be fulfilled. The nearly five-hundred-page book of tortuous Victorian prose was far from a best-seller, but influential people read it and were impressed. Croly's ideas about the economy, the state, culture, and patriotism were close to those of Theodore Roosevelt, and the former president appeared in the book as the exemplar of the heroic, disinterested, and exceptional democratic leader. Roosevelt appreciated the theoretical grounding it lent his politics—and the flattery. He adapted Croly's call for a "new nationalism" as the slogan for his return to the electoral fray and sought Croly's personal counsel. The attention won by the book elevated the reputation of the then unknown middle-aged architectural critic. (The national hubbub about the book shamed Harvard into awarding a degree to the forty-one-year-old Croly, who had wandered in and out of classes from 1886 to 1897 without ever completing the graduation requirements.) Croly's intellectual credentials and new political influence made him a logical choice for the editorship of the *New Republic*, financed by a Morgan banker and Rockefeller heiress who deemed it wise to "use your wealth to put ideas into circulation." Croly won editorial independence from his financial angels and sought as well to establish an independent voice, declaring, "We shall be radical without being socialistic." In due course, he would be neither. When he sought a staff of editors and writers for the magazine, it is not surprising that he approached Lippman. Despite their difference in age and personality, Lippman and Croly were natural allies. Croly had been impressed by the young writer's first book. No doubt his admiration was piqued by Lippman's acknowledged debt to his own idea of a nationalized democracy. The two writers also shared an intellectual universe, both having devoted themselves to philosophy at Harvard under William James and George Santayana.[44]

In his second and even more influential book, *Drift and Mastery* (1914), Lippman declared, "The battle for us . . . does not lie against crusted prejudice, but against the chaos of a new freedom."[45] Attacking the Democratic Party of William Jennings Bryan and Woodrow Wilson and underscoring the uncertainty of modernity, Lippman anatomized the temperament of true progressive social reform.

> There is a growing body of opinion which says that communication is blotting out village culture, and opening up national and international thought. It says that bad as big business is to-day, it has a wide promise within it, and that the real task of our generation is to realize it. It looks to the infusion of scientific method, the careful application of administrative technique, the organization and education of the consumer for control, the discipline of labor for an increasing share of the management. Those of us who hold such a belief are pushed from behind by what we think is an irresistible economic development, and lured by a future which we think is possible.

Lippman derided the narrow vision of those who hoped to restore a world of individualism and competition. In doing so, he in effect rejected the variant of progressive social reform most indebted to the producerist ideology of the farmer and labor movements of the nineteenth century. The promise of progress, however, depended critically on the fostering of a particular mentality, in which democracy and science must combine: "We don't imagine that the trusts are going to drift naturally into the service of human life. We think that they can be made to serve it if the American people compel them. We think the American people may be able to do that if they can adjust their thinking to a new world situation, if they apply the scientific spirit to daily life, and if they learn to coöperate on a large scale. Those to be sure, are staggering *ifs*."[46]

Would democracy bring drift or mastery? At the height of Lippman's progressive enthusiasm, he suggested that democracy informed by the scientific temper could yield a socialized democracy. Croly shared the faith. They derived their conception of the "scientific spirit" from the philosophy of pragmatism. Formulated in the last two decades of the nineteenth century, the philosophy of pragmatism became widely diffused among the American educated class in the Progressive Era. As one progressive put it, "We were all Deweyites before we read Dewey."[47] The theorists of pragmatism, William James, John Dewey, and Charles Pierce, were at work at the same time that economists, sociologists, and historians were all seeking new paradigms and professionalizing their disciplines. Pragmatism was thus one of the new bodies of knowledge, and, as in the other disciplines, its practitioners consciously sought to overthrow old systems seen as theoretically untenable and socially conservative. As a unified philosophical theory, pragmatism necessarily addressed questions of epistemology and ethics—subjects that, for the purposes of this analysis, can be bracketed. As a foundation for political theory and practice, pragmatism gave warrant to an expansive vision of democracy with its linkage of the ideal of individual self-realization, the analysis of the social embeddedness of the individual, and the method of experimental science. Pragmatism jolted young intellectuals such as Lippman and Croly out of inherited Victorian folkways, as well as tempering convictions of their own superiority that had been bred in them by parents and schools. It turned them, for a time, into ardent democrats.[48]

Although Croly and Lippman most often described the scientific method in pragmatist terms, their adulation of science had other sources as well. In Lippman's case, the uncommonly brilliant style masked the war between William James and Frederick Winslow Taylor that was being waged within. For several years at the height of the social ferment of the Progressive Era, Lippman's convictions about the veracity of the philosophy he had learned personally from James made him democracy's evangelist. But he was also a devotee of Taylorism, and *Drift and Mastery* was as much a hymn to the virtues of expertise and science as it was a credo of pragmatist democracy.[49] It helped that technocratic rule and democratic results could appear compatible in Taylor's rendering of scientific management. Taylor, who claimed to have found the path to industrial harmony through efficiency and abundance, helped Lippman to phrase his inherited cultural elitism in a modern and more popular key, while pragmatism endowed science with a universal and democratic character. But the democratic faith born of pragmatism was vulnerable on several counts. "Mastery," the solution to the ills of the modern world, could be gained through the cultivation of a democratic public skilled in the experimental method and the worldview of doubt. The tension, however, between public mastery via the pragmatic method and the mastery of the public by the pragmatist elite persisted. Lippman oscillated between the two possibilities. He projected a special educational mission for the scientific elite in democratic education, yet the internal ambiguity in the pragmatic notion of stewardship lent force to long-cultivated elitist sentiments. Should the people prove resistant to their education, surely the technically expert must assume command of the administration of government.[50]

Perhaps even more corrosive of the democratic spirit of pragmatism was the solution it offered to the psychic and social crisis besetting the educated middle class in the modern world. Pragmatism provided an intellectually compelling philosophy for a world shorn of faith and certainty. Yet, in addition, its revival of the old idea of individual authority and moral stewardship in the figure of the adept experimental scientist bestowed new authoritative social roles on a class put in limbo by the consolidating economy and modern politics. Croly made a persuasive case for a nationalized democracy, in which individual self-realization would be won through service to the "collective purpose." In theory, pragmatism envisioned the cultivation of a democratic public and the self-realization of all persons. A critic of economic inequality and a defender of the union worker, Croly was nevertheless most solicitous to the plight of the man with ability in a commercialized democracy. Disinterested service in the task of social reconstruction, through pragmatic methods, would give meaning and purpose to the life of the exceptional individual, whom the existing culture and practice of American democracy crushed. With the help of Santayana, who had unabashedly called for a "government of men of merit," Croly alchemized pragmatism into a rationale for the dominance of a meritocratic elite. "The disinterested and competent individual is formed for constructive leadership," Croly asserted, "just as the less competent and independent, but well-intentioned, individual is formed more or less faithfully to follow on behind. Such leadership, in a country whose traditions and ideals are sincerely democratic, can scarcely go astray."[51] "Men of superior merit" would assume their rightful places as managers of consolidated enterprises, as "critics" and artists, as political leaders and governmental administrators. To be a progressive was to serve one's ambition as one served the cause of social reform. Lippman, characteristically, had his feet planted more firmly on the ground. "The intelligent men of my generation can find a better outlet for their energies than in making themselves masters of little businesses," he wrote, mocking Wilson for his outmoded vision of entrepreneurial individualism. "They have the vast opportunity of introducing order and purpose into the business world, of devising administrative methods by which the great resources of the country can be operated on some thought-out plan. They have the whole new field of industrial statesmanship before them."[52]

Whether pragmatism is compromised by an inherently ambiguous conception of democracy or whether Lippman and Croly were insufficiently pragmatic is a question still debated. It seems clear, nevertheless, that even in their most expansive vision of democracy, the two progressive editors were bedeviled by a problem John Stuart Mill had long before identified at the core of liberal democracy: how to achieve efficient administration and scope for the activity of the superior individual under majoritarian democracy. Even though pragmatism suggested the most egalitarian solution imaginable to the conflict—that the scientific temper could be cultivated in everyone—Lippman and Croly leaned toward the administrative resolution of the problem. A reformed, progressive government would give expression to expertise and preferment to the experts. The infirmity of American democratic institutions could be cured by superseding the old ways of electoral politics with the new means of administration. While he was writing *Drift and Mastery*, Lippman gave expression to the significance of administration to the progressives. "The winter of 1914 is an important change for me. . . . Perhaps I have grown conservative. At any rate I find less and less sympathy with the revolutionists—with English Walling and Max Eastman—and an increasing interest in administrative problems. I come definitely nearer to the Progressives."[53] Radicals and "Progressives" parted company on the means and ends of politics. Just as differences over collective action and socialism had been the fulcrum of the Gilded Age debate, so too did one of the finest minds of the Progressive Era identify these issues as the pivot on which one's political allegiance turned. Although there was a dialogue between radicals and progressives in the first decades of the century, Lippman's reflection reminds us of the lines that were drawn between them.

The similarity between Lippman and Croly's linkage of science, expertise, and governance and the administrative mandate of the postbellum intellectuals is striking.[54] On a number of other issues, as well, their ideas closely resembled those that had emerged out of the postbellum debate between liberal reformers and social scientists. A strong and activist national state should steer a middle course between socialism and conservatism; reform, not revolution, was the order of the day. In Croly's famous formula, "Hamiltonian means" should be harnessed to "Jeffersonian ends"; the powerful state would not be socialistic but rather "unscrupulously and loyally nationalistic" with "the deepest interest in the development of a higher quality of individual self-expression."[55] For Lippman, intelligent mastery must triumph over the drift of the anachronistic individualism of the antimonopolists and the panaceas of the radicals.[56] Both agreed that the corporate revolution of the economy was inevitable and desirable and that management of the economy should be left in private hands under governmental regulation. Experience would determine if some industries should be subject to greater public control, but the relative talent of corporate managers as compared with public officials suggested that the resort to public ownership should be rare and confined to "natural monopolies." Efficiency, rational administration, and material abundance would eliminate inequality without revolution or forced redistribution. Collectively organized capital and labor were legitimate political actors, but society, acting through the government, had an obligation to define the rules of collective behavior. The narrower self-interest of labor and capital, in any event, would be counteracted by consumers, collectively organized into a new force of the public interest.[57] In the heady years between Roosevelt's adoption of the "New Nationalism" and Wilson's practical adaptation of the "New Freedom" into an advanced progressive program, optimism about the coming triumph of scientific mastery was joined to a faith in its democratic results.

Just as the new liberals of the late nineteenth century had done, Croly and Lippman legitimated the rise of corporate capitalism and looked to administrative governance to achieve social reform and guarantee social peace and progress. Their view of a new individualism, however, was both more profound and more complicated than the consuming individualism articulated by Clark and others and that was emerging as the practical reality of the new phase of capitalism. They subscribed to a more thoroughly socialized view of human beings and welcomed the collectivization of social life in ways that would have been astounding to the Victorians of both generations of postbellum liberals. Their criticisms of bourgeois manners and aesthetics, of the stultifying gender roles of the bourgeois family, of masculine acquisitiveness and patriarchalism and feminine domesticity and fecundity, were a measure of the truly new currents of thought in the Progressive Era: feminism, cultural modernism, and pragmatism. The differences were important, and I do not seek to minimize them. Nevertheless, Croly and Lippman considered themselves liberals, and they did so because of a classically liberal concern over the danger posed to the individual by collectivism and statism.[58] The new individualism they valued was the capacity and right of all persons to realize their life's goals. This ideal of self-realization, rooted in a long-standing tradition in Western thought of human beings as producers and actors, in fundamental ways rejected the emergent consumerist ideology. Self-realization, not self-satisfaction, was what mattered. Even as the consumer was a central figure in their revision of the body politic, it provided a new model for political activity rather than an excuse for a narrowed politics. During their pragmatist and progressive years, Lippman and Croly eschewed the materialistic and de-politicized version of consuming individualism and, in doing so, articulated a deeper and more liberating vision of progressive liberal democracy.

The egalitarian rendering of self-realization came to Lippman and Croly from pragmatism, and it is undeniable that pragmatism for a time infused progressive social theory with a more profound democratic substance than that encompassed in the new liberalism forged in the postbellum debates. By the early 1920s, however, Lippman, Croly, and many other progressives were apostates of the pragmatist philosophy and skeptics about democracy.[59] Old voices beckoned to those disappointed equally by Wilson's wartime abandonment of progressive ideals and the supposed irrationality of the American and European masses. Lippman heard Santayana's Cassandra-like prophecies of the failings of the masses. His *Public Opinion* (1922) was one of the sharpest indictments of democracy penned by a liberal in the twentieth century. Gone was the criticism of private property that had informed his acceptance of corporate dominance; abandoned was the vision of a rational public organized collectively to achieve mastery. His devastating critique of guild socialism, the most promising theory of industrial democracy then existing, laid to rest for good the youthful socialist ghost that had once spirited his progressive optimism.[60] Ironically, his reconception of the public as an undifferentiated mass, gullibly consuming whatever falsehoods were peddled to them, accepted some of the more negative premises of the new liberals' consuming individualism than pragmatism had allowed. No more profound repudiation of pragmatism was imaginable than Lippman's notion that only a knowledgeable elite could save civilization from the misapprehensions of reality by the irrational democratic masses.

World war and the revival of conservative Republicanism obviously took their toll on progressive intellectuals. But the resort to an administrative counter against a democratic public had its precedents, which suggests that the postwar position was not only a reaction against circumstances. The many similarities—even before the shocks of world war—between the progressive program of Lippman and Croly and the new liberalism forged in the Gilded Age suggest that the *New Republic* editors came to progressivism with some ideas already formed. Or, to put it more theoretically, the affinities give evidence of the emergence of a new hegemonic liberal ideology. The exact means through which Lippman and Croly acquired their ideas would require a biographical investigation beyond the scope of these concluding speculations. It seems reasonable to observe, at least, that the new liberalism had circulated freely within the social milieu of the cultured upper middle class of Manhattan and Harvard in which the two were raised and educated. I would suggest that Lippman and Croly inherited a social philosophy that was the product of the postbellum liberal debates and that it rendered them susceptible to cynicism about democracy when they faced the inevitable disappointments of practical politics.[61]

The *New Republic* progressives were not the only progressive "critical" intellectuals, nor did their interpretation of fundamental political questions represent the only possibility for progressive social reformers. Even among those whose progressivism was also rooted in the philosophy of pragmatism and who contributed to the magazine, there were significant differences. For example, John Dewey and Jane Addams denounced corporate economic power, sought to extend democratic participation in civil society and in politics, advocated an active state as a means to create a more substantive and equal democracy, warned of the bureaucratic and hierarchical implications of governance by experts, and sought to replace individualism with a true social ethic. Similar values and ideas animated many leaders of the social gospel movement, some of whom were also pragmatists.[62] Even though Dewey, Addams, and others shared in the dream of the special destiny of the educated elite, the relative absence of the technocratic fantasy placed them to the democratic left of intellectuals such as Croly and Lippman. It is thus clear that some progressives dissented from the new liberalism's legitimation of corporate capitalism, apotheosis of the consumer, and depoliticization of social life, even if they did tragically share in some of the assumptions.[63] I would argue, nonetheless, that among the dozen or so critical intellectuals generally identified as the leading progressive thinkers, Croly and Lippman were the ones who had the greatest success in translating their ideas into political influence. When all is said and done, however, in comparison with the policymaking social scientists ensconced in proliferating government agencies, even Lippman and Croly's practical power was quite limited.[64]

Part of the fascination with political intellectuals, by intellectuals, is that they seem to provide us with deeper insight into the society of their day. We go to them when we seek the underlying logic of a political movement or repressed possibilities that might have philosophical or practical relevance to our own problems. But as most intellectual historians would concede, if we wish to understand the success or failure of their program, we must look to the seats of power. Modern liberalism was not only a body of social thought but also the product of the Progressive Era's innovations in statecraft, and much of the historical interest in it derives from the recognition of its importance in twentieth-century American politics. After an examination of the historiography of the Progressive Era, the impact of liberal reform in progressive politics, the activity of social scientists in Progressive Era governance, and certain currents of progressive social thought, the final question remaining concerns the institutionalization of new liberalism in progressive politics. The careers of Roosevelt and Wilson, the presidents who inaugurated modern American liberalism in national politics, give powerful evidence of the political significance of the Gilded Age reconstruction of American liberalism.[65]

Roosevelt, born in 1858, was the contemporary of the ethical economists. He graduated from Harvard in 1880, but despite his proclivities to intellectual endeavor, his education affected him little, for the college had not yet taken up the modernizing tendencies of the day.[66] At the age of twenty-three, Roosevelt published his first of many books and was also elected to the New York State Assembly from his home district in New York City. He entered public service wholly committed to the ideals and practical programs of the liberal reformers. He believed it was the social duty of the "best men" to serve the public; he disdained the rank materialism of the "plutocracy" and feared the leveling tendencies of the uninformed masses. He favored civil service reform and rule by the elite and devoted himself to checking the class legislation of labor. But Roosevelt parted company with the "independent" liberal reformers on questions of political strategy. The story of his break with them is familiar: his experience in the legislature persuaded Roosevelt that "independence" from the Republican Party was quixotic and that the drive for reform must be conducted from within. Instead of joining the mugwump bolt to the Democrat Grover Cleveland in 1884, he led the New York State Republican delegation. Once the bright hope of the liberal reform movement, Roosevelt became their Judas. Nevertheless, despite the personal antagonism that grew between Roosevelt and many reformers (especially Godkin), Roosevelt remained largely true to the liberal reform agenda even as he grew into the consummate political administrator. After his sorry third-place showing in the famous mayoral race against Henry George, he continued in public service through appointment to several of the administrative bodies that were proliferating by the 1880s. He was chosen to serve on President Benjamin Harrison's civil service commission; he was appointed commissioner of the nonpartisan New York City board of police; and in McKinley's first term, he became assistant secretary of the navy. His exploits with the Rough Riders at San Juan Hill—and his self-promotion—catapulted him into the national limelight and into contention for top political offices. It also helped establish him as one of the nation's most influential imperialists.[67]

Roosevelt's popularity and his continuing association with the New York independents won him the Republican nomination for the New York governor's race in 1898. It was during his term as governor that he began to marry the liberal program of efficient, nonpartisan, elite rule to progressive causes. Roosevelt attributed his discovery of the "social question" to his partnership as police commissioner with the photographer and reformer Jacob Riis.[68] During his governorship, he promoted virtually all the measures that would come to define state-level progressivism: civil service reform; environmental conservation; corporate taxation; and labor legislation including factory inspection, the creation of a tenement house commission, the regulation of sweatshops, safety and hours legislation for railroad workers, the regulation of women's and children's labor, workmen's compensation, and the eight-hour day.[69] His success at gaining a number of these reforms threatened to destroy the New York Republican Party machine by striking at its lifeline to big business. In 1900, the party boss of New York, in order to stave off another term in which the party's perquisites would be further eroded, maneuvered Roosevelt onto the second spot on McKinley's ticket. Party considerations won out over the better judgment of Mark Hanna, the mastermind of McKinley's campaign, who warned, "Don't any of you realize that there's only one life between that madman and the Presidency?"[70]

Roosevelt's ascension to the presidency in 1901, on the assassination of McKinley, coincided with the "Great Merger Movement" in American industry and the consequent rise of the "trust problem" as the principal social question of the day. It was evident from Roosevelt's first public addresses as president that his position on the "trust question" was fully consonant with the political economy of new liberalism that the U.S. Industrial Commission report would articulate the following year. (Indeed, the lead economist on the USIC, Jenks, had served as Roosevelt's adviser during his governorship.) No individual did more than Roosevelt to shift the terms of national political debate about the trust question. We need not enter into the details of Roosevelt's methods of regulating trusts, as it has been amply documented elsewhere. It is well known that he viewed "combination" as "necessary and inevitable" and made the distinction between good and "evil" corporations the linchpin of his policy. He thought that the 1890 Sherman Act's attempt to restore competition, and its strict interpretation by the courts, was disastrous, even as he selectively employed it to strike at the most egregious violators of fair business practices. He sought not to destroy corporations or labor unions but rather to establish an efficient national control over them to prevent the "evil" practices in which some engaged. The power of congressional conservatives and anti-monopolists, as well as his temperamental dedication to rule by the elite, led him to circumvent Congress through executive agencies and to elaborate the as yet untapped powers of the presidency. He strengthened executive branch agencies, especially the Bureau of Labor, the Department of the Interior, and the ICC, encouraging their heads to investigate, regulate, and intervene. Upon his demand, Congress chartered the cabinet-level Department of Commerce and Labor, under which the Bureau of Corporations was created and through which his administration sought to work with corporate leaders to define the rules of the game. He parried Upton Sinclair's socialistic muckraking of the "beef trust," *The Jungle*, into eminently moderate health and safety regulation overseen by a newly created nonpartisan administrative agency. He exploited a less than monumental strike in the Eastern anthracite coal fields to establish a new federal approach to labor conflicts. Always alert to the danger that extremists on both ends of the class divide posed to the interests of the moderate middle, Roosevelt understood that the state could no longer be reflexively procapital. He put an end to the automatic dispatch of federal troops and instead sought to institutionalize permanent mechanisms for the government to oversee the mediation of conflicts between organized labor and organized capital. If his domestic approach to the preservation of social order was to "walk softly," affairs overseas more often called for the "big stick." Roosevelt's imperialistic bluster reflected his quest to brew social harmony out of the spirit of duty and nationalism, but his adventures, especially in Latin America, were undertaken with the interests of large business in mind.[71]

The trust question was the centripetal force in Roosevelt's presidency. Industrial growth and corporate consolidation created conditions demanding correction by social welfare legislation and governmental regulation; the virtual "sovereignty" inherent in consolidation and abused by some required sweeping political reforms to end the cycle of business's corruption of politics; the extremes of wealth it generated sowed class discord and national fragmentation, and the national government had to assume the lead in reform and the cultivation of a new spirit of public good over class interest. Measures that some progressives saw as a radical means to invigorate democracy, such as the initiative and referendum or the taxation of incomes and inheritances, were to Roosevelt moderate reforms that would preserve a fundamentally equitable and progressive economic system. The profound and idiosyncratic moralism of Roosevelt's approach also testified to his perception that "evolution" and "combination" had brought the nation to the brink of a new era. His notion of the "strenuous life," his belief that an imperialistic nationalism could be the solvent of social conflict, his preachments for the cultivation of masculine martial virtue and feminine rededication to birthing Anglo-American republican citizens—all can be interpreted as a projection of a new model of the moral self, a replacement for the bygone moral economy of entrepreneurial individualism. In this quality of his thought, Roosevelt was closer to the Victorian liberal reformers than to the modern salesmen of consumption (such as Clark and Jenks) who advised him on practical matters.

Roosevelt shared the procorporate, administrative, reformist worldview of the new liberals. He also worked closely with many liberal reformers and liberal social scientists and oversaw the institutionalization of some of the elements of their political program. Consistently, from his years as New York governor through his 1912 bid for the presidency at the head of a party of advanced middle-class progressives, he had believed "that reform is the antidote to revolution; and that social reform is not the precursor but the preventive of socialism."[72] He was convinced that he personally could rescue the Republicans from reactionaries and the progressives from reckless radicals. Had Roosevelt not been blocked by congressional conservatives during his presidency and opposed by party bosses in 1912, it is likely he would have done more to make new liberalism a going concern.

In the 1912 presidential race, American voters were presented with the choice of two progressives, a socialist, and a conservative. The Democrat, Woodrow Wilson, won because of the split in the Republican Party, not because his "New Freedom" was necessarily the most popular expression of reform sentiment. Wilson adopted progressive causes much later than did Roosevelt, and the circumstances in which he did so raise questions about the depth of his commitment. He emerged as an up-and-coming Democrat in 1909–10, after his much publicized fight for reform as president of Princeton University helped attract the attention of the party. Chosen by party leaders as their candidate for the governorship in his first entry into electoral politics, Wilson suddenly converted to progressive reform and pushed through one of the most ambitious progressive legislative programs in the country. With his proven political abilities and his reputation as a measured and respectable academic, Wilson was particularly appealing to moderate and conservative leaders of the party who chafed under the continued dominance of William Jennings Bryan. In a bruising convention battle, in which Wilson's backers maneuvered as well as any machine boss, Wilson became the Democrat's "progressive" candidate.[73]

There is fairly significant disagreement among historians about whether Wilson's progressivism was born of personal conviction or opportunism. According to some analysts, Wilson clarified and institutionalized the liberal variant of progressive social thought and in doing so was in concord with the fundamental sentiments of the American people.[74] According to others, Wilson's decision to push for virtually all the key demands of progressives grew out of calculations about how to keep himself and the Democratic Party in power—or, as Roosevelt observed, "Wilson is, I think, as insincere and cold-blooded an opportunist as we have ever had in the Presidency."[75] Even if Roosevelt's judgment was too harsh, political opportunism played a large part in Wilson's domestic progressivism. But, whatever his motives, the progressive legislation Wilson steered through Congress represented the institutionalization of modern American liberalism. His program also represented an accommodation to corporate hegemony and enhanced the administrative power of the national government in ways that facilitated the expansion of the corporate economic order.[76]

Although Wilson discovered progressive reform late in the game, his administrative and procorporate proclivities were long-standing. They originated directly in the debates in the 1880s among liberal reformers and social scientists, during which Wilson, as a political scientist, had been a minor contributor. Wilson, only five years younger than Henry C. Adams, earned his doctorate from Johns Hopkins seven years after Adams did. A peer of the ethical economists, a social scientist who shared much of their animating religious spirit, he was nevertheless closer in political sentiments to the more conservative thinkers among the young intellectuals and to the older liberal reformers. (A devoted reader of the *Nation*, he took notes in the margins and preserved his weekly copies.)[77] In his scholarship, the problem of the relationship between democracy and capitalism dominated his investigations. He was particularly attracted to the work of the historian Frederick Jackson Turner, whose theory of the frontier helped him phrase his own conviction that the critical questions facing the nation were "questions of economic policy chiefly." More in keeping with the fear of liberal reformers than with the enthusiasm of his peers, he proposed that the danger of democracy could be averted by removing governance from politics to the realm of administration, and he attacked the dominance of Congress over the other branches of the federal government. If modern administration might save democracy from itself, Wilson worried that other modern trends threatened to turn back the clock. As Wilson wrote, "Our own temperate blood, schooled to self-possession and to the measured conduct of self-government, is receiving a constant infusion and yearly experiencing a partial corruption of foreign blood: our own equable habits have been crossed with the feverish habits of the restless old world. We are unquestionably facing an ever-increasing difficulty of self command with ever-deteriorating materials, possibly with degenerating fibre." The new immigrants were erasing all the gains won by the "political evolution" of the "English race," thought Wilson in his own contribution to ascendant Darwinian racism. As one of his interpreters has noted, with his dichotomy between administration and politics, Wilson identified "a principled basis for checking the dangers to democracy—popular sovereignty, the spoilsmen, and the new immigrants—without simply destroying democracy."[78] As we have seen, the road on which he discovered the administrative solution was well traveled.

The major acts of legislation passed during Wilson's presidency give evidence that his fundamental notions of political organization and the importance of administration had not changed in his journey from Democratic conservative to the party's progressive standard-bearer. Ever wary of the close relationship between congressmen and the voters and the mediocrity of most legislators, Wilson sought to expand the powers of the presidency even further than did Roosevelt. Roosevelt had used the office as a "bully pulpit" and had recommended legislation to Congress; Wilson became intimately involved in crafting legislation and steering it through Congress. The major economic legislation of Wilson's first term—the Federal Reserve Act (1913), the Federal Trade Commission Act (1914), the Tariff Commission (1916)—displayed his preference for expert, nonpolitical administrative commissions.[79]

But to what ends did Wilson desire to regulate business through government administrative agencies? Contrary to the rhetoric of the "New Freedom" campaign of 1912, Wilson did not turn out to be a crusader for a return to small enterprise and competitive individualism. The hopes of the Bryanite wing of the Democratic Party that tariff reduction and antitrust legislation would destroy monopoly and that the income tax would redistribute income from the monopolists to the producers were dashed. If the tariff was the mother of trusts as antimonopolists liked to claim, Wilson's first legislative victory, the Underwood-Simmons Tariff (1913), ended special privileges that the trusts had enjoyed but did nothing to undermine consolidated industries. In recognizing that the stability and prosperity of American corporations depended on preserving a competitive position in international trade, and in adjusting government policy to the fact, tariff reform became part of the solution to "overproduction," as diagnosed by Wells.[80] Wilson's first income tax (made possible by the ratification of the Sixteenth Amendment before Wilson took office) was adopted to replace revenue lost to tariff reduction, not to meet the progressives' demands for progressive taxation. (Wilson later acceded to higher and progressive rates out of political necessity as war approached, not newfound egalitarianism.) The Bryanites also found themselves shut out of foreign policy, even though Bryan, the leading anti-imperialist, was appointed secretary of state. The interventionism of Wilson, in theory to defend the abstract freedom of trade, represented the underlying conviction that the national interest depended specifically on the international expansion of American corporations.[81]

In proposing trust legislation, Wilson explained to Congress, "The antagonism between business and Government is over. We are now about to give expression to the best business judgment of America, to what we know to be the business conscience and honor of the land. The Government and business men are ready to meet each other halfway in a common effort to square business methods with both public opinion and the law." To those who might doubt the moderation of his progressivism, he explained that he sought "nothing essential disturbed, nothing torn up by the roots, no parts rent asunder which can be left in wholesome combination." All agreed that "private monopoly" could not be tolerated.[82] What was called for was to specify what practices to prohibit, what powers a commission would hold. The Clayton Act (1914) settled the former, the Federal Trade Commission act (1914) the latter.

On banking legislation, on Wilson's prodding, Congress rejected the alternatives of a powerful, governmentally controlled central bank or an entirely private one and settled on a mix between public control and private management, lodged in a nonelective administrative agency dominated by experts mostly chosen by business. The Federal Reserve Act reorganized the national currency and banking system to achieve the "elasticity" and fiscal stability that reformers and businessmen had demanded since the depression of the seventies and that they believed would aid in the expansion of consolidated enterprises. The system ended the legislative meddling that, since the Civil War, had disturbed American capitalists; at the same time, they won state aid in easing the cyclical tendencies of the unfettered market and a guarantee—they thought—of stable growth.[83]

In less than two years, Wilson pushed through legislation that permanently settled three of the most contentious issues that had arisen with the transformation of the American economy: the tariff question, the money question, and the trust question. More tentatively, a resolution to the labor question was also in sight. The Clayton Act gave rhetorical endorsement to the right to unionize and strike, but it was in the realm of administrative government that the major innovations in labor policy occurred. Where Wilson had the opportunity to do so, he appointed prolabor advocates to government service, as in his choice of

William B. Wilson as secretary of labor and Frank P. Walsh as head of the U.S. Commission on Industrial Relations (CIR). In addition, the administration provided mediation services in labor conflicts, through which it deliberately promoted the responsible unionism of the American Federation of Labor as a counter to the radical Wobbly and socialist unions. The association of the AFL and the Democratic Party in the teens was in many ways a marriage of expedience. Nonetheless, there was much in common between Samuel Gompers's "pure and simple" business unionism and Wilson's brand of progressive reform.[84] The limits, however, could be glimpsed in the fate of the CIR. Issuing the most radical conclusions ever to come out of a government investigation, the CIR's majority report was ignored by the politicians—Wilson and Congress alike—who commissioned it.[85]

In 1914, after winning trust, tariff, and banking legislation, Wilson declined to attend to a whole host of progressive reforms—the abolition of child labor, woman suffrage, aid to farmers, and a broad spectrum of labor legislation—declaring, instead, that the New Freedom had been won. By the time Wilson embarked on the next wave of progressive reform in the winter of 1915–16, the outbreak of war in Europe had profoundly affected American domestic politics. Wilson's rediscovery of progressivism is only explainable in this particular political moment. Most important, Wilson needed to win over the advanced progressive constituency in order to triumph over a reunited Republican Party, but those voters only looked to him because Roosevelt had abandoned them to serve his more cherished cause of "preparedness." As many historians have documented, the administrative liberal state came into full flower during World War I. Even though many of the developments during the war years would, I think, support my interpretation of the character of modern liberalism—for example, the evolution of the regulative, propaganda, and administrative powers of the wartime state, the political resolution of a newly resurgent class conflict, the ideological construction of the national interest, the practical power in the wartime boards of corporate "dollar-a-year men"—the politics of wartime raise too many complicated questions to be dealt with adequately in the space remaining. And so, artificially but inevitably, this exploration of the influence of postbellum new liberalism over progressive liberal ideology and politics ends in the summer of 1914, when the most important and enduring domestic acts of Wilson's entire presidency had already been accomplished and war in Europe broke out.

In this survey of the Progressive Era, I have not intended to violate the now routine stricture against viewing "progressivism" as a unitary movement or a single ideology. But it is reasonable to pose the fundamental question of power: Who won, who lost, and what were the consequences? Antimonopolist producerists, the more radical social reform progressives, and the socialist radicals, all of whom fought for more democratic and radical changes to American society, lost. In contrast, virtually the entire program of Gilded Age liberal reform won legislative enactment, and the new liberal social scientists moved into the inner circles of power. The new liberalism, which originated among the two generations of postbellum liberal political intellectuals in their debate over the problem of the relationship between democracy and capitalism, was endorsed and promoted by many politically and culturally powerful progressives and, to a disproportionate degree, was politically institutionalized at the national level. The inauguration of the modern liberal state under Presidents Roosevelt and Wilson (and to a lesser degree, William H. Taft) promoted an administered democracy that secured corporate property against both democratic political challenge and the vagaries of the unregulated market and legitimated the dominance of corporate capital in American society. In the reconstitution and preservation of individualism, even as it accorded new legitimacy to the action of organized social forces, the new statecraft remained liberal.[86]

As I have attempted to demonstrate in this book, the fundamental question during the Gilded Age had concerned the meaning and content of democracy. In the first two decades of the twentieth century, the dividing line had continued to be between those who feared that democracy posed too many dangers to the institutions and practices of modern capitalism and those "radicals," socialists, and left social reformers who sought to limit (or abolish) capitalism in order to restore and expand democracy. The solution adopted in Progressive Era governance, which was inherited from the Gilded Age, was to circumvent the question of democracy by removing most of the important political decisions to the nonpolitical administrative realm.[87]

One of the principal claims made by the advocates of an administered democracy was that the complexity of the consolidated economy required that decisions be delegated to experts, freed from the pressures of democratic politics, in order to achieve the rationality and efficiency dictated by social scientific investigation. The relationship between democracy and bureaucracy remains a difficult and pressing question. In a technologically and economically complex world, what degree of expert authority and administrative, as opposed to self-governance, is required? The apparent inexorability of rationalization allows many commentators simply to dismiss the question, with the claim that it would be utopian, quixotic, and disastrous to insist that all politics be governed by the procedures of participatory democracy. To the traditional argument against participatory democracy has been added recently the resurgence of free market dogmatism. In its current incarnation, "market populism" (in the apt phrase of one of its critics) claims that only the market can dispense efficiency and guarantee real democratic results.[88] It is difficult to start a discussion about the processes of democracy within the active state when modern liberal and social-democratic governments are under siege by the publicists of neoliberalism, the corporations who hope to profit from it, and a new generation of politicians who have absorbed the teachings of market populism. Nevertheless, there are many ways to increase political participation, some of which were once common in America and cannot be so easily dismissed. Moreover, the patent failure of bureaucracy to deliver what it promises—neutrality, efficiency, and rationality—and the broader cultural consequences of a politics dominated by bureaucratic forms and procedures should at least be cause to reanimate the debate. A starting point would be an acknowledgment of the historical sources of administrative governance in the United States in an antidemocratic movement that was directed against citizens who had mobilized politically to win what they considered to be a more democratic society.

Late-nineteenth-century liberal political intellectuals, in order to resolve the problem of democracy in the age of capital, had invented an administered democracy, and the political innovations of the Progressive Era went quite far in institutionalizing the administrative solution. The settlement was premised on the conviction that individual satisfaction, the public interest, and national prosperity depended on the preservation of consolidated capitalist enterprise. With the triumph of corporate capitalism, the struggle for economic democracy necessarily proceeded on a new terrain, one in which the asymmetry in power between capital and the rest of the population had greatly increased. Just as significant, the administrative politics instituted to regulate and preserve corporate capitalism eliminated the forms of democratic participation and accountability that, for all their flaws and exclusions, had characterized American politics since the Jacksonian era. Even as, later in the twentieth century, the quite modest innovations in social welfare and economic regulation of the Progressive Era were extended and new social movements arose to expand democratic rights, so too were the forms of administration multiplied and the avenues of participation constricted. The current endemic political apathy and hostility toward liberalism and big government may be, in part, two sides of the same coin of administered democracy.

The founders of America's administered democracy offered a compensation to the people for their loss: the joys of a consuming individualism. Clark's promise that "mastership and plutocracy . . . yield by natural law a democratic result" was an exaggeration, not an aberration. The first inklings that consumption of the market's bounty is a *substitute* for democracy—not simply one of the great results of the American democratic system—came as the boastful self-congratulations of the forces of order after the 1896 election. Historians seem to have accepted that the death of politics by consumption was a Progressive Era phenomenon and that consumerism inevitably generates political apathy.[89] In fact, whatever position one takes on whether consumerism is good or bad, there is no logical, practical, or historical reason that high levels of consumption must sap the desire to participate in politics. Recognizing the origins of this notion in the fantasies of some of those who most wanted to rein in democracy should make us wary of the facile equation.

The Progressive Era, of course, was not the final word. The struggle to define and invigorate democracy continued in twentieth-century America, most notably in the labor movement of the thirties, the civil rights movement of the fifties and sixties, and the New Left movements of the sixties. Nevertheless, the twentieth century began under the terms of a particular settlement, and it is not self-evident that its basic elements have ever been successfully renegotiated. It seems that we have yet to reckon the price Americans paid for the eviscerated and anemic democracy bequeathed to us by late-nineteenth-century liberals. On the other side of a new century, when "consolidation" has given way to "globalization" and the hopes invested in the free market have become the new utopianism, the question of the relationship between democracy and capitalism is still burning.

NOTES

ABBREVIATIONS
The following abbreviations are used throughout the notes.

AER
American Economic Review
DAB
Dumas Malone and Allen Johnson, eds., *Dictionary of American Biography*
(New York: Scribner's, 1964)
ELGP
Edwin Lawrence Godkin Papers, Houghton Library, Harvard University,
Cambridge, Mass.
HCAP
Henry Carter Adams Papers, Bentley Historical Library,
University of Michigan, Ann Arbor, Mich.
HSUSA
U.S. Bureau of the Census, *Historical Statistics of the U.S.A., Colonial Times to 1957*
(Washington, D.C.: Government Printing Office, 1960)
JBCP
John Bates Clark Papers, Rare Book and Manuscript Library,
Columbia University, New York, N.Y.
JSS
Journal of Social Science
NAR
North American Review
NYPL
New York Public Library, New York, N.Y.
PAEA
Publications of the American Economic Association
PSQ
Political Science Quarterly
QJE
Quarterly Journal of Economics

INTRODUCTION

1. J. R. Lowell to C. E. Norton, Apr. 13, 1865, in Norton, *Letters of James Russell Lowell*, 1:344.

2. James Russell Lowell, "The World's Fair, 1876," *Nation*, Aug. 5, 1875, 82.

3. W. A. Rogers, "Around Columbia's Maypole," *Harper's Weekly*, Apr. 30, 1887, cover illustration.

4. For the classic work on free labor ideology, see Foner, *Free Soil*.

5. On the rise of corporate capitalism, see Sklar, *Corporate Reconstruction of American Capitalism*. On the defeat of the Populists, see Goodwyn, *Democratic Promise*. On the labor movement, see Montgomery, *Fall of the House of Labor*; Salvatore, *Eugene V. Debs*; and Hattam, *Labor Visions and State Power*.

6. The most influential interpretations of the Progressive Era from three different eras formulate the problem in this way. See Hofstadter, *Age of Reform*; Wiebe, *Search for Order*; and Sklar, *Corporate Reconstruction of American Capitalism*. For analyses specifically concerned with the nature of new liberalism and international comparisons, see Kloppenberg, *Uncertain Victory*; Furner, "Republican Tradition"; Furner, "Knowing Capitalism"; and Rodgers, *Atlantic Crossings*.

7. The political theorist C. B. Macpherson influentially argued that "possessive individualism" was at the core of liberalism and that liberalism was thus premised on assumptions about the workings and legitimation of a market society. Political theorists have effectively challenged the validity of Macpherson's interpretation of sixteenth-century political thought, on which he developed the thesis of possessive individualism. Yet it appears that Macpherson's linkage of capitalism, liberalism, and the assumptions of possessive individualism is evident in the writings of the late-eighteenth-century Scottish Enlightenment and that, with qualifications, the thesis of possessive individualism might reveal important assumptions carried forward in the subsequent evolution of liberalism (Macpherson, *Political Theory of Possessive Individualism*; Dunn, *Political Theory of John Locke*; Tully, "Possessive Individualism Thesis"). On defining liberalism, see Arblaster, *Rise and Decline of Western Liberalism*, chaps. 1–4, and Ross, "Liberalism." On the gendered quality of liberal theory, see the pioneering work by Pateman, *Sexual Contract*.

8. Arblaster, *Rise and Decline of Western Liberalism*, 15.

9. See, for example, Rawls, *Theory of Justice* and *Political Liberalism*. For a communitarian critique, see Sandel, *Liberalism and the Limits of Justice*.

10. This summary is based largely on Arblaster, *Rise and Decline of Western Liberalism*, chaps. 1–4. For a contrary view of liberalism, arguing that it can be understood not as a coherent tradition of thought but rather only as a distinctive "discourse," see Bowles and Gintis, *Democracy and Capitalism*, 14–17. Their specific discussion of liberalism as a discourse, nevertheless, is quite close to the definition put forward here. For further discussion of the controversial subject of the relationship between individualism and liberalism, see Lukes, *Individualism*, and Macpherson, *Life and Times of Liberal Democracy*.

11. Held, *Models of Democracy*, 1–9; Cohen and Arato, *Civil Society and Political Theory*.

12. Hofstadter, *Age of Reform*, 141–43.

13. Fine, *Laissez Faire*, quotation on 24–25. For an example of his opinion of laissez-faire liberals, see 30–31.

14. In many respects, Sproat's work is a sharply drawn analysis of the politics of Gilded Age liberalism. The problem, however, is that he treated it as a mood—of "nostalgia"—and failed to see the depth of the liberals' intellectual explorations (see Sproat, *"Best Men,"* chap. 10 and pp. 226–27). A recent work that accepts Sproat's and Fine's typology to present a different interpretation of the origins and character of modern liberalism than that offered herein is Schneirov, *Labor and Urban Politics*. For a dissent to the politics

implicit in the interpretation, which nonetheless agrees with the portrayal of the Gilded Age liberal reformers as classical liberals, see Benedict, "Laissez-Faire and Liberty."

15. Kloppenberg, *Uncertain Victory*; Furner, "Republican Tradition"; Furner, "Knowing Capitalism"; Rodgers, *Atlantic Crossings*. See, for example, Furner on Carroll D. Wright ("Knowing Capitalism," 246–62) and Kloppenberg on William James (*Uncertain Victory*, pt. 1). Both Wright and James began their careers within the political milieu of liberal reform, and their adaptation of liberalism was common among liberal reformers.

16. See especially Fine, *Laissez Faire*.

17. Sproat, *"Best Men,"* chap. 1; Riley, *American Magazine Journalists*, 160–73; Mott, *American Journalism*, 269, 284, 346–48; Mott, *History of American Magazines*, vol. 2, chaps. 1–2.

18. As in any attempt to apply a satisfactory label to a group that was diffuse in its own time, there are difficulties. The terminology of liberal reform was the most common among the liberal reformers themselves, and at this date, it is more neutral than some of the alternatives—"mugwump," "best men," "old liberals"—and appropriately narrower than the simple term "liberal."

19. See *DAB* on each individual mentioned in this paragraph. For full-length biographies and autobiography, see Armstrong, *E. L. Godkin*; Logsdon, *Horace White*; Ferleger, "David A. Wells"; Milne, *George William Curtis*; Leiby, *Carroll Wright and Labor Reform*; Henry Adams, *Education of Henry Adams*; Kirkland, *Charles Francis Adams*; and Bellomy, "Molding of An Iconoclast." On education, see McLachan, "American Colleges and the Transmission of Culture."

20. Jürgen Habermas's theory of the nineteenth-century bourgeois public sphere, presented in *The Structural Transformation of the Public Sphere*, serves as a perceptive and useful analytical framework for the examination of this particular group of Americans. See also Calhoun, *Habermas and the Public Sphere*.

21. This book will undoubtedly be criticized for its relative neglect of women and gender. In defense, I will say that no historian can do it all and that there are legitimate reasons for the absence. First, before the 1890s, women did not play any appreciable role in the debates on the questions at the heart of this study; they were simply excluded from the main social networks of intellectual production through which the new liberalism was forged, and although they read a number of the periodicals, the writers on these subjects displayed little interest in how women might have received their ideas. (For an opposing view, compare Leach, *True Love and Perfect Union*.) Although liberal ideology was gendered, I do not think that the transformation of liberalism hinged on such gendered conceptions (except in the case of the ideal of the masculine worker, discussed in chapters 1 and 2 below), and thus I have not discussed its gendered dimension in great depth. Women were influential in the sphere of the "social," and the second half of the nineteenth century was the period when the putative distinction between the social and the political seemed to have the greatest currency. The two would be joined back together in the twentieth century, most importantly in the emergence of the welfare component of modern American liberalism. But in the postbellum era, they constituted separate spheres of endeavor, and I have not been able to conduct primary research into both. For histories that directly address questions of women's public roles and gendered ideology that are related to the themes of this book, see Katz, *Shadow of the Poorhouse*; Leach, *True Love and*

Perfect Union; Stanley, *From Bondage to Contract*; and DuBois, *Feminism and Suffrage*. For analyses of the later period that emphasize the critical importance of women and gender in the development of the liberal welfare state, see Gordon, *Pitied but Not Entitled*, and Skocpol, *Protecting Soldiers and Mothers*. For a theoretical discussion of the role of nineteenth-century middle-class women in the creation of the "social" as a sphere of class control, see Riley, *Am I That Name?*

22. Earlier studies of these men, especially Fine's, credited them as the progenitors of progressivism, in sharp contrast to the older liberals who thwarted progressive reform. A fine study of the younger generation's involvement in professionalizing social science can be found in Furner, *Advocacy and Objectivity*. Ross, in *Origins of American Social Science*, offers a nuanced interpretation of the relationship between the professional ambitions of the young social scientists and the political milieu in which they worked. Furner, in her recent work, has turned to analyzing the influence of social scientists on policymaking. While she has appropriately foregrounded politics and proposed a suggestive analysis of the different strands of new liberalism, the work published to this date is relatively silent on the relationship between policymaking social scientists and the public social and political conflicts outside their rather exclusive circles. (See Furner, "Republican Tradition" and "Knowing Capitalism.")

23. See Weinstein, *Corporate Ideal*; Livingston, *Federal Reserve System*; Sklar, *Corporate Reconstruction of American Capitalism*; and Kolko, *Triumph of Conservatism*. For pointed statements of the central theses, see Weinstein's introduction and Livingston's appendix B.

24. For example, see *DAB* on Wells (10:637–38), Norton (7:569–72), and the Adams brothers (1:48–52, 61–67).

25. For alternative interpretations of American intellectuals, see Wilson, *Figures of Speech*, and Haskell, *Emergence of Professional Social Science*. On the trials of the young social scientists, see chapter 5 below and Hofstadter and Metzger, *Development of Academic Freedom*. For theoretical explorations that have influenced my formulation, see Weber, *Protestant Ethic and the Spirit of Capitalism*; Gramsci, *Selections from the Prison Notebooks*, 5–23; Habermas, *Structural Transformation of the Public Sphere*; and the debate about hegemony in Bender, *Antislavery Debate*.

26. See Kloppenberg, *Uncertain Victory*, and McClay, *Masterless*, for more typical intellectual histories of the same period with which I am concerned.

27. On Dewey, see Westbrook, *John Dewey and American Democracy*, chap. 1.

28. James quoted in Riley, *American Magazine Journalists*, 172.

29. Hoogenboom, *Outlawing the Spoils*; Sproat, *"Best Men,"* 60–88. For an important corrective to the dominant interpretation of Gilded Age corruption, see Summers, *Era of Good Stealings*.

CHAPTER ONE

1. *New York Tribune*, July 6, 1865, 6.

2. On Tammany Democracy and patriotism, see Bernstein, *New York City Draft Riots*, 196–99.

3. *New York Tribune*, July 4, 1865, 4; July 6, 1865, 6.

4. "The Great Festival," *Nation*, July 6, 1865, 5. It was E. L. Godkin's policy to publish articles in the *Nation* anonymously. A reliable index to authors is available, and wherever

an attribution is given without brackets, the source of authorship is Haskell, *Nation Index*. There are, however, other ways to determine authorship of some of the unattributed articles. In these cases, I have indicated authorship with square brackets.

5. *Nation*, July 6, 1865, 5.

6. On Radical Republicans, see Foner, *Reconstruction*, 228–39; Montgomery, *Beyond Equality*; and Trefousse, *Radical Republicans*. On the relationship between the antislavery movement and Radical Republicans, see Foner, *Free Soil*, chap. 4, and Stewart, *Holy Warriors*.

7. See, for example, Godkin, "The Danger of the Hour," *Nation*, Sept. 21, 1865, 357.

8. The recognition of this fact motivated three of the most important liberal treatises of the nineteenth century: John Stuart Mill's *Considerations on Representative Government* and *On Liberty* and Alexis de Tocqueville's *Democracy in America*. Mill and Tocqueville, as has often been observed, shared a deep ambivalence about this development.

9. In the United States, where almost all European American men had gained the suffrage during the Jacksonian era and the ideology of universal white manhood suffrage was pervasive, the extension of the franchise called for the inclusion of those who had been categorically excluded from the political nation: African American men and even, the more consistent and the more idealistic argued, women and Native Americans.

10. Wyatt-Brown, *Honor and Violence in the Old South*; Higginbotham, "Martial Spirit."

11. Berlin, Reidy, and Rowland, *Black Military Experience*, introduction.

12. Bensel, *Yankee Leviathan*, chap. 3. For the statistics on land grants, see *HSUSA*, 430. For the relationship between Republican Civil War economic legislation, free labor ideology, the growth of the state, and the transformation of the U.S. economy, see Richardson, *Greatest Nation of the Earth*.

13. On the relationship between Radical Republicanism and the woman suffrage movement, see DuBois, *Feminism and Suffrage*, chap. 2.

14. Montgomery, *Beyond Equality*.

15. Curtis, "Consolidation," *Harper's Weekly*, Dec. 9, 1865. See also Curtis, "The Good Fight," [1865–66], in Norton, *Orations and Addresses*, 151–77.

16. See Cohen, "Problem of Democracy," chap. 1.

17. The phrase "free labor civilization" was frequently used by contemporaries, and I think it best conveys what historians designate as free labor ideology. On free labor ideology, see Foner, *Free Soil*.

18. Among many compelling analyses of the conflicts of the Gilded Age that put the concept of producerism (explicitly or implicitly) to good use, see particularly Fink, *Workingmen's Democracy*; Salvatore, *Eugene V. Debs*; Hattam, *Labor Visions and State Power*; Berk, *Alternative Tracks*; and Kazin, *Populist Persuasion*.

19. Lincoln, "Address before the Wisconsin Agricultural Society," Sept. 30, 1859, in Lincoln, *Collected Works*, 3:477–82. For an exploration of the free contract strain of free labor ideology, see Stanley, *From Bondage to Contract*.

20. On the eight-hour-day movement, see Montgomery, *Beyond Equality*, chap. 6, and Glickman, *Living Wage*, chap. 5. For a study of the ideological debates surrounding the postbellum labor question that complements the analysis presented here, see Stanley, *From Bondage to Contract*, chap. 2.

21. Foner, *Free Soil*, chap. 1.

22. In 1870, although most Americans still lived in rural areas, approximately two out of every three working persons were employees—not property owners (Montgomery, *Beyond Equality*, 25–30). Montgomery's figures are based on a careful analysis of the landmark 1870 census, supervised by Francis Amasa Walker (who figured prominently in liberal reform), and the 1940 review of the errors of the 1870 census. As he notes, the 1860 census is too flawed to determine the occupational distribution of the prewar population.

23. The literature that treats the Civil War as a bourgeois revolution is certainly relevant to this issue. (See especially Genovese, *Political Economy of Slavery* and *World the Slaveholders Made*, and Moore, *Origins of Dictatorship and Democracy*, chap. 3.) The investigation of the cultural and ideological construction of free contract by Stanley in *From Bondage to Contract* perhaps comes closest to tackling this question (see especially chap. 2).

24. The term "labor reform" was used by workingmen to describe their movement. (See, for example, *Daily Evening Voice*, Mar. 2, 1866, editorial.) Thus the term "labor reformer" is as applicable to working-class activists as it is to their middle-class allies. When used in this chapter, "labor reformer" designates anyone involved in the movement, with no assumptions made concerning his or her class identity.

25. Montgomery, *Beyond Equality*, chap. 9.

26. The terminology of liberal reform was in use by its partisans by the early 1870s. In the 1860s, many future liberal reformers were still vying over who would be able to claim the valuable title "Radical." (See, for example, "True Radicalism," *Nation*, July 18, 1865, 50–51.) The vast majority of the leaders of the liberal reform movement were once Radical Republicans.

27. Nordhoff, "The Misgovernment of New York,—A Remedy Suggested," *NAR* 113 (Oct. 1871): 335.

28. See Massachusetts House of Representatives, *Report of the Special Commission on the Hours of Labor and the Condition and Prospects of the Industrial Classes*, 21–23 (hereafter cited as "1865 Mass. Labor Comm.").

29. Charles F. Adams, "The Protection of the Ballot in National Elections," *JSS* 1 (June 1869): 91–111.

30. Quoted in Montgomery, *Beyond Equality*, 238.

31. On Republican legislation, see Richardson, *Greatest Nation of the Earth*.

32. *Philadelphia Daily News*, Dec. 24, 1868, quoted in Montgomery, *Beyond Equality*, 239; "The Labor Problem," *Daily Evening Voice*, Nov. 4, 1865. On wage-slave rhetoric, see Stanley, *From Bondage to Contract*, chap. 2.

33. *DAB*, 8:326–27.

34. 1865 Mass. Labor Comm., 4. On the ASSA, see Haskell, *Emergence of Professional Social Science*, and Furner, *Advocacy and Objectivity*.

35. 1865 Mass. Labor Comm., 25.

36. Ibid.

37. The commission's formulation suggests that, in the United States, the theory of free contract was bound up with assumptions about male identity, democratic citizenship, and progressive civilization. For a historical examination of the relationship between free contract and gender, see Stanley, *From Bondage to Contract*. For a theoretical exploration

of the gendered character of liberal contract theory, see Pateman, *Sexual Contract*, chaps. 3–5.

38. 1865 Mass. Labor Comm., 35–40.

39. Ibid., 43.

40. Ibid., 48–49.

41. "The Report of the Commission," *Daily Evening Voice*, Mar. 6, 1866.

42. 1865 Mass. Labor Comm., 48.

43. *DAB*, 10:104–5; Ross, *Origins of American Social Science*, 43–44, 77. Walker's report, incidentally, gives cause to question Ross's portrayal of him as one of the optimistic American exceptionalists.

44. Massachusetts House of Representatives, *Reports of Commissioners on the Hours of Labor*, 22–23 (hereafter cited as "1866 Mass. Labor Comm.").

45. Ibid., 30.

46. Ibid., 31.

47. Ibid., 33–34.

48. For similar formulations being put forward in Radical journals and in organizations in which Radicals were prominent, see Edmund Quincy, "Insurance against Strikes," *Nation*, June 19, 1866, 777; T. G. Shearman, "Speculation," *Nation*, June 26, 1866, 809–10; Wendell Phillips Garrison, "Co-operative Societies," *Nation*, Mar. 22, 1866, 360–61; Rowland Hazard, "The Hours of Labor," *NAR* 102 (Jan. 1866): 195–209; Samuel Eliot, "Address to the Fifth General Meeting of the ASSA," Nov. 19, 1867 (Boston, 1867); and Curtis, "The Eight-Hour Law," *Harper's Weekly*, May 25, 1867, 323.

49. Logsdon, *Horace White*; Ashley, *American Newspaper Journalists*, 346–51.

50. For examples of this argument, see "The Eight-Hour Demonstration," May 1, 1867; "The Relations between Capital and Labor," May 8, 1867; "An Eight-Hour Party," May 10, 1867; "The Agrarian Philosophers," May 25, 1867; and "The Eight-Hour Business," June 13, 1867, all in *Chicago Tribune*.

51. "Eight-Hour Demonstration"; "Industrial Legislation," *Chicago Tribune*, May 1, 1867.

52. "Industrial Legislation."

53. "Freedom of Labor," *Chicago Tribune*, May 8, 1867.

54. "The Eight-Hour Riots," *Chicago Tribune*, May 5, 1867.

55. "How Fortunes Are Made," *Chicago Tribune*, May 7, 1867; quotations in "Freedom of Labor," *Chicago Tribune*, May 8, 1867.

56. Ross, *Origins of American Social Science*, 42–48.

57. "Relations between Capital and Labor."

58. Quotation in "Co-operation," *Chicago Tribune*, May 7, 1867; "Co-operation in Chicago," *Chicago Tribune*, May 26, 1867.

59. "Co-operation in Chicago."

60. "Agrarian Philosophers."

61. "Eight-Hour Demonstration."

62. "End of the Eight-Hour Strike," *Chicago Tribune*, June 2, 1867.

63. Hofstadter, *American Political Tradition*, 188–205.

64. Remarks of Wendell Phillips at the Mass Meeting of Workingmen in Faneuil Hall, Nov. 2, 1865, pamphlet, NYPL, 3.

65. Ibid., 12, 20–21.

66. Ibid., 21.

67. On Phillips's involvement in electoral politics, see Montgomery, *Beyond Equality*, 269–70, 369–71, 373.

68. Phillips, "The Foundation of the Labor Movement," speech delivered in 1871, pamphlet, NYPL, 6, 7.

69. Ibid., 11, 12.

70. Ibid., 15, 16.

71. On Godkin's life before he took over the *Nation*, see Armstrong, *E. L. Godkin*, chaps. 1–4.

72. Ibid., 38–39, 45–47, 49–52.

73. Godkin, in drafts of an essay solicited by Charles Eliot Norton for the *North American Review*, opposed extending the suffrage to freedmen unconditionally, recommending quite stringent literacy tests as a condition of enfranchisement. Norton refused to publish the essay until Godkin revised his position on black suffrage. Godkin balked but finally submitted an acceptable version. Immediately after Godkin complied, Norton recommended him for the editorship of the *Nation*. The backers of the enterprise interviewed Godkin, received satisfactory assurances that he supported the Radical view of Reconstruction, and hired him, agreeing to Godkin's condition that he have "autocratic" control over the content of the magazine. The essay in question was "The Democratic View of Democracy," *NAR* 101 (July 1865): 103–33. It is important to note that Armstrong's interpretation is based on a misreading of a key letter from Norton to Godkin. For further discussion of this essay, Godkin's conflict with Norton, and his hiring as the *Nation*'s editor, see Cohen, "Problem of Democracy," 47–58, and 58 n. 131.

74. Godkin was also considered for the professorship in political economy at the new Cornell University in 1867. As we have already noted Godkin's ambition, it cannot be ruled out that his attention to the labor question was guided by his desire to receive this job. (See Charles Eliot Norton to Edwin Lawrence Godkin, July 5, 1867, ELGP.) The topical distribution of Godkin's writings can be tracked in the *Nation Index*. His attention to the Northern labor question was particularly marked between 1868 and 1872. The panic of 1873 and the subsequent depression knocked out organized labor in the North, and Godkin had little to say in his editorials about unemployment and the different types of working-class activism that prevailed during these years. A serious depression in 1875 following the death of his wife also stilled his pen (Riley, *American Magazine Journalists*, 160–73).

75. Godkin, "Co-operation," *NAR* 106 (Jan. 1868): 172.

76. For a discussion of these essays, see Cohen, "Problem of Democracy," 44–58.

77. Godkin, "Tyranny of the Majority," *NAR* 105 (Jan. 1867): 224–25.

78. Charles Eliot Norton to Edwin Lawrence Godkin, May 22, 1867, ELGP; "True Radicalism," *Nation*, July 18, 1867, 50–51.

79. On education and cooperation, see Godkin, "Labor Crisis," *NAR* 105 (July 1867): 177–213; "Wages against Co-operation," *Nation*, Aug. 8, 1867, 111–12; "Why Political Economy Has Not Been Cultivated in America," *Nation*, Sept. 26, 1867, 155–56; and "Co-operation," *NAR* 106 (Jan. 1868): 172.

80. "Labor Crisis."

81. On national organization, see Montgomery, *Beyond Equality*, chaps. 4, 8, 9–11, app. C.

82. Godkin was by no means the only one linking national to international developments. See also "The Tyranny of Trades-Unions," *Chicago Tribune*, May 5, 1867; "Progress in Economic Education," *JSS* 1 (June 1869): 137–40; "General Intelligence—Social Reform Movements in the United States," *JSS* 2 (1870): 201–17; Richard J. Hinton, "Organization of Labor: Its Aggressive Phases," *Atlantic Monthly*, May 1871, 544–59; Charles Francis Adams, "The Butler Canvas," *NAR* 114 (Jan.–Apr. 1872): 147–70; and E. Gryzanowski, "On the International Workingmen's Association: Its Origin, Doctrines, and Ethics," *NAR* 114 (Apr. 1872): 309–76.

83. Godkin, "The Condition of France," *Nation*, Apr. 23, 1868, 325–26.

84. Quotation in Godkin, "The Annexation Fever," *Nation*, Apr. 15, 1869, 289–90.

85. Quotations in Godkin, "The Latest Phase of the Labor Trouble," *Nation*, Apr. 1, 1869, 249–50. See also "The Working-men's Congress," *Nation*, Sept. 24, 1868, 244–46; Godkin, "The Working-Man's View of Capital," *Nation*, Feb. 4, 1869, 85–86; "The Printer's Strike," *Nation*, Feb. 11, 1869, 108–9; and [Godkin], "The Social Future As Foreshadowed by the French Elections," *Nation*, June 17, 1869, 468–69.

86. "Social Future."

87. Ibid.

88. See "The Latest Phase of the Labor Trouble" for this formulation. He had equal disdain for "social" legislation of behavior, especially coercive temperance laws (Godkin, "Puritanism in Politics," *Nation*, Nov. 3, 1867, 65–66).

89. Godkin, "The Difficulties of Economical Discussion," *Nation*, July 22, 1869, 65–66; quotation in "Legislation and Social Science" (paper presented at March 1870 meeting of the ASSA), *JSS* 3 (1871): 133. It was in this context in 1869 that the *Nation* argued that "reform," especially civil service reform, was now a pressing issue. For the linkage between sentimentalist politics, corruption, and the need for reform on scientific principles, see "The Reform Movement," *Nation*, Jan. 21, 1869, 46.

90. Godkin, "The Labor Movement in Europe," *Nation*, May 12, 1870, 298; "Working-men's Congress"; "Legislation and Social Science"; "The Caesarists and Sentimentalists," *Nation*, Sept. 29, 1870, 200–201.

91. The shifting position of Godkin and other liberal reformers on state regulation is the subject of chapters 3 and 4 below.

92. Godkin, " 'Cornering' the Public," Mar. 2, 1871, 136–37; Godkin, "The True History of the Coal Trouble," Mar. 9, 1871, 152–54; Godkin, " 'What Are We Going to Do about It?,' " Apr. 13, 1871, 252–53, all in *Nation*; Bernstein, *New York City Draft Riots*, 228–36; Mandelbaum, *Boss Tweed's New York*, 77–80.

93. Hicks and Tucker, *Revolution and Reaction*, xv–xvii.

94. Mill came in for censure for his advocacy of land reform in England (Godkin, " 'The Commune' and the Labor Question," *Nation*, May 18, 1871, 333–34).

95. Montgomery, *Beyond Equality*, 370–74; Foner, *Reconstruction*, 372–78, 454–59, 497–99. In addition to editorials cited above, see Godkin, "The Problem at the South," Mar. 23, 1871, 192–93; "An Illustration of Government at the South," Mar. 30, 1871, 212–13;

" 'What Are We Going to Do about It?,' " Apr. 13, 1871, 252–53; "Sex in Politics," Apr. 20, 1871, 270–72; "A Southern View of the Southern Problem," July 6, 1871; and "Municipal Caesarism," Sept. 28, 1871, 205–6, all in *Nation*.

96. Godkin, "How Protection Affects Labor," *Nation*, May 25, 1871, 352–53.

97. Ibid.

98. Ibid.

99. Godkin, "The Future of Capital," *Nation*, June 22, 1871, 429–30.

100. "How Protection Affects Labor."

101. "The Future of Capital."

102. Ibid.

103. Phillips sympathetically reported the activities of the International and praised the Paris Commune in his newspaper, and he was an exponent of socialism from the 1870s until his death (Hofstadter, *American Political Tradition*, 204–10).

104. Mill, *On Liberty*, introduction; *Principles of Political Economy*, bk. 5, chap. 11; *Utilitarianism*. For an analysis of Godkin's exposition and adaptation of Mill, see Cohen, "Problem of Democracy," 48–56. For Mill's influence on Godkin, see Armstrong, *E. L. Godkin*, 9, 195.

105. By the end of his life, Godkin had become a true, classical conservative. The shift from philosophical liberalism to philosophical conservatism probably occurred in the late 1880s, long after the peak of his influence in liberal reform and over middle-class public opinion in the seventies. I would argue that the fundamental reversal hinged on his pessimism about the mutability of human nature and his rejection of a progressive conception of history, the seeds of which are both evident in his early seventies writing on the labor question. The more he dwelled on these elements, the less his voice was heeded. Godkin's reign of public influence corresponded with his promotion of liberalism. For a view of Godkin as a conservative, see Kirk, *Conservative Mind*, 294, 304–10.

CHAPTER TWO

1. Curtis, "The Good Fight," in Norton, *Orations and Addresses*, quotations on 153, 166, 172, 177.

2. Frederick Douglass, "Reconstruction," *Atlantic Monthly*, Dec. 1866, 761–62; Douglass, "The Color Line," (*NAR*, 1881), reprinted in Foner, *Writings of Frederick Douglass*, 4:344.

3. C. F. Adams, "The Protection of the Ballot in National Elections," *JSS* 1 (June 1869): 91–111.

4. Quoted in Foner, *Politics and Ideology*, 135.

5. On the process of transforming slaves into free workers and the issue of land redistribution, see Berlin et al., *Destruction of Slavery* and *Wartime Genesis of Free Labor*.

6. Berlin et al., *Destruction of Slavery* and *Wartime Genesis of Free Labor*; Cohen-Lack, "Struggle for Sovereignty."

7. E. Quincy, "Reconstruction through Bankruptcy," *Nation*, Nov. 2, 1865, 550–51.

8. W. F. Allen, "A Trip in South Carolina," *Nation*, July 27, 1865, 106–7. Allen wrote about New York City government under the pseudonym "Marcel." See, for example, "Town Meetings for Great Cities," *Nation*, May 19, 1866, 684–85.

9. Atkinson, "Probable Effects of Southern Free Labor on Northern Industry," *Nation*, Aug. 17, 1865, 198–99.

10. Quincy, "Reconstruction through Bankruptcy."

11. Powell, *New Masters*, chap. 5.

12. See, for example, A. W. Kelsey, "The Future Relations of North and South," *Nation*, Jan. 18, 1866, 79–91. On antislavery ideology, see Olmsted, *Cotton Kingdom*, and Foner, *Free Soil*, chap. 2.

13. For a more detailed discussion of how Northerners implemented the free labor system in the South during Reconstruction, see Foner, *Reconstruction*, chap. 4.

14. W. F. Allen, "Cotton Culture," *Nation*, Sept. 7, 1865, 295.

15. The context of Quincy's remarks makes it clear that Quincy used the terms "whites" and "blacks" as shorthand references for different nationalities. Nevertheless, the language itself reveals the ambiguity of the Radical idea of race as national origin (Quincy, "General Cox and the Negroes," *Nation*, Aug. 24, 1865, 229–30).

16. Fields, "Slavery, Race, and Ideology."

17. Curtis, "Electioneering in the South," *Harper's Weekly*, July 25, 1868, 467.

18. Allen, "The Feelings of the Southern Negroes," *Nation*, Sept. 28, 1865, 393.

19. "The Republican Party in the South," *Nation*, July 18, 1867, 50.

20. Foner, *Politics and Ideology*, 141–42.

21. Ibid., 138–43.

22. Norton to Godkin, May 22, 1867, ELGP.

23. White, "Mr. Stevens' Letter in the South," *Chicago Tribune*, May 10, 1867. White again shifted ground in June when President Johnson showed resistance to the congressional military plan. His position on confiscation, however, did not change (Logsdon, *Horace White*, 143–44).

24. Godkin, "The Labor Crisis," *NAR* 105 (July 1867): 198–99.

25. "True Radicalism," *Nation*, July 18, 1865, 50–51.

26. Ibid.

27. Ibid.

28. "Republican Troubles," *Nation*, Oct. 17, 1867, 314–15.

29. From the summer of 1867 until Grant's election in November 1868, the editors of these papers differed significantly on specific issues, such as on Johnson's impeachment. Their relationship with the Radical congressmen fluctuated according to events during this period. This summary should be understood as a generalization about a tendency in a politically complex era. For more detailed assessments of the eclipse of the Radical Republicans, see Foner, *Reconstruction*, chaps. 6–9. Logsdon is particularly informative about the political relationships of this period, for Horace White was one of Grant's most influential early supporters (*Horace White*, 144–57).

30. Jaynes, *Branches without Roots*. For a study of those freed families able to acquire land, see Oubre, *Forty Acres and a Mule*.

31. For one of the best recent studies of the ideas and actions of freed men and women in local Reconstruction politics, see Saville, *Work of Reconstruction*.

32. The *Nation* specifically condoned a tax on wasteland. The failure to use resources it deemed an unnatural act, and thus such a tax was fair game. Furthermore, within the

persisting commitment to state activism, taxation for the general good—in this case, a policy favoring rational economic development—was commonplace. At a later date, this too would be deemed an illegitimate infringement on sacred rights of private property ("Southern Politics," *Nation*, Aug. 1, 1867, 110–11).

33. De Forest, "The Man and Brother," *Atlantic Monthly*, Sept.–Oct. 1868, 337–48, 414–25. An alternative theory of De Forest's access to the *Atlantic Monthly* is necessary to explore. De Forest was a writer and a novelist, and his first novel after the war, *Miss Ravenel's Conversion from Secession to Loyalty* (1867), gained the admiration of William Dean Howells, then a subeditor at the magazine, for its "realism." The two writers began a long friendship and correspondence, in which laments about the unpopularity of their small, beleaguered school of realist writers figured prominently. Nevertheless, that De Forest's writings of this sort could gain publication in the magazine attests to something more than an editor's admiration for the style of a writer. On De Forest and Howells, see Wilson, *Patriotic Gore*, 684–701.

34. De Forest, "Man and Brother," 344.

35. Ibid., 342.

36. Ibid., 425.

37. Sedgwick, "The Constitutional Amendment," *Nation*, Feb. 18, 1869, 124–25.

38. Foner, *Reconstruction*, 352–78.

39. See, for example, Curtis, "Business Reviving," *Harper's Weekly*, Mar. 7, 1868, 147.

40. Parton, "Reviving Virginia," *Atlantic Monthly*, Apr. 1870, 432–44, quotation on 441.

41. Godkin, "The End at Last," *Nation*, May 19, 1870, 314. This declaration appeared a week after an editorial reporting that the French trade unions were organizing for a general strike (Godkin, "The Labor Movement in Europe," *Nation*, May 12, 1870, 298).

42. Shaler, "An Ex-Southerner in South Carolina," *Atlantic Monthly*, July 1870, 53–61, quotation on 61.

43. *DAB*, 9:17–19.

44. A further, rather technical point in scientific theory gave even greater force to a Darwinian theory of divergent races. In the 1860s, contemporary geological research—later proved wrong—dated the earth as much younger than Darwin had posited in his initial researches. The younger age of the earth posed problems for Darwin's anti-Lamarckian theory of natural selection: it seemed impossible to conceive of such large evolutionary changes in such a short period of time. Thus, in later editions of the *The Origin of Species*, Darwin himself had tentatively acceded to the Lamarckian idea that environmental or socially induced changes during an individual's lifetime could be passed on to future generations. The implications of this theory could go in different directions when applied to African Americans. Either the two centuries under "civilization" had contributed substantially to their natural improvement, or enslavement had only stamped their African deficiencies more deeply into their natural character. As no one who accepted Darwinian theory knew the biological basis for evolution—Mendel's pioneering work on genetics lay in obscurity until the early twentieth century—evolutionary theory provided a kind of blank field for all sorts of psychological and ideological projections. For a lucid and bracing account of the disreputable history of Darwinian and other forms of scientific racialism, see Gould, *Mismeasure of Man*.

45. Shaler, "Ex-Southerner in South Carolina," 60–61.

46. Curtis, "Good Fight."

47. Powell, *New Masters*, chaps. 6–7, epilogue. One of the richest sources for tracing the communication between Northern planters and Northern men of influence is the Edward Atkinson Papers at the Massachusetts Historical Society, Boston, Mass.

48. "The Race Question," *Nation*, July 21, 1870, 39.

49. Jacob Cox to James Garfield, Mar. 27, 1871, quoted in Foner, *Reconstruction*, 499.

50. Godkin, "The Problem at the South," *Nation*, Mar. 23, 1871, 192–93.

51. Pomeroy, "The Force Bill," *Nation*, Apr. 20, 1871, 268–70. On Pomeroy, see *DAB*, 8:52–53, and Pomeroy, *Constitutional Law*.

52. See chapter 4 below.

53. Foner, *Reconstruction*, 499–511; Sproat, *"Best Men,"* 76–88.

54. For a discussion of the federal judiciary's postwar shifts on the protection of civil rights, see Smith, *Civic Ideals*, 325–37; for a relevant interpretation of the Slaughterhouse cases, see Forbath, "Ambiguities of Free Labor," 772–82.

55. Foner, *Reconstruction*, 539–54.

56. Ibid.

57. Ibid., 535–36. On the importance of Northern capital in the early resurrection of the plantation system, see Powell, *New Masters*, chap. 3.

58. Foner, *Reconstruction*, 526–27.

59. Nordhoff, *Cotton States*, 11–25. References to Pike's *Prostrate State* are from the modern reprint, edited and introduced by Robert F. Durden (New York: Harper and Row, 1968). This account is drawn from Durden's introduction, reconstructing the history of the production and reception of Pike's book. On Reid, see Powell, *New Masters*, 152.

60. C. Vann Woodward demonstrated that Redeemer governments and those that followed them were as corrupt as Reconstruction governments, if not more so. And their corruption took forms that liberal reformers opposed—excessive debt and the corruption of politicians for the personal favor of special interests (*Origins of the New South*, chap. 3).

CHAPTER THREE

1. Chandler, *Visible Hand*; Sklar, *Corporate Reconstruction of American Capitalism*.

2. James Livingston offers provocative reflections on the ideal of selfhood inherent in the ideology of possessive individualism. His interpretation of this problem, though I disagree with some of his related arguments, has influenced my formulation of liberal reformers' response to the economic transition (Livingston, *Pragmatism*, chap. 2).

3. Bensel, *Yankee Leviathan*.

4. *DAB*, 19:637–38; Ferleger, "David A. Wells," 1–16, quotation in uncited private letter on 4; "Report of a Memorial Meeting of the Economic Conference of the Johns Hopkins University," Nov. 22, 1898, E. R. A. Seligman Collection, Rare Book and Manuscript Library, Columbia University, New York, N.Y.

5. Wells joined the ASSA no later than 1866, served as an officer of the organization in 1867 and following years, and was a regular speaker at annual meeting panels on the labor question. This information can be found in Samuel Eliot, "Address before the ASSA at the Fifth General Meeting, New York," Nov. 19, 1867 (Boston, 1867), pamphlet, NYPL.

6. Curtis, "Custom-House Fraud," *Harper's Weekly*, Mar. 3, 1866, 130; "The Way the Government Is Served," *Nation*, Feb. 15, 1866, 198.

7. See, for example, "Mr. Wells's Report for 1868," *Nation*, Jan. 14, 1869, 24–25.

8. Ibid.; Atkinson, Broadside no. 19, Nov. 17, 1869, p. 1, Edward Atkinson Papers, Massachusetts Historical Society, Boston, Mass.

9. U.S. Congress, House, *Report of the Special Commissioner of the Revenue* [for 1869] (hereafter cited as "Rev. Comm. Report for 1869").

10. C. F. Adams, "A Chapter of Erie" (orig. *NAR*, July 1869), and Henry Adams, "The New York Gold Conspiracy" (orig. *Westminster Review*, Oct. 1870), both reprinted in Adams and Adams, *Chapters of Erie*.

11. Ferleger, "David A. Wells," 274–79.

12. Rev. Comm. Report for 1869, xxxi.

13. Ibid., xxxv.

14. Hobsbawm, *Age of Capital*, 46.

15. In 1872, for example, 7,432 new miles of railroad tracks were laid, more than twice that of the peak year of construction before the war. See Berk, *Alternative Tracks*, 35, and *HSUSA*, 200–204.

16. Sproat, *"Best Men,"* 172–82; Keller, *Affairs of State*, 380.

17. Wells, "The Meaning of Revenue Reform," *NAR* 113 (July 1871): 104–53, quotation on 106.

18. Ibid., 151. See also Dorfman, *Economic Mind in American Civilization*, 3:15.

19. Wells, "Meaning of Revenue Reform," 130–32, 145, 151–53.

20. Images produced for the middle-class market attest to the symbolic significance of the railroad (Takaki, *Iron Cages*, chap. 8, and illustrations on 172, 192).

21. Chandler, *Visible Hand*, chap. 3.

22. On the close relationship between government fiscal policy, private finance, and railroad policy, see Berk, *Alternative Tracks*, chaps. 2, 4, and Bensel, *Yankee Leviathan*, chap. 4.

23. On railroads and corporate theory and practice, see Berk, *Alternative Tracks*, 48, and Dunlavy, "Political Structure," 114–54. On the legal history of the corporation, see Hurst, *Legitimacy of the Business Corporation*, esp. chaps. 1, 3. On the erosion of the grant theory of the corporation in the first half of the nineteenth century, see Horwitz, *Transformation of American Law, 1780–1860*, 111–13. For the history of developments in legal doctrine regarding the corporation, see Horwitz, *Transformation of American Law, 1870–1960*, chap. 3.

24. Gordon, Edwards, and Reich, *Segmented Work, Divided Workers*, 107–8.

25. Horwitz argues that the theory did not, as conventionally assumed, emerge from the *Santa Clara* case of 1886 but rather was articulated around the turn of the century as a response to a "crisis of legitimacy" in the market system (*Transformation of American Law, 1870–1960*, chap. 3, esp. 66–68). This chapter and chapters 5 and 6 demonstrate that liberal reformers and political economists grappled with this crisis of legitimacy much earlier and that their legitimating theory of the corporation exerted a powerful influence.

26. Cooley, *Constitutional Limitations*, 351–59. Later editions noted that the Fourteenth Amendment incorporated the principle into national law. See also Horwitz, *Transformation of American Law, 1870–1960*, 29, 158–59, and Wolfe, *Rise of Modern Judicial Review*, chap. 6. For an important revisionist interpretation of the origins of laissez-faire constitutionalism, see Benedict, "Laissez-Faire and Liberty."

27. The *Nation* listed the treatise as one of its books received but never reviewed it (Notice of Books Received, *Nation*, June 17, 1869, 472). The *North American Review*, which was one of the few other nonspecialist journals that dealt with legal writing, also did not review it. For historical appraisals of Cooley, see Benedict, "Laissez-Faire and Liberty," 330–31; Jacobs, *Law Writers and the Courts*, 27–58; and Twiss, *Lawyers and the Constitution*, chap. 2.

28. J. C. Hurd, "Pomeroy's Constitutional Law," *Nation*, July 16, 1868; Pomeroy, "The Power of Congress to Regulate Railway Commerce," *Nation*, July 30, 1868, 86–88.

29. Sedgwick, "Monopolies and the Fourteenth Amendment," *Nation*, Dec. 1, 1870, 361–62. The debate seems to lend support to Forbath's interpretation of *Slaughterhouse* (Forbath, "Ambiguities of Free Labor," 792–94, quotation on 792).

30. Wells, "How Will the United States Supreme Court Decide the Granger Railroad Cases? Correspondence," *Nation*, Oct. 29, 1874, 282–84; Stephen J. Field to David A. Wells, June 29, 1877, David Ames Wells Papers, NYPL.

31. See below, chapters 6 and 7.

32. Hurst, *Legitimacy of the Business Corporation*, chap. 1; Horwitz, *Transformation of American Law, 1780–1860*, 111–14; Horwitz, *Transformation of American Law, 1870–1960*, chap. 3; Berk, *Alternative Tracks*, 47–51.

33. Hurst, *Legitimacy of the Business Corporation*, chap. 1; Horwitz, *Transformation of American Law, 1780–1860*, 111–14; Horwitz, *Transformation of American Law, 1870–1960*, chap. 3; Berk, *Alternative Tracks*, 47–51; Gunn, *Decline of Authority*, chap. 8.

34. Berk, *Alternative Tracks*, 49.

35. Quotation in Adams and Adams, *Chapters of Erie*, 100–101.

36. Hodgskin, "The Railroad Fraternity," *Nation*, May 21, 1868, 406–8; Hodgskin, "One Reason Why Railroads Are Badly Managed," *Nation*, June 11, 1868, 464–66. Between 1867 and 1871, Hodgskin wrote most of the articles in the *Nation* that contained specific economic analysis about the national debt, the currency, and national banking.

37. Hodgskin, "One Reason Why Railroads Are Badly Managed."

38. Parton, "Log-Rolling at Washington," *Atlantic Monthly*, Sept. 1879, 361–78, quotations on 377.

39. Ibid., 376.

40. Kirkland, *Charles Francis Adams*, 23–35.

41. Quoted in ibid., 35. George Fredrickson explores the cultural and personal dimension of the shift from antebellum humanitarianism and anti-institutionalism, exemplified in Emerson's towering influence over the young men of the period, to the institutionalism and more limited horizons of the postbellum generation. Though there is much of value in his analysis, he tends to give insufficient attention to the intellectual content of postbellum reform (Fredrickson, *Inner Civil War*, chaps. 12–13).

42. Kirkland, *Charles Francis Adams*, chaps. 3–4. For a sympathetic view of Adams's thought on railroads and his career as a regulator, see McCraw, *Prophets of Regulation*, chap. 1. Adams's evolution from railroad reformer to speculator and director of one of the main transcontinental railroads is a significant one in the collective biography of liberal reformers. Kirkland's narrative of Adams's life emphasizes his vested interests and career goals, suggesting that these were determinative of his ideas about railroads. There is a tremendous amount of evidence for Adams's less than lofty motivations, but once said,

there is still more intellectual and political significance in his theories of corporate development and state regulation that is not reducible to self-interest.

43. C. F. Adams, "The Railroad System," *NAR* 104 (Apr. 1867): 476–511; C. F. Adams, "Railroad Legislation," originally published in *American Law Review*, pamphlet (1868), NYPL.

44. Adams, "Railroad Legislation," 14.

45. Ibid., 23.

46. C. F. Adams, "Boston," *NAR* 106 (Jan. 1868): 14.

47. Ibid., 15.

48. Ibid., 17.

49. Ibid., 18.

50. Ibid., 21.

51. In 1868, Vanderbilt attempted to gain control of the major lines linking New York and Chicago and soon found himself challenged by Gould, Fisk, and Drew, working together to achieve the same end. The struggle focused on control over the Erie Railroad, which appeared to both sides to be a crucial asset if a system, eliminating competition, was to be successfully created. Adams and the historian Matthew Josephson have recounted the details of the story. Suffice it to say that it involved watered stock, the virtual theft of stockholders' funds by the directors of corporations, the bribery of judges and legislators in New York and New Jersey, the alliance of the "Erie Ring" (Fisk and Gould) with the "Tammany Ring" (Peter B. Sweeney and William M. Tweed) to take over the directorship of a major corporation, and even a fantastical night escape across state lines with trunk-loads of greenbacks by some of the malefactors to avoid arrest. This was the stuff of great satire and a platform for easy denunciation. And Adams did extensive research, and apparently some fine investigative reporting, to uncover the minutiae that added up to grand scandal. Matthew Josephson, who popularized the view of the Gilded Age as one lorded over by "robber barons," credited Adams's article as "substantially correct" (*Robber Barons*, 121).

52. Henry Adams to C. F. Adams, May 8, 1867, in Levenson et al., *Letters of Henry Adams*, 1:532; C. F. Adams, "Boston," 7–12; Kirkland, *Charles Francis Adams*, chap. 3, esp. 77–78.

53. "A Chapter of Erie" (orig. *NAR*, July 1869), reprinted in Adams and Adams, *Chapters of Erie*, 8.

54. Ibid., 12. Admittedly, Adams's tone in this essay was uncommonly dark.

55. Kirkland, *Charles Francis Adams*, 41–43. Adams's recommendation was made in "Railroad Inflation," *NAR* 108 (Jan. 1869): 162.

56. McCraw, *Prophets of Regulation*, 17–47.

CHAPTER FOUR

1. "Politics," *Atlantic Monthly*, Jan. 1872, 124–26 (emphasis added). Although the passage is broken up by commentary, the quotations in this and the succeeding paragraph present three continuous, unedited paragraphs. Howells's article proposed to explain the more limited Liberal Republican campaign to oust Grant in the 1872 election, but it stands as well as a summation of the broader liberal reform program and ideology.

2. Karl Polanyi's interpretation of the forced creation of the so-called self-regulating

market examines the historical record of nineteenth-century English economic liberalism and demonstrates that the same kind of administrative tendencies grew out of the doctrinaire politics of laissez-faire (*Great Transformation*, chaps. 12–13, esp. 139).

3. J. N. Pomeroy, "The Power of Congress to Regulate Railway Commerce," *Nation*, July 30, 1868, 86–88.

4. For the history of the fiscal revolution and the politics attendant on it, see Unger, *Greenback Era*, chap. 1, and Sharkey, *Money, Class, and Party*, chaps. 1–3; on war financing, Bensel, *Yankee Leviathan*, chap. 4; and on postwar conflicts, Brock, *An American Crisis*, 215–28.

5. Godkin, "What Inflation Means," *Nation*, Dec. 12, 1867, 480; "Business Reviving," *Harper's Weekly*, Mar. 7, 1868, 147; "Currency Contraction," *Chicago Tribune*, June 1, 1867; Logsdon, *Horace White*, 157; Edward Atkinson to Edwin Laurence Godkin, June 24, 1867, Horace White to Edward Atkinson, Sept. 25, 1867, and Edward Atkinson to Horace White, Sept. 30, 1867, all in Edward Atkinson Papers, Massachusetts Historical Society, Boston, Mass.; Bensel, *Yankee Leviathan*, 255–60, 284–85. The divisions closely correspond to Livingston's distinctions between metropolitan and continental capital (*Pragmatism*, 31–40).

6. Unger, *Greenback Era*, 17, 73–85; Sharkey, *Money, Class, and Party*, 96, 102–4; Montgomery, *Beyond Equality*, 177, 345–50, 425–45.

7. Charles Eliot Norton to Edwin Lawrence Godkin, Feb. 4, 1868, ELGP. The *Nation* frequently used the expression "extreme Radicals" in the period when it was searching for a way to distinguish its own correct Radical position from illegitimate ones.

8. Godkin, "Who Are the Bondholders?" *Nation*, Feb. 6, 1868, 104–5. See also Curtis's almost weekly editorials on the debt in the 1868 issues of *Harper's Weekly*.

9. "The Nomination of Grant," *Nation*, Dec. 19, 1867, 504.

10. The last two points had been in doubt for a short time; when they were cleared up satisfactorily, emergent liberal publicists were enormously relieved and convinced that they had found the right candidate. The momentum for Grant's nomination can be tracked in the *Atlantic Monthly*, *Harper's Weekly*, and the *Nation* from the fall of 1867 through 1868.

11. Logsdon, *Horace White*, 155–57.

12. On the Republican and Democratic campaigns, see Foner, *Reconstruction*, 337–43, and Montgomery, *Beyond Equality*, 350–54. For the liberal Radicals' interpretation of the issues at stake in the 1868 election, see "The Destructive Democracy," *Atlantic Monthly*, Feb. 1868, 133–46, and "The Next President," *Atlantic Monthly*, May 1868, 628–32. For a history of the bond question, see Dewey, *Financial History*, 332–49.

13. Noyes, *Thirty Years of American Finance*, 17. The lame-duck Forty-Ninth Congress, in recognition of the election verdict, had passed a similar bill for redemption of the bonds in gold that was pocket-vetoed by Johnson (Montgomery, *Beyond Equality*, 355).

14. "True Radicalism," *Nation*, July 18, 1867, 50–51.

15. "The Reform Movement," *Nation*, Jan. 21, 1869, 46.

16. U.S. Congress, House, *Report of the Special Commissioner of the Revenue* [for 1868] (hereafter cited as "Rev. Comm. Report for 1868"); for its reception, see Ferleger, "David A. Wells," 274–79.

17. On Wells's change in mood and opinion, compare Rev. Comm. Report for 1868 and

Rev. Comm. Report for 1869. His analysis of the inefficiency of patronage appointees can be seen as early as the commission's report for 1866 (U.S. Revenue Commission, *Reports of a Commission* [for 1866], 4–8 [hereafter cited as "Rev. Comm. Report for 1866"]); it was already far developed in the report for 1867 (U.S. Congress, House, *Report of the Special Commissioner of the Revenue* [for 1867], 72–78).

18. Bensel, *Yankee Leviathan*, 318–20.

19. For a defense of the importance of the Supreme Court and its role as a check on legislatures, see J. N. Pomeroy, "The Use of the Supreme Court to the Union," *Nation*, Feb. 20, 1868, and "The New United States Judges," *Nation*, Dec. 2, 1869, 477–78. The question remained a live one, as attested to by Godkin's inclusion of the opposition of one of his main editorial writers to the strengthening of the Court, even as he publicly defended it. See C. C. Nott, "The Burden on the Supreme Court," *Nation*, Jan. 13, 1870, 22–23; Godkin, "The Legal Tender Decisions," *Nation*, Feb. 25, 1869, 145–46; and "The Legal Tender Decision," *Nation*, Feb. 17, 1870, 100. The disagreement among liberal reformers over *Hepburn* and the reconsideration and reversal of the decision in *Knox v. Lee* concerned primarily the question of national power in a wartime emergency, not disagreements over fiscal management. For a further discussion, see Cohen, "Problem of Democracy," 229–31.

20. Walker, "The Report of the Special Commissioner," in Dewey, *Discussions in Economics and Statistics*, 1:55–68.

21. Sedgwick, "Commissions," *Nation*, Mar. 31, 1870, 203–4, and "The Political Prospect," *Nation*, Sept. 1, 1870, 132.

22. Sproat, *"Best Men,"* 78.

23. Wells, "The Meaning of Revenue Reform," *NAR* 113 (July 1871): 104–53.

24. Ibid., 132.

25. See, for example, E. Atkinson, "Inefficiency of Economic Legislation," *JSS* 4 (1872): 122–32.

26. Wells, "Meaning of Revenue Reform," 145.

27. Ibid., 105.

28. Favoring Senator George Hoar's recommendation that Congress appoint a commission to investigate the condition of labor in the United States, because it was also affected by commerce, finance, and the currency, the *Nation* curtly reminded readers that when Wells had made a similar investigation and recommendation, he was roundly criticized and that the president had succumbed to popular pressure and removed him (Sedgwick, "The 'Condition of the Laborer,' " *Nation*, Dec. 21, 1871, 397–98).

29. For a particularly pointed example of this interpretation of the liberal reformers, see Hoogenboom, "Spoilsmen and Reformers."

30. Parton, "The Government of the City of New York," *NAR* 103 (Oct. 1866): 413–65; Curtis, "The New York 'Ring' Revealed," *Harper's Weekly*, Nov. 3, 1866; Curtis, "Custom-House Fraud," *Harper's Weekly*, Mar. 3, 1866; Rev. Comm. Report for 1866, 4–8. From a thorough survey of the *Nation* and *Harper's Weekly*, it is clear that corruption in the Republican Party and national government emerged as a central issue in 1869. This was the year of the "Erie Raid" and "Gold Corner," the third-party labor bids for office, Grant's quest to annex Santo Domingo, and the alienation of Wells from the administration over tariff policy. On the importance of efficient governance, see "Mr. Wells's Report for 1868,"

Nation, Jan. 14, 1869, 24–25; "The Way the Income Tax Ought to Be Collected" and "The Way It Ought Not to Be Collected," *Nation*, Nov. 25, 1869, 452–53; and "Economy," *Nation*, Mar. 24, 1870, 187–88. On the connection between the focus on corruption, concerns over taxation, the need for rule by the best men, and the rise of popular movements, see "The Next Work for the Republican Party," *Nation*, Aug. 19, 1869, 144–45, and "The Ring in the West," *Nation*, Oct. 28, 1869, 358–59.

31. Sproat, *"Best Men,"* 85–88.

32. Fels, *American Business Cycles*, 99–101; Josephson, *Robber Barons*, 168–71.

33. No accurate statistics on unemployment were yet compiled, and contemporary assessments of the numbers of unemployed varied widely. See Bernstein, "American Labor in the Long Depression," 60–61, 81–82.

34. Wright, *Old South, New South*, 57, 76; Woodward, *Origins of the New South*, chap. 7.

35. U.S. Congress, House, *Investigation by a Select Committee*, quotation on 1.

36. U.S. Congress, Senate, *Upon the Relations between Labor and Capital*. References in card catalogs and the indexes to the publications of the U.S. Congress list the publication as 5 volumes. The Library of Congress card for this publication, however, quotes from Senator Henry W. Blair's letter to explain that no fifth volume was published.

37. On the 1874 elections and party competition, see Foner, *Reconstruction*, 523–24, and Summers, *Era of Good Stealings*, 253–55. On theories of late-nineteenth-century political parties, see McCormick, *Party Period and Public Policy*, chaps. 1–4, esp. 171–76. For a characteristic condemnation of the lassitude of Gilded Age politicians, see Hofstadter, *Age of Reform*, 60. For an argument for stalemate that joins the use of the concept of critical elections to the ethnocultural thesis, see Kleppner, *Third Electoral System*, and Kleppner, "Political Revolution of the 1890s." For a structural analysis of the American state that recasts the terms of the debate and offers a more persuasive analysis of political stalemate, see Skowronek, *Building a New American State*.

38. Gutman, "Movement by the Unemployed"; Gutman, "Tompkins Square 'Riot,'" quotation on 56.

39. The most significant case was that of the Molly Maguire trial. See Kenny, *Making Sense*.

40. Bernstein, "American Labor in the Long Depression," 76–77, 82; Katz, *Shadow of the Poorhouse*, 86. On Chicago, see Sawislak, *Smoldering City*, 265–77.

41. Curtis quoted in Gutman, "Tompkins Square 'Riot,'" 56; Kenny, *Making Sense*; Massachusetts, Railroad Commission, *R.R. Commissioners' Special Report*, 15.

42. Foner, *Great Labor Uprising of 1877*, 231–40.

43. Keller, *Affairs of State*, 176–79; Miller, *Railroads and the Granger Laws*, 78–79.

44. See above, chapter 3. Compare McCraw, *Prophets of Regulation*, chap. 1.

45. C. F. Adams, "The Protection of the Ballot in National Elections," *JSS* 1 (June 1869): 91–111.

46. C. F. Adams, "The Government and Railroad Corporations," *NAR* 112 (Jan. 1871): 31–61.

47. "The Regulation of All Railroads through the State-Ownership of One," speech of C. F. Adams on behalf of the Mass. Board of Railroad Commissioners, made before the joint standing legislative committee on railways, Feb. 14, 1873.

48. Quotation in Godkin's response to Edward F. Adams, "The Wisconsin Method of Railroad Reform: Correspondence," *Nation*, Aug. 20, 1874, 121–22. Other articles on the Grange laws in the *Nation* are Godkin, "Corporations and Monopolies," June 4, 1874, 359–60; Sedgwick, "The Right to Confiscate," Sept. 24, 1874, 199–201; Godkin, "Potter and His Law," Oct. 8, 1874, 231–33; C. F. Adams, "The Experience of a Great Corporation," Oct. 22, 1874, 264–65; Wells, "How Will the United States Supreme Court Decide the Granger Railroad Cases? Correspondence," Oct. 29, 1874, 282–84; and C. F. Adams, "The 'Bloated Bondholder,'" Nov. 26, 1874, 345–46. The importance of the panic can be seen by comparing the tone of these above-cited articles with Adams's measured rhetoric in one of his prepanic articles, "The 'Farmers' Clubs' and the Railroads," *Nation*, Apr. 10, 1873, 249–50.

49. C. F. Adams, "The Last Railroad Grievance," *Nation*, Mar. 23, 1876, 190–91; Mc-Craw, *Prophets of Regulation*, 48–49. On Adams's subsequent career, see McCraw, chap. 1; Kirkland, *Charles Francis Adams*; and Skowronek, *Building a New American State*.

50. Wells, "How Will the United States Supreme Court Decide the Granger Railroad Cases? Correspondence," *Nation*, Oct. 29, 1874, 282–84; Stephen J. Field to David A. Wells, June 29, 1877, David Ames Wells Papers, NYPL; Miller, *Railroads and the Granger Laws*, 95–96, 116, 170–71, 187–93, quotations on 188, 187.

51. Godkin, "The Granger Collapse," *Nation*, Jan. 27, 1876, 57–58; Keller, *Affairs of State*, 193–95; Thomas Nast, "Public Opinion," *Harper's Weekly*, May 23, 1874, 432.

52. Keller, *Affairs of State*, 110–21.

53. Sedgwick, "The Future of Legislatures," *Nation*, May 20, 1875, 341–42.

54. Godkin, "Municipal Government," *Nation*, May 30, 1867; C. C. Nott, "The Bottom of the Great City Difficulty," *Nation*, Sept. 7, 1871, 157–59. Godkin reported that he received many favorable letters on Nott's article treating the city as a "joint-stock association" ("Municipal Government," *Nation*, Sept. 21, 1871, 188–90).

55. The proposals sought to amend the state constitution, which required a favorable vote in two successive legislatures. The plan passed in the fall of 1877 but was rejected in the spring of 1878 and hence never adopted. See New York Assembly, *Report of the Commission to Devise a Plan for the Government of Cities*; Mandelbaum, *Boss Tweed's New York*, 169–72; and compare Keller, *Affairs of State*, 119–20. For liberal reform opinion, see "[The Tilden Commission]," *Nation*, Mar. 22, 1877, 170–71.

56. Norton, *Orations and Addresses*, 2:20.

57. Walker, "American Industry in the Census," *Atlantic Monthly*, Dec. 1869, 678–701. The interpretation put forward in this paragraph is based on extensive reading of the *Nation*, *North American Review*, *Atlantic Monthly*, *Harper's Weekly*, and personal papers of liberal reformers in the formative years of the civil service reform movement, 1866–72. Much reform activity was directed at state and municipal governments, which, after the repeal of most wartime taxes by 1872, stood as the primary taxing authorities in the country. For an exemplary analysis of the politics of civil service reform, see Yearley, *Money Machine*. For a revisionist interpretation of Gilded Age corruption, see Summers, *Era of Good Stealings*.

58. Sproat, *"Best Men,"* 90–103.

59. For a history of civil service developments, see Skowronek, *Building a New American State*, 57–65.

60. See Mill, *Considerations on Representative Government*, chaps. 5–7.

61. "Minority representation" proposed that the vote of a taxpayer or property owner be weighted, thus counting for more than one vote. See, for example, Nordhoff, "The Misgovernment of New York,—A Remedy Suggested," *NAR* 113 (Oct. 1871): 321–43.

62. J. M. McKim, "The Vexed Question: Correspondence," *Nation*, Apr. 14, 1870, 237.

63. In the context of the discussion in this chapter, it is worth noting that the debates in 1879 were triggered by the Republican proposal to enact additional laws to supervise elections in the South to ensure that black men were not defrauded of their right to vote. The debates raised questions about patronage, legislative activism, and federalism, thus placing the issue of black suffrage in the middle of other issues of liberal reform. For works referred to here, see James G. Blaine, L. Q. C. Lamar, Wade Hampton, James A. Garfield, Alexander H. Stephens, Wendell Phillips, Montgomery Blair, and Thomas A. Hendricks, "Ought the Negro to Be Disfranchised? Ought He to Have Been Enfranchised?," *NAR* 128 (Mar. 1879): 225–83; *Nation*, Feb. 13, 1879, 113–14; Apr. 3, 1879, 226–27; *Harper's Weekly*, Feb. 1, 1879, Apr. 12, 1879, 282, 292–93.

CHAPTER FIVE

1. George, *Progress and Poverty*.

2. David A. Wells to Edward Atkinson, Mar. 20, 1880, Edward Atkinson Papers, Massachusetts Historical Society, Boston, Mass. George, however, had been a participant in the Liberal Republican movement and was personally acquainted with Horace White (Logsdon, *Horace White*, 354 n. 53).

3. George, *Progress and Poverty*, 11.

4. For example, several conservative national business organizations, once bastions of hard-money orthodoxy, voted against specie resumption in 1870 and 1871, as their members were enjoying the speculative boom encouraged by the government's soft-money, inflationary policy (Unger, *Greenback Era*, 165–69).

5. In the United States, serious depressions occurred during the years 1873–79, 1883–85, and 1893–96, while the intervening years witnessed one short-lived boom and a longer period of stagnation. The scholarly debate over whether the economic statistics of the period justify designating the period as a depression has continued over several decades. It is clear, at least, that those who lived through the period viewed it as one of secular crisis. For different theoretical approaches supporting the theory of crisis, see Fels, *American Business Cycles*; Gordon, Edwards, and Reich, *Segmented Work, Divided Workers*, 18–47, 94–127; and Livingston, "Social Analysis."

6. As in so many other ways, the *Slaughterhouse* decision and dissent set a precedent in this regard (Twiss, *Lawyers and the Constitution*, chap. 3).

7. George, *Progress and Poverty*; Bellamy, *Looking Backward*; Harvey, *Coin's Financial School*; Twain, *A Connecticut Yankee*; Donnelly, *Caesar's Column*; Washington Gladden, "Is Labor a Commodity?," *Forum*, July 1886, 468–76; quotations in Washington Gladden, "Socialism and Unsocialism," *Forum*, Apr. 1887, 127, 128.

8. On the professionalization of social science and the transformation of higher education, see Furner, *Advocacy and Objectivity*, Ross, "Socialism and American liberalism"; Ross, *Origins of American Social Science*; Haskell, *Emergence of Professional Social Science*; and Veysey, *Emergence of the American University*. The still indispensable history of American economic thought is Dorfman, *Economic Mind in American Civilization*.

9. Both terminologies are used by the historians of the debate in political economy. For reasons that should be clear by now, I avoid the term "classical liberal" in favor of "classical economist" or "liberal reformer." I use "new school" and "ethical economist" interchangeably. The terms "old school" and "new school" were in contemporary use but had rather ambivalent connotations to the men of the new school, as evidenced by one of its practitioners referring to a request for writing from "the 'new school' of political economy, if there is such a thing" (H. C. Adams to Mother, Mar. 1, 1886, HCAP).

10. For an alternative interpretation of the rise and significance of expertise, see Haskell, *Emergence of Professional Social Science*, esp. 44–88.

11. The literature on this subject is extensive. For an introduction, see Levy, *Socialism and the Intelligentsia*, 1–34. It is perhaps worth observing that Marxist theory was largely the product of middle-class intellectuals associated with the movement, starting, of course, with Marx and Engels themselves. For a comparison of some American intellectuals with their European counterparts that addresses some of these questions, see Kloppenberg, *Uncertain Victory*.

12. For analyses of the conflict as a matter of intellectual history and the cultural transmission and transformation of ideas, see Furner, *Advocacy and Objectivity*, and Ross, *Origins of American Social Science*, chaps. 3–4.

13. Quoted in Fink, *Workingmen's Democracy*, 4.

14. Bellomy, "Molding of an Iconoclast," 45–47.

15. Hofstadter, *Social Darwinism in American Thought*, 53–54; quotation in Bellomy, "Molding of an Iconoclast," 290–91.

16. This brief review is based on the reading of Sumner's essays from the late 1870s to the mid-1880s, particularly the books directed at a popular audience, *What Social Classes Owe to Each Other* and *Collected Essays*. Bellomy, who focuses on Sumner's early life, found his subject to be a "reactive" thinker. Hofstadter's elegant and devastating portrait of Sumner has not been surpassed in style, wit, and perspicuity. For an opposing view of Sumner that argues that he was not a social Darwinist and that he was an important and original intellectual, see Bannister, *Social Darwinism*, chap. 5. In my opinion, neither of Bannister's appraisals of Sumner is sustainable.

17. Sumner, *What Social Classes Owe to Each Other*, 145.

18. Sumner, "Socialism," *Scribner's Monthly* 16 (Oct. 1878): 887–93, quotations on 892, 893.

19. Sumner, *What Social Classes Owe to Each Other*, 141, quotation on 88.

20. Ibid., chaps. 6 and 3, respectively. Chapter 3 is Sumner's clearest articulation of the relationship between capital and civilization, though the idea is woven through the argument of the entire book.

21. *DAB*, 10:342–45.

22. For an alternative view of the importance of organizational changes and their effects on humanitarian reform, see Fredrickson, *Inner Civil War*.

23. Walker, "The Wage-Fund Theory," *NAR* 120 (Jan. 1875); Walker, *Wages Question*. The wage-fund doctrine had been refuted in England by William Thornton, and John Stuart Mill had abandoned the doctrine after being persuaded by Thornton's refutation. But despite such overwhelming authority for consigning the theory to oblivion, American

liberals clung tenaciously to it—for good reason, given the political conditions of the United States. Walker's refutation was not therefore the first, but it was highly persuasive.

24. Walker, *Wages Question*, 143.

25. The substance of Walker's refutation of the wage-fund doctrine is in ibid., chaps. 8 and 9.

26. Dobb, *Theories of Value and Distribution*, chap. 7. The most renowned of these economists were Stanley Jevons, Carl Menger, and Léon Walras; the three independently developed utility theory in the 1870s. In the United States, John Bates Clark independently developed a version of marginal utility theory in the late 1870s. When he did so, he was unaware of the work of the European economists. For this reason, opinion varies on whether Clark should be considered one of the several independent inventors of marginalism. Dobb did not consider him to be one. In addition to the development of marginal utility theory, a school of German historical economics had been internationally recognized since the late 1860s. There are many histories of international economic thought. For one containing clear expositions of economic doctrines, see Gide and Rist, *History of Economic Doctrines*.

27. A mixed review appeared in the *Nation*, written by the eminent scientist and economist Simon Newcomb. The crux of Newcomb's criticism was that Walker failed to credit the importance of capital's contribution to "civilization" and consequently the laborer's interest in capital's access to its just share of distribution (Newcomb, "Walker on the Wages Question," *Nation*, July 6, 1876, 12–13).

28. On Sidgwick's review of Walker, see Livingston, "Social Analysis," 89 and 89 n. 45.

29. Dobb, *Theories of Value and Distribution*, chap. 7; Ross, *Origins of American Social Science*, chaps. 4, 6.

30. Walker, *Wages Question*, chaps. 4, 8, 9, 13.

31. On the importance of the moral claims made by producers through the labor theory of value, see Livingston, *Pragmatism*, 41–50. The vision of the moral superiority of the producer was perhaps even stronger in the South among freedmen and the white yeomanry. But Walker carefully defined the "wages question" as an issue only of the class that was paid cash wages. He thus in effect limited his study to the industrial working class, and without explicitly addressing alternative definitions, he rejected the broader notion of the "producing classes" held by many Americans. His definition enabled him to exclude an analysis of most of the nation's agricultural production in his study.

32. He did so by recategorizing employers as the "entrepreneurial class," providing the indispensable service of management. For a further discussion of this aspect of his thought, see Cohen, "Problem of Democracy," 281–85. For an appraisal of the weakness of Walker's economic ideas as they were elaborated in subsequent decades, see Dorfman's comments in Dewey, *Discussions in Economics and Statistics*, 13–16.

33. The liberal reformer who took on this task most avidly was the textile manufacturer and insurance industry leader Edward Atkinson. See especially the speeches in Atkinson, *Labor and Capital, Allies Not Enemies* and *Addresses Upon the Labor Question*. For an analysis of the publicity and educational activities and organizations of the liberal reformers, see Sproat, *"Best Men."*

34. See chapter 1 above.

35. This biographical sketch is drawn primarily from Adams's personal papers. For

additional information, see the perceptive analyses by Dorfman in Dorfman, *Essays by Henry Carter Adams*, introduction; Coats, "Henry Carter Adams"; and Ross "Socialism and American Liberalism."

36. Adams, Andover Diary, Apr. 19, 1876, p. 41, HCAP.

37. Adams, Baltimore Diary, Aug. 2, 1877, HCAP.

38. On his relationship to Walker, see F. A. Walker to H. C. Adams, Aug. 30, 1877, HCAP.

39. H. C. Adams to Mother, Oct. 21, 1877, HCAP.

40. H. C. Adams to Mother, Apr. 18 and 30, 1878, HCAP.

41. Gide and Rist, *History of Economic Doctrines*, bk. 4, chap. 1; Ross, *Origins of American Social Science*, chap. 4, esp. 104; Dorfman, *Economic Mind in American Civilization*, 3:87–98, 160–64.

42. H. C. Adams to Mother, Berlin, Oct. 12, 1878, HCAP.

43. H. C. Adams to Mother, Oct. 29, Nov. 10, "Sunday morning Nov. [illeg.]," Dec. 1, 1878, and Jan. 18, 1879; H. C. Adams to Father, June 20 [mistakenly dated 1878, written in 1879]; Berlin Diary, [late Dec. 1878 or early Jan. 1879], p. 20; quotation in Berlin Diary, Dec. 7, 1878, p. 9, all in HCAP.

44. Berlin Diary, Monday, [Dec.] 10, 1878, pp. 25–26, HCAP.

45. On agnosticism, see 1877 diary, Mar. 17, 1882, HCAP. (The bizarre dating is explained by the fact that Adams wrote a few entries in his 1877 diary after he returned from Europe. Most of the entries were commentaries on his entries from youth.) Adams rarely used the term "proletariat," but at the same time he finished his first article on socialism, he was searching for a means to limit large property and preserve the independence of "personalized personal production" as opposed to "capitalized personal productive activity" (Berlin Diary, in entry titled "For Miscellaneous," Dec. 20, 1878, HCAP). The language is convoluted—perhaps to trick the German censors—but underneath we can see Adams's concern that abstract property claims and the creation of a mass proletariat were linked.

46. Adams, "The Position of Socialism in the Historical Development of Political Economy," *Penn Monthly*, Apr. 1879, 285–94; "Democracy," *New Englander* 40 (Nov. 1881): 752–72. The admission was made in H. C. Adams to Mother, Jan. 18, 1879, HCAP.

47. For a brief collective biography, see Ross, *Origins of American Social Science*, 102–3. Contemporaries of the ethical economists who held more closely to the tradition of classical political economy and were trained in American universities by conservative professors such as W. G. Sumner and Charles F. Dunbar included Arthur T. Hadley, J. Laurence Laughlin, Frank W. Taussig, and Henry W. Farnam.

There were other men and women emerging as intellectuals in the seventies and eighties as well. At the time, however, only those who entered the social sciences (political economy, political science, history, and, later, sociology) engaged in broadly political debates and had an influence over government policy. A slightly younger cohort of intellectuals began their careers later in philosophy and psychology, and although some were publishing in the late 1870s and 1880s, they hardly ever addressed political questions proper. By the 1890s, a number of them would be active in the progressive movement and agitating for political reforms. The most important figure who fits in this category was John Dewey. Robert Westbrook, one of Dewey's most sympathetic recent biographers, points out that Dewey was preoccupied with the epistemological issues raised by Hegel's idealism from the time he began to publish (1882) until 1892, and only in the late 1880s did he begin to think about democracy and politics (Westbrook, *John Dewey and American Democracy*, 14–15). A more problematic figure to categorize in the intellectuals' political spectrum is William James. One of his recent defenders has categorized James as a socialist (Livingston, *Pragmatism*, 166). But before the turn of the century, James called himself a liberal individualist and considered Godkin his political guide. An intellectual history of the late nineteenth century would have to account for activity in all disciplines and the arts. The focus of this work, however, is on political intellectuals, and as it has already been argued, the political intellectuals who came of age and exerted influence from the late 1870s through the mid-1890s—with rare exceptions—were amateur or professional social scientists.

48. For an astute inquiry into the centrality of socialism in the early work of the American ethical economists, see Ross, "Socialism and American Liberalism," and Ross, *Origins of American Social Science*, chap. 4. Ross, I think, underestimates their break with the conventional wisdom of the liberal reform intellectuals. For example, in correctly noting their ambiguity about socialist programs, she observes that "liberal reformers" also favored programs such as profit sharing, cooperation, and arbitration. But as her study does not include nonacademic intellectuals, she misses the differences in the ways these types of programs were conceived by the two groups.

49. H. C. Adams, "Democracy," *New Englander* 40 (Nov. 1881): 752–72.

50. Clark, "How to Deal with Communism," *New Englander* 37 (July 1878): 533–42.

51. Clark, "Business Ethics, Past and Present," *New Englander* 38 (Mar. 1879): 157–68.

52. Clark, "The Nature and Progress of True Socialism," *New Englander* 38 (July 1879): 565–81, quotations on 566.

53. Ibid., quotations on 580, 571.

54. Ibid., 572–78, quotations on 577, 578.

55. H. C. Adams, "Democracy," quotation on 765.

56. Ibid., 756–57. Adams noted that Russian local government was the sole exception to the historical fact that democracy originated in individualism.

57. Ibid., 761.

58. Ibid., 763–65, 770–72.

59. In one letter, Adams described to his mother a visit to the Bowery home of a tailor active in the Knights of Labor. He was virtually dumbstruck by his experience, and his praise of the man demonstrates that, for him, the visit was an excursion into an exotic, unknown world (H. C. Adams to Mother, New York City, June 8, 1882, HCAP).

60. Ely, "Past and Present in Political Economy," *Johns Hopkins University Studies in History and Political Science* 2 (Mar. 1884): 143–202.

61. For the earlier attack on the German school, see Godkin, "The New German Political Economy," Sept. 9, 1875, 161–62, and Godkin's response to Allen, "The New German Economists: Correspondence," Sept. 23, 1875, 195–97, quotation on 197; for the review of Ely, see "Notes on R. T. Ely's 'The Past and Present of Political Economy,'" July 24, 1884, 74, all in *Nation*. For an extended critical review by a frequent contributor to the *Nation*, see Newcomb, "The Two Schools of Political Economy," *Princeton Review* 60 (Nov. 1884): 291–301.

62. See especially the essay, "Sociology," in Sumner, *Collected Essays*, 77–97.

63. R. T. Ely to H. C. Adams, June 18, 1885, and Arthur T. Hadley to R. T. Ely, Sept. 26, 1885, encl. with Arthur T. Hadley to H. C. Adams, Oct. 19, 1885, HCAP; R. T. Ely to E. R. A. Seligman, June 9, 1885, E. R. A. Seligman Papers, Rare Book and Manuscript Library, Columbia University, New York, N.Y.

64. The meeting is reported in Ely, "Report of the Organization of the American Economic Association," *AER* 1 (Mar. 1886): 5–46, quotations on 6, 19.

65. Ibid., 35.

66. For a more extensive discussion of the formation of the AEA, see Furner, *Advocacy and Objectivity*, chap. 3.

67. For the most pointed theoretical debate between the two schools of political economy, see Adams et al., *Science Economic Discussion*.

68. H. C. Adams to Mother, Nov. 7, 1883, HCAP.

69. For membership figures for both organizations, see Hattam, *Labor Visions and State Power*, 116 n. 6; for strike statistics, see Montgomery, "Strikes in Nineteenth-Century America," 92–93.

70. Constitution of the Knights of Labor, in Commager, *Documents of American History*, 1:546–47.

71. Hattam, *Labor Visions and State Power*; Fink, *Workingmen's Democracy*; Leiby, *Carroll Wright and Labor Reform*, 69–73.

72. On Haymarket, see Foner, *Great Labor Uprising of 1877*. An example of the use of Haymarket to delegitimize the whole labor movement can be found in the *Nation*, May 6 and 13, 1886, esp. 392–93, 396. Examples of the other tendency, to distinguish between the un-American violent immigrant and the true American laborer, can be found in Andrew Carnegie, "Results of the Labor Struggle," *Forum*, Aug. 1886, 538–51; J. L. Spalding, "Are We in Danger of Revolution," *Forum*, July 1886, 405–15; and Curtis, *Harper's Weekly*, May 8, 1886, 290.

73. In addition to planning meetings and organizing the business of the association, Ely chose which articles to publish in the AEA journal. The three articles published in 1886 were by the members most sympathetic to the labor movement. One turned the liberal reformers' criticism of municipal corruption on its head to demand public ownership of gas companies, and two others positively portrayed experiments in cooperative enterprise. See Edmund J. James, "The Relation of the Modern Municipality to the Gas Supply," *PAEA* 1 (May/July 1886): 7–76; Albert Shaw, "Coöperation in a Western City," *PAEA* 1 (Sept. 1886): 7–106; and Edward W. Bemis, "Coöperation in New England," *PAEA* 1 (Nov. 1886): 7–136.

74. Newcomb, "Dr. Ely on the Labor Movement," *Nation*, Oct. 7, 1886, 293–94; Ely wrote Clark that "men like Godkin of the Nation are putting pressure to . . . drive me out of J.H.U." and asked Clark to help him in whatever way he could (R. T. Ely to John Bates Clark, Dec. 1, 1886, JBCP). The following letters demonstrate that Clark tried to do so: Alexander Johnston to John Bates Clark, Dec. 17, 1886; quotation in H. C. Adams to John Bates Clark, Dec, 16, 1886; Washington Gladden to John Bates Clark, Dec. 25, 1886, all in JBCP. See also Ross, *Origins of American Social Science*, 116–18.

75. H. C. Adams, "Democracy," 770.

76. Adams, "On the Education of Statesmen," *Princeton Review* 60 (Jan. 1884): 16–35.

77. Adams, "The Labor Problem," in "Silbey College Lectures—XI," *Scientific American Supplement*, [Aug. 1886], 8861–63. See also an abbreviated version of the speech, which Adams had promised to a newspaper publisher, entitled "What Do These Strikes Mean?," encl. in H. C. Adams to James B. Angell, Mar. 25, 1887, James B. Angell Papers, Bentley Historical Library, University of Michigan, Ann Arbor, Mich.

78. Adams, "Labor Problem."

79. The account of Adams's academic travails in this and the following two paragraphs is based on the following unpublished sources. Quotations from Angell are in James B. Angell to H. C. Adams, Mar. 19, 1886, and Mar. 12, 1887, HCAP; quotations from Adams are in H. C. Adams to J. B. Angell, Mar. 25, 1886, and Mar. 15, 1887, Angell Papers. Other sources revealing Adams's ordeal at Cornell and Michigan are speech of Henry Sage, in "The Sibley Lectures," second session, *Scientific American Supplement*; H. C. Adams to James B. Angell, May 26, 1887, Angell Papers; Charles Henry Hull to H. C. Adams, Sept. 19, 1886; James B. Angell to H. C. Adams, Mar. 26, 1887, all in HCAP. See also T. M. Cooley, diary entry, Mar. 30, 1886, in Personal Memoranda, 1879–94, Thomas McIntyre Cooley Papers, Bentley Historical Library, University of Michigan, Ann Arbor, Mich., in which Cooley wrote that Dr. Angell "also took occasion to talk with me about Dr. H. C. Adams & his peculiar notions which seem to verge on Socialism. Dr. Adams has thus far had only temporary appointments here, the fear that he might do & say foolish things preventing anything more." Adams explained the circumstances of the Cornell speech and Sage's role in the affair in his scrapbook (vol. 2, HCAP), though his account of his own subsequent behavior does not accord completely with the evidence from the contemporary letters. The scrapbook entry, though undated, was clearly written a number of years after the incident. For another account, see Furner, *Advocacy and Objectivity*, chap. 6.

80. H. C. Adams, "Shall We Muzzle the Anarchists?," *Forum*, July 1886, 445–54.

81. R. Mayo-Smith to H. C. Adams, June 10, 1887, HCAP.

82. Ross, *Origins of American Social Science*, 111–17.

83. In 1881, Godkin, along with Carl Schurz, Horace White, and Henry Villard, bought the late William Cullen Bryant's *New York Evening Post*. Wells and the former secretary of the treasury, Benjamin Bristow, served as trustees (Armstrong, *E. L. Godkin*, 142–45).

84. On these cases, see Hofstadter and Metzger, *Development of Academic Freedom*, chap. 9.

CHAPTER SIX

1. On the theoretical debates raised during the process of reconciliation, see, for example, Adams et al., *Science Economic Discussion*. Walker's role is illustrated in his 1889 presidential address to the AEA, "Recent Progress of Political Economy in the United States," *PAEA* 4 (July 1889): 254–68. The *PAEA* volumes for the years 1887–95 contain many articles germane to the debate. For a representative statement of Godkin's position in these years, see Godkin, "Economic Man" (orig. *NAR*, 1891), in *Problems of Modern Democracy*, 156–79. The account here is focused on an analysis of the three primary theoretical questions listed above. A number of excellent studies of the debate in political economy exist. For an account of the economists' debate as a cultural process and its effect on the professionalization of social science, see Furner, *Advocacy and Objectivity*, chaps. 4–6. For an analysis of the many theoretical issues raised in the debate and their impor-

tance in the history of American social science, see Ross, *Origins of American Social Science*, chaps. 4–6.

2. Dorfman asserted that "Adams was in a very real sense the philosophical parent of much of the political-economic legislation of the next fifty years" (*Economic Mind in American Civilization*, 3:174). Skowronek discusses Adams as one of the key figures in the development of a "progressive theory of regulation" (*Building a New American State*, 132–38). Furner treats Adams as one of the most significant theorists in the "democratic statist" variant of "new liberalism" (Furner, "Republican Tradition").

3. For a more accessible introduction to his work in finance, see Adams, "Refunding the Public Debt," *Forum*, Dec. 1887, 367–75. On Adams's motivation in writing on finance, see H. C. Adams to Mother, May 10, 1880, HCAP.

4. Adams's "Relation of the State to Industrial Action" was first presented in February 1886 in a speech to the Constitution Club of New York and printed as a pamphlet, entitled "Principles That Should Control the Interference of the States in Industries," E. R. A. Seligman Collection, Rare Book and Manuscript Library, Columbia University, New York, N.Y. The revised monograph was published in *PAEA* 1 (Jan. 1887): 465–549. The edition referred to here is the *PAEA* version, reprinted in Dorfman, *Essays by Henry Carter Adams*, 56–133.

5. Adams, "Relation of the State," 66–67.

6. Ibid., 125–33.

7. Ibid, 105–14.

8. Ibid., 95.

9. Ibid., 79–83, 127–33.

10. Quotations in ibid., 129–30. This account is based on a comparison of the speech, "Principles," and the published version, "Relation of the State." Dorfman discusses the reception of the work, but it should be noted that he wrongly dates the speech, at least if the printed pamphlet is to be trusted (ibid., 28–37).

11. Ibid., 114–25.

12. Livingston, "Social Analysis."

13. Wells's *Recent Economic Changes* appeared first as a series of articles in *Popular Science Monthly*. The book did receive some negative reviews. See, for example, S. N. Patten, "Wells' Recent Economic Changes," *PSQ* 5 (1890): 84–103. Horace White defended Wells in the same volume, in "Wells' Recent Economic Changes," *PSQ* 5 (1890): 309–26. Patten, however, was something of a renegade. Almost alone among professional political economists, he was a protectionist. (And, indeed, it seems that his animus against Wells was based primarily in his hostility to Wells as a leader of the free trade movement.) While Patten also developed an economics based on the primacy of consumption, he rejected marginal utility theory as much as he did Wells's "eighteenth century" reasoning. On Patten, see Ross, *Origins of American Social Science*, 196–200. Ross's observation that Patten's importance as a " 'discoverer of abundance' " has been exaggerated by his biographer is to the point here as well.

14. Wells, *Recent Economic Changes*, 25–26.

15. Ibid., 85–86. Livingston details the similarity between the diagnoses of Wells and several other late-nineteenth-century economists and the interpretations of twentieth-century economic historians in "Social Analysis," 72–76; a "neoclassical" confirmation

of Wells's analysis is contained in Williamson, "Late Nineteenth-Century American Retardation."

16. Wells, *Recent Economic Changes*, 74.

17. Ibid., 404–5.

18. Ibid., 75.

19. On the currency reform movement, see below; on its role in the creation of a new banking system in the United States, see Livingston, *Federal Reserve System*, esp. chaps. 1, 3–4.

20. Among the liberal reform political intellectuals, Edward Atkinson and Horace White developed their economic ideas in a direction most similar to that of Wells, and indeed, the three worked together and were close friends. Atkinson was always more of an activist than a theorist, and his articulation of ideas about increased and efficient consumption is highly fanciful. Eugene Debs had a ball pillorying Atkinson's scheme to solve the problem of the working class through the invention of what he called "Alladin's Oven," a device to prevent waste of fuel and food in the preparation of meals. Nevertheless, Atkinson's diagnosis of the problem of profitability and his solution through consolidation are similar to, if not as well theorized as, Wells's. He was also one of the few of the liberal reformers who was committed to a dogmatic laissez-faire policy. For Atkinson's ideas, see the collection of his pamphlets in the Edward Atkinson Papers, Massachusetts Historical Society, Boston, Mass. He also wrote many books and articles, gave speeches, and participated in government commissions during the 1880s and 1890s. White, in *Money and Banking*, elaborated on Wells's study of economic developments to develop a theory of the cyclical tendencies of capitalism and the role of countercyclical banking methods to avert and ease crises (Livingston, *Federal Reserve System*, 74–76).

21. Ross, *Origins of American Social Science*, 179.

22. Clark, *Philosophy of Wealth*, 68.

23. F. H. Giddings to John Bates Clark, Oct. 24, 1886; Woodrow Wilson to John Bates Clark, Aug. 26, 1887, JBCP; Ross, *Origins of American Social Science*, 260.

24. Clark, "Profits under Modern Conditions," *PSQ* 2 (1887): 603.

25. For some of the immediate reaction to Clark's new theory of distribution, see the following letters in JBCP: F. H. Giddings to John Bates Clark, Sept. 9, 1887; F. A. Walker to John Bates Clark, Nov. 3, 1887; and early 1888 letters from J. W. Burgess and Julius H. Seelye. Seelye was Clark's mentor at Amherst. On Clark's influence on American economists, see Ross, *Origins of American Social Science*, 178–79, and Dorfman, *Economic Mind in American Civilization*, 3:188–205. On his significance as a social theorist, see Livingston, *Pragmatism*, 49–56, 57–63. On the originators of the marginalist school of economics, see Dobb, *Theories of Value and Distribution*, chap. 7, and Gide and Rist, *History of Economic Doctrines*, bk. 5, chap. 1.

26. Ross, *Origins of American Social Science*, 118–22, 172–81; Livingston, "Social Analysis," 87–94; Livingston, *Pragmatism*, 49–51.

27. The English economist Alfred Marshall was the most important theorist synthesizing the new economics into a theory of equilibrium; Clark was influenced by Marshall, and the two corresponded regularly. See the various letters in Clark's papers, JBCP.

28. The problem, however, with the early theories of utility was that they could not account for how consumers' incomes were determined in the first place. Critics of mar-

ginalism in the twentieth century continue to insist that marginalism founders on its circular reasoning—its assumption of exactly what it must prove. If production is a "function" of effective demand, then the distribution of income is the crucial element in determining how much of any commodity is produced. Marginalism is premised on a calculation of income distribution, in order for demand to become effective, but it has no explanation for how that distribution came about. As Dobb explained, in marginalism, "income-distribution is made to appear as something independent of property institutions and of social relations: as something supra-institutional and supra-historical so far, at least, as income-distribution between *factors* [laborers, capitalists, and landowners] is concerned" (Dobb, *Theories of Value and Distribution*, 34–35).

29. Clark, "The Philosophy of Value," *New Englander* 40 (July 1881): 457–69.

30. Ibid.; Clark, *Philosophy of Wealth* (1886), chap. 3; "The Limits of Competition," *PSQ* 2 (Mar. 1887): 45–61; Clark, *Distribution of Wealth* (1899), quotation on iv. For Clark's original articles, see "Profits under Modern Conditions," *PSQ* 2 (1887): 603–19; "Capital and Its Earnings," *PAEA* 3 (Mar. 1888): 81–149; Clark and Giddings, *Modern Distributive Process* (1888); and "Possibility of a Scientific Law of Wages," *PAEA* 4 (Mar. 1889): 37–69.

31. See Clark, *Distribution of Wealth*, chaps. 11–13 (orig. *QJE*, 1891).

32. Ross, *Origins of American Social Science*, 118–22, 403–4.

33. Livingston, "Social Analysis," 93–94.

34. Clark's theories of competition and collective bargaining appeared first in "Limits of Competition" and "Profits under Modern Conditions."

35. Clark, "Modern Appeal to Legal Forces," presidential address, American Economic Association, Dec. 26, 1894, published in *PAEA* 9 (Oct. and Dec. 1894), quotation on 482–83.

36. On the Pullman boycott, see Salvatore, *Eugene V. Debs*, 126–49; Dubofsky, *State and Labor*, 27–31; and Schneirov, Stromquist, and Salvatore, *Pullman Strike*.

37. Quoted in Dubofsky, *State and Labor*, 29.

38. H. C. Adams to E. R. A. Seligman, Aug. 28, 1894, HCAP.

39. Mott, *History of American Magazines*, 4:511–23; *DAB* entries on Rice and Page.

40. Harry Perry Robinson, "The Humiliating Report of the Strike Commission," *Forum*, Dec. 1894, 523–24.

41. Quoted in Dubofsky, *State and Labor*, 30.

42. Ely, "Fundamental Beliefs in My Social Philosophy," *Forum*, Oct. 1894, 173–83.

43. On Cooley, see Skowronek, *Building a New American State*, 153–54; Forbath, *Law and the Shaping of the American Labor Movement*, 72; and Carrington, "Law and Economics in the Creation of Federal Administrative Law." On the ICC as an experiment in administrative governance, see Skowronek, *Building a New American State*, chaps. 5, 8. Cooley's response to the strike itself justified the military response after judging the union's actions illegal (Cooley, "The Lessons of the Recent Civil Disorders," *Forum*, Sept. 1894, 1–19).

44. Clark, "Modern Appeal to Legal Forces," 492.

45. Leiby, *Carroll Wright and Labor Reform*, 28–33.

46. Ibid., chap. 3, quotation on 63.

47. Ibid., chap. 3.

48. The following account is based on U.S. Congress, Senate, U.S. Strike Commission,

Report of the Chicago Strike (hereafter cited as "U.S. Strike Commission, *Report*"); Wright, "Steps toward Government Control of Railroads," *Forum*, Jan. 1895, 704–13; and Wright, "The Chicago Strike," *PAEA* 9 (Dec. 1894): 503–22.

49. U.S. Strike Commission, *Report*, xlvi.

50. Ibid., xli.

51. Ibid., xlviii.

52. Wright, "Chicago Strike," 511.

53. For a characteristic statement of conditions in the railroad industry from the industry's perspective, see O. D. Ashley, "The General Railroad Situation," *Forum*, Oct. 1895, 266–76.

54. Wright, "Chicago Strike," quotations on 510, 511.

55. Ibid., 512.

56. Ibid., 517.

57. U.S. Strike Commission, *Report*, l–li.

58. See, for example, Robinson, "Humiliating Report of the Strike Commission."

59. Wright, "Chicago Strike," 518.

60. Ibid., 516.

61. Ibid., 518.

62. Dubofsky, *State and Labor*, 30.

63. Dorfman, *Economic Mind in American Civilization*, 3:128–29.

64. See, for example, Wright, "May a Man Conduct His Business As He Please?," *Forum*, Dec. 1894, 425–32.

65. Montgomery, *Worker's Control in America*; Licht, *Working for the Railroad*, 264–70.

66. U.S. Strike Commission, *Report*, l.

67. Wright, "Chicago Strike," 508.

68. For a particularly sharp dismissal of the free-silver movement, see Goodwyn, *Democratic Promise*. One of the best explanations of the disjuncture between the Populists' success at the local and state levels and their decline *preceding* the emergence of the silver movement in their ranks can be found in McMath, *American Populism*.

69. For a negative report on the Omaha platform, see Frank B. Tracy, "Menacing Socialism in the Western States," *Forum*, May 1893, 332–42; for a report on the ouster of the Colorado Populists in 1894, see Joel F. Vaile, "Colorado's Experiment with Populism," *Forum*, Jan. 1895, 714–23.

70. Livingston, *Federal Reserve System*, 74–75.

71. This account is drawn from ibid., chaps. 1, 3–4.

72. Ibid., chap. 3.

73. Ibid, 87–88.

74. Ibid., 89–102.

75. "The Downfall of Certain Financial Fallacies," *Forum*, Oct. 1893, 131–49, quotations on 141, 144.

76. Symposium, "What Free Coinage Means," *Forum*, Oct. 1896, 129–51, quotation on 149; Andrew D. White, "Encouragements in the Present Crisis," *Forum*, Sept. 1896, 16–30.

77. Andrew D. White, "Encouragements in the Present Crisis," quotations on 16, 18, 20, 21; Andrew D. White, "Some Practical Lessons of the Recent Campaign," *Forum*, Dec. 1896, quotations on 417, 419, 420, 421.

78. The substance of Clark's vision of a consumer's paradise first appeared in *Philosophy of Wealth* in 1886 (see especially 40–41), then again in the 1888 article "Capital and Its Earnings," which, like so many others, began with Clark fretting about class conflict and promising that his theoretical practice would point the rational way to harmony.

79. Clark, *Distribution of Wealth*, chap. 3.

80. Clark, "Modern Appeal to Legal Forces," 501.

81. Among the many positive responses to his speech, one seems most important to Clark himself. The association's meeting took place at Columbia University, and shortly after the speech Clark received letters of congratulation from some of the most influential professors and administrators at Columbia. After brief negotiations, Columbia hired Clark as a professor of political economy. See J. H. Hollander to J. B. Clark, Feb. 28, 1895, JBCP.

82. Clark, "The Scholar's Political Opportunity," *PSQ* 12 (Dec. 1897): 590, 594, 596, 598, 599.

83. Ibid., 599, 600–601, 602.

84. Ibid., 600.

85. H. C. Adams to W. Salter, Aug. 17, 1896, HCAP.

86. Adams, "Economics and Jurisprudence," presidential address before the AEA, Dec. 1896, reprinted in Dorfman, *Essays by Henry Carter Adams*, 137–62.

87. Ibid., 162, 144, 159.

88. Ibid., 147. It is worth noting that Adams refuted the theory of corporate personality *before* legal theorists had settled on this theory of the corporation. On the evolution of legal realist theories of corporate personality, see Horwitz, *Transformation of American Law, 1870–1960*, 98–107.

89. Dorfman, *Essays by Henry Carter Adams*, 139.

90. Ibid., 152.

91. Ibid., 154, 155.

92. Ibid., 159.

93. Ibid., 160–61.

94. Ibid., 162.

CHAPTER SEVEN

1. Furner, "Republican Tradition," 228–34; Furner, "Knowing Capitalism," 268–74.

2. U.S. Congress, House, U.S. Industrial Commission, *Final Report*, 19:595.

3. Ibid., vii, 595, 649–52, 947–53.

4. Ibid., quotation on 645–46.

5. In the organizations of industrial labor, it was clear that the old and new coexisted uneasily. The decline of the Knights of Labor relative to the American Federation of Labor, Debs's straddling of "republicanism" and socialism after Pullman, and the internal battles in the AFL between Gompers and the socialists all testify to the importance of the nineties as a transitional decade (Montgomery, *Fall of the House of Labor*; Hattam, *Labor Visions and State Power*; Forbath, *Law and the Shaping of the American Labor Movement*; Salvatore, *Eugene V. Debs*). The debates among historians of the Populists about individualism versus the cooperative commonwealth, nostalgia versus rationality, might also be a reflection of the decline of old values and the uncertainty of what would succeed them.

6. The phrase is from Horace White, "Industrial Legislation," *Chicago Tribune*, May 1, 1867.

7. Chandler, *Visible Hand*, chaps. 7, 12; Leach, *Land of Desire*; Peiss, *Cheap Amusements*; Ross, *Working-Class Hollywood*; Lears, *Fables of Abundance*.

8. The issues were debated frequently in the *Forum*. Horace White, a leading anti-imperialist, favored the Open Door policy and made peace with Theodore Roosevelt on foreign policy during the latter's presidency (Logsdon, *Horace White*, 372, 387). On American foreign policy, see LaFeber, *New Empire*; Williams, *Tragedy of American Diplomacy*, chap. 1; and Healy, *US Expansionism*.

9. For an alternative approach to the rise of the administrative state that complements the one presented here, see Skowronek, *Building a New American State*.

10. James Huston has demonstrated the long stretch of Americans' belief in an equitable distribution of wealth and how it disintegrated during the economic transformation of the Gilded Age (Huston, *Securing the Fruits of Labor*). The vision described here was not a socialist one, nor do I mean to suggest that American producers were protosocialists. Indeed, there is nothing intrinsic to this egalitarian belief that is antithetical to the individualism that many historians claim American workers and farmers held to, especially in the economic conditions of precorporate America.

11. Frederick L. Hoffman, "Race Traits and Tendencies of the American Negro," *PAEA* 11 (Aug. 1896): 1–329.

12. Much of the extensive literature on the war of 1898 and the U.S. turn to imperialism demonstrates the congruence of domestic and international new liberalism. On the relationship between economic crisis, the emergence of corporate capitalism, and American foreign policy, see LaFeber, *New Empire*. On the ideology of American imperialism, see Healy, *US Expansionism*. On questions of race, politics, and ideology, see Woodward, *Origins of the New South*, chap. 12. On anti-immigrant nativism, see Higham, *Strangers in the Land*.

13. For an incisive analysis of the literature of the Progressive Era, see Rodgers, "In Search of Progressivism." Many of the most influential historical analyses of the Progressive Era argue that one or more of the three points identified here were central to the era's political economy. On the economic transformation from proprietary to corporate capitalism, see Chandler, *Visible Hand*; Lamoreaux, *Great Merger Movement*; and Sklar, *Corporate Reconstruction of American Capitalism*. On the cultural legitimation and political institutionalization of corporate capitalism, see Sklar, *Corporate Reconstruction of American Capitalism*; Weinstein, *Corporate Ideal*; and Livingston, *Federal Reserve System*. For a highly critical analysis of the relationship between corporate and new liberalism, see Lustig, *Corporate Liberalism*. On labor, see Montgomery, *Fall of the House of Labor*; Glickman, *Living Wage*; and Tomlins, *State and the Unions*, pt. 2. On bureaucratic and administrative tendencies, see Galambos, "Emerging Organizational Synthesis"; Wiebe, *Search for Order*; Hays, "Politics of Reform"; Skowronek, *Building a New American State*; Gilbert, *Designing the Industrial State*; and Haber, *Efficiency and Uplift*, and compare Haskell, *Emergence of Professional Social Science*, and Nelson, *Roots of American Bureaucracy*. There were parallel developments among women reformers and the origin of "welfare," especially on the issue of expertise and administration. For opposing views that nevertheless emphasize the importance of a gendered ideology, see Gordon, *Pitied but Not Entitled*,

and Skocpol, *Protecting Soldiers and Mothers*. Relevant to the question of the rise of nonpolitical administrative governance are the weakening of political partisanship and the sharp decline in voter turnout. Although the analysts of this aspect of American politics do not generally make a connection between the two, their work is suggestive. See Keyssar, *Right to Vote*; McCormick, *From Realignment to Reform*; McGerr, *Decline of Popular Politics*; Burnham, *Critical Elections*; and Oestreicher, "Urban Working-Class Political Behavior." On corporate capitalism as consumer capitalism and the shift in ideology and culture attendant on the rise of consumerism, see Cross, *All-Consuming Century*; Glickman, *Living Wage*; Leach, *Land of Desire*; Lears, *Fables of Abundance*; Livingston, *Pragmatism*; Marchand, *Creating the Corporate Soul*; and Sussman, *Culture as History*, 217–85. For the broad philosophical questions raised by consumerism, see the opposing views in Livingston's *Pragmatism* and Lasch's *True and Only Heaven*. The histories that address the nature of new liberalism confirm at least that there was a social dialogue about these ideas, even if they dispute the extent to which the real new liberals adopted these notions. For a more positive portrait of new liberalism than the one suggested in this book, see Kloppenberg, *Uncertain Victory* and *Virtues of Liberalism*; Furner, "Republican Tradition" and "Knowing Capitalism"; and Schneirov, *Labor and Urban Politics*. In a somewhat different vein, Rodgers in *Atlantic Crossings* presents a positive appraisal of progressive social reformers, while recognizing their limited success. For a defense of progressive intellectuals that recognizes the problematic nature of their conceptions of expertise and stewardship for democratic politics, see Fink, *Progressive Intellectuals*. For syntheses that confirm much of this literature, as well as foreground the pervasive social conflict that shaped the political solutions, see Dawley, *Struggles for Justice*, and Painter, *Standing at Armageddon*.

14. Thomas Haskell's review of Rodgers's book, which takes issue with the unifying framework of "exceptionalism" and raises significant questions about Rodgers's identification of the European roots of progressive reform, is germane to this argument. (See Haskell, "Taking Exception to Exceptionalism.")

15. Fine, *Laissez Faire*.

16. Wells and White had been two of the leading theorists of the currency and banking reform movement of the nineties, and White's *Money and Banking* remained the standard textbook on the subject into the 1930s (Ashley, *American Newspaper Journalists*, 346–51). Livingston identifies the direct roots of the Federal Reserve System in the 1890s, but the continuity between the earlier currency reform movement and the campaign of the nineties calls for a longer view (Livingston, *Federal Reserve System*, esp. chaps. 3, 8).

17. Quotation in Twiss, *Lawyers and the Constitution*, 18. Because of the constitutional division of powers and the conservative makeup of the Supreme Court throughout the Progressive Era, administrative law, an important aspect of new liberalism, did not achieve significant institutional success until the New Deal. On Cooley's role in administrative law, see Skowronek, *Building a New American State*, 153–54, and Carrington, "Law and Economics."

18. On the role of the old liberal reformers in New York, see McCormick, *From Realignment to Reform*, 46–56, 260–61. For a classic statement of this position, see Hays, "Politics of Reform." On electoral reforms, see Keyssar, *Right to Vote*, chap. 5. The antidemocratic potential of progressive reforms was particularly evident in the South, where progressivism and the entrenchment of Jim Crow often went hand in hand. See Kirby,

Darkness at the Dawning; Kousser, *Shaping of Southern Politics*; and Woodward, *Strange Career of Jim Crow*. Keyssar's *Right to Vote*, published as this book went into press, details the multifarious ways in which the suffrage was constricted in the late nineteenth and early twentieth centuries (see especially chap. 5 and 183–202).

19. On municipal ownership, see Rodgers, *Atlantic Crossings*, chap. 4, esp. 148–59.

20. Leiby, *Carroll Wright and Labor Reform*; Furner, "Knowing Capitalism," 246–58; Lacey, "World of the Bureaus," 135–36, 154–55; Furner, "Republican Tradition," 217–18; Dubofsky, *State and Labor*, 40–44; Fink, *Progressive Intellectuals*, 217; Dorfman, *Economic Mind in American Civilization*, 3:128–29.

21. For an early example of Wright's synthesis, see Wright, "Industrial Necessities," *Forum*, Nov. 1886, 308–15.

22. On the politics of the creation of labor bureaus, see Leiby, *Carroll Wright and Labor Reform*, chap. 3. For the liberal reform criticism of the Massachusetts bureau, see J. B. Hodgskin, "The Labor Question in Massachusetts," *Nation*, June 8, 1871, 398, and E. Atkinson, "The Condition of Labor in Massachusetts," letter to the editor, *Nation*, June 22, 1871, 433–34. It is pertinent to observe that Godkin's first proclamation of laissez-faire was issued two weeks before Hodgskin's article praising the bureau, that Atkinson took Hodgskin strongly to task and contradicted the bureau's report, and that Hodgskin, who had been the *Nation*'s lead writer on economic affairs, never wrote for the magazine again.

23. See chapter 6 above and Furner, "Republican Tradition."

24. On Clark, marginalism, and economic ideology, see Ross, *Origins of American Social Science*, 172–86; compare Livingston, *Pragmatism*, 52–62. On marginalism and progressive politics, see Sklar, *Corporate Reconstruction of American Capitalism*; Livingston, "Social Analysis"; and Furner, "Republican Tradition."

25. Clark, *Problem of Monopoly*; Clark and Clark, *Control of Trusts*.

26. On the Civic Federation initiative, see Sklar, *Corporate Reconstruction of American Capitalism*, 287–97, 324–25. On the question of statism and democracy, I find that Sklar's "state-society" paradigm basically evades the question of democracy. He leaves the impression that the more statist variant was inherently authoritarian. The middle term of the opposition, the people—central to the traditions of progressives, social democrats, and democratic socialists alike—is absent from his analysis. Furner has offered important correctives to the corporate liberal thesis advanced by Sklar, and she is closer to the international traditions and historical record on the point of statism, but her distinction between "corporate liberals" and "democratic statists" seems to have no place for the statist position enunciated by Clark for the corporate liberals of the Civic Federation.

27. Clark, *Social Justice without Socialism*, quotations on 31, 48.

28. Compare Fine, *Laissez Faire*.

29. Haber, *Efficiency and Uplift*, xii. On scientific management, see also Noble, *America by Design*, 267–320; Montgomery, *Fall of the House of Labor*, chap. 5; Nelson, *Managers and Workers*, chap. 4; and Chandler, *Visible Hand*, chap. 8.

30. Haber, *Efficiency and Uplift*, 54–55; Taylor, *Principles of Scientific Management*; U.S. Congress, House, Special Committee, *Taylor and Other Systems of Shop Management*.

31. Frederick W. Taylor, "A Piece-Rate System," *American Economic Association Economic Studies* 1, no. 2 (1896): 89–129.

32. The main disagreement is whether the drive was rooted in social or technological imperatives. Compare the opposing interpretations of Montgomery and Chandler.

33. Taylor, *Principles of Scientific Management*, 142–43.

34. Montgomery, *Fall of the House of Labor*, 249–56.

35. On the ideology of social efficiency, see Rodgers, "In Search of Progressivism," 123, 126–27. On Brandeis, Lippman, and Croly, see Haber, *Efficiency and Uplift*, chap. 5.

36. Montgomery, *Fall of the House of Labor*, 251.

37. On workers' protests, see ibid., chap. 5.

38. Recent exceptions are Furner, "Republican Tradition" and "Knowing Capitalism," and Fink, *Progressive Intellectuals*. The literature on corporate liberalism offers an important corrective to the tendency, but sometimes at the expense of failing to make important distinctions between business leaders, publicists, technical specialists, and critical intellectuals. A classic on progressive thought is White, *Social Thought in America*.

39. On the definition of the "critic," see Croly, *Promise of American Life*, 452.

40. Lippman, *Drift and Mastery*, chap. 7; Steel, *Walter Lippman*, 107.

41. See, respectively, Kloppenberg, *Uncertain Victory*; Livingston, *Pragmatism*, 69–75; and Forcey, *Crossroads of Liberalism*.

42. The four books referred to are Lippman, *Preface to Politics* and *Drift and Mastery*, and Croly, *Promise of American Life* and *Progressive Democracy*. For biographical information, see Steel, *Walter Lippman*, and Forcey, *Crossroads of Liberalism*. Much of the following discussion applies as forcefully to the third *New Republic* editor, Walter Weyl. Weyl was, however, less prominent and influential than his coeditors and for reasons of space constraints is omitted here.

43. Steel, *Walter Lippman*, chaps. 2–4.

44. Forcey, *Crossroads of Liberalism*, chaps. 1, 4; Willard Strait quoted in Steel, *Walter Lippman*, 60.

45. Lippman, *Drift and Mastery*, 17.

46. Ibid., 87.

47. Forcey, *Crossroads of Liberalism*, 21.

48. For an excellent intellectual history of the relationship between pragmatism and political theory and practice, see Kloppenberg, *Uncertain Victory*. The broader cultural significance of pragmatism is explored in Livingston, *Pragmatism*. Westbrook's *John Dewey and American Democracy* is an important examination of the centrality of democracy in Dewey's philosophy.

49. Steel, *Walter Lippman*, 77; compare Kloppenberg, *Uncertain Victory*, 392.

50. Kloppenberg engages in a perceptive analysis of the tension between bureaucracy and democracy in progressive thought. I do think, however, that he has understated the depth of the administrative tendency in the thought of Croly and Lippman and the toll it took on their conception of democracy (see Kloppenberg, *Uncertain Victory*, esp. 381–94).

51. Croly, *Promise of American Life*, chap. 13, quotations on 406, 441. On Santayana's influence, see Forcey, *Crossroads of Liberalism*, 18–19.

52. Lippman, *Drift and Mastery*, 85.

53. Croly, *Promise of American Life*, chap. 11; Lippman, *Drift and Mastery*, chaps. 14–15; quotation in Steel, *Walter Lippman*, 79.

54. The details differed, of course. For example, Croly rejected government by com-

mission, the favored method of the postbellum liberals. But he did so because he thought commissions too susceptible to the pressure of interest groups, and instead he called for an inordinately powerful executive, who would be better equipped to resist popular pressure (Croly, *Promise of American Life*, chap. 11).

55. Croly, *Promise of American Life*, 205–11, quotations on 209.

56. Lippman, *Drift and Mastery*, chaps. 9, 14.

57. Croly, *Promise of American Life*, chap. 12; Lippman, *Drift and Mastery*, chaps. 2–6.

58. A number of historians argue that the progressives articulated a new theory of the social self and rejected individualism (see Livingston, *Pragmatism*, and McClay, *Masterless*, chap. 5). While I agree that they rejected the possessive individualism of the Victorians, I see a redefinition, rather than a transcendence, of individualism. Kloppenberg, I think, strikes the proper balance in analyzing their collectivist and individualist tendencies and provides the best analysis of the ways in which liberal "progressives" differed from socialists, social democrats, and old liberals (Kloppenberg, *Uncertain Victory*, 3–8, 395–401).

59. Kloppenberg, *Uncertain Victory*, 390–93; Forcey, *Crossroads of Liberalism*, 291–306; Steel, *Walter Lippman*, chap. 14.

60. Lippman, *Public Opinion*, 185–94.

61. Steel's biography reveals some of the sources of Lippman's shifts in personal temperament and ambition and suggests that his antidemocratic turning cannot be seen as solely a logical reaction to the barbarity of world war and the betrayal of the peace settlement (Steel, *Walter Lippman*, chaps. 9–14).

62. See, for example, the discussion of Walter Rauschenbusch in Kloppenberg, *Uncertain Victory*, chaps. 6–7.

63. The most influential criticism of Addams and Dewey can be found in Lasch, *New Radicalism in America*. For their defenders, see Kloppenberg, *Uncertain Victory*; Westbrook, *John Dewey and American Democracy*; and, in a somewhat different vein, McClay, *Masterless*, chap. 5. For Addams's social thought, see Addams, *Democracy and Social Ethics*.

64. Lippman reached the height of his influence, moreover, when he took a leave from the *New Republic* and the role of critic and entered the Wilson administration (see Steel, *Walter Lippman*, chaps. 12–13).

65. The limited scope of this survey prevents an examination of progressive social reform in state and local politics. The focus on the national level is justified by the fact that one of the central developments of modern liberalism is the growth of an activist national state.

66. Roosevelt, *Autobiography of Theodore Roosevelt*, 18–21.

67. Ibid., chaps. 3, 5–7; Sproat, *"Best Men,"* 133–37.

68. Roosevelt, *Autobiography of Theodore Roosevelt*, chap. 6.

69. Ibid., 156–58.

70. McCormick, *From Realignment to Reform*, 157–64; Roosevelt, *Autobiography of Theodore Roosevelt*, chap. 8; Dunn, *From Harrison to Harding*, 1:335.

71. Roosevelt's preoccupation with questions arising out of the corporate transformation of the American economy and his consistency on these issues can be gleaned from his addresses to Congress and to the public during his presidency. My summary is drawn

from the compilation of these public messages, Roosevelt, *Roosevelt Policy*. On his domestic policy as president, see Cooper, *Warrior and the Priest*, chap. 6; Sklar, *Corporate Reconstruction of American Capitalism*, chaps. 4–5; and Painter, *Standing at Armageddon*, 180–86. On his ideology of imperialism and implementation of foreign policy, see Roosevelt, *Strenuous Life*, title essay; Healy, *US Expansionism*, chap. 6; and LaFeber, *Inevitable Revolutions*, 34–40, 78–79. On Jenks, see Furner, "Republican Tradition," 231 n. 107.

72. Roosevelt, "Industrial Democracy," address delivered in Cairo, Ill., Oct. 3, 1907, in Roosevelt, *Roosevelt Policy*, 615.

73. Link, *Woodrow Wilson*, 8–14; Cooper, *Warrior and the Priest*, chap. 12.

74. The different interpretations of Cooper (*Warrior and the Priest*) and Sklar (*Corporate Reconstruction of American Capitalism*) converge on this point.

75. See, for example, Link, *Woodrow Wilson*, chap. 3. Roosevelt is quoted in Cooper, *Warrior and the Priest*, 253.

76. This conclusion is in accord with Martin Sklar's argument that Wilson "gave leadership to, and presided over, a movement beginning to lay the institutional foundations, in law, jurisprudence, and executive administration, of corporate capitalism at home and of its expansion abroad" (*Corporate Reconstruction of American Capitalism*, 425).

77. Armstrong, *E. L. Godkin*, 94.

78. Wilson, *Congressional Government* and "The Study of Administration," *PSQ* 2 (June 1887): 197–222. For analyses of Wilson's scholarship and the influence of Turner on Wilson, see Sklar, *Corporate Reconstruction of American Capitalism*, 384–401 (Wilson quoted on 391). On Wilson's theory of administration, democracy, and Darwinian racism, see Rohr, "Constitutional World of Woodrow Wilson," quotation on 44, Wilson quoted on 43.

79. On executive power, see Link, *Woodrow Wilson*, 34–35, and Cooper, *Warrior and the Priest*, 230–40. Had Wilson been able to achieve all his goals, the ICC would have been strengthened in ways and for purposes similar to those won in banking, antitrust, and tariff legislation (Skowronek, *Building a New American State*, 271–74).

80. Sklar, *Corporate Reconstruction of American Capitalism*, 423.

81. Williams, *Tragedy of American Diplomacy*, chap. 2.

82. "Special Message on Trusts and Monopolies," delivered before Congress in Joint Session, Jan. 20, 1914, in Wilson, *Messages and Papers*, 49–50.

83. Livingston, *Federal Reserve System*, chap. 8; Sklar, *Corporate Reconstruction of American Capitalism*, 423–24.

84. On Wilson's labor policy, see Dubofsky, *State and Labor*, 52–60. See also Gompers, *Seventy Years*, xxv, xxxiv–xxxvii, 129–35, 171–86.

85. Fink, *Progressive Intellectuals*, chap. 3; Furner, "Knowing Capitalism," 274–84.

86. One question raised by my portrayal of new liberalism is the importance of different strains within it, such as those identified by Furner or Sklar. I would argue that, although different and at times opposing ideas circulated within the universe of new liberalism, the assumptions, principles, and objectives shared by those who can be classified as new liberals are more significant. For an analysis of the content of policy and the options available, the distinctions need to be examined. For an understanding of the broader political culture and the ideology of modern liberalism, the similarities are more

revealing. I would add that the distinctions seem to me overdrawn. Sklar's portrayal of Roosevelt as a statist with a socialistic spirit, in contrast to Wilson, who was an "anti-statist" liberal, seems stretched beyond credibility. Furner's conceptualization of "a discourse" between "two *different* types or variants of American liberalism" ("corporate liberal voluntarism" and "democratic collectivist statism") is useful in illuminating subtle theoretical and political differences, but the distinction too often breaks down when applied to particular individuals and specific circumstances (see above, this chapter, n. 26). I also think the encouragement it gives to typology and an internalist analysis sometimes overshadows a more important analysis of the broader political dynamics in which new liberals confronted opponents with different views and values. (For Furner's definition of the discourse of new liberalism, see "Republican Tradition," 176 n. 10.)

Another debate is engaged with the question of individualism. Whereas most historians agree that the state remained liberal, there is a significant body of opinion arguing that modernist social thought transcended individualism. In different veins, this argument can be seen in Furner's thesis of two distinct but "collectivist" variants of new liberalism ("Republican Tradition"), Haskell's thesis on interdependence (*Emergence of Professional Social Science*), or Livingston's analysis of the modern conception of selfhood (*Pragmatism*). To compare, see Ross's analysis of the reconstitution of liberal individualism in progressive social science (*Origins of American Social Science*, esp. chaps. 5–6). My reading of the sources and interpretation of the broader debate about liberal pluralism persuade me of the persisting importance of individualism (albeit redefined).

87. The intentions of the progressives who lent prestige to the administrative solution or who implemented administrative measures, of course, varied widely. Furner's distinction between the two trajectories of new liberalism is relevant to this question ("The Republican Tradition" and "Knowing Capitalism"). James Kloppenberg demonstrates that the social democrats and progressives analyzed the problem of the dominance of experts, even if they never fully resolved their own ambivalence about democracy and bureaucracy. Yet, as he also makes abundantly clear, the intellectuals he analyzed failed to enact their vision in the new liberal states (*Uncertain Victory*, 267–77, 381–94). Fink, by examining experts who wielded practical power, has probed the question of the tension between "democratic commitment" and expertise explicitly in *Progressive Intellectuals*. I do think, however, that a recognition of the pivotal importance of conflicts about expertise and democracy during the Gilded Age social crisis, and the defeat of the more democratic visions (see chap. 5 above), would help illuminate the "dilemma" that these historians observe.

88. Frank, *One Market under God*.

89. See, for example, Cross, *All-Consuming Century*, 21.

BIBLIOGRAPHY

MANUSCRIPT COLLECTIONS

Ann Arbor, Michigan
  Bentley Historical Library, University of Michigan
    Henry Carter Adams Papers
    James B. Angell Papers
    Thomas McIntyre Cooley Papers
Boston, Mass.
  Massachusetts Historical Society
    Edward Atkinson Papers
Cambridge, Mass.
  Houghton Library, Harvard University
    Edwin Lawrence Godkin Papers
    North American Review Papers
    Charles Eliot Norton Papers
New York, N.Y.
  Rare Book and Manuscript Library, Columbia University
    John Bates Clark Papers
    E. R. A. Seligman Collection
    E. R. A. Seligman Papers
New York Public Library
  David Ames Wells Papers

STATE AND FEDERAL GOVERNMENT PUBLICATIONS

Massachusetts. House of Representatives. *Report of the Special Commission on the Hours of Labor and the Condition and Prospects of the Industrial Classes.* 1866. Mass. House Doc. 98.

——. *Reports of Commissioners on the Hours of Labor.* 1867. Mass. House Doc. 44.

Massachusetts. Railroad Commission. *R.R. Commissioners' Special Report.* 1877. Mass. House Doc. 102.

New York Assembly. [Tilden Commission Report.] *Report of the Commission to Devise a Plan for the Government of Cities in the State of New York.* 1878. Assembly Docs., New York State 6, no. 68.

U.S. Bureau of the Census. *Historical Statistics of the U.S.A., Colonial Times to 1957.* Washington, D.C.: Government Printing Office, 1960.

U.S. Congress. House. *Investigation by a Select Committee of the House of Representatives Relative to the Causes of the General Depression in Labor and Business, Etc.* 45th Cong., 3d sess., 1879. H. Misc. Doc. 29.

——. *Report of the Special Commissioner of the Revenue* [for 1867]. 40th Cong., 2nd sess., 1868. H. Exec. Doc. 81.

——. *Report of the Special Commissioner of the Revenue* [for 1868]. 40th Cong., 3d sess., 1869. H. Exec. Doc. 16.

——. *Report of the Special Commissioner of the Revenue* [for 1869]. 41st Cong., 2nd sess., 1869. H. Exec. Doc. 27.

U.S. Congress. House. Special Committee. *The Taylor and Other Systems of Shop Management.* 62nd Cong., 2nd sess., 1912. H. Rep. 403.

U.S. Congress. House. U.S. Industrial Commission. *Final Report.* 19 vols. 57th Cong., 1st sess., 1902. H. Doc. 380.

U.S. Congress. Senate. *Report of the Committee of the Senate upon the Relations Between Labor and Capital, and Testimony Taken by the Committee.* 5 vols. Washington, D.C.: Government Printing Office, 1885.

U.S. Congress. Senate. U.S. Strike Commission. *Report of the Chicago Strike.* 53d Cong., 3d sess., 1895. S. Exec. Doc. 7.

U.S. Revenue Commission. *Reports of a Commission Appointed for a Revision of the Revenue System of the United States, 1865–66.* Washington, D.C.: Government Printing Office, 1866.

NEWSPAPERS AND PERIODICALS

American Economic Review

Atlantic Monthly

Chicago Tribune

Daily Evening Voice (Boston)

Forum

Harper's Weekly

Johns Hopkins University Studies in History and Political Science

Journal of Social Science

Nation

New Englander

New York Tribune

North American Review

Penn Monthly

Political Science Quarterly

Princeton Review

Publications of the American Economic Association

Quarterly Journal of Economics

Scientific American

Scribner's Magazine

PUBLISHED WORKS

Adams, Charles F., Jr., and Henry Adams. *Chapters of Erie and Other Essays.* 1871.

Adams, Henry. *The Education of Henry Adams.* 1918. Reprint, Boston: Houghton Mifflin, 1961.

Adams, Henry Carter. *Public Debts.* 1887.

——. *The Science of Finance.* 1898.

Adams, Henry Carter, Richard T. Ely, Arthur T. Hadley, E. J. James, Simon Newcomb, Simon N. Patten, Edwin R. A. Seligman, Richmond Mayo-Smith, and Frank W. Taussig. *Science Economic Discussion*. 1886.

Addams, Jane. *Democracy and Social Ethics*. New York: Macmillan, 1902.

Arblaster, Anthony. *The Rise and Decline of Western Liberalism*. Oxford: Basil Blackwell, 1984.

Armstrong, William M. *E. L. Godkin: A Biography*. Albany: State University of New York, 1978.

Ashley, Perry J., ed. *American Newspaper Journalists, 1873–1900*. Vol. 23, *Dictionary of Literary Biography*. Detroit: Gale Research, 1983.

Atkinson, Edward. *Addresses Upon the Labor Question*. 1886.

——. *Labor and Capital, Allies Not Enemies*. 1879.

Bannister, Robert C. *Social Darwinism: Science and Myth in Anglo-American Social Thought*. Philadelphia: Temple University Press, 1979.

Bellamy, Edward. *Looking Backward*. 1890.

Bellomy, Donald. "The Molding of an Iconoclast: William Graham Sumner, 1840–1885." Ph.D. diss., Harvard University, 1980.

Bender, Thomas, ed. *The Antislavery Debate: Capitalism and Abolitionism as a Problem in Historical Interpretation*. Berkeley: University of California Press, 1992.

Benedict, Michael Les. "Laissez-Faire and Liberty: A Re-evaluation of the Meaning and Origins of Laissez-Faire Constitutionalism." *Law and History Review* 3, no. 2 (1985): 293–331.

Bensel, Richard Franklin. *Yankee Leviathan: The Origins of Central State Authority in America, 1859–1877*. New York: Cambridge University Press, 1990.

Berk, Gerald. *Alternative Tracks: The Constitution of American Industrial Order, 1865–1917*. Baltimore: Johns Hopkins University Press, 1994.

——. "Corporate Liberalism Reconsidered: A Review Essay." *Journal of Policy History* 3, no. 1 (1991): 70–84.

Berlin, Ira, Barbara J. Fields, Thavolia Glymph, Joseph P. Reidy, and Leslie S. Rowland, eds. *The Destruction of Slavery*. Ser. 1, vol. 1, *Freedom: A Documentary History of Emancipation, 1861–1867*. New York: Cambridge University Press, 1985.

Berlin, Ira, Joseph P. Reidy, and Leslie S. Rowland, eds. *The Black Military Experience*. Ser. 2, *Freedom: A Documentary History of Emancipation, 1861–1867*. New York: Cambridge University Press, 1982.

Berlin, Ira, et al., eds. *The Wartime Genesis of Free Labor: The Lower South*. Ser. 1, vol. 3, *Freedom: A Documentary History of Emancipation, 1861–1867*. New York: Cambridge University Press, 1982.

Bernstein, Iver. *The New York City Draft Riots: Their Significance for American Society and Politics in the Age of the Civil War*. New York: Oxford University Press, 1990.

Bernstein, Samuel. "American Labor in the Long Depression, 1873–1878." *Science and Society* 20 (Winter 1956): 60–82.

Bowles, Samuel, and Herbert Gintis. *Democracy and Capitalism: Property, Community, and the Contradictions of Modern Social Thought*. New York: Basic Books, 1986.

Brock, W. R. *An American Crisis: Congress and Reconstruction, 1865–1867*. New York: Harper and Row, 1963.

Burnham, Walter Dean. *Critical Elections and the Mainsprings of American Politics.* New York: W. W. Norton, 1970.

Calhoun, Craig, ed. *Habermas and the Public Sphere.* Cambridge: MIT Press, 1992.

Carnegie, Andrew. *The Gospel of Wealth.* 1890.

Carrington, Paul D. "Law and Economics in the Creation of Federal Administrative Law: Thomas Cooley, Elder to the Republic." *Iowa Law Review* 83 (Jan. 1998): 363–90.

Chandler, Alfred Dupont. *The Visible Hand: The Managerial Revolution in American Business.* Cambridge: Harvard University Press, Belknap Press, 1977.

Clark, John Bates. *The Distribution of Wealth.* 1899.

———. *The Philosophy of Wealth.* 1886.

———. *The Problem of Monopoly: A Study of Grave Danger and the Natural Mode of Averting It.* New York: Columbia University Press and the Macmillan Company, 1904.

———. *Social Justice without Socialism.* Boston: Houghton Mifflin, 1914.

Clark, John Bates, and John Maurice Clark. *The Control of Trusts.* 1912. Reprint, New York: Macmillan, 1914.

Clark, John Bates, and Franklin H. Giddings. *The Modern Distributive Process.* 1888.

Coats, A. W. "Henry Carter Adams: A Case Study in the Emergence of the Social Sciences in the United States, 1850–1900." *Journal of American Studies* 1 (Oct. 1967): 177–97.

Cohen, Jean L., and Andrew Arato. *Civil Society and Political Theory.* Cambridge: MIT Press, 1992.

Cohen, Nancy. "The Problem of Democracy in the Age of Capital: Reconstructing American Liberalism, 1865–1890." Ph.D. diss., Columbia University, 1996.

Cohen-Lack, Nancy. "A Struggle for Sovereignty: National Consolidation, Emancipation, and Free Labor in Texas, 1865." *Journal of Southern History* 58 (Feb. 1992): 57–98.

Commager, Henry Steele, and Milton Cantor. *Documents of American History.* Englewood Cliffs, N.J.: Prentice-Hall, 1988.

Cooley, Thomas M. *A Treatise on the Constitutional Limitations Which Rest Upon the Legislative Power of the States of the American Union.* 1868.

Cooper, John Milton, Jr. *The Warrior and the Priest: Woodrow Wilson and Theodore Roosevelt.* Cambridge: Harvard University Press, Belknap Press, 1983.

Croly, Herbert. *Progressive Democracy.* New York: Macmillan, 1914.

———. *The Promise of American Life.* New York: Macmillan, 1909.

Cross, Gary. *An All-Consuming Century: Why Consumerism Won in Modern America.* New York: Columbia University Press, 2000.

Darwin, Charles. *The Origin of the Species.* 1859.

Dawley, Alan. *Struggles for Justice: Social Responsibility and the Liberal State.* Cambridge: Harvard University Press, Belknap Press, 1991.

Dewey, Davis R. *Financial History of the United States.* New York: Longmans, Green and Co., 1934.

———, ed. *Discussions in Economics and Statistics by Francis A. Walker.* 2 vols. 1899. Reprint, New York: Augustus M. Kelley, 1971.

Dobb, Maurice. *Theories of Value and Distribution since Adam Smith.* Cambridge: Cambridge University Press, 1973.

Donnelly, Ignatius. *Caesar's Column: A Story of the Twentieth Century.* 1890.

Dorfman, Joseph. *The Economic Mind in American Civilization, 1865–1918*. Vol. 3. New York: Augustus M. Kelley, 1969.

——, ed. *Two Essays by Henry Carter Adams: Relation of the State to Industrial Action and Economics and Jurisprudence*. New York: Augustus M. Kelley, Reprints of Economic Classics, 1969.

Dubofsky, Melvyn. *The State and Labor in Modern America*. Chapel Hill: University of North Carolina Press, 1994.

DuBois, Ellen C. *Feminism and Suffrage: The Emergence of an Independent Women's Movement in America, 1848–1869*. Ithaca, N.Y.: Cornell University Press, 1978.

Dunlavy, Colleen A. "Political Structure, State Policy, and Industrial Change: Early Railroad Policy in the United States and Prussia." In *Structuring Politics: Historical Institutionalism in Comparative Analysis*, edited by Sven Steinmo, Kathleen Thelen, and Frank Longstreth, 114–54. New York: Cambridge University Press, 1992.

Dunn, Arthur Wallace. *From Harrison to Harding: A Personal Narrative Covering a Third of a Century, 1888–1921*. New York: G. P. Putnam's Sons, 1922.

Dunn, John. *The Political Theory of John Locke: An Historical Account of "The Two Treatises of Government."* Cambridge: Cambridge University Press, 1969.

Ely, Richard T. *French and German Socialism in Modern Times*. 1883.

——. *The Labor Movement in America*. 1886.

Fels, Rendigs. *American Business Cycles, 1865–1897*. Chapel Hill: University of North Carolina Press, 1959.

Ferleger, Herbert Ronald. "David A. Wells and the American Revenue System, 1865–1870." Ph.D. diss., Columbia University, 1942.

Fields, Barbara J. "Slavery, Race, and Ideology in the United States of America." *New Left Review* 181 (May/June 1990): 95–118.

Fine, Sidney. *Laissez Faire and the General-Welfare State: A Study of Conflict in American Thought, 1865–1901*. Ann Arbor: University of Michigan, 1956.

Fink, Leon. *Progressive Intellectuals and the Dilemmas of Democratic Commitment*. Cambridge: Harvard University Press, 1997.

——. *Workingmen's Democracy: The Knights of Labor and American Politics*. Urbana: University of Illinois Press, 1983.

Foner, Eric. *Free Soil, Free Labor, Free Men: The Ideology of the Republican Party before the Civil War*. New York: Oxford University Press, 1969.

——. *Politics and Ideology in the Age of the Civil War*. New York: Oxford University Press, 1980.

——. *Reconstruction: America's Unfinished Revolution*. New York: Harper and Row, 1988.

Foner, Philip S. *The Great Labor Uprising of 1877*. New York: Monad Press, 1977.

——, ed. *The Life and Writings of Frederick Douglass*. Vol. 4. New York: International Publishers, 1950.

Forbath, William E. "The Ambiguities of Free Labor: Labor and the Law in the Gilded Age." *Wisconsin Law Review*, July–Aug. 1985, 767–817.

——. *Law and the Shaping of the American Labor Movement*. Cambridge: Harvard University Press, 1991.

Forcey, Charles. *The Crossroads of Liberalism: Croly, Weyl, Lippman, and the Progressive Era, 1900–1925*. New York: Oxford University Press, 1961.

Frank, Thomas. *One Market under God: Extreme Capitalism, Market Populism, and the End of Economic Democracy*. New York: Doubleday, 2000.

Fredrickson, George M. *The Inner Civil War: Northern Intellectuals and the Crisis of the Union*. New York: Harper and Row, 1965.

Furner, Mary O. *Advocacy and Objectivity: A Crisis in the Professionalization of American Social Science, 1865–1905*. Lexington: University Press of Kentucky, 1975.

——. "Knowing Capitalism: Public Investigation of the Labor Question in the Long Progressive Era." In *The State and Economic Knowledge: The American and British Experiences*, edited by Mary O. Furner and Barry Supple, 241–86. New York: Cambridge University Press, 1990.

——. "The Republican Tradition and the New Liberalism: Social Investigation, State Building, and Social Learning in the Gilded Age." In *The State and Social Investigation in Britain and the United States*, edited by Michael J. Lacey and Mary O. Furner, 171–241. New York: Cambridge University Press, 1993.

Galambos, Louis. "The Emerging Organizational Synthesis in Modern American History." *Business History Review* 44, no. 3 (1970): 279–90.

Genovese, Eugene. *The Political Economy of Slavery: Studies in the Economy and Society of the Slave South*. Middletown, Conn.: Wesleyan University Press, 1989.

——. *The World the Slaveholders Made: Two Essays in Interpretation*. 1969. Reprint, Middletown, Conn.: Wesleyan University Press, 1988.

George, Henry. *Progress and Poverty*. 1879.

Gide, Charles, and Charles Rist. *A History of Economic Doctrines from the Time of the Physiocrats to the Present Day*. Translated by R. Richards. Boston: D. C. Heath and Co., 1947.

Gilbert, James. *Designing the Industrial State: The Intellectual Pursuit of Collectivism in America, 1912–1925*. New York: Random House, 1969.

Glickman, Lawrence B. *A Living Wage: American Workers and the Making of Consumer Society*. Ithaca, N.Y.: Cornell University Press, 1997.

Godkin, Edwin L. *Problems of Modern Democracy: Political and Economic Essays*. 1896.

Gompers, Samuel. *Seventy Years of Life and Labor: An Autobiography of Samuel Gompers*. Edited by Nick Salvatore. Ithaca, N.Y.: Cornell University Press, 1984.

Goodwyn, Lawrence. *Democratic Promise: The Populist Moment in America*. New York: Oxford University Press, 1976.

Gordon, David M., Richard Edwards, and Michael Reich. *Segmented Work, Divided Workers: The Historical Transformation of Labor in the United States*. New York: Cambridge University Press, 1982.

Gordon, Linda. *Pitied but Not Entitled: Single Mothers and the History of Welfare, 1890–1935*. New York: Free Press, 1994.

Gould, Stephen Jay. *The Mismeasure of Man*. New York: Norton, 1981.

Gramsci, Antonio. *Selections from the Prison Notebooks*. New York: International Publishers, 1971.

Gunn, L. Ray. *The Decline of Authority: Public Economic Policy and Political Development in New York, 1800–1860*. Ithaca, N.Y.: Cornell University Press, 1988.

Gutman, Herbert G. "The Failure of the Movement by the Unemployed for Public Works in 1873." *Political Science Quarterly* 80 (June 1965): 254–76.

——. "The Tompkins Square 'Riot' in New York City on January 13, 1874: A Re-examination of Its Causes and Its Aftermath." *Labor History* 6 (Winter 1965): 44–70.

Haber, Samuel. *Efficiency and Uplift: Scientific Management in the Progressive Era, 1890–1920*. Chicago: University of Chicago Press, 1964.

Habermas, Jürgen. *The Structural Transformation of the Public Sphere: An Inquiry into a Category of Bourgeois Society*. Translated by Thomas Burger. Cambridge: MIT Press, 1989.

Harvey, William H. *Coin's Financial School*. 1894.

Haskell, Daniel C., comp. *The Nation: Indexes of Titles and Contributors, 1865–1917*. 2 vols. New York: New York Public Library, 1951–53.

Haskell, Thomas L. *The Emergence of Professional Social Science: The American Social Science Association and the Nineteenth-Century Crisis of Authority*. Urbana: University of Illinois Press, 1977.

——. "Taking Exception to Exceptionalism." *Reviews in American History* 28, no. 1 (2000): 151–66.

Hattam, Victoria C. *Labor Visions and State Power: The Origins of Business Unionism in the United States*. Princeton: Princeton University Press, 1993.

Hays, Samuel. "The Politics of Reform in Municipal Government in the Progressive Era." *Pacific Northwest Quarterly* 15 (Oct. 1964): 157–69.

Healy, David. *US Expansionism: The Imperialist Urge in the 1890s*. Madison: University of Wisconsin Press, 1970.

Held, David. *Models of Democracy*. Stanford: Stanford University Press, 1987.

Hicks, John, and Robert Tucker, eds. *Revolution and Reaction: The Paris Commune of 1871*. Amherst: University of Massachusetts Press, 1973.

Higginbotham, R. Don. "The Martial Spirit in the Antebellum South: Some Further Speculations in a National Context." *Journal of Southern History* 58 (Feb. 1996): 3–26.

Higham, John. *Strangers in the Land: Patterns of American Nativism, 1860–1925*. New York: Atheneum, 1963.

Hobsbawm, Eric. *The Age of Capital, 1848–1875*. New York: New American Library, 1984.

Hofstadter, Richard. *The Age of Reform: From Bryan to F.D.R.* 1955. Reprint, New York: Knopf, 1985.

——. *The American Political Tradition and the Men Who Made It*. 1948. Reprint, New York: Vintage Books, 1974.

——. *Social Darwinism in American Thought*. 1944. Reprint, Boston: Beacon Press, 1955.

Hofstadter, Richard, and Walter P. Metzger. *The Development of Academic Freedom in the United States*. New York: Columbia University Press, 1955.

Hoogenboom, Ari A. *Outlawing the Spoils: A History of the Civil Service Reform Movement, 1865–1883*. Urbana: University of Illinois Press, 1961.

——. "Spoilsmen and Reformers: Civil Service Reform and Public Morality." In *The Gilded Age: A Reappraisal*, edited by H. Wayne Morgan, 69–90. Syracuse, N.Y.: Syracuse University Press, 1976.

Horwitz, Morton J. *The Transformation of American Law, 1780–1860*. Cambridge: Harvard University Press, 1977.

——. *The Transformation of American Law, 1870–1960: The Crisis of Legal Orthodoxy*. New York: Oxford University Press, 1992.

Hurst, James Willard. *The Legitimacy of the Business Corporation in the Law of the United States, 1780–1970*. Charlottesville: University Press of Virginia, 1970.

Huston, James L. *Securing the Fruits of Labor: The American Concept of Wealth Distribution, 1765–1900*. Baton Rouge: Louisiana State University Press, 1998.

Jacobs, Clyde E. *Law Writers and the Courts: The Influence of Thomas M. Cooley, Christopher G. Tiedeman, and John F. Dillon upon American Constitutional Law*. Berkeley: University of California Press, 1954.

Jaynes, Gerald David. *Branches without Roots: Genesis of the Black Working Class in the American South, 1862–1882*. New York: Oxford University Press, 1986.

Josephson, Matthew. *The Robber Barons: The Great American Capitalists, 1861–1901*. New York: Harcourt Brace, 1962.

Katz, Michael B. *In the Shadow of the Poorhouse: A Social History of Welfare in America*. New York: Basic Books, 1986.

Kazin, Michael. *The Populist Persuasion: An American History*. New York: Basic Books, 1995.

Keller, Morton. *Affairs of State: Public Life in Late Nineteenth Century America*. Cambridge: Harvard University Press, Belknap Press, 1977.

Kenny, Kevin. *Making Sense of the Molly Maguires*. New York: Oxford University Press, 1998.

Keyssar, Alexander. *The Right to Vote: The Contested History of Democracy in the United States*. New York: Basic Books, 2000.

Kirby, Jack Temple. *Darkness at the Dawning: Race and Reform in the Progressive South*. Philadelphia: Lippincott, 1972.

Kirk, Russell. *The Conservative Mind, from Burke to Santayana*. Chicago: H. Regnery Co., 1953.

Kirkland, Edward. *Charles Francis Adams, Jr., 1835–1915: The Patrician at Bay*. Cambridge: Harvard University Press, 1965.

Kleppner, Paul. "The Political Revolution of the 1890s: A Behavioral Interpretation." In *Essays on the Age of Enterprise: 1870–1900*, edited by David Brody, 272–87. Hinsdale, Ill.: Dryden Press, 1974.

———. *The Third Electoral System, 1853–1892: Parties, Voters, and Political Cultures*. Chapel Hill: University of North Carolina Press, 1979.

Kloppenberg, James T. *Uncertain Victory: Social Democracy and Progressivism in European and American Thought, 1870–1920*. New York: Oxford University Press, 1986.

———. *The Virtues of Liberalism*. New York: Oxford University Press, 1998.

Kolko, Gabriel. *The Triumph of Conservatism: A Reinterpretation of American History, 1900–1916*. New York: Free Press, 1963.

Kousser, J. Morgan. *The Shaping of Southern Politics: Suffrage Restriction and the Establishment of the One-Party South, 1880–1910*. New Haven: Yale University Press, 1974.

Lacey, Michael J. "The World of the Bureaus: Government and the Positivist Project in the Late Nineteenth Century." In *The State and Social Investigation in Britain and the United States*, edited by Michael J. Lacey and Mary O. Furner, 127–70. New York: Cambridge University Press, 1993.

LaFeber, Walter. *Inevitable Revolutions: The United States in Central America*. New York: Norton, 1984.

——. *The New Empire: An Interpretation of American Expansion, 1860–1898*. Ithaca, N.Y.: Cornell University Press, 1963.

Lamoreaux, Naomi. *The Great Merger Movement in American Business, 1895–1904*. New York: Cambridge University Press, 1988.

Lasch, Christopher. *The New Radicalism in America, 1889–1963: The Intellectual as a Social Type*. New York: Knopf, 1965.

——. *The True and Only Heaven: Progress and Its Critics*. New York: Norton, 1991.

Leach, William. *Land of Desire: Merchants, Power, and the Rise of a New American Culture*. New York: Pantheon, 1993.

——. *True Love and Perfect Union: The Feminist Reform of Sex and Society*. New York: Basic Books, 1980.

Lears, T. J. Jackson. *Fables of Abundance: A Cultural History of Advertising in America*. New York: Basic Books, 1994.

Leiby, James. *Carroll Wright and Labor Reform: The Origin of Labor Statistics*. Cambridge: Harvard University Press, 1960.

Levenson, J. C., et al., eds. *The Letters of Henry Adams*. Vol. 1. Cambridge: Harvard University Press, Belknap Press, 1982.

Levy, Carl, ed. *Socialism and the Intelligentsia, 1880–1914*. London: Routledge and Kegan Paul, 1987.

Licht, Walter. *Working for the Railroad*. Princeton: Princeton University Press, 1983.

Lincoln, Abraham. *The Collected Works of Abraham Lincoln*. Edited by Roy P. Basler. 9 vols. New Brunswick, N.J.: Rutgers University Press, 1953–55.

Link, Arthur S. *Woodrow Wilson and the Progressive Era, 1910–1917*. New York: Harper and Row, 1954.

Lippman, Walter. *Drift and Mastery*. 1914. Reprint, Madison: University of Wisconsin Press, 1985.

——. *A Preface to Politics*. 1913. Reprint, Ann Arbor: University of Michigan Press, 1965.

——. *Public Opinion*. 1922. Reprint, New York: Free Press, 1997.

Livingston, James. *Origins of the Federal Reserve System: Money, Class, and Corporate Capitalism, 1890–1913*. Ithaca, N.Y.: Cornell University Press, 1986.

——. *Pragmatism and the Political Economy of Cultural Revolution, 1850–1940*. Chapel Hill: University of North Carolina Press, 1994.

——. "A Reply to Gerald Berk." *Journal of Policy History* 3, no. 1 (1991): 85–89.

——. "The Social Analysis of Economic History and Theory: Conjectures on Late Nineteenth-Century American Development." *American Historical Review* 92, no. 1 (1987): 69–95.

Logsdon, Joseph. *Horace White: Nineteenth Century Liberal*. Westport, Conn.: Greenwood, 1971.

Lukes, Steven. *Individualism*. Oxford: Basil Blackwell, 1973.

Lustig, R. Jeffrey. *Corporate Liberalism: The Origins of Modern American Political Theory, 1890–1920*. Berkeley: University of California Press, 1982.

McClay, Wilfred M. *The Masterless: Self and Society in Modern America*. Chapel Hill: University of North Carolina Press, 1994.

McCormick, Richard L. *From Realignment to Reform: Political Change in New York State, 1893–1910*. Ithaca, N.Y.: Cornell University Press, 1981.

——. *The Party Period and Public Policy: American Politics from the Age of Jackson to the Progressive Era*. New York: Oxford University Press, 1986.

McCraw, Thomas K. *Prophets of Regulation: Charles Francis Adams, Louis D. Brandeis, James M. Landis, Alfred E. Kahn*. Cambridge: Harvard University Press, Belknap Press, 1984.

McGerr, Michael. *The Decline of Popular Politics: The American North, 1865–1928*. New York: Oxford University Press, 1986.

McLachan, James. "American Colleges and the Transmission of Culture: The Case of the Mugwumps." In *The Hofstadter Aegis: A Memorial*, edited by Stanley Elkins and Eric McKitrick, 184–206. New York: Knopf, 1974.

McMath, Robert C. *American Populism: A Social History, 1877–1898*. New York: Hill and Wang, 1993.

Macpherson, C. B. *The Life and Times of Liberal Democracy*. Oxford: Oxford University Press, 1977.

——. *The Political Theory of Possessive Individualism: Hobbes to Locke*. 1962. Reprint, Oxford: Oxford University Press, 1964.

Malone, Dumas, and Allen Johnson, eds. *Dictionary of American Biography*. New York: Scribner's, 1964.

Mandelbaum, Seymour J. *Boss Tweed's New York*. 1965. Reprint, Westport, Conn.: Greenwood Press, 1981.

Marchand, Roland. *Creating the Corporate Soul: The Rise of Public Relations and Corporate Imagery in American Big Business*. Berkeley: University of California Press, 1998.

Mill, John Stuart. *Considerations on Representative Government*. 1861.

——. *On Liberty*. 1859.

——. *The Principles of Political Economy*. 1849.

——. *Utilitarianism*. 1863.

Miller, George H. *Railroads and the Granger Laws*. Madison: University of Wisconsin Press, 1971.

Milne, George. *George William Curtis and the Genteel Tradition*. Bloomington: Indiana University Press, 1956.

Montgomery, David. *Beyond Equality: Labor and the Radical Republicans, 1862–1872*. Urbana: University of Illinois Press, 1981.

——. *The Fall of the House of Labor: The Workplace, the State, and American Labor Activism, 1865–1925*. New York: Cambridge University Press, 1987.

——. "Strikes in Nineteenth-Century America." *Social Science History* 4 (Feb. 1980): 81–104.

——. *Workers' Control in America: Studies in the History of Work, Technology, and Labor Struggles*. New York: Cambridge University Press, 1979.

Moore, Barrington. *Social Origins of Dictatorship and Democracy: Lord and Peasant in the Making of the Modern World*. Boston: Beacon Press, 1967.

Mott, Frank L. *American Journalism: A History of Newspapers in the United States through 260 Years, 1690–1950*. New York: Macmillan, 1950.

——. *A History of American Magazines.* 5 vols. Cambridge: Harvard University Press, 1938–68.

Nelson, Daniel. *Managers and Workers: Origins of the New Factory System in the United States, 1880–1920.* Madison: University of Wisconsin Press, 1975.

Nelson, William E. *The Roots of American Bureaucracy, 1830–1900.* Cambridge: Harvard University Press, 1982.

Noble, David F. *America by Design: Science, Technology, and the Rise of Corporate Capitalism.* New York: Oxford University Press, 1977.

Nordhoff, Charles. *The Cotton States in the Spring and Summer of 1875.* 1876.

Norton, Charles Eliot, ed. *Letters of James Russell Lowell.* 1894.

——. *Orations and Addresses of George William Curtis.* 3 vols. 1894.

Noyes, Alexander Dana. *Thirty Years of American Finance: A Short Financial History of the Government and People of the United States since the Civil War, 1865–1896.* New York: G. P. Putnam's Sons, 1901.

Oestreicher, Richard. "Urban Working-Class Political Behavior and Theories of American Electoral Politics, 1870–1940." *Journal of American History* 74 (Mar. 1988): 1257–86.

Olmsted, Frederick L. *The Cotton Kingdom.* 1853.

Oubre, Claude F. *Forty Acres and a Mule: The Freedmen's Bureau and Black Land Ownership.* Baton Rouge: Louisiana University Press, 1978.

Painter, Nell Irvin. *Standing at Armageddon: The United States, 1877–1919.* New York: Norton, 1987.

Pateman, Carol. *The Sexual Contract.* Stanford: Stanford University Press, 1988.

Peiss, Kathy Lee. *Cheap Amusements: Working Women and Leisure in Turn-of-the-Century New York.* Philadelphia: Temple University Press, 1986.

Pike, James Shepherd. *The Prostrate State: South Carolina under Negro Government.* 1874. Reprint, edited and with an introduction by Robert F. Durden, New York: Harper and Row, 1968.

Polanyi, Karl. *The Great Transformation.* 1944. Reprint, Boston: Beacon Press, 1957.

Pomeroy, John Norton. *An Introduction to the Constitutional Law of the United States.* 1868.

Powell, Lawrence N. *New Masters: Northern Planters during the Civil War and Reconstruction.* New Haven: Yale University Press, 1980.

Rawls, John. *Political Liberalism.* New York: Columbia University Press, 1993.

——. *A Theory of Justice.* Cambridge: Harvard University Press, Belknap Press, 1971.

Richardson, Heather Cox. *The Greatest Nation of the Earth: Republican Economic Policies during the Civil War.* Cambridge: Harvard University Press, 1997.

Riley, Denise. *"Am I That Name?" Feminism and the Category of "Women" in History.* Minneapolis: University of Minnesota Press, 1988.

Riley, Sam G., ed. *American Magazine Journalists, 1850–1900.* Vol. 79, *Dictionary of Literary Biography.* Detroit: Gale Research, 1989.

Rodgers, Daniel T. *Atlantic Crossings: Social Politics in a Progressive Age.* Cambridge: Harvard University Press, Belknap Press, 1998.

——. "In Search of Progressivism." *Reviews in American History* 10 (Dec. 1982): 113–32.

Rohr, John A. "The Constitutional World of Woodrow Wilson." In *Politics and*

Administration: Woodrow Wilson and American Public Administration, edited by Jack
Rabin and James S. Bowman, 31–49. New York: Marcel Dekker, 1984.

Roosevelt, Theodore. *The Autobiography of Theodore Roosevelt*. 1913. Reprint, edited by
Wayne Andrews, New York: Farrar, Straus, and Giroux, Octagon Books, 1975.

———. *The Roosevelt Policy: Speeches, Letters and State Papers, Relating to Corporate Wealth
and Closely Allied Topics*. With an introduction by Andrew Carnegie. 2 vols. New
York: Current Literature Publishing Co., 1908.

———. *The Strenuous Life: Essays and Addresses*. New York: Century Co., 1905.

Ross, Dorothy. "Liberalism." In *Encyclopedia of American Political History: Studies of the
Principal Movements and Ideas*, edited by Jack P. Greene, 2:750–63. New York:
Scribner's, 1984.

———. *The Origins of American Social Science*. New York: Cambridge University Press,
1991.

———. "Socialism and American Liberalism: Academic Social Thought in the 1880s."
Perspectives in American History 11 (1977–78): 5–79.

Ross, Steven J. *Working-Class Hollywood: Silent Film and the Shaping of Class in America*.
Princeton: Princeton University Press, 1998.

Salvatore, Nick. *Eugene V. Debs: Citizen and Socialist*. Urbana: University of Illinois Press,
1982.

Sandel, Michael J. *Liberalism and the Limits of Justice*. New York: Cambridge University
Press, 1982.

Saville, Julie. *The Work of Reconstruction: From Slave to Wage Laborer in South Carolina,
1860–1870*. New York: Cambridge University Press, 1994.

Sawislak, Karen. *Smoldering City: Chicagoans and the Great Fire, 1871–1874*. Chicago:
University of Chicago Press, 1995.

Schneirov, Richard. *Labor and Urban Politics: Class Conflict and the Origins of Modern
Liberalism in Chicago, 1864–1897*. Urbana: University of Illinois Press, 1998.

Schneirov, Richard, Shelton Stromquist, and Nick Salvatore, eds. *The Pullman Strike and
the Crisis of the 1890s: Essays on Labor and Politics*. Urbana: University of Illinois Press,
1999.

Sharkey, Robert P. *Money, Class, and Party: An Economic Study of Civil War and
Reconstruction*. Baltimore: Johns Hopkins University Press, 1967.

Sklar, Martin J. *The Corporate Reconstruction of American Capitalism, 1890–1916*. New
York: Cambridge University Press, 1988.

Skocpol, Theda. *Protecting Soldiers and Mothers: The Political Origins of Social Policy in
the United States*. Cambridge: Harvard University Press, Belknap Press, 1992.

Skowronek, Stephen. *Building a New American State: The Expansion of National
Administrative Capacities, 1877–1920*. New York: Cambridge University Press, 1982.

Smith, Rogers M. *Civic Ideals: Conflicting Visions of Citizenship in U.S. History*. New
Haven: Yale University Press, 1997.

Sproat, John G. *"The Best Men": Liberal Reformers in the Gilded Age*. New York: Oxford
University Press, 1968.

Stanley, Amy Dru. *From Bondage to Contract: Wage Labor, Marriage, and the Market in
the Age of Slave Emancipation*. New York: Cambridge University Press, 1998.

Steel, Ronald. *Walter Lippman and the American Century*. Boston: Little, Brown, 1980.

Stewart, James B. *Holy Warriors: The Abolitionists and American Slavery*. New York: Hill and Wang, 1976.

Summers, Mark Wahlgren. *The Era of Good Stealings*. New York: Oxford University Press, 1993.

Sumner, William Graham. *Collected Essays in Political and Social Science*. 1885.

——. *What Social Classes Owe to Each Other*. 1883.

Sussman, Warren I. *Culture as History: The Transformation of American Society in the Twentieth Century*. New York: Pantheon, 1984.

Takaki, Ronald T. *Iron Cages: Race and Culture in Nineteenth-Century America*. New York: Oxford University Press, 1979.

Taylor, Frederick Winslow. *The Principles of Scientific Management*. New York: Harper and Row, 1911.

Tocqueville, Alexis de. *Democracy in America*. 2 vols. 1835–40.

Tomlins, Christopher L. *The State and the Unions: Labor Relations, Law, and the Organized Labor Movement in America, 1880–1960*. New York: Cambridge University Press, 1985.

Trefousse, Hans L. *The Radical Republicans: Lincoln's Vanguard for Racial Justice*. New York: Knopf, 1969.

Tully, James. "The Possessive Individualism Thesis: A Reconsideration in the Light of Recent Scholarship." In *Democracy and Possessive Individualism: The Intellectual Legacy of C. B. Macpherson*, edited by Joseph H. Carens, 19–34. Albany: State University of New York Press, 1993.

Twain, Mark. *A Connecticut Yankee in King Arthur's Court*. 1889.

Twain, Mark, and Charles Dudley Warner. *The Gilded Age: A Tale of Today*. 1873.

Twiss, Benjamin R. *Lawyers and the Constitution: How Laissez Faire Came to the Supreme Court*. With a foreword by Edward S. Corwin. Princeton: Princeton University Press, 1942.

Unger, Irwin. *The Greenback Era: A Social and Political History of American Finance, 1865–1879*. Princeton: Princeton University Press, 1964.

Veysey, Laurence R. *The Emergence of the American University*. Chicago: Chicago University Press, 1965.

Walker, Francis A. *The Wages Question*. 1876.

Weber, Max. *The Protestant Ethic and the Spirit of Capitalism*. Translated by Talcott Parsons. London: Allen and Unwin, 1958.

Weinstein, James. *The Corporate Ideal in the Liberal State, 1900–1918*. Boston: Beacon Press, 1968.

Wells, David Ames. *Recent Economic Changes*. 1889.

Westbrook, Robert B. *John Dewey and American Democracy*. Ithaca, N.Y.: Cornell University Press, 1991.

White, Horace. *Money and Banking*. 1895.

White, Morton. *Social Thought in America: The Revolt against Formalism*. New York: Oxford University Press, 1947.

Wiebe, Robert H. *The Search for Order, 1877–1920*. New York: Hill and Wang, 1967.

Williams, William Appleman. *The Tragedy of American Diplomacy*. 1959. Reprint, New York: Norton, 1972.

Williamson, Jeffrey G. "Late Nineteenth-Century American Retardation: A Neoclassical Analysis." *Journal of Economic History* 33 (1973): 581–607.

Wilson, Edmund. *Patriotic Gore: Studies in the Literature of the American Civil War*. New York: Farrar, Straus, and Giroux, 1962.

Wilson, R. Jackson. *Figures of Speech: American Writers and the Literary Marketplace, from Benjamin Franklin to Emily Dickinson*. New York: Knopf, 1989.

Wilson, Woodrow. *Congressional Government*. 1885.

——. *The Messages and Papers of Woodrow Wilson*. Edited by Albert Shaw. 2 vols. New York: Review of Reviews Co., 1924.

Wolfe, Christopher. *The Rise of Modern Judicial Review: From Constitutional Interpretation to Judge-Made Law*. New York: Basic Books, 1986.

Woodward, C. Vann. *Origins of the New South, 1877–1913*. 1951. Reprint, Baton Rouge: Louisiana State University Press, 1971.

——. *The Strange Career of Jim Crow*. New York: Oxford University Press, 1955.

Wright, Gavin. *Old South, New South: Revolutions in the Southern Economy since the Civil War*. New York: Basic Books, 1986.

Wyatt-Brown, Bertram. *Honor and Violence in the Old South*. New York: Oxford University Press, 1986.

Yearley, Clifton K. *The Money Machine: The Breakdown and Reform of Government and Party Finance in the North, 1860–1920*. Albany: State University of New York Press, 1970.

INDEX

Civil War, 1–2, 4, 18

Clark, John Bates, xiv, 179, 197; as ethical economist, 14, 159–62, 164, 165–66, 169; and marginalism, 180, 186–92, 231; legitimation of corporate capitalism, 186, 190–91, 217, 231–32; and politics, 186–88, 191–92, 210–14, 215–16, 231–32; on consumption and consuming individualism, 188–92, 209–12, 214, 216, 243, 249, 256

Clayton Act, 252

Cleveland, Grover, 12, 26, 192–93, 196, 200, 204–5, 206, 246

Coin's Financial School, 145

Compromise of 1877, 139

Congress. *See* U.S. Congress

Conservatism, 7, 8, 60

Consolidation, economic. *See* Economic development

Constitutions: revision of state, 132–33

Consumers/consumption: economic theories of, 93–94, 185, 186, 188–92, 199–200; political ideology of, 202, 209, 218, 223, 225, 226, 229, 234; and individualism, 209–12, 214, 216, 243–44, 256

Cooley, Thomas McIntyre, 11, 96–97, 131, 175, 179, 183, 194–95, 238

Corporate capitalism/corporation: legitimation of, 2–5, 15, 87, 96, 178, 184–92, 217–19, 222–24, 226, 243, 247–49, 250, 254–56; opposition to, 2–5, 45, 98, 101, 167, 177, 180, 192, 222, 245; legal status of, 80, 96–100; and politics, 162, 198–99, 203–9, 213–16, 231–32, 247–53. *See also* Economic development; Monopoly; Railroads

Corruption: and liberal reform politics, 18, 53, 100, 101, 105–6, 110, 117–30 passim, 137, 140, 183; and Reconstruction, 40, 75, 79, 82, 85; in Progressive Era, 228, 248

Courts: role of judges and, 70, 98–99, 126, 131–32, 137, 145, 192–93, 195, 197, 219, 228, 247. *See also* U.S. Supreme Court

Croly, Herbert, 235–45

Currency. *See* Fiscal policy

Curtis, George William, 28, 49, 168, 174, 235, 237; as liberal reformer, 11, 12, 115, 126, 136, 137–38, 219; on Reconstruction, 61–62, 67, 69, 79; and civil service reform, 133–35

Darwinism, 13, 73–74, 76–78, 80, 84, 150–51, 200, 219, 251. *See also* Racial ideology

Debs, Eugene V., 192–93

Democracy: and capitalism, 2–6, 30–33, 44–46, 59–60, 62, 70, 82, 84–85, 137–40, 144–48, 150–51, 160, 162–63, 167–68, 173–76, 250, 254–56; defined, 8–9; social scientists' view of, 14, 160–76 passim; liberal reformers' view of, 19, 31–33, 37, 57, 61, 62, 70, 74, 82–83, 84–85, 92, 107, 110–13, 129, 134–40, 150; effects of Civil War on, 24–34 passim; and socialism, 157–76 passim; in new liberalism, 180, 184, 200–202, 209–16, 219–26, 229, 254–56; progressives and, 235, 239–42, 244–45, 248, 250, 254–56. *See also* Citizenship; Godkin, Edwin Lawrence: on democracy, laissez-faire, and liberalism; Liberalism: and democracy; Producerism: ideas of

Democratic Party: in New York City, 25; in Reconstruction and Redemption, 70, 79, 80–81; and 1868 election, 114–16; and Liberal Republicans, 121; competitiveness of in Gilded Age, 124; free-silver and election of 1896, 178, 204–5, 206, 207, 208–9; during Progressive Era, 239, 249–50, 251–52, 253

Depression, economic. *See* Economic conditions

Dewey, John, 17–18, 236, 240, 245

Donnelly, Ignatius, 145

Douglass, Frederick, 43, 61–62, 73

Dred Scott v. Sanford, 117

Dunbar, Charles F., 179

Eaton, Dorman, 134–35

Economic conditions, 72, 81, 86, 92, 122–

Grant, Ulysses S.: and liberal reformers, 51, 71, 79, 92, 116–19, 132; campaign of 1868, 71, 115–16; "Independent" and Liberal Republican movement against, 79, 82, 93, 119–22; Reconstruction policies of, 81

"Great Merger Movement," 96, 217, 222, 247

Great Strike of 1877, 126, 127–28, 139–40, 150, 194, 208

Greeley, Horace, 24–25, 79, 82, 121

Greenbacks, politics of, 51, 89, 114–16, 117–18, 132, 203

Haber, Stephen, 233

Hadley, Arthur T., 179, 232–33

Hanna, Mark, 70

Harper's Weekly, 1–2, 11, 28, 61, 69, 82, 90, 136, 193

Harrison, Benjamin, 246

Hayes, Rutherford, 127, 135

Haymarket Affair, 2, 168–69, 172, 177, 187, 206

Hepburn v. Griswold, 118

Hewitt, Abram S., 123

Higginson, Thomas Wentworth, 69

Hoar, Ebenezer R., 119, 122

Hodgskin, James B., 100–101, 102

Hofstadter, Richard, 9

Horwitz, Morton, 96

Howells, William Dean, 11, 110–12, 137

Immigrants: views of, 74, 126, 136, 155, 168, 225, 250–51

Income tax, 87, 114, 203, 232, 251–52

"Independents." *See* Liberal Republicans

Individualism: and liberalism, 6–7, 178, 182, 254; economic and atomistic, 32, 37, 50, 53, 57, 58, 59, 149–50, 195; versus socialism, 41, 157–76 passim; entrepreneurial and competitive, 85, 86–87, 90–95, 100–101, 106–9, 110, 137, 161, 210, 211, 214, 220, 239, 241, 249, 251; revisions of, 109, 191, 209–16, 221–22, 226, 242–44, 245, 254, 295 (n. 86); ethical econo-

mists' criticism of, 147, 161–63, 164, 165, 166, 173; consuming, 209–12, 214, 216, 243, 256

Initiative and referendum, 232, 248

Intellectuals: defined, 14, 15–18; changing role of, 146–48, 149, 169–70, 174–75, 232–33, 235–37, 245–46

Interstate Commerce Act/Commission, 96, 175, 183, 195, 197–98, 218, 233

Jacksonianism, 98, 134, 226, 235

James, Edmund J., 14, 159, 165, 179

James, William, 17, 239, 240

Jenks, Jeremiah W., 217, 232, 247, 249

Johnson, Andrew, 26, 115

Kelley, William D., 70

Kloppenberg, James, 10

Knights of Labor, 145, 166–68, 170–71, 172, 177, 182, 187

Ku Klux Klan, 55, 76, 78

Labor movement: politics of, 8, 32, 33, 36, 38, 59, 60, 219, 230; impact on Reconstruction, 18, 62, 69–71, 82–83, 84, 110; ideology of, 29–31, 33, 40, 43, 59, 145–48, 166–68, 171, 222; effect of 1870s depression on, 123, 125–28, 132, 139–40; repression of, 125–28, 140. *See also* Eight-hour day; Liberal reformers: on workers and labor movement; Producerism; Progressives/progressivism: and labor; Pullman Strike; Social scientists: relationship to labor

Labor unions, 38, 50, 51, 53, 233; and collective bargaining, 49, 191, 215, 218; during 1870s depression, 125; in 1880s, 140, 145–46, 166–68; in 1890s, 177, 192–93, 198–99, 200; government policy toward, 192–93, 195–96, 218–19, 229–30, 247–48, 252–53; and conservative or business unionism, 197–202, 233, 253; and scientific management, 233, 235. *See also* Eight-hour day; Labor movement; *names of individual unions*

Laissez-faire, doctrine of: liberal reformers on, 32, 79, 85, 97, 122, 150–51, 173, 185, 220–21; challenge to, 146, 158, 164, 165, 170, 176, 180–84, 194, 198, 221, 222, 223, 228. *See also* Administrative governance/mandate: liberal reformers on; Godkin, Edwin Lawrence: on democracy, laissez-faire, and liberalism

Legal Tender Act, 118

Liberalism: revision of American, 4–6, 9–15, 87, 109, 159–76, 219–26, 230; historiography of American, 4–6, 9–15, 294–95 (n. 86); classical, 6, 58–59, 92, 121, 219; defined, 6–8; view of the state, 7, 113, 128, 182–83; new or modern, 7–8, 176, 182–83, 216, 219, 222, 226, 227, 231, 233, 235, 244–55 passim; and democracy, 7–8, 231, 237–38, 244; in Europe, 8, 52, 154; economic, 87, 89, 92, 131, 138, 148, 159, 161, 164, 185. *See also* Individualism: and liberalism; Liberal reformers

Liberal reformers: historiography of, 9–11, 13, 18, 227; constituency and role of, 9–13; and women, 12–13, 136–37, 259 (n. 21); influence of, 13–15, 112, 122, 125, 132–33, 135, 139–40, 147–48, 151, 173–76, 221–22, 227–30, 233; relationship to Radical Republicans, 31–33, 38–48 passim, 62, 68–78 passim, 112, 115–16, 121, 136, 137; on workers and labor movement, 34–43, 47–60, 90–91, 93–94, 105, 107–8, 110, 113, 120, 121, 125–28, 134, 138, 228, 246; on freedmen and Reconstruction, 61–85; on economic development, 86–109, 134, 138, 144, 147; on state regulation, 100–109; politics of, 113–22, 125–40; on U.S. financial system, 113–22, 134, 138, 202–9, 223; on farmers' movements, 128–32; challenged, 139–40, 146–49; and political economy, 143–51; and social scientists, 159–76; and formation of new liberalism, 184–86, 195–202, 219–26; and progressivism, 227–30, 246–47. *See also* Administrative governance/mandate: liberal reformers on; Civil service reform: and liberal reformers; Darwinism; Laissez-faire: liberal reformers on; Liberalism; Socialism: liberal reformers on; Tariff reform; *names of individuals*

Liberal Republicans, 78, 79, 93, 119–22, 134

Lincoln, Abraham, 27, 29, 89

Lippman, Walter, 235–45

Locke, John, 6–7, 58–59

Lodge, Henry Cabot, 225

Lowell, James Russell, 1–2, 11

McKinley, William, 205, 206, 207, 209, 210, 217, 246, 247

Marginalism/marginal utility theory. *See* Economic theory

Marx, Karl, 166

Massachusetts Commission on the Hours of Labor, 34–38, 59, 135

Massachusetts Railroad Commission, 102, 107, 119, 127, 128, 131

Mayo-Smith, Richmond, 159, 179

Mill, John Stuart, 54, 59, 135, 242

Miller, Samuel, 79–80

Minority representation, 111, 136, 137

Molly Maguires, 126

Monopoly, 2, 4, 98–100, 101, 102, 106, 128, 129, 180, 184, 190, 191, 192, 204, 218, 226, 228, 230, 232, 243, 251, 254

Muckraking, 238, 248

Mugwumps. *See* Liberal reformers

Municipal reform, 121, 132–33, 135–37, 228, 235

Munn v. Illinois, 131–32

Nation, 11, 25, 48, 66, 69–82 passim, 97, 100, 119, 120, 169, 182, 193, 237, 250. *See also* Godkin, Edwin Lawrence

National Civic Federation, 217, 218, 231

National debt. *See* Fiscal policy

Nationalism. *See* Patriotism

Newcomb, Simon, 11, 169

New York City, 23–24, 25, 51, 55, 126, 133–34, 237–38, 247

New York Tribune, 24, 25, 82

Revenue reform. *See* Fiscal policy; Tariff
reform
Rice, Issac, 193
Riis, Jacob, 247
"Robber barons," 90
Rodgers, Daniel, 10, 226–27
Roosevelt, Theodore, 217, 229, 231–32, 237,
238, 246–49

Sanborn, Franklin B., 34, 37, 38
Santayana, George, 241, 244
Schurz, Carl, 119
Scientific management, 233–35, 240–41
Scribner's Monthly, 11, 82, 149, 150
Sedgwick, Arthur G., 74, 97, 130, 132
Seligman, Edwin R. A., 14, 159, 165–66,
179, 193, 232
Seymour, Horatio, 116
Sherman Antitrust Act of 1890, 218, 247
Sherman Silver Purchase Act, 203, 204
Sidgwick, Henry, 154
Sinclair, Upton, 248
Sixteenth Amendment, 251
Slaughterhouse Cases, 79–80, 97
Slavery: abolition of, 19, 24–26, 27, 30–31,
43–44, 219; and wage labor, 33, 158;
effect of on South, 63–68. *See also*
Freedmen; Racial ideology
Social Darwinism. *See* Darwinism
Social gospel, 236, 245
Socialism, 43, 58, 206; and new liberalism,
5, 14, 179, 182–84, 198, 202, 210, 211, 221,
222; and progressivism, 5, 228, 232, 237–
38, 239, 242, 244, 248, 249, 253, 254; in
Europe, 8, 51, 59, 147–48, 176, 222; liberal reformers on, 51, 150, 185, 198, 202;
Christian, 145, 173, 210; social scientists
on, 157–76 passim. *See also* Anticommunism; Paris Commune
Social science: liberal reformers and, 34,
37–38, 48, 50, 53, 80, 118–19, 133, 144,
147, 201; professionalization of, 148–
66 passim, 174–75, 187, 221; role of in
governmental policymaking, 213, 248
Social scientists: background and role of,

13–17, 146–48, 155–59; challenge to
Gilded Age liberalism, 146–48, 159–76;
on role of state, 157–76; on socialism
and individualism, 157–76 passim; relationship to labor, 160, 165, 166–73, 175–
76, 194, 195; in formation of new liberalism, 176, 179–84, 186–92, 210–16, 217,
219, 221–22, 225; in Progressive Era,
230–33, 235–36, 245, 249, 250–51. *See
also* Administrative governance/man-
date: social scientists on; Democracy:
social scientists' view of; *names of
individuals*
Spanish-American War, 225
Sproat, John G., 10, 122
Steffens, Lincoln, 238
Stevens, Thaddeus, 68, 70, 115
Suffrage: black, 25–26, 28–29, 44, 48, 55,
61–62, 66–85 passim, 136; woman, 28,
55, 111, 135–36, 253; efforts to restrict,
135–37; disfranchisement of African
Americans, 139, 225
Sumner, Charles, 11, 68, 73, 119
Sumner, William Graham, 11, 18, 148–
52, 154, 157, 158, 161, 163, 165, 174, 179–
80

Taft, William H., 254
Tammany Hall, 23–24, 55, 133, 135
Tariff reform, 89, 92–93, 111, 118, 120, 138,
155, 185, 227–28, 251–52. *See also*
Protectionism
Taussig, Frank W., 179, 232
Taxation. *See* Fiscal policy; Income tax;
Municipal reform; Tariff reform
Taylorism, 233–35. *See also* Scientific
management
Thirteenth Amendment, 26, 27, 80
Tilden, Samuel, 11, 133, 135
Tilden Commission, 133
Trade unions. *See* Labor unions
Trusts. *See* Corporate capitalism/
corporation
Turner, Frederick Jackson, 250
Twain, Mark, 11, 18, 145